THE ONCE AND FUTURE NEW YORK

The Once and Future New York

HISTORIC PRESERVATION AND THE MODERN CITY

Randall Mason

University of Minnesota Press
Minneapolis
London

The University of Minnesota Press gratefully acknowledges the financial assistance provided for the publication of this book from the University Research Foundation of the University of Pennsylvania.

Published by the University of Minnesota Press
111 Third Avenue South, Suite 290
Minneapolis, MN 55401-2520
http://www.upress.umn.edu

Library of Congress Cataloging-in-Publication Data

Mason, Randall, 1963–
   The once and future New York : historic preservation and the modern city /
Randall Mason.
      p.   cm.
   Includes bibliographical references and index.
   ISBN 978-0-8166-5603-5 (hc : alk. paper) — ISBN 978-0-8166-5604-2 (pb : alk. paper)
   1. Historic preservation—New York (State)—New York—History—19th century.
2. Historic preservation—New York (State)—New York—History—20th century.
3. Architecture—Conservation and restoration—New York (State)—New York.
4. New York (N.Y.)—Buildings, structures, etc. I. Title.
NA108.N48M37   2009
363.6'909747109034—dc22

                                                                    2009000573

Printed in the United States of America on acid-free paper

The University of Minnesota is an equal-opportunity educator and employer.

18 17 16 15 14 13 12 11 10 09   10 9 8 7 6 5 4 3 2 1

Walking in Varick Street, I find that I am sometimes haunted by the image of St. John's Chapel. When I last saw it, between the Sixth Avenue El and the freight-yards of the Central Railroad, it presented, with its fine proportions and the dignity of its brown façade, a solitary architectural visage among the faceless constructions that outbulked it. There was still a placard on the door which said, "Seats Free. St. John's Chapel. Trinity Parish"; but the steps and the floor of the portico had already been taken down to make room for the new subway, and the pillars lifted tarnished foliation straight from the dirt of the road. Many of the small square panes had been broken in the round-arched windows; the clock in the spire had lost its hands, and its face was obliterated. The old spire itself, with its multiplied tiers, was beginning to lurch a little, like the mast of a sinking ship. And now, indeed, the office buildings, the freightyard, and the factories have closed over it and swallowed it up, imposing a monotony as blank as the sea.

EDMUND WILSON, 1919

Contents

Introduction

Preservation and Its History in New York

THE FRONT PAGE OF THE *NEW YORK TIMES* ON OCTOBER 29, 1963, READ "Demolition Starts at Penn Station; Architects Picket." Pennsylvania Station was a civic monument by any measure. Designed by the country's leading architects, McKim, Mead, and White, to bring the powerful Pennsylvania Railroad straight into Manhattan, upon completion in 1910, the station won immediate fame as a gateway, technological marvel, and symbol of New York City's ascendance. Modeled after the Roman baths of Caracalla, the station's refined neoclassical facades were matched by soaring interior spaces. Destruction of the vast structure was controversial and painstaking, and it was documented in detail—especially the fate of the monumental stone sculptures of eagles and angels.

In the popular mind, the destruction of Penn Station marked the beginning of historic preservation in New York and gave credence to the idea that change, development, and modernity are the enemies of memory and preservation. A shiny new generation of skyscrapers dominated midtown, enabled by the 1961 zoning ordinance. The arrival of architectural modernisms, the sweep of the public works of Robert Moses, the realities of urban renewal, and the gathering politics of social unrest threatened the historic fabric of the city like never before. The environmental cataclysms of this period seemed to reach a tipping point with the destruction of Penn Station.

This event achieved mythic proportions because it solidified support for the excellent Landmarks Law (perhaps the most powerful protective local-preservation regulation in the country), because the stark visual drama of the station's demolition was captured in great detail, and because the generation of preservation advocates involved in the aftermath of Penn Station's destruction associate 1963 with their awakening and therefore consider it a signal moment for the field. But this was not the beginning of historic preservation in New York City. Far from it. In fact, historic preservation thrived in New York from the 1890s onward.

As New York ascended, in the decades around 1900, to become the "capital of capitalism" and an iconic modern metropolis, historic preservation was part of the conversation about building a great modern city. Sustained by some of New

York's leading reformers and city builders, preservation was asserted as a key urbanistic strategy—creating places that represented stability and continuity with a noble past, providing a cultural counterweight to the often chaotic growth of the metropolis. More than a conversation about the past, historic preservation gave the past visual, formal presence through dozens of projects—restored buildings, protected parks, new memorials—adorning New York's everyday landscape. Preservation was imagined as an integral *part* of modernity and modernizing cities—not a means of resisting them.

The mythology surrounding Penn Station—that its tragic end was the origin of New York's virtuous, vigorous preservation field—has obscured the roots of preservation in the nation's leading city.[1] Historic preservation had been a persistent force in the development of New York since the turn of the twentieth century, when preservationists organized a reform movement and memory sites were created around the city to build a sense of the past into the changeful urban environment. "In the midst of the many changes in our fluid city, we need some permanent landmarks to suggest stability," a preservation group declared in 1912.[2] These sites included colonial houses, old parks, the sites of historic events, new memorials, public buildings, and public spectacles—a *memory infrastructure*. This early-twentieth-century legacy of historical consciousness, preserved places, and preservation was a signal contribution to city building. It brought balance to the modernizing city, and it surely made the possibility (even the expectation) of preserving Penn Station more real to New Yorkers when it was threatened in the 1960s.

The Once and Future New York documents the history of preservation in New York between 1890 and 1920 and debunks several myths about historic preservation: that preservation was nothing more than antiquarian collecting (preservationists were even more interested in social reform and collective memory), that preservation began in opposition to urban renewal in the postwar period (in fact, it began in the late nineteenth century), that preservationists were concerned only with individual buildings (their interests encompassed parks and landscapes, too), and that preservationists opposed the growth and development of modern cities (early-twentieth-century preservationists more often allied themselves with urban expansion).

While the myths about preservation's origins are founded in reality, they are only the beginning of the story. Preservationists have been strangely blind to the history of their own field, preferring to regard their efforts as flowing from a timeless ethos of connoisseurship and moral outrage at the excesses of urban development.[3] Of course, contemporary historiography demands that one frame preservation in critical terms: Preservation is a product of its times, interpretations of the past are contested, and the places and narratives constructed by historic preservation are meaningful cultural documents. These explorations are at the heart of this book.

Recovering a more complete history of preservation forces one to reconsider the widely held impression that preservation's purpose has always been "to resist modernity's brutal assault on New York's architectural history."[4] This latter-day antidevelopment ideology of preservation, rooted in the story of Penn Station's destruction, played a minor part in the early history of the field. In the early twentieth century, historic preservation did not simply oppose development—it framed, animated, and enabled development. Those advocating preservation created new places designed to be memorable in addition to protecting and redesigning extant historic places. Reformers channeled urban development, without stopping it[5]—and for preservationists this meant imbuing the modern city with cultural meaning: sometimes by preserving a historic building from the path of destruction; sometimes by creating a new landscape leavened with a measure of historical memory; always by inserting historic preservation into the discourse of modernizing New York.

Preservationists accomplished a great deal between 1890 and 1920: restoring buildings, creating historic sites, commemorating events, protecting landscapes, writing histories, staging festivals, forming organizations, raising funds, and lobbying public officials. Memory sites stretched across the five boroughs. Preservationists established historic preservation as a field of urbanism decades before the better-known watersheds in the history of preservation: Williamsburg in the 1920s, the first historic-district ordinances in the 1920s and '30s, the New Deal programs such as the Historic American Buildings Survey in the 1930s, formation of the National Trust for Historic Preservation in the late 1940s, and of course the demolition of Penn Station in 1963.

At its roots, preservation was not isolated as a singular, stand-alone cause. Preservation was envisioned as *part of* the development of modern cities, not as a reaction against city building; preservationists connected their work to the fields of city planning, landscape architecture, and urban design emerging in the same historical moment. As Columbia University architecture professor A. D. F. Hamlin declared in 1901, "The preservation of historic monuments is no mere fad, it is no mere concession to the poetic but impractical and visionary notion. It is a duty, as truly as is the preservation of our forests as a protection for the sources of our water supply, or the erection of libraries to stimulate and minister to the appetite for knowledge."[6]

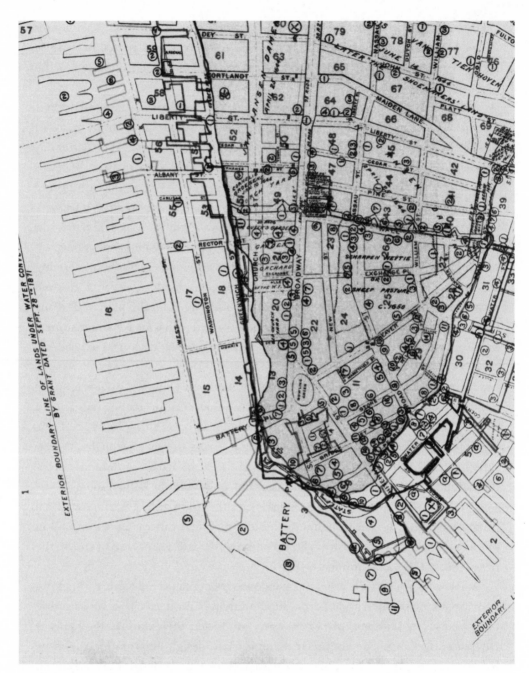

Figure I.1. In the eyes of Isaac Newton Phelps Stokes—architect, philanthropist, reformer, collector—New York at the turn of the twentieth century was already rich in historic sites and layers. This map, an example of his own cartographic work, is from his masterful six-volume compendium, The Iconography of Manhattan Island, 1498–1909, *which reproduced his large collection of maps and images, a chronology of the city's history, and his own cartographic tour de force. Courtesy of University of Pennsylvania Libraries.*

The Progressive reform impulse propelled preservation beyond its nineteenth-century roots in antiquarianism (which was concerned primarily with collecting remnants of a dead past). The preservation field drew inspiration from many different sources—social reform, history, art, architecture, urbanism—in responding to the marked changes in New York's scale, density, intensity, and complexity in the early twentieth century. One should think of the founding New York preservationists using historical memory as a lever against the "juggernaut" of urbanization, as a tool to address problems of overdevelopment, anomie, alienation, and social cleavage.

WHERE DID PRESERVATION COME FROM?

How, exactly, did preservation first take root in New York? To most historians, Gotham is infertile soil for preservation. The headline of New York's urban biography is the hegemony of commerce and the real estate market. In keeping with this seemingly self-evident truth, such a keen observer as Kenneth Jackson has argued that "history is for losers"—historic preservation was a preoccupation of social factions that were losing out in the contest to control New York's future.[7] Turning the old adage "History is written by the winners" on its head, the "History is for losers" notion stems from the idea that cultural hegemony was, in the early twentieth century, falling like sand through the fingers of older, established elite groups and being collected by new elite groups led by entrepreneurs without Old New York social ties. As the "winners" were busy writing the future of the city, the "losers" busied themselves by trifling in the past. Richard Hofstadter promoted this view of preservation in his 1955 *Age of Reform,* and serious historical works have followed his lead, marginalizing preservation as "a decidedly un–New York sort of enterprise."[8]

The archives paint a different picture. The preservation field was created in the period surrounding the turn of the twentieth century by some of the winners—not the losers—and was built into a serious and fairly successful reform movement. By dramatically overstating the case that the economy determines everything of consequence in New York, historians mistakenly suggest that the city's culture and landscape resulted from a zero-sum game in which commerce and memory are in competition, the latter ever beholden to the former. The story of preservation's emergence reminds us that historical memory has long been cultivated (by preservationists among others) despite the power of the market to erase the past.[9] The pace of market-fed destruction has never been fast enough to eclipse memory altogether, and the fusion of commerce and historical memory formed in this period has proven more lasting than competition between them.

Who were these "winners" behind preservation? The preservationists were a fascinating and somewhat surprising mix of people. In the vanguard were a remarkable group of New York's city builders—influential citizens who were also its first and foremost preservers.[10] Public officials and civic leaders such as Andrew Haswell Green, George McAneny, Robert De Forest, and Madison Grant built the roads, subways, parks, government agencies, and civic institutions supporting the economic and political development of New York while *also* working to restore historic buildings, preserve public parks, and save wilderness and natural areas. In addition to these leaders, a cadre of professionals—some men of means, others solidly middle-class—devoted themselves to preservation. They included Isaac Newton Phelps Stokes, Charles Rollinson Lamb, Henry Kirke Bush-Brown, Edward Hagaman Hall, George Frederick Kunz, Melusina Fay Peirce, Alexander McMillan Welch, and Reginald Pelham Bolton. As a group, they fit the typical profile of Progressives, but their individual achievements are little remembered today. The stereotypical blue-blooded members of patriotic societies, such as the Daughters of the American Revolution and the Sons of the American Revolution, were also among the preservationists, but they were in the minority. While hereditary groups undertook preservation projects to advance their own interests, the driving forces of preservation were reformers and public leaders who regarded historic places as one among many public goods needed to build a modern city balancing commerce and culture.

Influential Progressive writer Herbert Croly remarked on the imbalance characterizing New York at the turn of the century: "It still represents rather the formlessness and incoherence of our American past than the better defined and more fully rounded and proportioned creation of the future."[11] The problem, as George McAneny put it, was that "many of our cities have grown up wild in Topsy-like fashion. I speak, for one, with frank admission that that is our trouble in the city of New York."[12] Preservation brought order to urban culture and thus seemed a useful tool for these city builders. The city's rapidly shifting culture could be anchored by buildings, parks, and memorials representing noble, celebratory narratives of past achievement.

Historic places were fancied as anchors against unwanted change. Artist and preservationist Frederick Stymetz Lamb, around the turn of the twentieth century, articulated the broadly shared sense of disorder fueled by the disappearance of historic places:

> Old landmarks are obliterated; historical monuments destroyed; buildings of national importance sold for second-hand building material;

rivers, fields and commons of the old villages swept away, and in their place factory or rear tenement appears. The most impressive river front ever granted a city is bereft of all natural beauty. Remember Manhattan of the past, and look at it now! Central Park . . . and Riverside Drive alone remain. City Hall Park, one of the few of the early reservations, has been encroached upon because the city officials were too parsimonious to pay a moderate sum for a suitable site for the New York Post Office. City economy has been matched by corporate greed, and the beautiful St. John's Park, absorbed by the New York Central, has been forever lost to Greater New York, thus eliminating another of the few remaining breathing places.[13]

Lamb and fellow preservationists and reformers worried that single-minded and individualistic pursuit of wealth would fail because the resulting city would lack beauty and memory. The "old landmarks" and "rivers, fields and commons" of the colonial city were missed because they could keep the future character of the city in balance. Out of context, Lamb's lament might sound simply antidevelopment, but he and his colleagues lobbied not *against* development but for a *different kind* of development: not to halt change, but to modify or design it, to produce a "Greater New York" at once more beautiful, more efficient, and more clearly rooted in its own past.

Preservation was a cause championed by a group of city builders who were fully committed to growth, expansion, and the hegemony of the business elite in urban affairs. They embodied Progressive politics and embraced public service while maintaining connections to J. P. Morgan Sr., John D. Rockefeller, Andrew Carnegie, and the city's other leading capitalists.[14] They supported preservation because it helped stabilize urban culture, celebrating commercial growth and innovation against the countervailing threats of immigration, radical politics, immorality, and "the street." Historic preservation was one current in the larger stream of Progressive urban reforms.[15] The idea behind all these reforms was reining in laissez-faire urban development by creating public spaces, third-sector institutions, and other public goods. Like their kindred reformers in other sectors (health, politics, education), preservationists embraced pragmatism, impartiality, and professionalism, not mere sentiment. And they shared a basic faith in environmental determinism: Shaping the city would reshape the lives of its citizens.

The preservationist version of urban reform held that preventing change and cultivating historical memory in some parts of the city was deeply connected to redevelopment and erasing memory in (most) other parts. Preserving relatively few sites would support the march toward "improvement," a concept that held great allure for reformers (preservationists included) because it meant cultivating the many different values of the urban landscape—economic, social, environmental, aesthetic, cultural—in a holistic way. The American Scenic and Historic Preservation Society (ASHPS), founded by Andrew Haswell Green, typified this attitude. Disavowing the idea that preservation was merely an antiquarian hobby, it proclaimed itself "a national society for the protection of natural scenery, the preservation of historic landmarks *and* the improvement of cities."[16]

Preservationists were prone to moral exhortation—"What few memorials of the past we have should be preserved for the lessons they teach!"[17]—yet they did not suggest that cultivation of historical memory needed to come at the cost of prosperity. In fact, the balance they struck tilted decidedly toward business and economic growth. George McAneny, while serving as president of the Board of Aldermen, told a friendly audience of the Fine Arts Federation and the Architectural League in 1915:

> I may as well be frank with you, and say that the material or practical aspects of any question involving the development of New York City are bound to outweigh the artistic [or historical] aspects. . . . [It is], in the language of the street, a one-sided proposition.[18]

Or was it? McAneny's career in politics and preservation, and the results of the preservation debates and projects from these three decades, suggest that "material" and "artistic" forces were not locked in a zero-sum game of winners and losers. In contrast, the success of preservation in this period demonstrated the kinds of balance that could be achieved in the urban landscape between the forces for collective memory and metropolitan growth.

THE NEW NEW YORK

To appreciate fully the emergence of preservation in New York around the turn of the twentieth century, one must appreciate this period of extraordinary growth, change, and upheaval in the city's history. The period from 1890 to 1940 has been called "New York's most important period of change and development." Since the 1820s, New York had been on the path to become "the capital of capitalism"—exploding in size and complexity, a magnet of people and money and ideas, unmatched in national and global prominence.[19] By 1890, the city had 1.4 million residents. The newly consolidated metropolis had 3.4 million people in

1900; by 1920, the number had grown to 5.6 million. New York was the largest and most powerful metropolis in the country and perhaps the world, and arguably the most exciting, creative, convulsive, and problematic, too.[20]

In this period, the physical city grew upward and outward, concentrating masses of capital, people, and buildings in the Manhattan and Brooklyn cores while spreading development throughout the outer boroughs. New York—particularly Manhattan—became the emblem of modern cities' potentials and problems, a notion captured by the art historian John Van Dyke in his popular 1909 book *The New New York*:

> There is a great movement going on about you, a surge of struggling humanity; and there is a great roar, the metallic-electric hum of power in action. If you are a stranger within the gates perhaps this means chaos to you, sheer mob madness; and possibly before nightfall you will have concluded that Manhattan, like Constantinople, is lacking in homogeneity, wholly wanting in structural unity, in fact a mere agglomeration of buildings on a point of land. The checkerboard "blocks," the recurrent regularity of streets, you admit, point to something planned; but the buildings are eruptive and the whole city abnormal—something again that apparently just "happened."[21]

Historic preservation is often regarded as a protest against such hyperbolic accounts of "the new New York"—against development, modernization, and modernity[22] generally—as grasping, against the "chaos," for the simpler world of the past. Preservationists today still rely on this sense of aggrieved opposition to evil developers for a sense of purpose and a rallying cry for political support. But historical evidence from New York suggests the opposite; preservation was really *part of* New York's modern approach to city building, part of the "great movement" Van Dyke sought to capture. Indeed, the emergence of a coherent preservation field was one signal of the arrival of "the new New York"—like many other guidebooks of the era, generally praiseful of the new metropolis, Van Dyke's reserved a special chapter for "Historical Landmarks."

New York City's new municipal charter of 1898 consolidated a five-borough metropolitan region out of a far-flung collection of urban, suburban, and rural places. Talk of rationalizing growth and governance through municipal consolidation had been around for decades.[23] Andrew Haswell Green was a driving force behind the consolidation, and he later created the city's premier preservation organization. That Green's vision extended to both realms—for rationalizing the

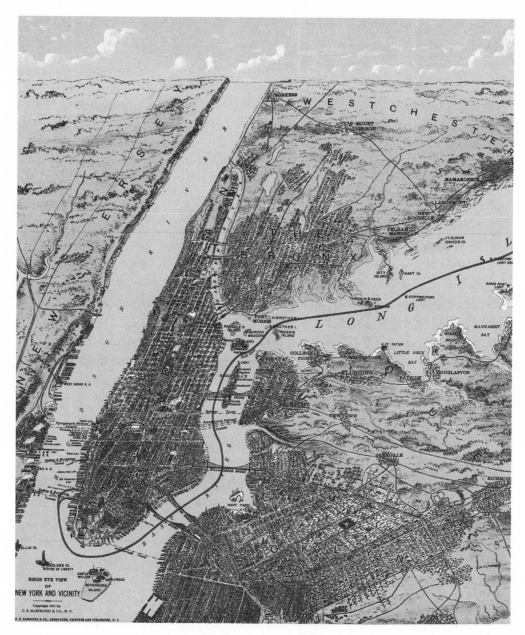

Figure I.2. This 1912 bird's-eye drawing captures the exploding scale and immense growth of Greater New York. Growth on the northern and eastern peripheries of the five-borough metropolis rivaled the constant redevelopment of the urban core as the driving force of metropolitanization. Courtesy of the Lionel Pincus and Princess Firyal Map Division, the New York Public Library, Aster, Lenox, and Tilden Foundations.

future growth of the city and for providing proper public amenities—was no coincidence. Balancing progress and tradition, private gain and public good, were the core problems of the city's remarkable growth.

Despite the massive expansion of city territory (including much undeveloped land), the crucible at the center of the metropolis—crowded Manhattan—barely cooled. The ethnicity of its people, the size and character of its buildings, the culture of the street, and the nature of work all presented problems. Polarized politics made everything worse. The Democratic machine, Republican business interests, labor groups, radical movements, good-government reformers, and numerous splinter and fusion groups inhabited a wide and contentious spectrum of municipal politics. And governance of the city continued to be shaped by the long-standing rift between state government and the city corporation.

These problems came to a head in the 1890s when reformers rallied behind a variety of urban-reform causes. Housing and tenement reform laws, public health and sanitation measures, civil service rules, urban design and beautification schemes, transit systems, roads and bridges, community centers, parks and playgrounds all attracted a distinct community of reformers and corresponding infrastructure. Progressive reform efforts shared an idealistic devotion to serving the best interests of society ("the public" or "the city"), an ethic of impartiality and objectivity (to oppose machine politics), and faith that reshaping the city's environment was the means for improving society in all its aspects—economic, social, political. The overarching political strategy of Progressives held that the government—populated by disinterested professionals and working in concert with enlightened citizens, charities, and philanthropies—could create a democratic public realm transcending corporate greed and political malfeasance. The emerging preservation movement developed along these lines, with activist private organizations leading most preservation efforts, most often in collaboration with government agencies and philanthropic, upper-class citizens.

Andrew Haswell Green, writing in 1901, articulated the connection between preservation and these other strains of reform urbanism: "We do not want the expensive and futile methods of past ages put upon us again [that is, the wasteful, shortsighted public works of Tammany politicians]. What we should have is one plan for the unified city that will provide conditions of living, methods of transit and travel, and features of adornment, suited to advance the comfort, convenience and happiness of the whole."[24] Among the "features of adornment" he envisioned were the preserved places where civic and national memory held sway.

The city's leaders were increasingly conscious of its new metropolitan character—at once vigorous, powerful, sprawling, liberating, dense, oppressive, and chaotic—and moved to address these new realities with environmental reform. In 1903, leading Progressive critic Herbert Croly evoked the city's chaos as well as its long history and future potential in his essay "New York as the American Metropolis." Though Croly wrote about society and architecture, he did not identify himself as a preservationist. However, the idea he voiced—that the urban past should be connected to the urban future—was the shared basis of preservation and myriad other reform efforts. He went on to praise "the quickening of public conscience [that] has naturally followed this awakening of municipal vanity"—in other words, the gathering influence of the reformers.[25]

"Congestion" was a compelling rallying cry for reform urbanism. As leading city-planning reformer Benjamin Marsh outlined the case against congestion, it was fundamentally an economic problem: "The causes of congestion of population are . . . largely the outcome of a system of laissez faire." The "evil of congestion" created other kinds of ill effects on the city: "all the human suffering, physical deterioration, and moral danger which congestion promotes and connotes."[26] But this discourse failed to capture another of the period's urban crises—a moment of deep cultural conflict as well as bursts of creativity. This moment at the beginning of the twentieth century found culture more loosened from its traditional moorings than it had previously been. The scope and depth of technological and social change breached the limits of cultural confidence and occasioned an intense period of searching for new cultural expression.[27] Immigration from overseas, internal migrations, technological innovation, and new modes of artistic expression stemmed from the economic power and social intensity concentrated in New York.

The visual culture of the period contrasted the chaotic and changeful present with an orderly, reposeful past in media ranging from widely seen Alfred Steiglitz photographs or George Bellows paintings, to more obscure representations such as Joseph Pennell's illustrations from *The New New York* or architect Raymond Hood's drawings of the emergent skyscraper city. Such contrasts could be read as conflicts between a dramatically changed present and a remote past, or as connections between the city's present development and the outlines formed by its past achievements. These contrasts formed a rich vein of cultural meaning exploited by preservationists to creative normative, consensual, comfortable stories about the city's past.

Preservationists called for a new urban culture drawing on both narrative and visual evidence of the past. The successes of modernity reshuffled the class system, questioned cultural norms rooted in rural and small-town life, and threatened the social order installed by the industrial economy of the post–Civil War

Figure I.3. Illustrator Joseph Pennell recorded urban scenes alive with tensions between the old and the new in the early twentieth century for popular audiences in newspapers, magazines, and books. Pennell's drawing of the Battery (one of many accompanying John Van Dyke's 1909 The New New York*) juxtaposes the city's historical layers with the dynamism of its street life and ascending skyline of modern buildings. Author's collection.*

Figure I.4. Architect Raymond Hood arrived in New York in 1914 and gained fame in the 1920s for futuristic skyscraper projects, including Rockefeller Center and the American Radiator and McGraw Hill buildings. In a series of annotated drawings from the early 1920s, Hood wrestled with the same fundamental problem confronting preservationists: modernizing the city while drawing meaning from the inherited built environment. Did modernity require wholesale architectural and urbanistic invention? Or could a modern city be coaxed, piecemeal, from gradual redevelopment? Provoked by the 1916 zoning ordinance, Hood's concern in this unpublished project extended beyond the form of new architecture to drawing meaningful contrasts with the existing older buildings brooding in the foreground and fading into the background of this drawing. Courtesy of the Architectural Archives, University of Pennsylvania.

period. The new norms reformers promoted—republican citizenship, patriotism, domesticity, beauty—were really a rehabilitation of old themes (some imagined, some real, drawn from a newly remote past).[28] Typical of modern culture, contradictions abounded: between desire for a technological future and appeal to the values of a lost past, between republican ideals and stark class divisions, between American patriotism and the reality of a polyglot population. Preservationists' recovery and reconstruction of a "usable past" was a way of papering over these contradictions.

MODERNITY BEGETS PRESERVATION

Tracing the roots of historic preservation to the urban and cultural crises of the first decades of the twentieth century, *The Once and Future New York* rests on two major historical arguments: First, there *was* a substantial historic preservation field in New York as early as 1890–1920, which placed preservation squarely within the Progressive movement and seems at odds with the celebrated notion of New York as the "capital of capitalism." Second, historic preservation should be seen as part of the broader cultural foment of modernity, not as a reaction against it. Why did preservation emerge at this time, in these decades around 1900? Interest in preservation was a sign of cultural crisis. The faster the pace of modernization, the more intensely were connections to the past sought.[29] Preservation wrestled with perhaps the central conflict in the cultural history of this period—new relationships to the past, marked by a growing cleavage between memory and history. Preservation was part of this tumultuous process, and memory sites were imagined as part of the very fabric of modernity.

Turn-of-the-century modernity transformed all aspects of American society, cutting across cultural, artistic, economic, political, and environmental realms. Modernity ushered in an era in which the experience of space and time were transformed. The spread of such innovations as railroad travel, telecommunications, electric lighting, and high-quality image printing allowed new sorts of communication and social relations, and it untethered cultural expression from the bounds of tradition. This phenomenon was most readily perceived first in the work of artists and writers (Georges Braque, Pablo Picasso, T. S. Eliot) and steadily infiltrated more spheres of culture and everyday life. With the strictures of tradition loosened, if not altogether torn, by technology and markets and migration, new cultural forms and themes dominated American culture. Novelty and nostalgia competed for influence. Modern art and the commercial cultures of mass marketing betrayed a new freedom to invent culture, not just inherit it. While the skyline boasted ever more steel-frame towers, colonial revival and other backward-looking cultural expressions thrived.

New relations to the past were central to all these cultural transformations. Traditional notions of memory—as something lived and passed down through experience—were steadily eclipsed by created, "constructed" associations with the past: Memory gave way to history. While deeply meaningful, this shift was not sudden. Transitional forms of memory and history—the term "historical memory" is favored here—satisfied cultural needs for new versions of the past. Revival architectural styles, restored and reconstructed house museums, and other "uses" of the past became hallmarks of modern culture. Cultural critic Van Wyck Brooks coined the notion of a "usable past" in 1915 to legitimize the search for meaning, reference, continuity, or stability in the past. The notion accurately described a dynamic expressed in every aspect of American culture in these decades and foregrounded the utilitarian aspect of historical memory: It was created to be useful, to perform a social function.[30] Modernity had made tradition a dead letter, but figures like Brooks, Theodore Dreiser, Edward Hopper, and many others purposefully remade American culture, often by regaining or reimagining the past.[31]

In New York, historic preservationists contributed to this modern cultural evolution by forging new forms of collective memory—popularizing narratives, images, buildings, monuments, and landscapes representing the city's past. They sought to shape and control urban culture by literally building historical memory into public space by preserving old places and creating new memorials. Translating historical consciousness into urban forms and spaces—"spatializing" historical memory—was a key to preservation strategy. Whereas modernity tended to estrange people from their past, preservation attempted to repair and invent social connections across time by rooting historical narratives in the actual urban environment of buildings, streets, and parks. Preservationists placed themselves at the center of modern culture in another sense by fusing celebrations of the city's past with spectacles of the city's commercial future—exploiting the new freedom to reassemble and reuse aspects of the past to make new meanings and cultural forms in the present.[32] "It becomes a part of the education of a people to have the great events of our history put before them in enduring and beautiful forms," wrote sculptor and preservationist Henry Kirke Bush-Brown in 1899. Historical memory should be "made definite and permanent in the mind by a living picture that shall endure."[33] So Manhattan's oldest and most prominent public buildings were restored; sites of Revolutionary War events were carefully marked and commemorated; the city's great urban parks were protected from encroachment. These memory sites communicated an interpretation of the past useful for reformers, trumpeting the need for civic patriotism, ancestor worship, and celebration of the city's commercial prowess. Meanwhile, evidence of slavery, racism, class conflict, violence, and other narratives that might challenge civic patriotism were ignored; they were not "usable" to reformers on political grounds. Preservationists' memorial gloss on New York's evolution nevertheless created a lasting legacy of historic places.[34]

A MEMORY INFRASTRUCTURE

The wave of modernity cresting around the turn of the century brought two sorts of crisis, paving the way for an urban preservation movement. In one sense, modernity engendered a cultural crisis in the relationship between past and present. Traditional ties of memory and community were strained or broken altogether, and the preservation movement responded by trying to heal the rupture, creating narratives rooted in place, heroism, and progress to replace what was perceived as having been lost. Modernity also instigated a new scale and complexity of urban problems—material problems such as not enough mobility, too much density, and environmental degradation, as well as immaterial issues such as the religious, linguistic, and other cultural stresses of immigration. New ideas about dealing with urban problems fueled can-do Progressive attitudes to addressing the whole range of urban issues: the philosophy of environmental determinism, faith in technical knowledge and objective professionals, the confidence to fix problems. Professionals and reformers from engineering, architecture, planning, political science, and other fields created new infrastructures in response. The different kinds of infrastructure shared some attributes: They comprised a geographically extensive system made of many parts; they included material aspects, such as physical structures, as well as immaterial aspects, such as rules, laws, and discourses, and aspects combining both, such as government agencies or philanthropic institutions; and they were designed to perform specific functions. Each family of urban problems engendered an infrastructure to fix it: Housing problems begot tenement laws, model housing projects, architectural competitions, and government agencies to monitor and regulate housing; congestion problems were addressed by zoning laws, transit systems, and park systems.

The result of preservationists' efforts could be regarded as a memory infrastructure: a collection of buildings, places, and public art establishing frameworks of collective memory for New Yorkers. Memory infrastructure was intended to perform the important cultural function of building civic identity by fusing celebrations of the past with optimism about the future. While the first stirrings of preservation reflected an antiquarian interest in curating old buildings as rare objects, the robust urban preservation of this period was animated more by the reform impulse to deploy historic sites as agents of cultural change and social stability. Preservationists were part of the broad cohort of "positive environmentalists," as historian Paul Boyer termed them, pursuing "benevolent social control through environmental change" to create "the kind of physical environment that would gently but irresistibly mold a population of cultivated, moral, and socially responsible city dwellers."[35]

Preservation addressed the cultural crises of modern cities by making a spectacle out of the past. Public consciousness of the past, preservationists believed, was anchored by materiality—the spatial, visual presence of recognizably old places and memorials—and displaying lessons of history before the common citizen in the form of a statue or an old building was considered a sure strategy for shaping the public mind. The experiential aspect of these memory sites was key: If the past could be experienced immediately and personally, its reforming power would be more effective. So the memory infrastructure consisted of places contrasting the stability and certainty of the past with the very changeful present.

Out of the relative chaos and disorder of the fast-growing city's built environment, preservationists designed and preserved relatively few memory sites, but those sites were orderly and coherent in terms of both visual representation and historical narrative. The collection of memory sites studded the expanding metropolis. Preservation advocates believed that "imagineering" a consensus history of the city, literally inscribing it into the built environment by preserving old buildings and creating new monuments, would counterbalance the tumultuous political and economic forces producing disorder and "congestion."

The varied and loosely related collection of places and projects "spatializing" historical memory created remarkably similar versions of the usable past—narratives and images conveyed through buildings, landscapes, artworks, and historical interpretation to imbue the everyday built environment with historical memory. Monuments such as City Hall, preserved Dutch farmhouses, memorial public art, bronze plaques marking historic places, and didactic school tours emanated from the same sources and served the same purpose.

Historic preservation encompassed a variety of constructions and activities giving form and durability to interpretations of the past: exhibits, memorials, battlefields, parks, and public spectacles as well as the saving of old buildings from decay and destruction. Many of these places are described below and still function today: Dyckman House, Morris–Jumel Mansion, Fraunces Tavern, City Hall Park, Riverside

Drive, Battery Park, and many more. Memory sites were located ad hoc, though some in the preservation movement—Bush-Brown, for instance—imagined a memorial geography spanning the whole city, with particular narratives assigned to particular zones: "Our public monuments should be studied as a whole, both as to subject and conception of treatment, in which location should form a part."[36] A glance at the voluminous annual reports of the American Scenic and Historic Preservation Society reveals preservationists' dizzying assortment of projects, issues, and activities: reports on threatened buildings, the progress of restoration projects, and the unveiling of new historical plaques; histories of New York City parks; and management reports on battlefields, plus ideological pronouncements and the occasional reflections on theory. Another sign of preservation's place at the center of modern culture and urbanism was the thoroughly modern organization of the preservation field: Professionals and experts created bureaucratic organizations, created a legal basis for their activity (mostly as state-chartered organizations), maintained political impartiality, and used the media (mostly newspapers) to garner support.

Were preservationists successful in creating a civic memory for all New Yorkers to rally around? The accomplishments of the preservation field were many, providing the city a durable legacy of reform, design, and collective memory—many of these places remain landmarks today. Dozens of memory sites were created and opened to the public, to be visited by substantial numbers of people. These sites did meet the goal of creating some buoys in the sea of change that dominated New York culture. They served as landmarks but were dwarfed by the places of commerce, work, and everyday life that made up most of the New York landscape. But this did not hinder the project of cultivating New Yorkers' collective memory. Preservationists did not seek control over big chunks of the city. To establish a canon of civic memory at the core of urban culture, they needed to shape relatively few, but strategically chosen, sites. There were relatively few places considered worthy of preservation, after all. City Hall, Central Park, Washington's Headquarters, the Battery, and a handful of others were essential; all others were icing on the cake. The historical memory constructed was narrow, paternalistic, largely authoritarian, and rigorously "on message": projecting norms of patriotism and respect for powerful institutions and people while admitting few dissenting narratives.[37] Today's preservation ideal of protecting all the most valuable buildings via regulatory, statutory power was never considered. Creating a view of the past literally shared by all citizens would have been a false hope—far from attainable in famously changeful, chaotic, and pluralistic New York. Preservationists had great faith that their monuments would be received as they intended, so the public needed just a smattering of well-designed memory sites to achieve the desired civic effect. Large-scale preservation orchestrated by government agencies was in its nascent stages and was considered either unnecessary or inappropriate in the dynamic urban milieu of New York.[38] The preservation ideology motivating the creation of these memory sites held that preservation was not an end in itself but rather a *means* to the end of "improvement."

The memory infrastructure built before 1920 laid the groundwork for the very robust historic preservation field of today. But preservation efforts in the early twentieth century were far from totally successful—St. John's Chapel was among the important historic buildings lost. And it would be misleading to think that preservation is successful only when buildings are saved from destruction. Collective memory in modern capitalist culture is a *process*—a continual ebb and flow of remembering and forgetting—and only one among many processes shaping the built environment as citizens experience it. A certain amount of selection, destroying old memory sites and creating new ones, is to be expected as part of this process. The memory infrastructure at the center of this book was an important expression of the desire for collective, historical memory among urban reformers—a desire animated by the Enlightenment notion that education would uplift citizens but motivated by creation of enforceable social norms of patriotism and citizenship. It involved preservation of old urban fabric in a literal sense (defending, protecting, and restoring buildings), as well as destruction of other fabric (demolishing buildings with associations contrary to preservationists' desired messages), and, of course, constant efforts to interpret the meaning of the past and the historical places representing it.

Preservation history should be concerned with the whole process of preservation unfolding within urbanization. Thus, history concerned only with successes—or with preservationists only as heroes—misses the point. This book is not a story of heroes.[39] As much can be learned about the ideas and impact of the preservation field through its failures as through its successes. *The Once and Future New York* brings to urban history a critical analysis of preservation's emergence as a distinct field around the turn of the twentieth century and of its impact on modern New York City.[40] While documenting the field and putting it in context, the book aims to rescue preservation from its marginal position vis-à-vis scholarship on urbanism and urbanization and to remind today's preservationists that their field was born with clear social purposes and vast civic ambition—not just a taste for old buildings.

PLAN OF THE BOOK

More often than not, New York has been on the leading edge of American urbanism. And in the decades surrounding 1900, New York was perhaps the most interesting emergent world city—and a laboratory for a new era of historic preservation. Here preservation was first transformed from an occasional hobby of elites into an urban reform movement. The preservation history of other regions and places has been studied in detail.[41] New York's extensive story is largely unwritten.[42] And in New York, there remains to be told an important part of the national story of preservation.

Research for this book drew on a diversity of historical sources, primary and secondary, both graphic and manuscript. These included records of civic groups and government agencies, historic maps and photographs, land records and condemnation proceedings, the letters and personal papers of civic leaders and others involved in the case studies, newspapers and other periodicals, oral history, and the secondary historical literature on New York City, reform movements, public history, architectural history, and a host of other topics. The secondary research on which the historiographical and theoretical arguments are based draw from a number of disciplines and fields, including human geography, sociology, historiography, and urban and architectural history.

Chapter 1 aims to define and describe the memory infrastructure imagined and constructed in turn-of-the-century New York. After laying out some of the rationales for new memory sites—the disorienting nature of urban change, the modern uses of history, ideals of civic patriotism—the chapter describes the leading institution behind the preservation movement (the American Scenic and Historic Preservation Society) and briefly catalogs the sorts of buildings, parks, monuments, and festivals created as urban aide-mémoire.

The visual legacy of preservation is an important aspect of the field's history. The actual spaces and environments shaped by preservationists—in the city's parks, on the streets, in the interiors of house museums—were critical to preservation theory and cannot be fully captured in the narrative description of book chapters. Following chapter 1 is a portfolio of photographs by Frank Cousins, whose work demonstrates the visual contributions of historic preservation to New York's discourse on urbanism.

Cousins was hired by New York's Art Commission in 1913 to record fifty historic places considered to be valuable—and threatened—expressions of the city's historical memory. Though they could not preserve or redesign each of these places, Art Commission members Isaac Newton Phelps Stokes and Robert De

Forest[43] archived Cousins's images of memorable buildings, "selected with a view to illustrate old buildings famous either for historical associations or interesting for architectural style or for some artistic detail."[44] The list included obvious landmarks—such as City Hall, Morris–Jumel Mansion, St. Paul's Chapel, and St. John's Chapel—as well as ordinary Federal townhouses in Manhattan and colonial farmhouses from the outer boroughs. In addition to individual buildings, Cousins took "portraits" of architectural details—doors, primarily. Such images formed a large part of Cousins's photographic business: He sold pictures of fine colonial architectural details to architects who reproduced them in colonial-revival designs.

Cousins's photographs contrasted the old and the new as seen in 1913, capturing authentic colonial and Federal period architecture as it existed "on the street." The images idealize colonial remainders, while unintentionally capturing the modern moment in which they were made. Cousins was neither a preservationist nor an artist;[45] he possessed insufficient skill to abstract these buildings from their settings. In a passing trolley car, malingerers on a doorstep, or a child staring at the camera, Cousins's images incidentally capture modernity by helping bring these old places into focus as an everyday infrastructure for cultural and social reform.

St. John's Chapel is the subject of chapter 2. St. John's was a large Episcopal church on Varick Street, built in 1803 and destroyed in 1918 after ten years of efforts to preserve it. The story of St. John's, largely unknown today, showcases the contestedness of public memory in urban space, the emergence of a distinctly modern conception of spatialized memory, and changes in the ideology of historic preservation, from an emphasis on associational values toward a focus on aesthetic values. These preservation debates pitted preservationist-reformers and the working-class congregation against the building's owner, Trinity Parish. City officials, prominent citizens, and architects also intervened, offering different arguments and strategies for preserving the building, but to no avail.

City Hall Park was the touchstone site of civic identity and power and a place characterized by a layering of buildings from many periods, as set forth in chapter 3. The park was the subject of many proposals for redevelopment and preservation between the 1880s and 1920s, including an ironic insistence by preservationists that some old buildings (with undesirable associations, such as the Tweed Courthouse) be demolished. Civic memory was at stake in multiple ways here: the endangered City Hall itself; other historic sites and buildings in the park; the sanctity of park space, which was threatened by proposals for new buildings; and City Beautiful urban design proposals, which presented an alternative to place-specific historic preservation as an ideology for spatializing public memory.

Figure I.5. St. John's Chapel before 1914, from the pages of the Nineteenth Annual Report of the American Scenic and Historic Preservation Society (1914, plate 13). This view looks east, across Varick Street. Courtesy of University of Pennsylvania Libraries.

Figure I.6. The paradox of looking forward and backward is artfully frozen in this remarkable image of City Hall Park circa 1913 made by Irving Underhill. City Hall (center) anchored the city's most important public space, symbolic center, and historic landscape. Surrounded by the Post Office and Woolworth Building (left), the Tweed Courthouse (immediately behind City Hall, just to the right), and the Brooklyn Bridge terminal (right), it was set within the park occupying much of the historic Commons. To merge past and future even more convincingly, two airplanes and the Municipal Building (right) were later spliced onto the photograph's negative. Courtesy of Library of Congress, Prints and Photographs Division.

Chapter 4 tells the story of the Bronx River Parkway. The world's first automobile parkway, it was planned and built between 1906 and 1925 on the edge of metropolitan expansion. The goal of the parkway project was the reconstruction of the ecology, economy, appearance, and social character of the Bronx River valley. Plans called for cleaning up and redeveloping the valley, as well as for creating a recreational park and a roadway connecting city and suburbs. To implement their multifarious vision, the Bronx Parkway Commission used a number of strategies to shape public memory, including the use of naturalistic design, photography, and storytelling about the valley's history and the commission's work in transforming it. In the process, the existing landscape, and its more recent past of "slums and Italian shacks," was erased. One valley landscape was creatively destroyed to be replaced with a new one embodying the cutting edge of both heritage (combining memory and nature) and modernity (combining movement and separation).

The conclusion summarizes the lessons of this history and connects this period to contemporary issues and research themes in historic preservation. There are

Figure I.7. Traffic on the Bronx River Parkway in 1922, when the project was mostly constructed and parts of the roadway were open. Note the river just behind the roadway and the newly made natural landscape in the foreground. Courtesy of Library of Congress, Prints and Photographs Division, Historic American Engineering Record.

many parallels between the challenges facing the early history of urban preservation of New York and those facing preservation early in the twenty-first century. The connections between historic preservation and other social issues and urban practices (architecture, city planning, economic development, social policy, cultural conflict) continue to be among the most promising, problematic, and misunderstood aspects of the preservation field.

Exploring the history of historic preservation raises the same question that plagues the contemporary pursuit of preservation: How is one to square the desire to save aspects of the existing environment with the overwhelming forces behind creating new buildings and new urban environments? The relationships between creating the new and saving the old are, as the following pages show, quite a bit more complex and contradictory than they appear on the surface. Fundamentally, historic preservation was deployed as a way to imagine a new city. It was a kind of planning, a kind of design, a way of acknowledging and asserting the public realm. This reality stands in contrast to the reputation of historic preservation as an arcane, hermetic practice of antiquarians.

New York's historic preservation advocates left a great legacy, a sampling of which is captured in the following chapters. But the landscape of their achievement went well beyond what is documented here—myriad historic places were created, historicist designs imagined, debates enjoined, demolitions averted, and public spaces sustained. And, more impressive, the places they cared for remain vibrant parts of contemporary New York. Like Edmund Wilson, preservationists today often feel "haunted" by disappeared buildings and lost memories. The preservation leaders whose stories follow leave us with another, more hopeful idea, though: that the rich, extant environments help us remember our shared past as citizens, can serve as inspirations, and should take their legitimate place as part of the infrastructural bones and guts of the great city.

One

Memory Sites: Buildings, Parks, Events

> Every collective memory unfolds within a spatial framework. . . . space
> is a reality that endures: . . . we can understand how we recapture the
> past only by understanding how it is, in effect, preserved by our physical
> surroundings.
>
> Maurice Halbwachs, *The Collective Memory*

E VERY CITY HAS ITS MEMORIALS, MARKED SITES, TREASURED PLACES, MUSE-
ums, stories, rituals, ruins, places left behind; they are inscribed in the life
of the city "like the lines of a hand," as Italo Calvino famously wrote.[1] Historians,
architects, and urbanists have long given short shrift to the aspect of city building that deposits and erodes historical memory, assuming that historic places are
found rather than made.[2] It follows that historic places have been regarded as
hidden treasures or adornments rather than purposeful infrastructure. But New
York's memorial landscape was purposely constructed to meet social needs and
political desires — markers of a period when memory and history loomed large in
American culture and urbanism and cities were rife with conflict and change.

What exactly was New York's memory infrastructure? What were its parts, and
what glue held them together? By whom, how, and why was it made? This chapter
describes the scope and character of the memory infrastructure and some of the
people and organizations behind its creation.

DEFINING MEMORY INFRASTRUCTURE

New York's memory infrastructure was a broad and diverse collection of memory
sites.[3] The traditional tropes of historic preservation — house museums, restored
works of fine architecture, battlefield sites, historical markers and plaques — formed
the core of the city's memory infrastructure and extended to include urban parks,
natural landscapes, and public artworks. They ranged from colonial farmhouses
in Brooklyn and Staten Island, to the thick cluster of historic buildings in Lower

Manhattan, to the parks network in Manhattan and the Bronx. Memory sites were found in the urban core as well as on the periphery. Locating memory sites in such prominent, obvious places—especially in parks—gave them a presence in the everyday experience of New Yorkers. While the locations of some sites could not be manipulated, some buildings were resituated to make them more accessible to the public (either by moving them to preserve them or by creating a parklike setting around them to visually emphasize their extraordinary value or to contrast the old placed among the new). All such places were set apart from the juggernaut of urbanization—visually (by design) and economically (by purchasing sites and protecting them from the market)—because of their extraordinary cultural value.

The process of building memory infrastructure was ad hoc but drew on a consensus of ideologies and methods: attitudes toward treating historic fabric (restoration was preferred, relocation was fine), toward designing the context of memory sites (monuments surrounded by lawn and park space), toward including select figures in the pantheon of civic patriotism (founding fathers, civic leaders, generals, and assorted other moral paragons, such as Joan of Arc, who was sainted in 1909) and excluding others. These principles gave the memory infrastructure a remarkable consistency even though many people, groups, agencies, and artists were involved in its making without formal rules or regulations.

The uses and functions of memory sites were explained in 1901 by Andrew Haswell Green, founder of the American Scenic and Historic Preservation Society (ASHPS) and fountainhead of preservation ideology:

> Within the limits of our own city, in the dramas of the past, have been enacted tragedies that are inspirations to lofty undertakings, the memories of which are fast fading from mind and of which no visible memorials have yet been established. Such landmarks are too rapidly yielding to the obliteration of time, and to preserve them is a sacred duty, akin to that of teaching the children of our public schools or maintaining libraries for the education of our people. Where there are no such existing memorials, we believe in fostering patriotic sentiment by the erection of monuments and tablets in appropriate places.[4]

Physical, historic fabric and "visible memorials" connected people and the past. The "lofty undertakings" were positive moral lessons of patriotic self-sacrifice, occasioned by "tragedies" such as British colonial oppression or Tammany political corruption. The moral power of historic places was unfailing and unexamined, and there was never a clear discussion of whether a particular place was "historic" or

Figure 1.1. Schenck House in Brooklyn, St. Paul's Chapel in Manhattan, and Van Cortlandt Manor in the Bronx, as photographed for the Historic American Building Survey in the 1930s. These seventeenth- and eighteenth-century buildings were typical of greater New York's surviving historic places around the turn of the twentieth century. Courtesy of Library of Congress, Prints and Photographs Division, Historic American Buildings Survey.

not—one just knew. The power of historic places had several dimensions—political (lionizing "lofty undertakings" of city building), social (socialization of school-children as citizens), and historical (stories or "memories . . . fast fading from mind"). Reflecting the evolution of reformist thinking over Green's career (from the 1850s through 1903), the preservation imperative was framed in unabashedly spiritual terms—as a "sacred duty."

Valuing buildings and places for aesthetic or artistic reasons was another of the drivers behind preservation activity. Architectural value, though it dominated preservation discourse by the end of the twentieth century, gradually influenced preservation, only becoming significant in the second decade of the twentieth century. Aesthetic or architectural significance of two kinds was acknowledged: a building's value as an artwork (its beauty, originality, and so on) and its association with a famous architect. (The two did not always come together: Not all famous architects' buildings have equal artistic value.) An aesthetic taste for ruins, so important in the development of European preservationist thinking, was not a strong influence in New York.

Preservationists sought to create public environments where historical memory could be put on display for the city's men, women, and children to soak in. Preservationists subscribed to theories of environmental determinism and artistic associationism. How transmission and reception of historical meaning happened was not explicitly questioned or examined. Historic places' moral transference worked in miraculous ways; the uplifting power of brave examples and good ideas would somehow find their way into the souls and minds of those needing uplift. The belief that history's lessons would be transmitted relied on the same kind of imagined rationality that supported a (misplaced) faith in an invisible hand of the market that would create an equitable as well as efficient economy. Some preservationists preferred biological metaphors of transmission: "Historic sites and buildings . . . exhale the subtle influences which refresh patriotism, civic virtue, piety and love." Or, with a more anthropomorphic twist: "A historic edifice is an unceasing teacher of history. . . . To affix to a building occupying such a [historic] site a conspicuous tablet recording a glorious name or deed is to open a perennial fountain of inspiration, to establish a silent but effective preacher of virtue."[5]

Andrew Haswell Green (1820–1903) typified the positive environmentalist strain of Progressive reform as it evolved from the previous reform model aimed at individual morals.[6] Green was a lawyer and political associate of Samuel Tilden; his public career was marked by his contributions to civic institutions and public spaces that framed New York's ascendance to be the capital of capitalism: His devotion to anti-Tammany political reform led to his work on state education and city public works and finance systems; he bore great responsibility for creating civic institutions such as the New York Public Library and Central Park; he was behind the planning of new neighborhoods in northern Manhattan and the Bronx and of Riverside Park; he earned the moniker "Father of Greater New York" by advocating the consolidation of the five boroughs into one metropolis (finally effected in 1898); he took a leading hand in the preservation of Niagara Falls and the New Jersey Palisades; and he organized the nascent preservation field, founding the ASHPS.[7]

Green's achievements—battling for political reform, modeling the public sector's responsibilities, building institutions and infrastructures—made New York at the dawn of the twentieth century as livable a city as it was economically successful. To the extent Green is remembered these days, he is lionized. But he had more adversaries in his career than just the ones at Tammany Hall. Tough treatment of Central Park workers and difficult relations with Frederick Law Olmsted and Calvert Vaux over park construction stemmed from his relentless drive for efficiency. Roy Rosenzweig and Elizabeth Blackmar concluded that Green's "managerial regime served the interests of the city's wealthiest taxpayers and businessmen, and the park workers understood this deeper level of political antagonism."[8]

Having stamped out corruption and having scrutinized every contract and contractor, Green "came out of his office [as City comptroller] one of the most unpopular men in the city."[9] Building a public realm did not necessarily translate into fair treatment for all constituent parts of the public.

Upon his untimely death in 1903 (gunned down, mistakenly, by a jealous husband), much reform work remained to be done, but Green's achievements set the framework for the generations of reformers and city builders to follow

Figure 1.2. Andrew Haswell Green. Courtesy of University of Pennsylvania Libraries.

in the fields of city planning, parks, and historic preservation. Though Robert
Moses eclipsed Green in the next generation as a renowned city builder, Moses's
achievements were prefigured by Green's (in the regional scale and comprehensive scope of his efforts and in the creative use of quasi-public corporations).

In a career spanning the second half of the nineteenth century, Green advocated the expansion, improvement, and political consolidation of the city. Two concerns drove his thinking and work. The animating force of Green's work in all fields
was the immorality of "political partisanship" and its "sinister influence" on the city:
the corruption of Tammany politicians whose patronage had come to dominate
New York's politics by midcentury.[10] Green's second major concern was "improving" the city comprehensively, by building parks and other cultural infrastructure
to accompany growth. That historic preservation was part of his broad, ambitious
vision for the city speaks clearly to the view among early leaders of the field that
preservation should be an active part of the city's growth and modernization—a
way to shape the growing city, not rebel against it.

Green was instrumental in preserving City Hall in situ, when support for moving
or replacing it ran high in the 1890s. Responding to threats to City Hall, he wrote
a pamphlet, published by the Sons of the American Revolution in 1894, articulat-
ing his preservation philosophy—a hybrid of individually and socially focused reform movements, the positive environmentalism that characterized the last third
of the nineteenth century, and a zealous pursuit of fiscal responsibility.[11]

Realizing a more general need to inject this sort of preservationist thinking
into city-planning debates, in 1895 Green founded the ASHPS, a quasi-public
group organized to preserve historic places, conserve natural sites, and advocate
for historic preservation in New York and nationally. Using his deep political connections to garner state sanction for his group, Green forged a political niche for
historic and scenic preservation. The ASHPS managed some state-owned parks,
brokered historic preservation projects, and served as a clearinghouse for the
emergent preservation field. Green led the ASHPS until his tragic death in 1903,
after which the ASHPS became a kind of living memorial to Green and his preservationist vision. The ASHPS trustees, in their November 13, 1903, memorial on
the death of Green, wove together the many strands of Green's public service and
moral forthrightness: "Pure in heart, lofty in ideals, gentle in spirit but strong of
deed . . . the standard of American citizenship is higher for the mark which he
attained." For his stewardship of the preservation movement, Green was remembered as "the devoted patriot, in whose veins flowed the blood of an heroic ances-
try, [who] took intense pride in the history of his country, the monuments and re-

cords of whose progress he strove to preserve."[12] The moral tone and Progressive bias clear in this encomium to their leader spoke volumes about the preservation field as it took hold in the heyday of environmental reform that followed in the first two decades of the twentieth century.

Preservation was a matter of public good to Green, who linked preservation of buildings, landscapes, and other memory sites to other kinds of urban infrastructure he was directly involved in building for New York—parks, libraries, and schools. While the memory infrastructure included a variety of forms and locations, the historical content of sites was narrowly focused on a few related themes. In keeping with the consensual notion of history that predominated in the public history practices of this period,[13] the historical narratives conveyed by memory infrastructure fell into just a few categories. Patriotism was the umbrella for these narratives, which included ancestor worship, most often focused on the founding fathers and Revolutionary War heroes (George Washington, of course, but Alexander Hamilton and Nathan Hale had important ties to New York City, which elevated their importance), whose stories were useful for "promoting good citizenship by perpetuating the memories of good citizens."[14] Houses and other sites related to these heroes were perhaps the most predictable sites of preservationist interest. Revolutionary War events had particular allure; battle sites around the city were marked, though they often bore little resemblance to their condition during historic events. One of the many aspects of reverence for City Hall Park was its history as the site where the Declaration of Independence was first read to the American army and to Washington himself. New York also had its requisite "Washington's Headquarters" (the Morris–Jumel Mansion). Other Revolutionary War narratives specific to New York included the erection of liberty poles in the Commons as a protest against the British and the "martyrdom" of American prisoners, whose sites included a mausoleum in Brooklyn's Fort Greene Park and the old Hall of Records (also known as the Martyrs' Prison) in City Hall Park.

"Civic patriotism" was preservation's overarching, consensus theme, consisting of narratives relating specifically to the rise of New York as a great city. Patriotism would be inspired, reformers believed, by celebrating the sites of great historic events (such as the Revolutionary War); the homes of the founding fathers; the city as a cradle for political, technical, and economic greatness (such as Stamp Act protests, Robert Fulton's invention of the steamboat, the Croton water system); and a forward-looking model for the kind of cultivated, balanced urbanism that preservationists saw themselves trying to perpetuate (the great urban parks, especially Central and Riverside parks, as well as older parks like the Battery and Fort Greene parks). Preserving historic fabric or erecting new memorials in these places defined the city's genius loci or, as in the phrase of sociologist Robert Bellah, the community's "constitutive narrative."[15]

The civic patriotism narrative wove together political and economic threads seamlessly as hand-in-hand historical achievements—a theme of boosterish, forward-looking confidence that the greatness of New York's past, if carefully balanced with progress, would translate into an illustrious future. Celebrating commercial success had its limits, though. The enemies of Progressive reformers included rapacious capitalists and their fellow travelers, the corrupt machine politicians. Narratives associated with such characters—Cornelius Vanderbilt or William Marcy "Boss" Tweed, for example—were assiduously avoided, and the canon of civic patriotism was largely formed in opposition to them. Finally, civic patriotism drew on sites expressing the persistence of Old New York, places distinguished by age-value and antiquarianism, the kind of old places fundamentally of interest to preservationists as a source of insight on the past.[16] The antiquarians were mostly upper-class elites, and the sites they championed included neighborhoods of typical Federal houses in and around Greenwich Village, old churches, and cemeteries. Old New York icons were increasingly rare, not only because of destruction by development or physical deterioration, but because of New York's series of devastating fires (especially those of 1776 and 1835).

Preservationists' reliance on natural and scenic places *as well as* buildings and designed landscapes as elements of memory infrastructure was a striking aspect of the early field. Scenic, natural, and historic places were closely related in preservationist ideology—"there is an intimate and fundamental relation between scenery and history"[17]—and the main historic preservation group of the period fused the two concepts in practice: the American Scenic *and* Historic Preservation Society. Nature, and the arrangement or preservation of natural places to make them sufficiently "scenic," was an important source of materials and meaning for preservationists. "Scenic" simply meant that a natural place met with conventional ideas about aesthetic value—the picturesque, or more prominently, the sublime. Assessments of natural beauty relied on canonical views of wildness, the sublime, and contrast to urban places. As with Olmstedian parks, the fusion of scenic beauty and the blocks and streets of urbanism was purposeful—a consciously designed landscape, balancing the salutary influences of nature with the cultivation possible in cities.

The core of modern culture draws on the past: heritage, patrimony, collective memory, and other forms of inheritance. To the Transcendentalists and other artists and thinkers who helped define American culture in the first half of the nineteenth century, the natural splendors and riches of the continent were a key part of this inheritance. In the twentieth century, at the national scale, nature still contributed to the emergent sense of heritage (with the creation of national monuments and parks in the West), and at the metropolitan scale designed parks contributed to civic patriotism.

The following sections summarize the main forms of memory infrastructure through which preservationists displayed civic patriotism: first, the institutions created to marshal preservation activity and communicate the need for memory infrastructure; second, the buildings, parks, monuments, and public festivals making up the infrastructure.

American Scenic and Historic Preservation Society

Institutions were an important part of the memory infrastructure—the means of creating memory sites, as essential as the ends themselves. Not only did institutions and their leaders advocate for and manage the places and monuments created, but they also represented lasting investments in the role of preservation as part of the larger practice of city building. Perhaps the most surprising achievement of this period was an organization devoted singularly to preservation, defining the preservationist mind-set of the period and opening a window for historians on this period of development in the historic preservation field. A dozen or more institutions worked on preservation goals in this period—some wholly created, others adapted to preservation from other goals. These included the city's Parks Department and Art Commission, the Fine Arts Federation, the Architectural League, the City History Club, and the Daughters of the American Revolution (DAR). One institution in particular is featured here—the ASHPS—of overwhelming importance because Green invented it specifically to give preservation a presence in city building.

The end of the nineteenth century saw the awakening of historical consciousness all over the country, and in New York as well.[18] Published histories flourished, including Teddy Roosevelt's *New York* of 1890, Charles Hemstreet's *Nooks and Corners of Old New York*, and many others.[19] A number of historical organizations formed for collective remembering, including hereditary groups (Daughters of the American Revolution, Sons of the American Revolution), antiquarian groups (Society of Old Brooklynites, Society of Iconophiles), the City History Club (focused on immigrant education), the august New-York Historical Society (founded in 1804), and the ASHPS.

The ASHPS was the most interesting and important organization advocating historic preservation in early-twentieth-century New York.[20] Describing itself as "a National Society for the Protection of Natural Scenery, the Preservation of Landmarks and the Improvement of Cities," the ASHPS was organized in 1895 as a voice for historic preservation, natural conservation, and urban reform in New York State as a whole, and for New York City in particular.[21] As an advocate, lobbyist, expert, and "information bureau," the ASHPS advanced the cause of preservation as part of the broader reform agenda. (Active into the 1940s, the society was dissolved in the 1970s.) The society's archive is the best window on the emergent ideology of preservation, the scope and intent of preservationist activities, and the political economy of preservationist institutions in the Progressive Era.

The ASHPS was chartered by the New York State legislature in 1895 and headquartered in New York City.[22] The state charter was significant, giving the society land-management responsibilities for a few state-owned park and historic properties, political leverage in the abiding political struggle between state and city, and a public mandate to issue annual reports and other missives. State funding was secured only for management of the few specific state-owned sites; all general operating funds were privately raised by the society, and the society was not afforded the power to issue bonds. This organizational model grew from Green's decades of experience as a political entrepreneur working with the pioneering Central Park Commission, the state commissions on preserving Niagara Falls and the Adirondack Mountains, and other forerunners of today's public-benefit corporations, all hybrid institutions with measures of private as well as public power and support.

In an 1895 "Memorial to the Legislature," Green proposed creating an organization specializing in historic preservation and natural ("scenic") conservation issues, using private initiatives backed by state sponsorship to transcend political interests and protect the public interest in historical memory and its expression in the built environment and landscape. "It would seem a fitting time that conservative methods be devised by means of which objects of historic value, localities where patriotic struggles have taken place, where peculiar natural scenery obtains, or made interesting by association with illustrious personages, should be rescued from the grasp of private speculation and preserved for public enjoyment." Referencing narratives of the French and Indian War and Revolutionary conflicts, he went on, "It cannot be but that the intelligent administration of these [scenic and historic] objects and areas will tend to quicken the spirit of patriotism to act as an example and stimulus to a higher standard of care of public grounds in the villages and towns throughout the State, and to cultivate attachment to localities—a most desirable influence to be fostered."[23]

The Trustees of Reservations, a group formed in Massachusetts in 1891 for the mission of preserving the grounds on which patriotic deeds had been performed, served as a model for Green (a Massachusetts native) when he formed the ASHPS. The mandate of the Trustees of Reservations was to preserve the natural places that give the state its particular character, along with the cultural landscapes—battlefields, farms—that built local and state identity. Keeping with this model, the ASHPS took interest in all sorts of natural and scenic places: battlefields, natural wonders, urban parks, river valleys, and village squares.[24]

In keeping with Green's obsession with fiscal responsibility (his penny-pinching made him Olmsted's nemesis in the process of building Central Park), his "Memorial to the Legislature" was framed as a money-saving suggestion, not as a request for money. The society's legislated mandate included powers to acquire and hold property, receive donations, administer lands given it by the state, act in concert with other states (that is, in organizing the Palisades Interstate Commission with New Jersey), and report bills and other recommendations directly to the legislature. The society traded on its close connection to the state, as well as its separateness from government agencies, to engage the public (mostly fellow professionals and reformers) on issues regarding preservation.

The society pursued three kinds of work, and it was remarkably consistent in these priorities between 1895 and 1925. First, it promoted preserving specific buildings and erecting memorials on specific sites. This was accomplished by cultivating public support (through publishing reports and maintaining connections to newspapers),[25] fund-raising, and lobbying public officials. Second, it promoted the beautification and improvement of cities by various means beyond preservation (including advocating for the new field of city planning, creation of parks, and the "landscape adornment" of open spaces and thoroughfares). Third, it administered places of scenic or historic interest (five battlefields and scenic parks) as a trustee designated by the state. The society had no regulatory power and little statutory power.[26]

The society was a modestly sized organization, and it is something of a wonder that such a range and variety of work was sustained between 1895 and 1925 and that its annual reports were so voluminous.[27] In its first couple decades, there were times of financial need and appeals for new members. Subscribing membership hovered between three hundred and five hundred; most activities were managed by a group of seven to ten officers and a few other activist members heading up a changing set of committees. The board of trustees met monthly and consisted of a few dozen members; task-specific committees expanded this group by another score. The first five years brought two reorganizations, the accumulation of some operating funds through subscriptions, and a small endowment from J. P. Morgan Sr. With these resources, historian and newspaperman Edward Hagaman

Hall was hired in 1898 as full-time secretary, and Hall became the workhorse of the society for decades thenceforth.[28]

The ASHPS allied its preservation-centered reform mission with other environmental reform and design movements. The society's 1923 mission statement read:

> The activities of most historical societies deal with events of the past. But the American Scenic and Historic Preservation Society was organized to deal with the past, the present, and the future. The work of the Society is designed to minister to both the physical and spiritual well-being of the people. Parks and playgrounds and good civic conditions tend to promote the health and happiness of the community. The cherishing of our historical landmarks and the perpetuation of our patriotic traditions tend to make better citizens of our people and to stabilize our cherished political institutions. The preservation of the beautiful places and the wonderful works of Nature serves to raise the people's thoughts to the Author and Giver of all good things.[29]

The society was part of a "whole group of organizations devoted to the cultivation of 'municipal aesthetics,' including not only the village improvement and rural art societies that are now so numerously scattered throughout the country, but the larger bodies like the ASHPS, and the Municipal Art Society of New York."[30] The ASHPS and these other organizations often had overlapping membership and leadership, and their missions often converged. For instance, the 1912 ASHPS report endorses the emerging science of city planning and George McAneny's 1912 proposal to establish a city planning commission, declaring "City Planning 'Pays'"—the ultimate New York endorsement.

Leading architect and planner Arnold Brunner, also an ASHPS member, voiced the idea that preservation and planning could easily be balanced: "We know that good city planning is especially careful to preserve local traditions, old buildings of historic value, and everything that accentuates the individuality of a city."[31]

The ASHPS participated in most of the prominent preservation debates in this period, including over St. John's Chapel, City Hall Park, Morris–Jumel Mansion, Hamilton Grange, and Central Park. Its role was often one of advocacy, and it cultivated contacts with politicians and public officials.[32] As George McAneny put it, though, owning historic sites was the name of the game: "The idea, of course, is to get possession of the titles of things that are in danger."[33] It mattered little who actually owned and controlled the sites, as long as they retained their memory function. It some cases, the society played a material role—for instance, acquiring Hamilton Grange. More often, the society argued that city and state government had a responsibility to acquire and maintain—with the help of civic associations and citizens—lands and buildings clearly of public value for their memory and beauty.

The society's most frequent role was as cheerleader and reporter—spreading the word that the people learn from historic places and are made healthier by scenic places. By communicating this appreciation of history and of the cultural value of historic places and environments, acts of stewardship would grow.

Decisions on what projects to advocate came ad hoc from the officers and active membership of the society, and there was no evident contention over which projects to favor or what positions to take. The society's record was very mixed: There were substantial victories, such as Morris–Jumel Mansion, Poe Cottage, and Philipse Manor; failures, such as St. John's Chapel and Fraunces Tavern; and mixed results, including City Hall Park. The society office was periodically approached by nonmembers requesting help in preserving sites. Sometimes the board rejected such suggestions, on the grounds that the appeals were motivated by "business purposes" or that the site in question was "not historic," but there were no explicit criteria for acceptance or rejection.[34] It also sought to build on its New-York-centric network by organizing the Hudson–Fulton Celebration and helping create and administer the Palisades Interstate Park Commission, and to widen its circle of influence by working with the Association for the Preservation of Virginia Antiquities on Jamestown Island[35] and inviting lectures and reports on such subjects as the state of historic preservation in foreign countries, the work of the English National Trust, or wartime destruction in European cities.

Parks and open spaces were just as important as buildings to the ASHPS. Both kinds of place supported public remembering. By the early twentieth century, preservationists of all kinds regarded "scenic and historic" qualities as strongly linked, an idea embedded in American culture in the writings of Thomas Cole and Frederick Law Olmsted, in popular images of historic and natural landscapes, and in the dual mandate of federal laws and the National Park Service to protect and provide access to both "natural" and "cultural" parks.[36] The encroachment of new buildings, infrastructure, or uses in any city park alarmed the ASHPS as much as any threat to a colonial house. Annual reports detailed the defeats and victories in this vein, framing them as issues of scenic conservation, recreational need, and valuable memory. Efforts to prevent encroachments on parks protected a legacy of nature-in-the-city and the Herculean efforts of various reformers to create the parks, which (then as now) were crucial to the form, meaning, and memory of the city. And in the cases of Central and Morningside parks, preservation efforts protected the legacy of the society's founder, Andrew Green, who had been instrumental in their creation.

Managing "state reservations" was an important aspect of the society's work. The five properties managed by the ASHPS represented its interests in scenic preservation beyond the issues of urban parks.[37] Each annual report related detailed plans, expenditures, visitation statistics, and photographs for each of the five places: Stony Point Battlefield State Reservation on the west shore of the Hudson River, site of a Mad Anthony Wayne's successful raid on British forces in the Revolutionary War; Watkins Glen State Reservation, a natural reserve at the head of Seneca Lake in the Finger Lakes region; Fort Brewerton State Reservation, a French and Indian War and Revolutionary War site on Oneida Lake; Letchworth Park, including the falls of the Upper Genesee River (containing Native American historic sites and second to Niagara Falls as a sightseeing destination); and Philipse Manor Hall, a vestige of the Dutch patroon landscape in Yonkers, which the society transformed from use as city hall to a historic site and museum. These places, though not in New York City proper, illustrated the society's larger goals: the advancement of patriotism as a cultural reform, a holistic view of natural and historic places as objects of conservation, and stewardship through a combination of "disinterested" management and government ownership.

In any given year, the ASHPS studied and researched preservation projects, issued reports, advocated positions, lobbied publicly and privately, helped organize campaigns, and more. It kept vigil over dozens of projects at a time, mostly in New York State but spanning the country and the world. The society envisioned itself as a clearinghouse for the burgeoning preservation field—a "Bureau of Information."[38] Members were encouraged to use the society and its office, so that "efforts for local projects of a public nature find their effectiveness still further increased by their association with an influential body of advisers and colaborers."[39]

The ASHPS complemented the isolated, ad hoc projects that preservationists pursued on the ground with regular publications. Information on historic preservation nationally, internationally, and in New York was published primarily through annual reports. Hundreds of copies of the annual reports were printed and bound, distributed widely, and "Transmitted to the Legislature" each year between 1896 and 1930.[40] The society's self-conscious archive—annual reports and board minutes—present a wealth of information about the ambition and scope of preservationist activities. In 1908, ASHPS president George Frederick Kunz, introducing another annual report hundreds of pages thick, noted that it recorded "numerous other matters which have engaged our attention from time to time [including] . . . the condition of the parks and monuments and other municipal conditions in New York City . . . Tree protection, tree labeling, the care of neglected monuments, the recommendation of tablets, the identification of sites, the preservation of many buildings not mentioned herein."[41] ASHPS reports included lengthy histories of important threatened sites (Central Park, City Hall Park, the Morris–Jumel Mansion, Hamilton Grange, St. John's Chapel); the 1914 edition included a lengthy report on the New York Commercial Tercentenary Celebration (organized by Edward Hagaman Hall) and Reginald Bolton's archaeological digs in northern Manhattan. Pamphlets and monographs on specific sites and buildings were published for wider dissemination. The histories presented were straightforward chronologies for the most part, clearly written and well illustrated. They included graphic documentation: Photographs are part of every history the society commissioned (often written by Hall), and maps were presented demonstrating a keen archaeological sense of the relationships between extant and destroyed historic resources. Such diachronic representations of the built environment represented the city that preservationists wished to commemorate; in the case of City Hall Park, for instance, preservationists' maps have proven to be of lasting scholarly value.[42]

The ASHPS differed significantly from the Daughters of the American Revolution, the Sons of the American Revolution, and other organizations, lacking the hereditary groups' singular ideological bias toward patriotic narratives (not to mention their hereditary requirements for membership). The ASHPS certainly advocated national patriotism and supported Americanization, but it reached beyond these to focus on a broad agenda of urban improvement and the cultivation of scenic and historic values. The ASHPS realized that preservation should do more than save the houses of the founding fathers. It promoted a more expansive, engaged, positive view of historic preservation than its nineteenth-century antiquarian predecessors or heredity-besotted contemporaries.[43] Choosing pragmatism over stridency (especially after Green's death), ASHPS leaders ignored the advice of Charles Ashbee, an acolyte of William Morris who lectured to the society in 1900. America was fertile ground, he saw, for preservation as a protest against industrialization and "materialism":

An appeal to the American citizen against . . . materialism has in it a special piquancy and meaning. . . . It is in the United States that the problems of modern civilization are being worked out & given consideration before all things else. It is here that the battle with the hard facts of life, the battle with natural forces, the stress of individual and racial development is fiercest. . . . This materialism [the American] has built up for himself, is it going to destroy him? What will he shape it to? What will it shape him to? It is his Sphinx riddle.

Preservation, Ashbee suggested, was an answer: "We, indeed, are wearying of the empty objectless life of great cities, we are searching for another side in human development that modern materialism denies us."[44] While the ASHPS was more progressive than William Sumner Appleton and his Society for the Preservation of New England Antiquities (SPNEA), by comparison,[45] it rejected the more conservative and more radical approaches—it was not about to give up on "materialism," the culture of business that was a core New York sensibility.

The ASHPS took steadfastly conservative interpretations of history, cultivating normative historical narratives to reinforce heroic traditions and create social cohesion: "As a nation we have three centuries of precious political traditions, affecting our social conditions and rights of property. At the present time these traditions are seriously threatened and we feel that every important instrumentality for cultivating sentiment in favor of their maintenance should be encouraged. The ASHPS endeavors to be such an instrumentality."[46] Society policy was sometimes frankly dismissive of dissent or departure from consensus views. At the annual meeting of January 18, 1910, ASHPS members passed a resolution *against* the use of Central Park (and presumably other public places) for "public speaking, where strikers, woman suffragists, single-tax advocates, and propagandists . . . may meet for the discussion of their causes." The resolution was "unanimously supported."[47]

Andrew Green was the icon of the ASHPS, an enduring influence even after his death. Green had tried to resign as president of the society in 1899, claiming he was too busy, but the other board members talked him out of it.[48] After his death, the ASHPS maintained a voice in city planning, urban beautification, administrative reform, and park issues. But it dropped the moralizing, religious tones, which sounded more like artifacts of the nineteenth century (Green's century) in the face of the "City Efficient" ideology that peaked in the first decade of the twentieth century. The ASHPS became, in a way, a monument to Green, preserving the memory of reform by lionizing the memory of a chief reformer in a form of civic filiopietism.[49]

The officers and trustees represented a "new" elite of upper-middle-class professionals and artists, whose collective mission was enacting a whole range of public, nonpartisan reforms. This leadership group overlapped a great deal with those of the Municipal Art Society, the Fine Arts Federation, the National Arts Club, and other visual arts and reform societies. They inhabited the more conservative branches of the Progressive reform movement, seeking to ameliorate the worst excesses of capitalist development and build a society of democratic culture as well as economic prosperity. For instance, the society counted a leading housing reformer among its members—but that reformer was conservative Robert De Forest, not the more radical Benjamin Marsh. Advocates for reform of poverty were absent from the society. Other prominent members included engineer Nelson Lewis, landscape architect Samuel Parsons, architects Arnold Brunner and Thomas Hastings, the head of the American Museum of Natural History Henry Fairfield Osborn, and even national experts such as civic improvement writer Charles Mulford Robinson and architect-planner Daniel Burnham.

Following Green's death, Tiffany and Company executive George Frederick Kunz long served as president of the ASHPS. Kunz was a prominent and well-connected professional—a mineralogist with a doctorate from a German university and a national authority on gems who corresponded with such scientists as William Morris Davis, Hiram Bingham, and Bashford Dean, philanthropists Samuel Avery and Cleveland Dodge, City History Club founder Catherine Abbe, reformer Robert De Forest, and Columbia University president Nicholas Murray Butler.[50] Professionally, Kunz led the New York Academy of Sciences and was curator of precious stones at the American Museum of Natural History. His public history efforts ventured more broadly than historic preservation per se: He launched the campaign to build New York's Joan of Arc memorial, was a member of the Board of American Pageant Association, and helped lead the enormous efforts to organize the Hudson–Fulton and Commercial Tercentenary celebrations (with Hall, in 1909 and 1914, respectively). As part of his work leading the ASHPS, Kunz became an authority on park preservation and its social benefits.[51] On other fronts, Kunz was appointed by George McAneny to sit on the Fifth Avenue Commission (a body advising the borough president on matters of "architectural regulation"), and, under the leadership of banker and conservation philanthropist George Perkins, he raised funds for the YMCA and other civic ventures.[52]

Though driven by professionals of the reformer-elite class, the society had the tacit (and sometimes active) support of the city's financial elite, too. Even a glance at some of the names help locate the society: Besides Green, the most prominent name is that of the Morgans, John Pierpont Morgan Sr., who was longtime honorary president, and John Pierpont Morgan Jr., who, with partner George F. Baker, bought and donated Hamilton Grange to the ASHPS in 1924; another prominent figure was Samuel P. Avery, art collector, philanthropist, and donor of Columbia's Avery Library. The board actively invited prominent people to become members, including John D. Rockefeller and Olivia Sage (Mrs. Russell Sage). The ASHPS sometimes requested support from people in high places: New York State governor Frank W. Higgins and President Theodore Roosevelt responded by writing brief encomiums for inclusion in the 1905 Annual Report; a 1907 brochure included endorsements from the presidents of Harvard (Charles Eliot), Yale (Arthur Hadley), and Columbia (Seth Low), Bishop Henry Potter of the Episcopal Diocese of New York, and the archbishop of the Roman Catholic See of St. Paul.[53]

Women played a small role in the ASHPS, though they were prominent in the preservation field in the nineteenth century.[54] A few women were subscribing members of the society, and they tended to be women of means as opposed to professionals or reformers, but the active work was almost exclusively done by men. The exception was Melusina Fay Peirce, who forged interesting points of contact between the increasingly male-dominated preservation field and women's reform traditions. When the ASHPS formed a "sister" organization, the Women's Auxiliary, in 1900, Peirce was its head. She had been an accomplished reformer for decades, a prominent advocate of cooperative housekeeping and other issues, since living in Boston in the 1870s when she was married to Harvard philosopher Charles Sanders Peirce. The Women's Auxiliary was created to sustain the work of some New York women in preservation; it began as a Fraunces Tavern committee of the Mary Washington Chapter of the DAR.[55] And despite the fact that the ASHPS took a paternalistic attitude toward them, the women's preservation work was impressive. The auxiliary, like the DAR chapters, raised money and created and curated historic house museums, focusing on themes of patriotism and domesticity, working veins of historical narrative effectively the same as those of interest to the ASHPS as a whole: national patriotism filtered through local experience and merged with local place attachment.[56] The auxiliary was a "separate organization" in membership and management and pursued three projects from its beginnings: Fraunces Tavern, Morris–Jumel Mansion, and Poe Cottage in the Bronx.[57] Their activities are not widely reported in the ASHPS reports, though Peirce gave presentations to the society's annual meetings as president of the auxiliary. These women were very successful in selecting a few preservation projects and implementing them well—which contrasted starkly with the society's strategy of advocating many things and implementing very little (only Hamilton Grange).[58]

Several writers have concluded that historic preservation was an activity of the elite, and while this seems largely true, the "elite" formulation hides a good deal of complexity.[59] The people forming organizations, lobbying politicians, raising money, and preserving buildings were indeed financially secure, socially comfortable, well-bred, and well-educated. The most active preservationists were *not* the most wealthy—they represented the socially ascendant professional class and the new experts who were coming to dominate urban reform. The idea that preservation was simply an antiquarian hobby of the waning, old-money elite is disproved by the collective biography of the ASHPS membership and leadership.

The scope and process of the ASHPS's work was more important than the actual results. Comprehensive results would have been impossible to achieve; as the city-planning field demonstrated, there were many obstacles to marshaling the financial or political power needed to implement comprehensive environmental reform. The ASHPS articulated a vision of the city's memory infrastructure. It carved out quasi-public responsibilities and goals that effectively (if not with complete success) asserted the concerns of a nascent historic preservation movement as part of public debate over the shaping of the city and its public space. It did more to constitute a "field" than any other group by sustaining public discourse about preservation and tirelessly enlisting others in spatializing collective memory and cultivating it in historic and scenic places. More often reacting than working proactively, it left a legacy of preserved sites as well as discourse about preservation and a tradition of concern about the need for spatialized memory as part of the modern city. A 1910 *Literary Digest* editorial noted, "No other so-called patriotic society is doing work quite so disinterested and intelligent."[60] This was high praise indeed for the Progressives and professionals driving the preservation field through the work of the ASHPS. The ASHPS embodied the early-twentieth-century ideal of landscape preservation as social reform, and when the era of Progressive reform waned in favor of more professionalized, bureaucratic City Efficient urban management, the ASHPS found itself on the sidelines.[61]

BUILDINGS

Preserving and restoring individual works of architecture was the primary form of historic preservation in this period. The buildings chosen were generally the oldest remaining in the city or those with the highest symbolic value. While a local connection was fundamental—place-specific narratives were, in preservation theory, always preferred to narratives without some organic, authentic connection to the specific site—the additional significance of a national theme (association with a founding father, for instance) was highly desirable. Architectural distinction elevated the importance of a house but was not essential—public buildings and vernacular farmhouses, if old enough, were highly valued. The survival of any historical context was unimportant; many of the buildings, once rural, were by 1900 existing in thoroughly urban contexts. Between 1890 and 1910, preservationists were more interested in historical associations than in fine architectural specimens.

House museums were the charismatic species of preservation. They memorialized a range of historical narratives—patriotic events, ancestors and founding fathers, local history, colonial design, and pioneer families and domesticity—and dramatized them through architectural, interior, and landscape design. They wore their reform intentions on the sleeves of their colonial costumes: The colonial-revival and ancestor-worship message of these memory sites revealed their makers' desire to Americanize immigrants—a motive with benign beginnings that became more coercive after World War I.[62] Though methods of preservation got more professional in the second decade of the twentieth century and though the municipal government contributed to preservation in many cases, creation of building-restoration memory sites abided by the circa-1900 model. As the number of house museums and other restored buildings grew, they became more entrenched as the core of preservation in New York and elsewhere.

The four examples briefly described in this book are the Morris–Jumel Mansion (in northern Manhattan), Hamilton Grange (the home of Alexander Hamilton, located in Harlem), Dyckman House (in far northern Manhattan, an eighteenth-century farmhouse associated with an old Dutch family), and Fraunces Tavern (a colonial-era tavern in Lower Manhattan, which was the site of Washington's farewell to his troops).[63] They illustrate the most common strategies for designing and managing memory sites: restoration of the building and its interiors to evoke a period of the distant past, creation of a parklike buffer around the building, and management and interpretation by a dedicated preservation group, which could sustain the interpretation of the building, hold events, and so on.

The ideal way to spatialize memory was to take ownership of the property (either by a private group or government agency) and redesign, preserve, or restore it to maximize its function as a didactic memory site, an image evocative of the past, a "preacher" of history. Restoration was placed in the hands of professional architects, though preservationists and amateur historians contributed to the interpretations leading to restoration decisions. Restoration was more speculative than scientific, though there are remarkable examples of very scientific restorations in this period (premised on thorough historical research and detailed investigations into extant historic fabric of the buildings)—in particular, Grosvenor Atterbury's restoration of City Hall in 1913–15 (see chapter 3). The more desired result vis-à-vis memory infrastructure was an evocative environment, not an accurate restoration.

Urbanistically, preservationists relied on the creation of green buffers to heighten the visual impact of the memory site. Arranging a historic house on a green lawn with a stage set of specimen trees was akin to placing a jewel in a jewel box, the buffer physically setting the site of cultural value apart from the everyday landscape

Figure 1.3. This scene of colonial domestic life was re-created at the Dyckman House in northern Manhattan. Such idealized environments were used to teach visitors proper models of domestic labor. Author's collection.

surrounding it. These framed views of historic houses highlighted the diachrony of the memory site—the contrast between historic house and contemporary context—so visitors would more directly experience a different time.

The management of restored buildings sometimes fell to preservation groups, sometimes to genealogical societies such as the DAR or the Sons of the American Revolution. The ASHPS took on management of Hamilton Grange after St. Luke's Episcopal Church (which had purchased the building when city improvements encroached on it) stopped using it as a rectory and sold it to J. P. Morgan Jr. and George F. Baker, who donated the building to the society. The New York City government played an important role in some cases, taking ownership and contributing to the maintenance of such places as the Morris–Jumel Mansion and Dyckman House and the Poe Cottage in the Bronx. Public–private partnership was a fairly common model in this period. Day-to-day management of visitors, interpretation, and curatorial duties was assumed by private associations of volunteers specific to the site, while legislative sanction, funds for acquisition, and some maintenance work were contributed by municipal officials (the Parks Department).

The Morris–Jumel Mansion was an unalloyed success of the early New York preservation community. "This property [Morris–Jumel Mansion] was acquired by the city in deference to the strong public sentiment which sought its preservation because it was Washington's Headquarters during a portion of the momentous year of 1776 and because it is an interesting specimen of Colonial architecture,"

Figure 1.4. The Morris–Jumel Mansion was the embodiment of the historic colonial house preserved within a jewel-box park. The Harlem River is visible in the distance. Courtesy of Library of Congress, Prints and Photographs Division, Historic American Buildings Survey.

said Manhattan Parks commissioner Henry Smith on dedicating the new public museum in 1910.[64]

Preservation of this "beautiful specimen of classic colonial architecture and interesting historical building"—also known as Washington's Headquarters, owing to George Washington's brief stay there in 1776—was mainly the work of two intertwined women's organizations: the Mary Washington Chapter of the DAR and the ASHPS's Women's Auxiliary.[65] In 1903, the city purchased the house and a few acres of land surrounding it on the heights overlooking the Harlem River around 161st Street. The purchase, instigated by preservationists, also advanced the Parks Department's efforts to increase the number of small neighborhood parks, formalized in the Small Parks Act of 1887. The city's purchase gave the DAR an opportunity to create a museum, as it assumed management responsibility for the house.

"Washington's Headquarters" was certainly an important Revolutionary War narrative—he stayed here briefly as his troops were retreating northward in

1776—but this property also gave the DAR the opportunity to interpret its favored narratives of colonial domestic life and Georgian architecture, through period rooms and tableaux featuring mostly reconstructed interiors arranged as didactic displays. Morris–Jumel became a model for future preservation efforts, for its canonical narratives, fine architecture and furnishings, and park setting and views and for the successful private lobbying effort leading to government action. This was a public–private partnership of the sort common in this period.

Hamilton Grange is a Federal-style country house in northern Manhattan (Convent Avenue and 141st Street), designed and built by John McComb for Alexander Hamilton around 1803.[66] Hamilton was New York's own founding father, and though he lived in this house briefly, it was strongly associated with him—a filiopietistic sentiment prompting preservation efforts spanning more than forty years.[67]

In 1889, after ownership passed out of Hamilton's family, the Grange fell "in the pathway of improvements" and was moved a few hundred feet out of the way of the advancing grid of residential streets.[68] Purchased by St. Luke's Episcopal Church, a congregation that had moved uptown from Greenwich Village, the house was saved, though preservationists lamented the loss of thirteen gum trees,

Figure 1.5. This postcard view of the room where the Marquis de Lafayette slept in the Morris–Jumel Mansion captures the essence of house museum restoration, attempting to convey authenticity by matching significant historical narratives with completely designed environments. Author's collection.

a

Figure 1.6. Hamilton Grange in its original landscape as a country house (a), with the ring of thirteen gum trees in the right foreground. In 1889 the Grange was jacked and moved out of the way of row house developments and Manhattan street grid construction (b; note the newly graded street in the foreground). Courtesy of Library of Congress, Prints and Photographs Division, Historic American Buildings Survey.

b

a gift from George Washington planted in a circle representing the original thirteen colonies.[69] In its new location, the Grange was used temporarily as a church, then as the rectory for the new St. Luke's, built next door in 1892. Moved from its original, bucolic setting and crammed against the new stone church, the integrity and value of the house as a memory site devoted to Hamilton was compromised, and this became the abiding issue for preservationists to resolve.

Preservationists protested that a house with such eminent associations deserved a more respectful site. In preservation ideology, this meant arranging the house on a green lawn with a stage set of specimen trees. This jewel-box effect would restore something like the historical setting of the house at the time Hamilton occupied it; more importantly, it would contrast the house with the surrounding streets and building, heightening its visual power as a memory site.

The ASHPS and various partners (including the Washington Heights Taxpayers Association) attempted to buy the house, move it a second time to a more open, parklike setting, and create a museum commemorating Hamilton's life. Unable to raise the funds themselves, the ASHPS lobbied the city Parks Department to buy and move the house and then allow a private preservation group to operate it as a museum for schoolchildren.[70] The State Legislature (1908) and Manhattan Parks commissioner Charles Stover (1912) approved such a move, but the money to carry it out could not be secured.[71]

The building continued in use as St. Luke's rectory until 1924, when the ASHPS convinced two of its board members (and two of New York's wealthiest men), J. P. Morgan Jr. and his partner George Baker, to donate $25,000 to buy the building, plus a $25,000 endowment for maintenance. Thereafter, it was restored and opened as a museum of Hamiltoniana and used as the headquarters of the ASHPS. Plans for moving the house to St. Nicholas Park were again drafted in the 1940s and '50s, and again by the National Park Service (which had acquired it in 1962) in the 1990s. Community protests marked the plans of the mid-1990s, and until recently the Grange remained on its crowded Convent Avenue site. In June 2008 the Grange was moved to St. Nicholas Park. Though some ascribe the tortured history of the building's partial preservation to the fact that it is located in Harlem, and therefore looked down upon by the mostly white preservation establishment, the halting efforts to effect its preservation predate Harlem's transformation into a center of African American society.[72] It remains a monument to Hamilton, but more strikingly an unintentional monument to the frequency of less-than-perfect results in historic preservation.

Dyckman House was a common kind of memory site constructed by early-twentieth-century preservationists—a colonial-era building restored as a didactic

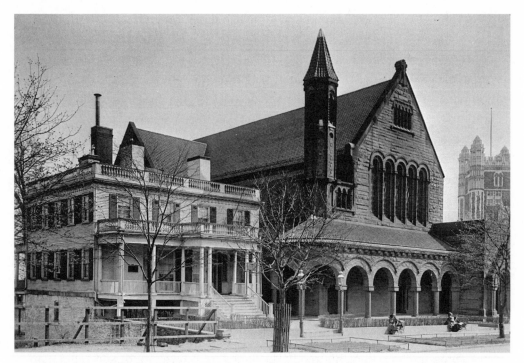

Figure 1.7. Hamilton Grange, on Convent Avenue near the corner of 141st Street, next to St. Luke's Episcopal Church. Courtesy of Library of Congress, Prints and Photographs Division, Historic American Buildings Survey.

house museum situated in a small park—but its preservation is also a remarkable story.[73] The house was built after the Revolutionary War to replace a seventeenth-century farmhouse burned by British occupiers (see Figure 1.8 and Plate 3). Built of fieldstone, brick, and wood, it featured low-pitched gambrel roofs and a basement kitchen. The early twentieth century brought apartment-house development fueled by subway construction to the area (the house occupies a corner of Broadway and 204th Street). Against this threat, Dyckman descendants bought back the house and some surrounding land, restored the building and grounds, and donated them to New York City as a museum. The restoration, carried out in 1915–16, was based on architectural, historical, and archaeological research and yielded reconstructed period rooms with family heirlooms and re-created gardens (featuring a hut, of the sort supposedly used by Revolutionary War soldiers, as a didactic exhibit based on the work of amateur archaeologist Reginald Pelham Bolton).[74]

The restoration was carried out by the husbands of the two Dyckman sisters who purchased the house—architect Alexander McMillan Welch (married to Fannie

Figure 1.8. Dyckman House, seen across Broadway (near 204th Street) after its restoration in 1915. Courtesy of Library of Congress, Prints and Photographs Division, Historic American Buildings Survey.

Fredericka Dyckman Welch) and scientist–museum curator Bashford Dean (married to Mary Alice Dyckman Dean).[75] This extraordinary pair brought professional museum and architectural skills to the project, elevating the sisters' substantial philanthropy (dedicating a public park and museum to their parents, commemorating their family's genealogical claim to colonial New York).

Initial plans to move the house to a nearby park were technically not feasible.[76] House and grounds were restored to a late-eighteenth-century appearance by Welch, based on historic images, investigations in the house, and Welch's sense of what it would have looked like in the early nineteenth century. An 1830 wing was removed, porches were restored, and the few interior modernizations were removed and replaced with details copied from elsewhere in the house. Walls and finishes were mostly stripped; electricity and modern plumbing and heating systems were introduced. A new stone retaining wall was constructed, and the house was filled with family heirlooms and arranged as a museum by Dean.[77]

Dean and Welch also reconstructed the *story* of this place in a small, self-published guidebook.[78] Based on their research (and the archaeological work of

Bolton, which revealed a nearby burial ground that included the graves of Indians and Negroes), Dean and Welch traced the site's history to a nearby Indian village, through Revolutionary War events on and around the site, and through a detailed history of the Dyckman family. The history concludes with a detailed description of the house's restoration, completing the continuous narrative weaving together past and present. This book was integral to the creation of the memory site; it fulfilled the preservationist ethic of documenting one's work while assuring that the public was presented with a compelling narrative to be learned and respected. The lessons of Dyckman House were laid out in detail to be visually soaked in by visitors.

The restoration of Dyckman House married a classic antiquarian preservation approach to modern curatorial preservation techniques to create a memory site with clear social-reform intentions. Such house museum projects were cen-

Figure 1.9. Bashford Dean and Alexander McMillan Welch published this small book documenting their work on the Dyckman House and explaining the significance of the restored house and the Dyckman family. Author's collection.

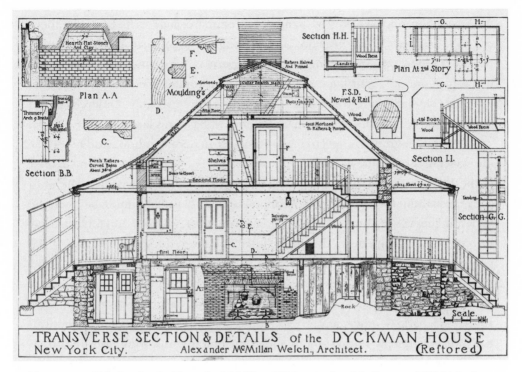

Figure 1.10. This drawing by Alexander McMillan Welch, reproduced in Dean and Welch's book The Dyckman House Park and Museum, *reflects the painstaking documentation and professional restoration process undertaken for the house. Author's collection.*

tral parts of the memory infrastructure, re-creating a bygone setting to educate the public and present models of domesticity and citizenship. The restoration of Dyckman House—like most early preservation projects—ignored and destroyed as much of the past as it preserved. When it opened to the public as a museum in 1916, it was not colonial, but colonial revival, an idealized representation of what the Dyckmans, Dean, and Welch wanted to present about colonial life and their family history. This site was promoted as a place to learn about colonial, rural New York—in vivid contrast to the quickly urbanizing neighborhood in which the modern historic site was created.[79]

Fraunces Tavern, a commercial building at Pearl and Broad streets in Lower Manhattan, possessed highly valuable historical associations but proved a challenge to preserve. Built in the first quarter of the eighteenth century, the building's most important association was with George Washington and the earliest U.S. government: In 1783 Washington, soon to resign his commission as general of the army and smooth the transition to democratic governance, bade farewell to his officers over dinner at the tavern. Also, the Sons of Liberty met at the tavern before the Revolution, and New York's Chamber of Commerce held its first meeting there in 1768.[80] *Harper's Weekly,* in 1896, began a long illustrated article titled "Historic New York Houses" by describing Fraunces Tavern as "with little doubt, the oldest building in the city . . . fitting reminder of the New York of a century and a quarter ago." Its colonial and Revolutionary associations were carefully rendered, but its architectural condition—much changed since 1783—was lamented.[81]

Preservation groups rallied to make Fraunces, in poor condition and hidden in the skyscraping downtown, a visible memory site. The Mary Washington Chapter of the DAR organized a campaign in 1894 to rescue Fraunces from a fate as "a cheap restaurant for foreign men of foreign tongue."[82] Collaboration between the DAR and the ASHPS, brokered in 1901 between Andrew Green and Melusina Fay Peirce, gave new impetus to the effort.[83] Peirce delivered a speech exhorting the preservation of Fraunces (also issued as a pamphlet and published in the ASHPS Annual Report for 1901): "Let the tavern . . . be forever preserved as the MECCA of American Patriotism!" If Fraunces were preserved properly—restored in place and set in a park—"modern New York would possess a reminder of her American past not only deeply interesting as such, but potently inspiring also toward an equally American future."[84]

The New York City Board of Aldermen passed an ordinance in 1903, at the behest of the ASHPS, creating a park of the block bordered by Pearl, Water, and Broad streets and Coenties Slip in which Fraunces would be preserved and surrounded by green. Never mind that this would have destroyed a number of old buildings and altered the context of the tavern to look nothing like its condition in the 1780s—such was the preservationists' design strategy of segregating historic buildings from contemporary context so as to heighten their historical and aesthetic value. The next year, the Board of Estimate and Apportionment (which held the purse strings of the municipal government more firmly than did the aldermen) rescinded the ordinance, leaving Fraunces and the block unaltered.[85]

The Sons of the American Revolution swept in where the ASHPS had failed and purchased the building in 1904, hiring architect William Mersereau to rebuild and restore it as a colonial-revival structure housing a museum and a restaurant. Very little of the building's eighteenth-century fabric was extant.[86] Mersereau's work consisted of deconstructing post-eighteenth-century additions "to restore the building so far as possible to its original form," following the evidence of "old roof lines and rafters." The top story was removed, as were "modern" bricks and other material; yellow bricks from Holland and red bricks scavenged from some old houses in Baltimore, Maryland, were imported to restore the walls. The first floor was raised, windows were replaced with ones of original dimension, and

Figure 1.11. Fraunces Tavern after restoration in 1907. Courtesy of University of Pennsylvania Libraries.

special care was taken to re-create the original dimensions and retain the original timbers of the Long Room—actual site of Washington's farewell. When the building was opened as a museum and restaurant in 1907, it was a reconstructed rather than a preserved building. Amid the tall buildings and hurried street life of downtown Manhattan, it was a vivid reminder of colonial roots, a memory site of the first order.[87]

PARKS

Urban parks figured strongly in efforts to make New York a balanced and memory-rich landscape. "The original conception, purpose, and even long traditional use of a park are also important factors in regulating the individual characteristics of a park. . . . Ceaseless vigilance is necessary to counteract this growing tendency to use public parks for purposes for which they were not intended."[88] Natural, or "scenic," value was among the foremost concerns of early-twentieth-century preservationists; along with colonial, filiopietistic, and commercial narratives of

Figure 1.12.
Fraunces Tavern
before restoration,
showing additions
and modifications
made during its
continuous use
in the nineteenth
century. Courtesy of
University of Penn-
sylvania Libraries.

buildings, scenic places contributed to the overarching message of civic patrio-tism. Scenic places were part of the American legacy, threatened by unfettered development and requiring protection in times of change.[89] The tropes of histori-cal memory were as much natural as architectural: the primeval forest, natural wonders (Niagara, the West), the pioneer homestead, the family farm, the battle-field. As these places receded from everyday experience—whether they were be-ing destroyed or were simply too remote to be seen—preservationists stepped in to protect them. In New York City, the thirst to preserve parks as well as buildings was reflected in ASHPS annual reports, each covering the city's parks as exten-sively as it covered buildings.

The creation of new parks in the second half of the nineteenth century rep-resented the clearest idea for creating balanced urbanism—leavening the break-neck growth, bustle, and crush of the commercial city with places for repose and recreation, letting the salutary influences of natural scenes salve the enervated urban soul, reducing congestion by making "a more openly built environment."[90] Central, Riverside, Prospect, Morningside, and other parks reshaped the sort of metropolis New York could become. A few smaller open spaces remained from the colonial era—the Battery, Bowling Green, the Commons (City Hall Park). New York's urban parks provided recreation and respite from the built-up city, and they served memorial functions too: They represented the pastoral landscape waning as the city grew, they represented wild nature (a strong influence on American character), they had become historic places in themselves (some had been built in colonial days, while Central Park was nearly fifty years old), they were respected as a public works legacy of past city governments, and they had become a setting for memorial artworks unrelated to the parks themselves. Preservationist thinking asserted the sanctity of parks—both recently created and colonial—as places of great public value, including these uses as memory sites.

Preservationists found parks to be ideal public environments, places where ordinary citizens could be routinely exposed to the positive influence of nature as well as of historical memory. Landscaped parks, urban squares, and other green spaces were considered an important part of the city's memory infrastructure. In some respects, they were destinations for visitors, like house museums, but, perhaps more powerfully, parks, squares, and other scenic places were part of the everyday landscape experienced by New Yorkers.

Some parks were old enough—in some cases, older than any building in the city—to qualify as colonial landmarks: the Battery, Bowling Green, the Commons (which later became City Hall Park). Having remained open spaces in such long, continuous use, the parks were considered true landmarks and historic places: sites most worthy of preservation. As sites of historical memory, the Commons, Bowling Green, and the Battery were sites of Revolutionary War events, while Union Square was (since 1856) home of Henry Kirke Brown's statue of George Washington.

The great nineteenth-century naturalistic parks were tacitly considered landmarks and memory sites in that they represented a legacy of civic works—part of the narrative of civic greatness–cum–civic patriotism. In this sense, they were regarded in the same light as historic public buildings like City Hall. By 1900, after all, Central Park was already two generations old. At the same time, Central Park and Prospect Park included sites sanctified by Revolutionary War and War of 1812 activities.

Parks were also used as a stage for memorials. Most memorials of the time—such as the many figurative statues of great men—were not site specific, so they could be placed anywhere the public would see them. While most parks became collecting points for memorials in this heyday of memory infrastructure, Riverside Park emerged as a memorial parkway: a new hybrid urban form combining functions of road, park, and memory site.

As landscapes, these parks and squares rightfully were not treated like buildings and restored to their condition in some earlier period. Park landscapes were managed to preserve their value as recreational place *and* memory site. The preservation strategy centered on modulating change—preventing encroachments or "intrusions" such as new structures,[91] or the selling off of park land for development.

The primary theme in park preservation was protecting parks against "encroachments." In Morningside Park, for example, a proposal for a stadium in the park was decried because it threatened the park's artistic beauty (it was designed by Olmsted and Vaux) and the public's use of the open green space and would be detrimental to surrounding land values. Preservationists also celebrated the historical value of the park: For Morningside, Edward Hall constructed a detailed history and documentation of the site as if it were a modern preservation project. Revolutionary War associations formed a base of historic value, but the overarching story was a narrative of civic achievement, of the park as a rallying point for civic patriotism.[92] And the 1909 ASHPS report rejected the site of a new courthouse in Washington Square Park: "For the past forty years—ever since the city committed the unfortunate mistake of selling a large portion of City Hall Park to the Federal government for a post office—the citizens have had to keep up an almost constant warfare for the protection of their public places from dismemberment or perversion to uses for which they were not designed."[93]

With their focus on parks and squares, preservationists sought to prove wrong Herbert Croly's observation (mainly instigated by City Hall Park's condition around 1903) that "there are no public squares which, either because of the sacredness of their associations or the excellence of their encircling buildings, have aroused in the minds of its inhabitants any feelings of pride and affection."[94]

Like restored buildings, parks were a device of positive environmentalism: Encounters with scenic places—like encounters with places or artworks linked to patriotic people or acts—were believed to transmit ideals of good citizenship, republican self-regulation, appreciation of beauty, spirituality, and so on. The status of parks in the New York preservation movement was doubtless enhanced by the active part leading preservationists played in creating parks. Andrew Green was centrally involved in the creation of Central Park, Riverside Park, Morningside Park, and plans for the Twenty-third and Twenty-fourth wards in the Bronx, and he regarded parks as essential urban infrastructure. Park preservation continued (preserved) the legacy of men such as Green. Through the beginning of the twentieth century, into the 1920s, the ASHPS became more and more involved in park issues—protesting against intrusions, writing histories, speaking to the multiple values that parks provide the city. Beginning in 1902, the ASHPS also included a "Landscape Architect"—longtime member Samuel Parsons—among its officers.

Preservation of three regional landscapes elsewhere in New York State served as critical precursors to the urban preservation movement in New York City. Andrew Green led the preservation of Niagara Falls, the Adirondacks, and the New Jersey Palisades beginning in the 1880s. In each case, a special-purpose state commission was created to be the hub of a coalition of groups (women's clubs, wealthy landowners, reformers, and others) working for the protection of an iconic natural landscape. This was the political model later employed by Green's ASHPS and other partnerships for preservation in New York City.[95]

Arguments for park preservation and against intrusive development highlighted the multivalence of parks—sources of aesthetic, public health, historical, and sometimes economic values—and revolved around struggles to balance the different values. The value of parks as memory sites is illustrated by brief descriptions of preservation issues surrounding Central Park, Fort Greene Park, the Battery, and Riverside Drive.

The story of Central Park's creation and preservation has become a famous part of the New York narrative. Olmsted and Vaux's visionary 1858 plan set the standard for urban parks, bringing balance, aesthetic delight, and reform to Manhattan's dense urban design. Intrusions, adaptations, and other depredations threatened to compromise the park's integrity while the park grew to be wildly popular. The "original" vision was restored by the Central Park Conservancy in the late twentieth century. The story of the park's evolution and preservation is far more complicated than this, but by the end of the nineteenth century, preservationists had helped define and defend the values of this public landscape.[96]

By 1900, Central Park was more than two generations old, enough to be considered "historic," and preservationists were protective of its age value as well as its scenic value. More important, the park was a potent political symbol for Progressives, evidence of the city having created a truly democratic public space and—just as important—a tempting resource for machine politicians and other political ne'er-do-wells to mine: There was a constant danger of government-supported building projects being located in public parks to avoid land-acquisition costs.

Intrusions proposed for the park were many—and were visually cataloged in a cartoon published in the *New York Times* in 1924—and included an academy of design, racetracks, a music and art center, and many other buildings and uses. Between 1890 and 1919, the city and its government expanded rapidly, bringing pressure on any available building sites.

Preservationists made up a substantial part of a citizen's committee formed by the Parks and Playgrounds Association to oppose city plans to build new structures in the park; their successful appeal noted that "a good many of us would like to have Central Park as it was originally designed by Olmsted & Vaux."[97] In a 1924 letter to the editor, George Kunz and Edward Hall invoked the park's seventy-five years of history and its open, green character. Testifying at City Hall against a plan to place a music and art center in the park, Hall reiterated, "The sole argument advanced for putting the buildings in Central Park was that such a course was cheaper than buying private property," and he rebuffed arguments in favor of the intrusion by in-

Figure 1.13. A typical scene in Central Park at the Mall, circa 1902. Central Park had acquired value as a landmark of civic achievement and public works as well as a space for recreation and socializing. Courtesy of Library of Congress, Prints and Photographs Division.

voking the memory of Andrew Green, relating an 1863 quote by this "other" author of Central Park.[98] A 1924 newspaper headline echoed earlier fights, touting the public's interest in park preservation: "Fight to Save Park Arouses Entire City . . . Appeal Also Sent to Estimate Board to Keep the 'People's Heritage' Intact."[99] Reporting on yet another encroachment suggested for Central Park, this article repeated the rationale offered many times over by preservationists.

Against these threats, preservationists touted the park's legacy of public use (its political value) as well as its historical associations and age value. In his 110-page history of Central Park published in 1911, Edward Hagaman Hall described the park not only as possessing "a history of its own" but also as "[having] inherited from the years before its creation a history which well deserves to be preserved," referring to old military fortifications within the park.[100] Detailing the park's several historical layers helped justify preservationists' diligence in preventing intrusions.[101] Central Park "should be preserved for what it was intended to be — a quiet, rustic retreat from noise, confusion, hubbub, and organized crowds; and as

one of the greatest examples of landscape art in America, it should also be protected from devastation."[102] The "original conception" argument helped construct
the historic value of Central Park, too—parallel to the "artistic intent" argument
lately used by the Central Park Conservancy.

While preservationists were mainly concerned with protecting the integrity
of the park as a historic landscape, they made their own intrusions in the park
landscape by placing monuments and memorials. Between 1890 and 1920, a number of new memorials were added to Central Park, continuing a tradition of the
1870s and 1880s: Columbus Circle, 1892; a statue of Danish sculptor Albert
Thorvaldsen, 1894; the Maine Monument, 1913; the Sherman Monument at
Grand Army Plaza, 1916; a memorial to William T. Stead (a journalist who died
on the *Titanic*), 1920. These pieces of infrastructure—connected visually to each
other as well as to the naturalistic and formal landscapes of the park—illustrated
the theory that memorials are best experienced among the green settings of parks,
which enable public contemplation and reflection.

Adding memorials to the edges of the park was more controversial: Whereas a variety of statues or tablets could be fit unproblematically within the naturalistic and romantic worlds created inside the park, memorials at the edge were more aggressively debated. Being more clearly part of "the street" perhaps made them vulnerable to public opinion, from which they were in a way protected if they fell within the park; giving Columbus pride of place at the southwest gateway to the park, for instance, did not pass without protest.[103]

Throughout this period, preservationists contributed to the larger movement to protect the park's integrity. Preservation leader Edward Hagaman Hall, writing to the *New York Times* in 1924, intoned, "If Central Park is to be preserved at all, it must be preserved intact. If its dismemberment begins now, it is doomed."[104] Preventing intrusions and encouraging the placement of new memorials ensured that Central Park's central place in the city's memory infrastructure would be preserved.

Fort Greene Park, just north of downtown Brooklyn, up the hill from the Navy Yard, was created as Washington Park in 1847.[105] Brooklynite Walt Whitman advocated for creating the park as the "lungs" for this fast-growing part of Brooklyn. Olmsted and Vaux redesigned it in 1864, inserting a rural, naturalistic place into the urban grid in order to reform and balance it. They created a number of different experiences for visitors, including meandering walks connecting pasture-like grounds and wooded copses, thick plantings on the park edges, and long views from the heights. This new scheme also promoted historical memory by placing the Prison Ship Martyrs Monument in a prominent site.

The story of the Prison Ship Martyrs is a tragic Revolutionary War narrative. Thousands of American prisoners were held by the British in old ships anchored in Wallabout Bay (near the Navy Yard), where many died of disease and starvation in dreadful conditions.[106] For decades afterward, their bones periodically washed up on the shore and were collected by local residents and interred in a crypt. The suffering of the patriots at the hands of the occupiers stirred feelings of pity and recalled the glories of sacrifice and duty. This was perhaps the most violent and vivid story in the canon of New York's Revolutionary War narratives.

Fort Greene Park became one of the clearest expressions of scenic and historic landscape values and of the preservationist synthesis of park and memory infrastructure, particularly as the park was redesigned in advance of the dedication of the Prison Ship Martyrs Monument in 1908. The redesign not only gave the park a general renovation, but it also reimagined it as a memory site for a citywide audience (whereas it had before functioned mostly as a neighborhood park). The new Prison Ship Martyrs Monument was the centerpiece, a skyscraper of a memorial

Figure 1.14. The Prison Ship Martyrs Monument in Fort Greene Park, Brooklyn, was the site of large celebrations, such as this one attended by cavalry and a substantial public audience in an undated photograph (probably from 1910–19). Courtesy of Milstein Division of United States History, Local History, and Genealogy, the New York Public Library, Astor, Lenox, and Tilden Foundations.

designed by Stanford White and dedicated in front of twenty thousand spectators in 1908.[107] (The new memorial replaced a modest crypt close to the Navy Yard.) Broad stairways led to a plaza featuring the 148-foot Doric column with a bronze lantern atop the crypt for the martyrs' remains (previously buried in a small vault along Hudson Street); bronze eagles stood guard at the corners of the plaza; a stairway and elevators gave access to the observation deck.

At a ceremony marking the interment of newly found martyrs' bones in 1900 (excavated from the Navy Yard), Gen. Stewart Woodford, leader of the Prison Ship Martyrs Monument Association,

> briefly reviewed the history of the attempts made to erect a fitting monument to the Revolutionary Martyrs. "And as to these sacred remains," he continued, pointing down at the seven polished oak boxes, "they are those of martyrs, more than heroes. When knives flash and men spring at each other's throats and into death, it is the hour when heroes are born.

But when men, silently, patiently, calmly, unwaveringly refuse to leave their prison house, with its lingering death of starvation and privation, then is the hour when martyrs are made. And thus were these martyrs made over 120 years ago. Let them breathe to us their lesson of patriotism, let them breathe to us their lesson of fidelity, and let them breathe to us their lesson of duty."[108]

General Woodford (1835–1913) was a New Yorker and Civil War veteran (he led New York volunteers and a regiment of "colored infantry"), a postwar military governor of Charleston, South Carolina, a congressman and U.S. attorney, and a U.S. envoy to Spain.[109] His words, spoken by a leader of the convulsive war between the states, riveted the audience of ten thousand.

Compelled by the need to teach a "lesson of duty" in the built environment, preservationists transformed this neighborhood park into a formal, dramatic node in the memory infrastructure. The new monument spatialized patriotic and place-specific narratives as the central feature of the park. For decades afterward, the Martyrs Monument in Fort Greene Park was the site of Memorial Day, Flag Day,

Figure 1.15. Battery Park has long been a popular park in Manhattan. Here the western parts of the park are pictured circa 1902; the Statue of Liberty is visible in the center distance, with Ellis Island

and Evacuation Day celebrations drawing thousands of New Yorkers and a variety of politicians and historical, patriotic, and genealogical societies.[110]

The Battery was the geographic center of the town from the moment of European colonization in 1624, and it remains Manhattan's oldest public space. Named for the gun emplacements of the first Dutch fort, the Battery has served many public uses over the centuries—military installation, pleasure ground, transportation hub, stage for celebrations, and memory site. Throughout these changes, it has remained a place where New Yorkers can take a walk by the harbor, experience nature, see, and be seen.[111]

The Battery's significance as a memory site stemmed from three sources of value. First, the Battery was a rare open space in the midst of downtown, and it is the place where New Amsterdam started—the site most associated with the founding of the European settlement (an era from which no buildings survive).[112] The massive downtown business district that had grown by the end of the nineteenth century surrounded the Battery, striking a visual contrast valuable to preservationist strategy—old, open space against the backdrop of new, massive commercial buildings. The iconic role of the Battery was reinforced because it is foregrounded

Immigration Station to its right and the New Jersey docks far to the right. Courtesy of Library of Congress, Prints and Photographs Division.

in so many popular nineteenth- and twentieth-century panoramic views of the city. The main narrative implied by these views is the city's explosive uptown growth—the geography of progress—but an important counternarrative in these images is the preservation of the Battery as a remnant of the colonial city and as a scenic reserve contrasting with the newer urban fabric.

Second, the physical remainder of the Battery's military function—Castle Clinton—remained in situ and by 1900 had already been adaptively reused a number of times (as a theater, an immigration station, and an aquarium). The Battery expanded by landfill over the centuries and encompasses considerably more land than did the seventeenth-century Battery. So while the park did not have authenticity as it would be defined today, it did have the massive castle as its authentic antique. The red sandstone pile visually anchored the place, provided an in situ presence to contrast to the openness of the park landscape.

Third, there has been a long history of adding new structures and functions to the Battery. Most were decried as encroachments (elevated railroads, subway construction, vendors' stands, and commercial structures); new monuments were hailed as proper uses of a park. Open space afforded good sites for monuments and memorials—where artistic works could be set in a green context and attract an audience of park visitors. As one of the city's most valued parks, the Battery also held one of its most valued collections of memory infrastructure.[113]

Like many city parks, the Battery became a collecting point for monuments and memorials.[114] The Battery was near the top of the hierarchy of places to locate monuments—only City Hall Park and Central Park rivaled it as a prestigious location. The Commercial Tercentenary Celebration, when it opened in October 1914, chose the Battery as the site for official ceremonies, including the dedication of a memorial cannon by the City History Club.[115] For the 1909 Hudson–Fulton Celebration, a debate ensued over who had really discovered the Hudson River—the Dutch Hudson or the Italian Verrazano? (More about this below.)

The Battery adapted to the changing city—it grew through landfill; the fort was reused; the working harbor pressed at the edges; subways and elevated trains threaded the spaces above and beneath it; its abiding view of the harbor kept it a place for promenading and civic celebrations. Conflicts arose from proposals to consume park space with new transportation facilities or public buildings. But it had many defenders. "The elevated railroad recently demanded another piece of the Battery, and for every seizure of open land that any company or scheme may propose, some plausible pretence will be found," *Harper's Weekly* reported in 1891. "The obstruction at the Battery is a serious injury to the city. The ground is open to the sea air, and is susceptible of being made the most delightful of the smaller parks. It is the only resort open to the people in the lower wards for recreation and relief during the heats of summer."[116]

The contentious process of preserving and developing the Battery only seemed to reinforce its status as one of the city's richest memory sites. Preservationists reported in 1915 that "Battery Park is much disturbed by subway excavations. An interesting feature of these disturbances is the evidence which they give of old New York history. The raw earth, lying in heaps on the surface, reveals an abundance of old yellow Dutch brick, red brick, oyster and clam shells, meat bones, fragments of blue and other china, black bottles of the period of the Revolution."[117] In 1895, for instance, the Park Board announced its refusal to allow subway track tunnels to be four feet above ground in Battery Park.[118] These surrounding and encroaching changes threatened—while in some ways enhancing—the Battery's historic and aesthetic values. Later, in the 1940s, the Battery would play a central role in the history of preservation in New York as the fate of Castle Clinton became the subject of a "battle" pitting George McAneny and other preservationists and civic leaders against Robert Moses.[119]

Like the Battery, Riverside Park evolved into an important node of memory infrastructure. Riverside was created as an urban park and parkway—embodying the nineteenth-century park ideal of a more openly built environment[120]—but this was only part of its story and its raison d'être. By the early twentieth century, it had become a memorial landscape as well. Riverside was first imagined in the 1860s as a means of expanding New York rationally and artistically. Planned by boosters and civic officials like Andrew Green in collaboration with designers Olmsted and Vaux, the park converted marginal land along the river, topographically difficult to build on, into a naturalistic park, recreational drive, and elite residential district. Green put the Riverside Park/Drive project in the context of the broader urbanization process, saying in 1866, "The part of the city west of the [Central] park through which this drive is to pass will probably be built with dwellings of a costly character, and these, after having served their day and generation will give way, as in other locations, to the pressure of business."[121]

The residential heyday of Riverside Avenue (Riverside Drive's name until 1908) never passed. Opened in 1880, it was lined with new mansions and later (fueled by the opening of the West Side subway in 1904) with apartment buildings. Demand for memory infrastructure kept pace with the urban expansion and redevelopment of Manhattan, requiring sites publicly owned and well positioned in terms of urban design (within parks, in visually strategic locations, in accord with City Beautiful principles). The west side of Riverside Drive was transformed into a memorial landscape, a theater for the display of memory works. (The east side of the

Figure 1.16. The Soldiers' and Sailors' Memorial was one of several memorials placed along Riverside Drive in the 1880s and '90s. Author's collection.

drive remained exclusively residential; the park was mostly developed later, after riverfront railroad tracks were covered in the 1930s.) The transformation began with the siting of the Soldiers' and Sailors' Memorial at 89th Street (dedicated to the memory of Union troops in 1902, designed by Charles and Arthur Stoughton), and Grant's Tomb at 122nd Street, designed by John Duncan and dedicated in 1897.

Riverside Drive became a part of the memory infrastructure haltingly and gradually. The site of the Soldiers' and Sailors' Memorial was originally to be at one of the corners of Central Park and was moved to Riverside as a compromise; ditto the Firemen's Memorial. Not part of Olmsted and Vaux's original design, memorials were embraced by city officials and reform groups to reimagine and embellish this gentrifying edge of the island in keeping with the emergent memorial culture and urban-design style. More and more memory sites were located on Riverside Drive, most of them added between the 1890s and the 1920s. They formed a coherent group visually and thematically: All were neoclassical designs by leading artists, most employing figurative sculpture; all promoted ideas of patriotism and progress. Memory sites along the drive included memorials to financier Robert Hamilton (1906, 76th Street), banker and West Side booster Cyrus Clark (1911, 83rd Street), and Joan of Arc (1915, 93rd Street); the Firemen's Memorial (1913, 100th Street); and statues of Union general Franz Sigel (1907, 106th Street), politician Samuel J. Tilden (1926, 112th Street), and Hungarian patriot Louis Kossuth (1928, 113th Street).

MONUMENTS AND STATUES

"Monumental art has taken a great bound forward in this city," an 1895 *New York Times* article trumpeted. "Within the next two years the outlook is that at least a million dollars will be expended on monuments and statues of public men, everlasting lessons for the youth of coming generations." Celebrating this convergence of commemoration and public art as a sign of New York's ascendance to parity with "the European capitals," the article included sketches of new memorials giving durable form to founding father and New Yorker Gouverneur Morris, Hungarian patriot Louis Kossuth, and the founder of lithography Aloys Senefelder—new figures in the memory infrastructure.[122]

Two commemorative art traditions—one abstract and allegorical, the other place- and narrative-specific—contributed to memory infrastructure, and both were well established in New York City in the last third of the nineteenth century. The practice of spatializing memory in the form of realistic statues sprouted in the 1870s and by 1890 was in full blossom. Art historian Michele Bogart[123] ascribed the emergence of public sculpture, most of it commemorative, to the rising status of the sculptors' profession and the allied architectural-artistic-political movement to remake cities with "municipal art"—the City Beautiful movement. The 1893 Columbian Exposition was the coming-out of public sculpture, putting on display spectacular works by leading artists, and it initiated a raft of public commissions in New York (and elsewhere) contributing greatly to the memory infrastructure. New York exhibited "a body of municipal sculpture that would express the civic ideal: an urban vision of patriotism, civilization and good government."[124] These new memorials perfectly complemented in situ preservation of buildings and parks.

Erecting monuments was the most obvious way to create *lieux de mémoire*—a centuries-old tradition in Western culture. Setting up intentional totems to stimulate memory is an ancient human practice.[125] The creation of monuments, memorials, and other commemorative public art as part of the modern urban landscape is well developed and well studied.[126] In the period following the Civil War, a great number of war memorials and statues celebrating the lives of military heroes and political and cultural figures graced public parks and plazas. The ascendance of neoclassical, City Beautiful architecture and urban design following the 1893 Columbian Exposition, with its aggressive sculpture and public art programs, placed issues and works of public, commemorative art to the front of the

Figure 1.17. This monument to the Marquis de Lafayette, a bronze relief by Daniel Chester French on a granite pedestal by architect Henry Bacon, was dedicated at the edge of Prospect Park, Brooklyn, in 1917. The Lafayette Monument typified the three-dimensional public memorials built as part of the city's memory infrastructure. Combining fine artwork, park locations, and urban designs that positioned the memorials as focal points, these monuments were intended to uplift citizens by punctuating the everyday environment with extraordinary historical memories. Photograph by the author.

urban-reform agenda. Artists and architects created a debate about "municipal art," or "civic art," a movement that went well beyond the creation of artworks to encompass issues of urban design, high-quality public architecture, transportation, and what would today be called "streetscape" issues.[127]

While adorning buildings and urban landscapes of the city, monuments and statues added layers of historical memory. Figures, reliefs, tablets, and architectural assemblages by leading artists commemorated specific events, narratives, and people, complementing the somewhat more abstract forms of civic memory embodied in buildings and parks. As a collection of public artworks, these monuments reinforced dominant canons of civic patriotism. Behind these monuments was a gregarious collection of preservationists, artists, and advocates for myriad causes; monumental art grew out of collaboration among artists, designers, planners, and preservationists. Many of the artists and architects who designed and made public sculptures, arches, obelisks, fountains, murals, and other pieces were key figures in the municipal art organizations as well as the historic preservation field. They included men such as Henry Kirke Bush-Brown, Charles and Frederick Lamb, Thomas Hastings, Charles McKim, John LaFarge, Edwin Blashfield, Frederick MacMonnies, and J. Q. A. Ward.

Plaques were among the most common memorial artworks proliferating in this period. Fixing bronze plaques to buildings or placing stone markers to commemorate historical events at their authentic sites became the classic trope of preservation, the simplest and least-expensive way to expand the memory infrastructure. They required permission from the owners of land or buildings, but not ownership itself. Installing plaques was a simpler and more expedient way to spread the message of preservation and educate the public than was building preservation.

More than statues and architectural memorials, plaques built on the authenticity of specific sites, seeking the authority of the "You are there" idea that a particular site has greater purchase on one's memory if it actually bears witness to the narrative being commemorated. The plaques included pithy accounts noting the significance and moral lessons of the narrative commemorated: "The eminence overlooking McGown's Pass was once occupied by British troops"; "Here stood a bastion of the wall which between 1653 and 1699 extended from the East River along the line of the present Wall Street." They were placed at dozens of sites around the city, including McGown's Pass, site of Revolutionary War activities in Central Park, and on Wall Street. They were attempts to fix (literally) the meaning of historical events or people, erected by all sorts of "historical societies"—antiquarian, genealogical, ethnic, and ASHPS.

The strategy of plaquing—applying narrative content and visual form to make a public memorial—was also extended to new structures and infrastructures. In the stations of the original IRT subway, walls were adorned by decorative faience plaques integral to the mosaic tile wall surfaces. The subjects of the plaques were historical and site specific: beavers at Astor Place, referring to the original source of the Astor family fortune; tulips at 110th Street in the "Bloomingdale" section of Manhattan; and so on. This was one of many efforts to build memory into the everyday landscape as well as monumental New York.[128]

Placing monuments, statues, and plaques is simpler—shorter term and lower cost—than restoring a building or preserving a park. Being easier to establish, however, artworks also offered a way for more-marginal social groups (such as

McGown's Pass Monument, New York, looking north.

McGown's Pass Monument, New York, looking east, showing tablet.

Figure 1.18. This plaque marking the site of McGown's Pass was one of many subtle site-specific markers enthusiastically placed around the city by preservationists. Courtesy of University of Pennsylvania Libraries.

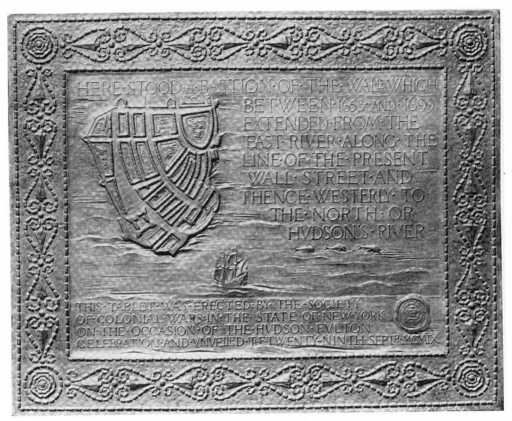

Figure 1.19. This plaque, placed at 48 Wall Street, maps the location of the original wall of the colonial town. It was erected by the Society of Colonial Wars (in which Madison Grant was an active member) during the Hudson–Fulton Celebration in 1909. Courtesy of University of Pennsylvania Libraries.

ethnic groups) to contribute to the memory infrastructure. While monumental art made the memory infrastructure more pluralistic, it never actually reflected the city's complicated social mosaic. Italian and other European groups expressed their social memory in monuments, for instance, while African Americans remained excluded.

Much of this proliferation of City Beautiful public art was allegorical, representing abstract ideas and principles near and dear to Progressive political and social reform. Allegorical municipal art remained primarily a matter of aesthetics and style and was universal as opposed to place specific—as appropriate to New York and Chicago as to Berlin and Budapest. Allegorical sculptures, specifically historical monumental art, complemented the "placeful," trumpeted broader civic themes, and were often located at prominent urban design points: parks, squares, public buildings.

Another tradition in commemorative art found its inspiration in specific historical narratives rooted in place. It was this type of memory work—whether building, park, battlefield, memorial, or statue—that would "quicken the spirit of patriotism" as Andrew Green wrote.[129] Place-specific works were important in preservationists' commemorative strategy. The historical memories embedded in them were rooted in New York's soil and people and stories, tapping the same narratives as building and park preservation.

The relationship between the meaning of a monument and its location was an important variable—site-specificity increased the impact of memorials. The meaning and relevance of monuments was increased by being located at or near the "authentic" site of a historical event. The "tightness" of the relation between specific narrative and specific site varied considerably; the connection did not have to be literal to give the monument greater relevance. A statue of Revolutionary martyr Nathan Hale was placed in City Hall Park in 1889, purportedly near the site of his hanging.[130] Not far from Hale, a modest stone marks the exact site of the Martyrs' Prison in the park—a building torn down over the protests of preservationists to make way for subway construction. Horace Greeley's statue was retained near his newspaper's headquarters on Park Row, instead of being moved to the Battery, a place with no particular resonance to his memory. But exact geographic accuracy was not essential to the memorials' success. The placement of memorials in an open park or plaza setting was more important.

By the early twentieth century, there were dozens, perhaps hundreds, of memorials to individuals, events, and civic ideals represented in statues across the city: the Italian explorer Giovanni da Verrazano, Revolutionary patriot Nathan Hale, and the collection of civic and patriotic monuments along Riverside Drive. Bogart relates the detailed stories of many other commissions in New York between 1890 and 1920, both freestanding memorials and architectural decoration projects. Some involved preservationists directly, including the Chelsea Park Doughboy Statue, designed by Charles Rollinson Lamb and Philip Martigny and dedicated in 1921, and several works by Henry Kirke Bush-Brown. Both Bush-Brown and Martigny contributed to the marvelous commemorative sculpture program on the new Hall of Records (also known as the Surrogate's Court)—perhaps the apex of this art/memory form.

The extensive sculpture program on the facade of the new Hall of Records incorporated historical figures as well as allegorical sculptures. Bush-Brown and Martigny made a row of New Amsterdam and New York mayors (from David de Vries of the seventeenth century to Abram Hewitt of the 1880s), as well as a row of allegorical figures including *Heritage, Maternity, Philosophy,* and *Poetry.* The statues

Figure 1.20. The new Hall of Records, at the corner of Chambers and Center streets, was completed in 1901 as part of a planned series of neoclassical office and court buildings surrounding City Hall Park. The facade's extensive sculptural program placed the building within the memory infrastructure. Courtesy of Library of Congress, Prints and Photographs Division, Historic American Buildings Survey.

were integrated into the building program, carefully placed as both adornments and organizing elements in John Duncan's Beaux-Arts facade. The sheer number of sculptures (and the perseverance displayed in the face of the exhausting and frustrating process of gaining the Art Commission's approval of the sculptures — multiple maquettes were rejected; meanwhile, the budget for the art was constantly pressured) was a measure of the seriousness with which reformers regarded these expressions of historical memory.[131]

The Hall of Fame of Great Americans capitalized on the memorial craze, attempting to create a new memory site by collecting a large number of filiopietistic statues under one roof. New York University created the hall on its Bronx campus in 1901 and filled it with filiopietistic monuments to great Americans. The interior of the neoclassical edifice (designed by Stanford White) housed tablets and busts memorializing the lives of the great—a pantheon of heroes in American memory. Separate areas were organized for women and heroes not of American birth. Decisions regarding admission to the Hall of Fame were made by boards of experts and nominations from the public; many preservationists were included in the selection process, and the ASHPS regarded the hall to be furthering the goal of stimulating patriotism and historical memory. As a novel and grand form of memory infrastructure, the Hall of Fame represented the yearning for new and more powerful forms of commemoration and spatialized memory to project and inculcate positive public memories in the civic mind. The success and power of monumental art on display in these decades drew from its presence in the landscape, in both extraordinary and ordinary locations throughout the city—an urbanistic quality of the memory infrastructure that the developers of the Hall of Fame apparently did not understand. Being quite remote from the rest of the city and from "the street," the hall has never been well visited by the public.

While art and decoration certainly were part of the raison d'être of these statues and monuments, the driving force in creating them was often public education. Charles Mulford Robinson explained:

Figure 1.21. The Hall of Fame featured bronze busts of great Americans displayed in an arcade. Courtesy of University of Pennsylvania Libraries.

That public sculpture necessarily is, in one way or another, educational, will not be, perhaps, entirely clear at once. But when to the long list of commemorative and memorial statues there is added a realization that ideas are embodied in all sculptural figures, it will be seen that the statues of a city are a record not only of its history but of its spirit, not only of its achievements, but of its ideals and aims.[132]

A nationally prominent purveyor of City Beautiful and village-improvement reforms, Robinson acknowledged the several functions of public sculpture: "to instruct, by embodying ideals and principles in allegory, symbolism or historical scenes . . . to record history . . . to be decorative."[133] While his explanation of *how* these artworks were believed to wield their reforming power is typically vague and opaque, there was no question that statues and monuments were imagined as elements of memory infrastructure.

Museums made up another kind of hall of fame serving commemorative functions in early-twentieth-century New York. The Metropolitan Museum of Art started its American Wing in this period, partly because of the success of other memory work such as the Hudson–Fulton Celebration. The Museum of the City of New York also got its start in this era, created expressly as a hall of fame, celebration, collection, and reflection for the city. The creation of historical museums and museum exhibits can be seen as part of the larger stream of memory work this study describes as an urban-scale, "open-air" phenomenon. Max Page argued that the memory works created inside the walls of museums were compensating for what preservationists failed to achieve in the city landscape.[134] This undersells the real successes of historic preservation, or perhaps it overestimates what the preservationists intended to achieve. They tried a million things at once, rarely considering which of the alternative forms of memory would be most effective. There is no question that the spirit behind the American Wing resonated with the spirit, goals, narratives, and ideology promoted by preservationists. Programmatically, the American Wing and preservationists' urban projects shared the same memorial purposes; the historical narratives selectively presented in the American Wing and in the works of the preservation field were fully aligned. In the words of American Wing organizer R. T. H. Halsey, speaking in 1925, the American Wing makes up for the diminished memorial capacity of the actual New York landscape:

Old New York has gone. Nothing of New Amsterdam remains. . . .
Hitherto New York has been bare of the background which would allow
a realistic visualization of America's traditions and history. . . . A journey

through this American Wing cannot fail to revive those memories and bring with it a spirit of thankfulness that our great city at last has a setting for the traditions so dear to us and invaluable in the Americanization of many of our people to whom much of our history has been hidden in a fog of unenlightenment.[135]

Halsey was far too dismissive of the work of preservationists. Preservationists had saved (or re-created) fragments of Old New York over the preceding thirty years, making up a collection of varied historical artifacts composed to present images of a respectful and proud past, to highlight some narratives over others—a result like the collection assembled in the American Wing, although perforce less aesthetically controlled, given the fact that it was not contained within the walls of a museum but spread over the many square miles of the burgeoning metropolis.

FESTIVALS AND CELEBRATIONS

Restored buildings, old parks, granite monuments, and bronze plaques were preservationists' stock-in-trade and the heart of memory infrastructure. Their durability suggested the lasting importance of the memories they represented. But the process of collective remembering took other, powerful, yet more ephemeral forms in the life of the city. The spectacle of public festivals and celebrations contributed to the memory infrastructure, adding the spectacular presence of historical memory in reformers' urban landscape, reinforcing the core messages of preservation—civic patriotism; place-rooted stories highlighting the continuities in New York's development—and endorsing New York's present and future economic power by connecting it to traditions of commercial growth, invention, and entrepreneurship.

Historical pageants, holiday festivals, and monument dedications were popular in the early twentieth century, meaningful if fleeting expressions of historical memory.[136] They afford a clear view of the official historical memory—staged, designed, scripted to transmit publicly what leaders thought were the important messages about culture, memory, and citizenship.

The Hudson–Fulton Celebration of 1909 and the New York Commercial Tercentenary Celebration of 1914—the two festivals highlighted here[137]—celebrated narratives of civic patriotism, preached place attachment, and activated New York's broad community of reformers, designers, and public officials to put on a great public show of their ideal visions—"building on a spectacle of the past a new city unity for the future."[138]

Lasting a few weeks or months, the festivals were no less real in the life of the city than buildings, statues, or parks. Festivals were an extraordinary opportunity to bring the visual and memorial culture of preservation to public audiences of many thousands. They were no less spatial: The most elaborate and successful celebration, the Hudson–Fulton Celebration, occupied many prominent sites around the city (the Battery, Broadway, Central Park, City Hall Park, the Hudson River) with literally spectacular events and designs. The celebration also afforded an opportunity to dedicate more-permanent memory works such as statues and memorials. The narratives celebrated were the same as well. Festivals afforded preservationists unprecedented opportunities to develop and display their ideas in detail and dramatically—for example, designing a series of thirty floats parading down Broadway to tell the comprehensive story of the city's history instead of being limited to the particular narratives of a building or a monument.[139]

The New York State government provided seed funding, and fund-raising among private citizens provided the lion's share. The chief organizers and chroniclers of the celebration were none other than George Frederick Kunz, president of the ASHPS, and Edward Hagaman Hall, secretary of the ASHPS. They possessed the historical imagination as well as the network of reformers, officials, and other powerful citizens to coordinate everything. The (mostly honorary) commissioners of the Hudson–Fulton Celebration were esteemed public figures: Grover Cleveland, Chauncey Depew, Seth Low, Cornelius Vanderbilt, and other captains of industry and government. The commission's president was Gen. Stewart Woodford.

The Metropolitan Museum of Art was one of many institutions participating in the celebration. Met chairman and millionaire civic reformer Robert De Forest noted that the establishment of the Met's American Wing, devoted to historic American visual arts, stemmed from the museum's having tested the ground through a temporary exhibit of American furniture organized as part of the Hudson–Fulton Celebration.[140]

The Hudson–Fulton Celebration of 1909 was typical of the historical pageantry popular in this period, combining public events (parades, speeches, plays, and performances), indoor and outdoor exhibits, complex organizational schemes and partnerships, and patriotically focused interpretations of local history.[141] The celebration commemorated the "discovery" of the city by explorer Henry Hudson along with the commercial growth spurred by Robert Fulton's steamboat invention (pegged, respectively, to the years 1609 and 1809).[142] The celebration's historical memory program went beyond these two stories to encompass the whole canon of civic patriotism, and indeed to deepen and broaden the stories usually presented.[143] The celebration's floats, exhibits, speeches, and publications exhibited preservation narratives seamlessly connected to New York's commercial ascendance.

The celebration looked backward and forward simultaneously—constructing a single, three-hundred-year narrative out of divergent themes to create a story of the commercial ascendance of modern New York City and touting the city's nascent moment of modernization as the continuation of that narrative. Perhaps the most exciting aspects of the Hudson–Fulton Celebration were displays integrating the technological future and the civic past: reconstructions of historic ships (Hudson's *Half Moon* and Fulton's *Clermont*) sailing alongside the Great White Fleet in naval parades; electric light displays on historic buildings (City Hall, presented by General Electric);[144] airplane demonstrations sharing the program with historical floats featuring Indians and faux colonial settlers.

The celebration was an ambitious array of parades, speeches, exhibits, displays, and performances lasting two weeks in September and October. Events were staged in dozens of locations, on land and water, spread across the five boroughs.[145] Didactic school programs and museum exhibitions "to inculcate civic virtue" through its history lessons supplemented the public entertainments.[146] The Hudson–Fulton was an ephemeral landscape of memory; few permanent elements remained after 1909.[147] And it was a huge popular success. More than a million people attended the celebration, many of them traveling to New York to do so. The major parades drew more than two million spectators. The main historical parade featured fifty-four floats, arranged chronologically and designed around themes ranging from colonial history (Dutch and English), to patriotic heroes and events, to commemoration of civic achievements (Hudson's explorations, Fulton's steamboat, the Erie Canal), and even to Native Americans. Each float incorporated live figures. Despite the profusion of messages and narratives, the hierarchy was made clear: The patriotic prevailed, and Native Americans were included seemingly to show how far civilization had advanced by colonization and technological development. The didactic messages emphasized personal virtue as well as civic pride.

The massive public undertaking of the celebration built upon a consensus that history was important as a tool for shaping public consciousness, not just as knowledge in itself. Despite being unabashedly didactic and driven by elite reformers, upper-class donors, and powerful public officials, the Hudson–Fulton Celebration revealed the extent to which the construction of historical memory could be a contested public process. The extent of public participation was impressive; millions attended over the weeks of scheduled events, making it an indisputably *public* spectacle. And an event associated with the celebration—the erection of a statue

Figure 1.22. The many activities in the Hudson–Fulton Celebration were cataloged in thick reports created by Edward Hagaman Hall, secretary of the ASHPS. The frontispiece of this report captures the fusion of modern city (the skyline of tall commercial buildings) and historical legacy (the working reconstruction of Fulton's pioneering Clermont steaming up the Hudson). Courtesy of University of Pennsylvania Libraries.

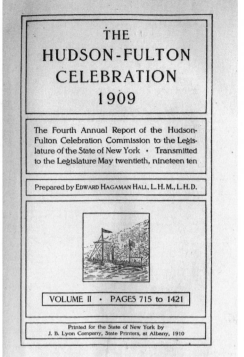

of Italian explorer Giovanni da Verrazano—demonstrated vividly the point that memory infrastructure was fraught with politics.

Charles Barsotti, Italian immigrant and publisher of the large newspaper *Il Progresso,* succeeded in expanding the canon of civic memory advanced by the Hudson–Fulton Celebration. In the midst of memory making centered on Hudson and Fulton, Barsotti brashly insisted that his countryman Verrazano be acknowledged as the true "discoverer" of New York City (and as part of the heritage of New York's large Italian community). A controversy ensued, played out in the newspapers. It was one of very few arguments over historical interpretation to emerge in all the discussions about memory infrastructure and civic patriotism in this period. Organizers of the Hudson–Fulton Celebration, overwhelmingly representing the WASP establishment, never questioned that it was Henry Hudson (the Dutch sailor often thought to be English) who should be celebrated as the discoverer of the Hudson River. Barsotti, through an Italian lens, took pride in Verrazano's earlier sighting (discovery?) of the river, even though it was not named for him, and challenged the celebration's organizers. Verrazano's inclusion in the celebration was "destined to challenge seriously the honors to be accorded to the

Figure 1.23. Floats from the Hudson–Fulton Celebration historical parade marked events and historical memories organizers regarded as important contributions to the development of New York. Of the dozens of floats (paraded in chronological order), the two pictured here idolize "the colonial home" (a) and the creation of the Croton water system in the 1840s (b). The photographs were taken by Jessie Tarbox Beals, the first woman photojournalist. Courtesy of University of Pennsylvania Libraries.

Figure 1.24. The Hudson–Fulton Celebration featured electric illuminations of public buildings and ships to make a spectacle of the fusion of new technology and modern progress with the city's historic legacy of commercial innovation. Courtesy of University of Pennsylvania Libraries.

Figure 1.25. Crowds of dignitaries, children, and the public assembled for events in the Hudson–Fulton Celebration. Courtesy of University of Pennsylvania Libraries.

Figure 1.26. The monument to explorer Giovanni da Verrazano in Battery Park in 1909. Later alterations to the granite base and bronze figures restrained the sprawling composition by Italian sculptor Ettore Ximenes. Courtesy of University of Pennsylvania Libraries.

intrepid Hudson."[148] Edward Hall, seeking accommodation instead of conflict, hedged that while Verrazano had indeed entered New York Harbor about a century before Hudson, that did not mean that Verrazano had "discovered" it: "The word 'discover' does not necessarily mean to see a thing first. Its primary meaning is to uncover or lay open to view; hence to exhibit or make known. So it was with Hudson," Hall was quoted (confusingly) as saying.[149]

Barsotti organized a subscription drive among his readers and fellow Italian immigrants to commission the bronze-and-granite memorial to a great figure in Italian history. He succeeded in putting up the monument, while Hall minced words. The grand, fourteen-foot Verrazano monument assumed a prominent site in Battery Park—the oldest open space in Manhattan and the center stage for the whole Hudson–Fulton Celebration. "Parade Route Thronged" read one newspaper headline: Twenty-five thousand Italians representing 250 societies marched in procession to the dedication. The crowd along the route, from Madison Square down to the Battery, was two hundred thousand strong; a thousand policemen kept order while dignitaries made speeches.[150] Barsotti managed to push back on the normative memory infrastructure and make it a bit pluralistic.

The issue of placing statues of ethnic-group heroes was an interesting sub-text and challenge to the story of the Hudson–Fulton Celebration and the whole construction of memory infrastructure in this period. The Art Commission prevented the Verrazano statue (an inferior piece of work, they felt, from sculptor Ettore Ximenes) from being placed in perhaps the only spot *more* esteemed than the Battery, next to Frederick MacMonnies's statue of revered American patriot Nathan Hale in City Hall Park.

Preservationist and sculptor Henry Kirke Bush-Brown had ideas about putting ethnic memory sites in their place: Washington Square could be the designated ghetto for not-quite-American heroes and narratives. "There is already here the statue of Garibaldi, adjacent to a district which has always been and is yet occupied by a foreign population. Might we not devote this space to the monuments of the lovers of liberty in other countries, which from time to time their compatriots in this country wish to erect[?]"[151]

Though few openly discussed the zoning of particular narratives in particular places—apart from Bush-Brown—there were tacit negotiations taking place about the geography of memory sites and their political symbolism. A few ethnic groups and associations worked to inscribe their own social memories into the civic canon, mirroring the plurality of ethnic voices on the street.[152] Elite preservationists generally countenanced and even encouraged this. However, as the Verrazano debate revealed, preservationists were unwilling to cede the ultimate meaning of memory infrastructure to non-"American" identities. Thus, while the Verrazano monument ultimately occupied an excellent site, the celebration was not renamed "Verrazano–Fulton."

The Verrazano statue flew in the face of the whole rationale for the Hudson–Fulton Celebration—enforcing the idea that New York's greatness stemmed from Dutch and English accomplishments, not from those of Italians or other non-WASPs—yet it was lodged in one of the most prominent memory sites in the city. And there it remains today, somewhat altered in form, but an unalloyed testament to the cultural pluralism of New York City and the public, contested character of creating historical memory and memory infrastructure.

The celebrations succeeded by bringing the memory infrastructure to life, even if briefly, in the public space of the city. For historians, the celebrations give a glimpse of the reception of memory infrastructure: The many small organizations collaborating to carry out the events, the large attendance at parades and ceremonies, the avid newspaper coverage all suggest a genuine engagement with the spectacles of public memory preservationists wished New Yorkers to witness.

Frank Cousins's Photographs
for the Art Commission, 1913

Plate 1. Three houses on State Street

Plate 2. Smith's Folly

Plate 3. Dyckman House

Plate 4. Weehawkin Street

Plate 5. Schenk–Crook House

Plate 6. Ferris House

Plate 7. Hamilton Grange

Plate 8. Morris–Jumel Mansion (Washington's Headquarters)

Plate 9. Nathan Hale Memorial

Plate 10. St. Paul's Chapel

Plate 11. Assay Office

Plate 12. St. John's Chapel

Plate 13. 122–124 William Street

Plate 14. 189–191–193 Hudson Street

Plate 15. Beach Street doorway

Plate 16. Watts Street doorway

Two

The Preservation and Destruction of St. John's Chapel

> There is little permanence upon which to fasten one's memories, affections and historical traditions. A city needs just such piles as old St. John's to give it some idea of firmness and stability in contrast with the fleeting changes around; to stand as monuments to the best and noblest human effort, and to serve as visible bonds to bind together generations and centuries of high endeavor.
>
> American Scenic and Historic Preservation Society,
> *Fourteenth Annual Report*, 1909

ST. JOHN'S CHAPEL, A LARGE EPISCOPAL CHURCH ON VARICK STREET, WAS designed by architect John McComb for Trinity Parish and completed in 1807. The chapel closed in 1909 and was torn down in 1918. The will of the chapel's owner, the Vestry of Trinity Church, to redevelop the site ultimately prevailed over the pleas of the congregation and historic preservationists to preserve the building. This chapter relates the long, complicated story of the preservation and destruction of St. John's Chapel, focusing on the years between 1908 and 1918 when the chapel was a prominent and contested memory site. The little-known story of the chapel is one of the best windows on the emergence of the urban-preservation field.

The closing of churches and consequent displacing of congregations is a common narrative in the story of American cities, and New York has its many examples.[1] But few provoked such outcry as that of St. John's. Efforts to close and destroy this century-old church stirred declarations of the importance of collective memory and public monuments from a wide range of groups. The debate over St. John's pitted Trinity Vestry against the chapel's congregation, reformers, and others wishing to see the building preserved. Trinity was among New York's oldest and most powerful institutions, so in many ways it was surprising that the preservation debate lasted as long as it did.[2] While preservationists sought the "permanence" and

Figure 2.1. The exterior and interior of St. John's Chapel, as published in Aymar Embury's Early American Churches *in 1914. Courtesy of Anne and Jerome Fisher Fine Arts Library, University of Pennsylvania.*

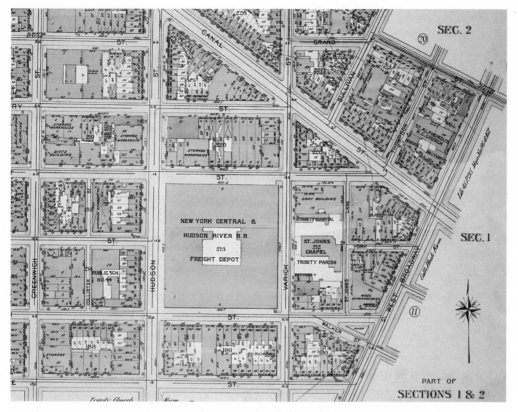

Figure 2.2. During the last third of the nineteenth century, the neighborhood of St. John's Chapel (on the east side of Varick Street) changed dramatically. Developed as an elite residential square at the beginning of the century, it became a warehousing and manufacturing district—most strikingly evident in this map from 1898 in the railroad freight depot occupying what was once St. John's Square. Courtesy of the Lionel Pincus and Princess Firyal Map Division, the New York Public Library, Aster, Lenox, and Tilden Foundations.

"stability" lent by the persistence of old, grand buildings in a furiously changing and commercializing environment, Trinity Vestry saw change and destruction as "natural," embraced land-use changes and the uptown movement of its chapels, and sought to marshal the momentum of the market for its own purposes. Trinity had few supporters in the St. John's case, though it mattered little in the end; the vestry was able to exercise its property rights, outlasting public opprobrium and selling the chapel site for redevelopment.

The fate of St. John's was debated for more than ten years before demolition contractors carried out their work in 1918. In this decade, New Yorkers debated the building's meaning and made many proposals, some based on its continuing use as a church, others on particular renderings of the building's history.

These agents involved in the preservation debate included the congregation and clergy who worshipped there, the chapel's "mother church" organization (Trinity Vestry), Episcopalian ministers and lay leaders, urban reformers of various stripes (especially historic preservationists), public officials, architects, newspapers, and concerned citizens. The chapel was meaningful to these groups in a correspondingly diverse set of ways: as a place for religious worship, as a center of the neighborhood, as an economically valuable site ripe for redevelopment, as a totem of Old New York, as beautiful or authentic architecture, as the testing ground for Trinity's civic responsibilities, as a potential work site for reform movements. The range of meanings ascribed to the building—religious and secular, associational memory, architectural and historic—and the politics and struggles over the building's fate vividly illuminate the engagement of historic preservation with larger issues of urbanization and modern culture. And preservationists' efforts to fix the building's history in the public mind nearly saved the building, but only after the memory of the chapel—as a living congregation, as opposed to a secular historical landmark—was inexorably changed.

Before the building was destroyed, the congregation removed elements of its interior to use in its new home, St. Luke's Chapel. The very different fate of the different parts of the St. John's fabric mirrored what was happening in the city as a whole: While astonishing growth often resulted in the destruction of buildings, elements of New York society believed that some artifacts, buildings, and landscapes were too meaningful to be so sacrificed. Memories of the place changed markedly but did not disappear altogether. And, as the chapter's opening quotation suggests, civic culture remained anchored by a past that seems to grow at once more distant and more stable. The debate about historic preservation illuminated so brightly by the St. John's Chapel case—over the selective salvation of material remnants of the city's urban past—was one way of reforming the character of the fast-growing modern city. New Yorkers sustained a vigorous, ever-shifting discussion about balancing the tendencies toward permanence and destruction constantly played out in the built environment—a discussion hashed out through private and public interests invested in such landmarks of Old New York as St. John's.

Between the onset of public debate in 1908 and the building's demolition in 1918, the public memory of the chapel was transformed in several ways: First, the chapel was understood at the outset as a site of community religious worship and later as a secular, civic historic site. Second, changes in the ideology of preservation were reflected in the drift in focus from the historical and associational values of the chapel and the congregation to the aesthetic and architectural values of the building itself. Underlying these shifts was an evocation of Old New York, a popu-

Figure 2.3. Demolition photographs from a report of the American Scenic and Historic Preservation Society. Courtesy of University of Pennsylvania Libraries.

lar and whitewashed image newly minted in the reform culture's historical memory that clearly contrasted with new New York, which was dense, ethnically varied, cacophonous, and full of contrasts. This cultural shift had both geographic and epistemological aspects: As the prevailing notion of the chapel's memory shifted from one of local to metropolitan relevance, it ceased to represent a *traditional* kind of memory, formed out of the community's continuous association with a shared past, and was transformed into *modern* memory, abstracted from the social webs that produced it and freely reassembled by civic discourse. The memory that had been sustained locally and traditionally by the congregation was replaced by a modern, metropolitan, "civic" conception of its past. By tracing the subtle shifts in how St. John's was remembered differently by a changing set of voices, this case traces the larger transformation in modern New York's use of historical memory to shape urbanization.

CREATING AN UPTOWN CHAPEL-OF-EASE

The history of St. John's begins on the social and geographic margins of the city. The chapel was completed in 1807 as part of Hudson Square, a planned neighborhood built by Trinity Church for the uptown migration of New York's wealthy, Episcopal elite. Located beyond the built-up town, on Varick Street just below Canal Street, the area was laid out as an English residential square, with a private landscaped park surrounded by a continuous facade of Federal townhouses and an elegant chapel.[3] Architects John and Isaac McComb built St. John's in high colonial–Georgian style, as a copy of James Gibbs's St. Martin-in-the-Fields in London. It was "the very finest church ever erected in the city," with imposing dimensions and fine decoration inside and out.[4] Decorative ironwork, carved details, and an impressive portico made the massive stone building an instant visual landmark. In contrast to other churches existing in 1807, St. John's was unmistakably urban: a design of great elegance and streetscape presence, conceived of a piece with its park and townhouse rows. The whole place—houses, chapel, park—was meant to be seen and experienced ensemble; only in the modern city of the twentieth century would the chapel be regarded as an individual landmark. It was a landmark in the premodern sense: a spire to define the skyline, an imposing entrance, surrounded by a foreground of open space.

Hudson Square's site was known as the Lispenard Meadows, a swampy margin of the growing post-Revolution town that was part of the Queen's Farm (the land grant that was the source of Trinity's vast wealth). The area was known for its skating ponds and snakes, and the land was so uneven and poorly drained that test piles had to be driven in several places before the site of the chapel was decided upon. The building of the chapel, park, and houses was a drastic transformation of swamp into elite residential district.[5]

By the 1830s, St. John's Park was the city's most fashionable district, and the chapel was known as New York's "Court Church." Families living around the park included the Mangins, Delanceys, Minturns, and Stuyvesants.[6] But New York's development continued rushing northward. Stalled at about City Hall, at Chambers Street, around the end of the Revolution, by 1840 the town had spread well past Madison Square.[7] As the city expanded, its social geography developed into a pattern of increasingly segregated functions and land uses and residential enclaves sorted by class. Areas of wealthy residences, once mixed in with other land uses near the tip of Manhattan, leapfrogged uptown in a succession of enclaves, leaving the poor concentrated near districts of commerce, shipping, and warehouses around downtown. By midcentury, the wealthy had regrouped on lower Fifth Avenue, and as New York boomed and grew to be the center of national and regional economies in the second half of the nineteenth century, demands for commercial and warehouse space grew as well. Across Lower Manhattan, townhouses gave way to tenements, warehouses, rail yards, and factories. By midcentury, the

Figure 2.4. John McComb's drawings for St. John's Chapel, as reproduced in I. N. P. Stokes's Iconography of Manhattan Island. *Courtesy of University of Pennsylvania Libraries.*

Varick Street neighborhood had changed drastically. The area's population and St. John's congregation had changed, too: By the 1870s, townhouses had been subdivided and were occupied by multiple working-class families, including many immigrant Germans and Italians.[8] The city's changing social geography threatened a number of Trinity's chapels—essentially, they were subsidiaries controlled by Trinity Vestry—as populations moved but chapels remained fixed in place.

St. John's Park and the Memory of Its Destruction

In the first half of the nineteenth century, St. John's Park was one of Manhattan's three most important urban green spaces, along with City Hall Park and the Battery. By the 1840s, a social hierarchy dictated how each park was used. The Battery was the most convivial and socially mixed; St. John's was the most polite and refined; City Hall Park was the least respectable place for women.[9] Things kept changing. St. John's Park became a de facto public park after the wealthy fled the area, popular with residents of crowded downtown neighborhoods.

This ended when the park was destroyed in 1867 with the reluctant permission of Trinity's new rector, Morgan Dix (a native of Manhattan and rising star in the Episcopal Church). The park was sold off by the Trinity Vestry (and the owners of surrounding houses), reneging on a long-standing promise to convey the park to the city if ever the owners decided not to care for it (which they long had not). The park was bought by shipping baron Cornelius Vanderbilt for $1 million—$400,000 of this went directly to Trinity coffers, and $600,000 was distributed to the other owners. Trinity was widely and publicly criticized for cashing in on what was de facto a public park and later expressed regret that the sale was "necessary . . . because of the inevitable growth of the city."[10] Vanderbilt immediately razed the park and built a Hudson River Railroad freight shed to the lot lines. The massiveness of the warehouse—featuring a block-long sculptural frieze celebrating Vanderbilt's empire—was a further insult to those who sensed the magnitude of the park's loss.

At the time of its destruction, the park's loss was seen as a loss of "nature," of a green space in the industrial quarter.[11] Within a couple of generations, the regret and outrage felt by New Yorkers in the 1860s had taken on a historical dimension, for it was remembered by early-twentieth-century New Yorkers as soon as St. John's Chapel was threatened. The destruction of the park was remembered as a blow to New York's heritage of civic life and public spaces. The park's destruction endured in the civic memory at least until the second decade of the twentieth century and served as a distasteful parable of private interests cashing in on a rare public resource: a green space downtown. Trinity's history of compromising its civic responsibility for corporate gain was clear to turn-of-the-century critics looking backward.

Trinity Vestry's attitude toward the park presaged its response to the public outcry about its plans to close the chapel. Trinity portrayed the destruction of both park and chapel as inevitable, part of the march of progress (which was "natural" and thus went unquestioned), and justified because the vestry needed money to continue its important work. Righteous about its policy of improving the overall financial health of the parish at the expense of poor and working-class congregants, Trinity regarded buying and selling its religious structures and other real estate holdings simply as a means of funding church work (that is, building new chapels uptown where the upper and middle classes were moving). In writing its own history, Trinity represented itself as a victim of the "juggernaut" of commercial progress, whereas it was actually a major player in the real estate market and a beneficiary of "progress": "Planned in wisdom . . . the speed of the city's growth and the insistence of the claims of commerce allowed [St. John's Park] to exist scarcely more than the life span of a generation . . . pressed upon on all sides by the rising tides of commerce."[12] Nevertheless, Trinity's policy was criticized, both inside and outside the religious community, as ruthless class discrimination. In the words of the Reverend Dr. William Rainsford—an outspoken, Progressive Episcopal minister—this was "a movement which I beg to think all thoughtful Christian men can agree in denouncing as the ignorant, unchristian and fatal retreat of the churches from the poor, the leaving of the poor, to follow the well-to-do."[13]

The chapel itself remained, facing Vanderbilt's giant freight warehouse instead of its park. The chapel congregation remained large and active, a center of religious worship in a district increasingly given over to warehouses, industry, and immigrant workers crowded into Federal row houses. St. John's carried on its "old traditions" of social service, ministry to the poor, and strongly Anglo-Catholic liturgy, despite the destruction of the park and other surrounding changes.[14]

The Chapel as Real Estate

The destruction of St. John's Park and Trinity's attitude toward its real estate holdings cast doubt on the status of St. John's Chapel well before the 1908–9 controversy. As early as 1893, Trinity's rector, Morgan Dix, announced the vestry's intention to build a new chapel on St. John's Burying Ground (later Walker Park, and located between Seventh Avenue, Hudson Street, and Clarkson Street, just north of Houston), consolidating the congregations of St. Luke's and St. John's chapels.[15] Dix was a beloved leader. And it is peculiar that he would have supported this change in St. John's because of his strong personal associations with and memories of the chapel. St. John's was in many ways Dix's home: He was baptized and confirmed at St. John's, was ordained there, first preached there, and lived there for ten years as rector. Pressure to close the chapel probably came from the vestry, the lay body composed of businessmen and other prominent citizens, who took a notoriously "business" approach to consolidating and selling excess property.[16] Two of the powerful and somewhat shadowy figures in the whole St. John's case—the vestry's comptroller Hermann Cammann (a real estate entrepreneur) and Col. William Jay (a Wall Street lawyer, Civil War veteran, and descendant of the prominent New York family of John Jay)—were said to have embodied this attitude.[17]

In 1894, Dix, on behalf of the vestry, proposed the consolidation of St. John's and St. Luke's and, according to canon, "respectfully ask[ed] the consent of the

Figure 2.5. This photograph circa 1913 captures the changed environment surrounding St. John's Chapel. Vanderbilt's railroad freight depot (left) faced the chapel across Varick Street; industrial loft buildings (right) increasingly replaced the early-nineteenth-century houses that had formed the chapel's original context. Courtesy of University of Pennsylvania Libraries.

Bishop ... to take down and remove the edifice known as St. John's Chapel."[18] Dix's written record suggests a deep reluctance to close St. John's; pressure from vestrymen played a strong role in decisions Dix announced about park and chapel.[19] In March 1894, Bishop Potter granted permission to demolish St. John's, acknowledging the considerable sentiment that this would crush and the outcry that would be raised. Potter, too, regretted parting with St. John's, but he agreed that the new arrangement would be more efficient. He gave consent to use the site "for other than sacred purposes," as required by canon. Potter's letter granting the permission lamented lost memory: "No one who knows and loves the elder New York can learn without unfeigned regret that the Corporation which you represent contemplates taking down St. John's and parting with its site or using it for other than sacred purposes."[20] Correspondence between Potter and the vestry explained that for some time the vestry, with "utmost pain and reluctance," had considered closing St. John's, destroying the buildings, selling the land, and arranging for its "improvement for business purposes." This was despite vestrymen's realization that "St. John's is among the most venerable churches in the city" and despite their recognition of "its great size and architectural merit and the historical associations which cling to this sacred edifice."[21] (As late as 1907, Dix still held out hope that St. John's congregation and landscape could be sustained: "I feel a deep interest in St. John's, and hope and pray that it may long continue as a centre of large work for Christ, and a landmark of religion in the region in which it had been so long situated."[22] Beyond his personal attachment to the chapel, Dix's use of "landmark" suggests the common awareness of environmental and cultural factors—the chapel's urban presence and historical memory—that were at the root of struggles to preserve St. John's.)

The vestry had researched the number of communicants at St. John's, where they lived, and which way the trends were moving (if communicants did not live very close to the chapel, that would constitute reason to close it, even if they willingly traveled to St. John's from afar). The chapel's vicar, Rev. Philip A. H. Brown, reported in March 1894 that the number of worshippers at St. John's continued to be in the hundreds. But the vestry concluded that the number of St. John's communicants living *above* Canal Street was "increasing very rapidly every year," and that the area south of Canal was warehouses, not tenements, so "all kinds of constituents are 'moving up.'"[23] The neighborhood had changed enough to render the work of the chapel "less efficient," the vestry concluded, a verdict outweighing the building's historic or other public value.

Demolition plans for St. John's were thwarted, however, by the city's condemnation of the St. John's Burying Ground to make what became Walker Park (under the Small Parks Act of 1887). This complicated the plans to consolidate St. John's and St. Luke's by taking away the site where their replacement was to be built.[24] Another reason why Dix probably resisted the consolidation plans between 1894 and 1908 is because he did not want to upset the worship of the congregation and especially of its beloved Civil-War-hero-turned-vicar, the Reverend Brown.

CLOSING THE DOORS OF "OLD ST. JOHN'S"

Redevelopment of the St. John's neighborhood into an industrial district of modern loft buildings continued apace, making the logic of closing the chapel ever more obvious. Dix acted in November 1907—probably under pressure from vestrymen—naming a committee to consider closing the chapel "in view of the changed conditions in the part of the City in the neighborhood of St. John's, and of the character and residentiary movements of the population of said district."[25] This was resolved on the same day that St. John's Vicar Brown—the congregation's revered, longtime leader—was given sick leave, and his assistant Charles Gomph was appointed temporary vicar. At this time, the congregation had several hundred communicants (those who had recently received communion), yet smaller Sunday congregations (less than a hundred on nonholidays).

In the public mind, Trinity had earned a tarnished reputation quite apart from the St. John's case. Stretching back to the 1860s, newspapers had publicized a number of scandals involving the church's considerable real estate holdings, accusing the city's most elite religious (and supposedly philanthropic) institution of financing itself as a slumlord—profiteering from "rookeries, which were manifestly unfit for human habitation."[26]

Trinity's public reputation again came to the fore when the parish's leadership changed in 1908—Morgan Dix died in April, and his assistant, Rev. William Thomas Manning, was quickly elevated to replace him. Dix and Manning had clashed in the past.[27] Separated by a generation and by geography,[28] they were quite different men with quite different ideas about Trinity's role as a New York City institution. The difference between Dix and Manning could be summarized as the difference between religious leadership by sentiment and leadership with a business mind. One could say they marked opposite sides of the historical divide between traditional and modern approaches to church leadership. Manning's mandate included modernizing the church, which, in a sign of the times, meant making it more "efficient."[29] It is not surprising, then, that he moved swiftly to bring Dix's foot-dragging on St. John's to an end. A standing committee of Manning's vestry—including Cammann and Jay—resolved on November 9, 1908, to close St. John's.[30]

The statement of Dix's reluctance to close St. John's was presented by Manning as proof that efficiency was a greater good than preserving the building and its memory: "No one ever felt more keenly the close associations which the work at St. John's has had with the life of the City" than Dix, Manning stated, "and yet, after long shrinking from it, he at last believed the facts to be so conclusive that he wrote out with his own hand and presented to the Vestry the resolution" suggesting the closing of the chapel.[31]

Manning announced the "consolidation" of St. John's and St. Luke's in letters to be read to all Trinity's chapels on Sunday, November 22. In his letter to St. John's, Manning recognized the depth and breadth of memories the congregation had of its "venerable House of Worship," noting the "painful and trying" experience the closing would cause worshippers and the "close and tender associations with it and the deep attachment to it of our late beloved Rector, the Revd. Dr. Dix, and of the relation of the Chapel through so many years to the life of the parish and of the Church in this city." But the fate of the chapel came down to this: "The Vestry feel that . . . The work which for some years past has been done at both Chapels can all of it be efficiently carried on at Saint Luke's."[32] The religious work of St. John's was insufficient to warrant the cost of keeping it open. This conclusion was contradicted not only by the evidence marshaled by the congregants (St. John's had 557 communicants) but also by data published in the vestry's own parish *Year Book*—which listed a music program, Sunday school for 280 children, and more than a dozen guilds and charity groups operated by St. John's.[33]

Manning's letter was leaked to the Saturday evening newspapers, and "in such a manner was Pandora's box opened!"[34]—ten years of protest and negotiation over the chapel ensued. Immediately put under the gaze of the newspapers, the vestry hedged about the fate of the building. Knowing its public image to be fragile, Trinity handled this as a potentially explosive public issue. And its image was not an idle worry: Vestry officials wrote of their concern that reformers' previous outcries raised over tenement conditions and unfairness in the handling of St. John's Park (however unfounded in the church's eyes) could lead to legal challenges to the church's charter and ultimately threaten its land-based wealth. The clearly stated parish policy of the 1870s was obviously being reconsidered:

> To prevent such a shame, disgrace and disaster [as leaving the downtown poor without places of worship], it is the policy of the Corporation to keep its churches on their ancient sites, in good repair, and in decent order, to make the services attractive, to provide the means of religious education for children, and to minister to all who can be reached . . . in a word, to maintain the public worship of Almighty God with due honor, and to sustain the institutions and ordinances of Christianity in those parts of the city which would otherwise be left nearly, if not quite destitute of spiritual and religious privileges. . . . it is held that the greater part of the means of the Corporation should be spent in ministering to their spiritual welfare.[35]

From this point onward, Trinity only referred to "closing" and "consolidation," abandoning the previously acknowledged intention to demolish the chapel and arrange its "improvement for business purposes." It was widely understood, though, that Trinity Vestry intended to demolish and redevelop the site, not just cease worship and ministry at St. John's. (Indeed, a January 16, 1909, article in the real estate magazine *Record and Guide* reported matter-of-factly that Trinity was preparing plans "for the improvement of the site of old St. John's Church, in Varick St., with a 7-sty. fire-proof warehouse.")[36] The reason for this public relations trickery was recognition of the public's feelings for the chapel and its associations and of the public relations costs of talking openly of destroying it. Like the destruction of St. John's Park forty years before, the passing of the chapel was interpreted by church officials as "natural," part of the growth of the city, whereas the critical public clearly saw Trinity's actions as a disagreeable matter of choice.

PROTEST

The outlines of the chapel controversy quickly took shape. At first, it was Trinity Vestry versus St. John's congregation, almost in the sense of a landlord–tenant dispute. To the congregants, the vestry's talk of "consolidation" directly threatened their religious life. While the vestry stressed the "natural" redevelopment and neighborhood change that made this necessary (if regrettable), the congregation saw the vestry exercising power unjustly, trading the economic value of the property for the chapel's meanings as a religious home to the congregants and an architectural-historical landmark.

The few accounts by historians of the St. John's case fail to convey the congregation's stake and experience in this controversy, leaving it invisible in a story primarily about the building as an artifact and object of professional reformers.[37] But the congregation and its attachment to the place is key to understanding how the St. John's case shed light on larger connections between collective memory and urbanization. The closing of the chapel marked a tipping point in the conversion of the chapel's cultural value from religious to civic, from local to metropolitan, and from traditional to modern.

The reaction of the congregation was immediate, energetic, and nuanced. It pursued several complementary lines of argument against the vestry's action: congregants' strong desire to continue worshipping in the same place, their desire to worship with the same clergy, their reverence for Dr. Dix and his lifelong association with St. John's, their property rights as a chapel congregation, the responsibility of Trinity to allow self-rule for chapels and to provide religious service to all parts of the city and all classes of its residents, and finally, the notion that the building had some public value as a historical and architectural landmark. This last rationale—that St. John's was a civic landmark—was asserted by the

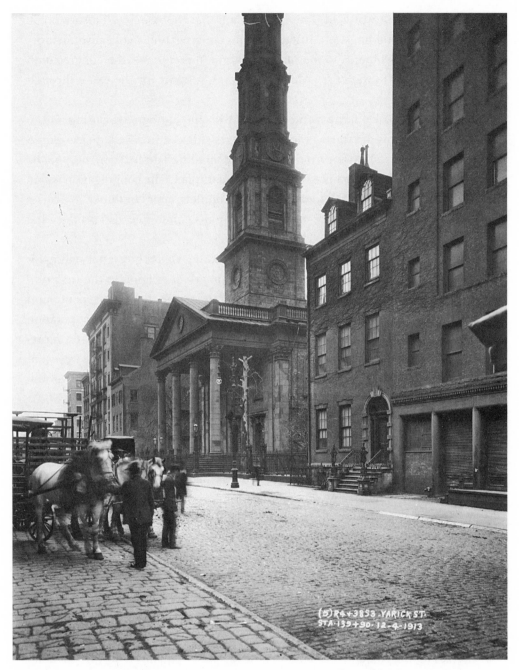

Figure 2.6. The streetscape of St. John's Chapel in 1913, captured by a photograph documenting preconstruction conditions for subway builders. Courtesy of the New York Transit Museum.

congregation's first words of protest, signaling that the visual and associational qualities of the building were fused with the congregation's collective memory and religious attachments to the place. To argue these points, the congregation appealed directly to the vestry while also sowing support for the cause through the newspapers.[38]

A committee was quickly formed to deal with the announced closing and to ask Trinity to reconsider the decision.[39] Like everyone else involved, the congregation assumed that the closing would lead to the building's destruction, despite the vestry's disingenuous insistence that this was not its plan. The congregation issued several private petitions, followed by public pamphlets, later continued as a series of legal actions against Trinity. The congregation's committee also produced at least two fund-raising letters to help pay legal fees.[40]

The congregation's first petition began by quoting Dix's 1907 letter stating his hope that St. John's would long remain "a landmark of religion in the region in which it has so long been situated."[41] It goes on to engage the vestry's main point of attack: that not enough people worshipped at St. John's to make its operation worth the cost. The document was sent to the vestry with 557 signatures, representing many of the 656 communicants, whose number had increased in recent years. The petition listed the number of communions on various holidays, as well as current attendance at the chapel's various schools, clubs, and guilds. These statistics illustrated the congregation's earnest belief that the vestry would "readily see the hardship and injustice of closing the Chapel when there is an opportunity of doing so much good."[42] The congregation argued that the number of worshippers had been increasing steadily since the disarray following Reverend Brown's 1907 departure. The vestry and congregation never agreed on these numbers: Trinity used more strenuous qualifications to define "active communicant," resulting in lower numbers of chapel users.[43]

Statistics were used by both sides of the fight to demonstrate that St. John's was or was not the center of an active, thriving ministry. The initial petition was signed by 557 congregants.[44] Records kept by the chapel clergy showed that St. John's had 1,073 baptized persons, 780 confirmed, and 621 communicants in good standing.[45] The vestry essentially tried to raise the bar, excluding many of these people by increasing the frequency of communion needed to qualify as a true "communicant." The congregation had declined steadily over the preceding decades, but this was due as much to changes in clergy as to neighborhood change. But in the year or two before the closing was carried out, St. John's was becoming a larger congregation, and it still exceeded the size of Trinity's most prized and jealously protected "historic chapel," St. Paul's.[46]

The petition also rejoined the vestry's contention that most of St. John's communicants lived at such a distance from St. John's that they would be more efficiently served by attending St. Luke's. The issue here was whether a place-based community still existed around the chapel. Indeed, a number of St. John's folks did travel from distant parts of the city—such as protest committee member Herman Gustow, who journeyed each Sunday from 180th Street—but a significant portion did reside in the immediate area.[47]

The petition concludes by enumerating the values of the building itself—constructing a collective memory of the chapel as seen by the congregation:

> St. John's, as is well known, is one of the historical buildings of New York City, noted for its architecture so distinctive, and of an epoch so interesting in the artistic life of the nation, of which so little remains, and possessing a cultural value which cannot be estimated in dollars and cents. It is a spiritual and not a commercial asset. . . . The destruction of such a building will indeed be a sad event for the Church and City.[48]

The dual nature of the building's value was an important point in the congregation's arguments—members sensed that the place was important to the city's memory as well as their own; the building's civic meaning supported its significance as a religious community.

On December 14, the vestry received a letter from St. John's clergy and staff formally protesting the closing and stating their commitment to the ongoing religious work of the chapel. Though the number of active congregants had been an overt bone of contention, the real appeal, the chapel's assistant vicar Charles Gomph wrote to Manning, was based on spiritual need, not statistics. St. John's had a great "moral influence" on the area. Staff members sought to balance their loyalty to the parish hierarchy with the clear sense that the congregation had been wronged: "We have endeavored to pacify the people in their feeling that a grave injustice has been done them."[49]

First among the congregation's arguments was that the chapel's religious life should be continued, which to the congregation meant staying in the chapel and keeping its doors open. This was the literal intention of the legal injunction it sought and was granted in January 1909. But the themes of preserving religious worship and the venerable old building were inseparable (at least as reflected in petitions and newspaper coverage). The congregation's essentially historical construction of the building's meaning is clear in the description of "a congregation of people who have been baptized and brought up in the chapel and who are deeply attached to it, and desire to continue to worship in it."[50] In its very first reaction to the vestry's decision, the congregation raised the historical associations of the building, and its status as a city landmark, as reasons for Trinity to reconsider. Referring to "dear old St. John's," the petition includes appeals to the memories of the building: "one of the historical buildings of New York City"; "architecture so distinctive, and of an epoch so interesting in the artistic life of the nation, of which so little remains." The building possessed "a cultural value which cannot be estimated in dollars and cents." And, recognizing the tension between market and memory coming to characterize the New York landscape, the congregation stated plainly that its chapel was "a spiritual and not a commercial asset." The court brief submitted in January to gain the injunction against the vestry noted that "for its beauty, grace and grandeur . . . and its age and historical associations, [St. John's] has become a monument of peculiar value and worth from both a religious and civic viewpoint."[51] By invoking the notion of "civic," the congregation clearly understood its building's value to extend beyond its own religious community.

Trinity ignored the congregation's first petitions. So more petitions followed, mostly reiterating the points of the original argument, though in tones that escalated from a polite request to reconsider into a counterattack on the vestry. A second, ten-page petition from the congregation committee was printed on December 29, 1908, presenting again the "facts" about Trinity Vestry in the eyes of the congregation. It retained a polite and hopeful tone, asserting that the religious work at St. John's was well needed, was increasing, and "[could not] possibly be conducted if St. John's [was] closed." This petition also detailed the congregation's attachment to its own building and dissatisfaction with St. Luke's building, which was too small to seat everyone from both congregations.

Who were the members of the congregation? There was no question that St. John's congregation was less well-off than most of Trinity Parish—and a clear contrast to large, powerful St. Agnes's Chapel on West 91st Street, where Manning had officiated before becoming rector at Trinity. Judge William Beckett, one of St. John's lawyers, described his clients as "poor," though data on occupation suggest they were of the laboring and clerical classes. The chair of the congregation committee, John Burke, was a bank manager and had been a member of St. John's for fifty-one years (forty-six of them living in the neighborhood). He was certain the congregation would scatter if the chapel doors were closed. The other members of the seven-man committee were Herman Gustow, an attorney whose family had worshipped at St. John's for twenty-five years (every significant event in their lives revolved around the chapel; he noted that "this announcement brought great consternation, surprise and sadness to the congregation"); William G. Rose,

(TO BE RELEASED APRIL 6, 4 P. M.)

The Case of St. John's Chapel.

THE FACTS OF THE CASE.

On a Sunday in the year 1807 St. John's Chapel was solemnly and forever consecrated and devoted to the honor and worship of Almighty God.

On a Sunday—November 22, 1908—the congregation of St. John's Chapel were officially notified that the Trinity Vestry had **decided that the Chapel should be closed** on the first of February following. Without previous notice or hearing, without even an intimation that such action was impending, they were told that after the first of February the doors of their Church would be shut against them.

On December 5, 1908, a meeting of the congregation was held, a committee was appointed and a petition was prepared praying that the Vestry reconsider its action and "that St. John's be allowed to remain open to the Glory of God and to continue the good work which is now being carried on among the poor of the vicinity." This petition with the signatures of 557 members of the congregation was presented to the Vestry and was **denied**.

On December 14, 1908, the Clergy and workers of St. John's Chapel presented

[3]

Figure 2.7. To plead their case to the public, to newspapers, and to fellow Episcopalians, members of St. John's congregation published this pamphlet that outlined their opposition to the closing of the chapel. Courtesy of Butler Library, Columbia University in the City of New York.

an examiner for the state comptroller, who lived at 114 King Street and who had worshipped at St. John's for more than thirty years and met his wife there (from his experience as a real estate clerk, he believed the whole tract to be worth $400,000); Philip L. Schell, a commission merchant at 80–82 Leonard Street, and a congregant for twenty-six years, who had also met his wife there (he noted that "the work that is being done by St. John's Chapel is a prospering and increasing religious work at the present time, and, furthermore, that it is a religious work much needed in that section of the City"); Lewis W. Smith, a twenty-three-year-old clerk for an importer on Beaver Street, who lived at 31 Vandam (his mother and father met and were married at St. John's by Dr. Dix); Henry G. Dickens, a thirty-five-year-old shipping clerk for a confectioner at Vandam and Hudson streets (he lived at 13 Dominick Street); and Otto Freyer, of 126 Varick Street, a postal clerk at the Wall Street Station and a St. John's congregant for twenty-five years. On average, the committee members had been part of the congregation for more than twenty-two years. Other congregants worked as bookkeeper, freight handler, truckman, watchman, and porter. Most of them lived in the surrounding Fifth Ward, and their surnames seem largely English and German.[52] Ethnically, the congregation's members were mainly German, English, and Irish, so the heated issues of immigration and Americanization—one of the important drivers behind the preservation movement—really did not come into play in the St. John's case.[53]

Where did the members of the congregation live? This question bore on Trinity's argument that St. John's was no longer needed because its congregants did not live in its immediate surroundings. The trend was in this direction—reflecting the area's transformation from a mixed-use neighborhood into one specialized in warehousing and industry—but a substantial number of congregants did live close by. "Although there are a few Communicants who are attached to St. John's through ties of many years, and who do come a great distance to worship in the old Chapel, the vast and large number of Communicants and attendants at St. John's live in the immediate vicinity."[54] Another congregation petition notes that 350 of 486 congregants lived closer to St. John's than St. Luke's.[55] It seems likely that the congregation was split but was still rooted in the blocks around the chapel: It was made up mostly of working-class and poorer folks from the more immediate area (though increasingly from further afield, as Trinity told it) and of some better-off folks who had moved up and out of the area (for example, Herman Gustow, of 180th Street) but came back to worship at Varick Street because of their deep associations, ties of religion and collective memory, with the place and the theology.

While the congregants' primary attachment to the building was as a center of their religious life, others valued St. John's and wished to preserve it whole because of the chapel's role in the larger urban landscape. William Rainsford (rector of St. George's Episcopal Church, strident social reformer, and advocate of churches' serving as community centers)[56] summoned all the values of St. John's meaning and memory as a religious and moral force against the more debased parts of the city. While Trinity argued that the building and its work were no longer needed or effective, Rainsford argued that the religious, cultural, and *environ-*

mental qualities of St. John's were needed more than ever in that particular section of the city. Echoing the logic behind the settlement-house movement, Rainsford argued, "Our great parish churches, our beautiful buildings, our most stately services, must be given to those who need them most. . . . Hundreds of thousands of lives bound in, bound down, by an environment sordid and debasing—it is these that need a church worship, large, beautiful, stately. . . . The strong forces of God should be placed where all evil things abound. . . . Anchor fast the churches that we have got where they are."[57]

Few archival sources speak in the voices of the congregation's members.[58] These voices can mostly be found in court records and self-issued pamphlets, secondhand through newspaper reporting or reformers' reports, and through the rare letter. What remains of the congregation's individual voices reveals a great depth of feeling about the chapel. An undated (probably from 1909) anonymous letter, mailed from Brooklyn by a St. John's congregant, savagely and personally attacked Manning:

> Rev. Mr. Manning:
>   You are not content in robbing us of our dear old Church which has been our hope and strength from our childhood up but on the last day deprive us of a farewell sermon from our beloved pastor, Mr. Gomph. We don't want to hear you, your words are meaningless to us and we all know that this whole thing started with you, you are jealous of the superior qualifications of Mr. Gomph and want to get him out of the Parish. When the Grand? and glorious? Corporation of Trinity selected a Head why didn't it get a native born and a man whose preaching and teaching would be an honor to the Church instead of a man who is incapable of giving a sermon that is worth listening to and that is written[,] too. This whole thing is going to do harm to the Church generally and the Roman Church will profit largely by it. Shame on you, shame on Trinity Corporation one and all. I hope that a just visitation will fall on each and every one who has deprived us of our rights. That money is not yours nor Trinity's and I hope you'll all find that fact out before long. I can't wish you a happy and successful career as Rector of Trinity Corporation.[59]

This letter suggests how deeply the closing struck the emotions of the congregation and how strong was its members' attachment to "our dear old Church."

Manning received a more temperate appeal to his "priestly side" in a January 1909 letter from a St. John's communicant of eleven years, J. M. Mackay.[60] Manning, he wrote, was responsible for the death of the Guild of St. John the Evangelist and St. John's bible class. "Are you aware that the breaking up of that guild is sure to start some souls on the road to Hell? . . . Is not the saving of those souls worth (how much is it?) $25000 a year of Trinity's money?" Against the idea that St. John's was a dying chapel, Mackay added, "The congregation of St. John's has come back amazingly. Why not give us a year's grace in which to make good?" Reinforcing the contrast of "priestly" feeling with Manning's businesslike prosecution of the chapel closing, Mackay added a note on an outside fold of his letter: "Please read this as a minister of Christ and not as a business man."

Another correspondent, though not from the congregation, related personal knowledge of the feelings running through St. John's: Annie Gould wrote several letters to Manning, pleading for the continuation of St. John's.[61] Several of Gould's letters to the editor regarding the St. John's case were published in the *New York Times,* but she also wrote personally to Manning as someone of his own social class. "The work done in St. John's is *living* work. The congregation is large and devotedly attached to their vicar Mr. Gomph," about whom she notes, "I have never heard more earnest Christian teaching than in the simple but masterly sermons he preaches." She reported, "I talked to some of the church members. They were so sorrowful over the approaching shutting off of their church privileges." She asked Manning—"in the name of civilization, of our civil hopes, I appeal to you"—to attend St. John's services (he had not) and to extend its life for at least one year. "It's so hard to get devoted parishioners anywhere," she implored, "it seems inconceivable that Trinity would actually turn some out." "New York will be so much poorer, if there is no St. John's." There is no record of Manning's reply.[62]

Legal Challenges

As 1908 ended, petitioning and letter writing had not budged Trinity Vestry from its decision to close the chapel. The congregation committee began exploring legal measures to preserve the chapel and the right to continue worshipping there as a community. The congregation's legal challenges centered on the issue of the vestry's property rights: Who had the right to decide the best allocation of Trinity's wealth, and thus to close the chapel? Under the legal constitution of Trinity Corporation (under laws stretching back to the colonial era and significantly amended owing to controversies in the mid-nineteenth century over the vestry's vast tenement holdings), the chapels remained essentially colonies of the vestry. Though chapel members in good standing (whether defined by pew rents or frequency of communion) were understood to be "corporators" of the parish, their economic and property rights were subsumed to those of the vestry, which acted as the board of directors of the parent corporation. Corporators could vote to elect vestrymen in annual parishwide elections, but, as the St. John's case determined, they were not otherwise empowered to decide parish policies or investments.

The congregation challenged the vestry's action on several legal grounds: asserting the chapel's rights to property and the congregation's right to continue worship in its own chapel, questioning the integrity of the vestry as a private corporation with full control over the chapels, and challenging the process of electing the vestry (and asking whether the chapels had fair representation). The congregation argued that all corporators (any male who had taken communion in the church or any of the chapels in the previous year) had a direct say in such matters and that decisions such as a chapel closing should be put to a referendum of the corporators. Trinity Vestry argued that it alone (twenty-two men) held absolute rights over church affairs and that it could close a chapel if it wished. In essence, the legal case boiled down to property rights: a matter of who controlled the property of the parish.

An injunction was granted in January 1909, preventing Trinity from actually closing the chapel doors while the case was litigated. Sufficient grounds were found to believe that Trinity was acting beyond its rights in closing the chapel. The case was argued in April and was decided in favor of Trinity. The vestry's lawyer and clerk, William Jay, disavowed any intention of tearing down and redeveloping St. John's—even though the vestry had just gone to great lengths to secure the right to do so. As to the congregation's challenge under ecclesiastical law, the vestry, Jay maintained (as his nose no doubt grew in length), had no intention of tearing down or selling the chapel "for worldly use" and so did not disobey the church canon requiring the bishop's permission to do so.[63] He added that the vestry had no thoughts of lessening its work in the St. John's area; instead, it actually was increasing that work: "Trinity Parish is merely re-arranging its work and changing its methods in order to meet in the largest and broadest way changed conditions and existing needs."[64]

According to Justice James O'Gorman's decision, the vestry's status as the board of directors gave it power to decide the best allocation of parish resources, and the corporators had no recourse except through the regular vestry elections. The annual vestry election thus became another battleground on which the congregation fought for survival. The election on April 13, 1909, was the first contested vestry election in two hundred years. Corporators from every part of the parish elected vestrymen, and the issues clearly revolved around the St. John's controversy. The St. John's contingent worked assiduously to rally support among the parish's other eight congregations, and they and their supporters lost.

The most pointed, comprehensive, and public statement of the congregation's case came in a pamphlet published on April 5, 1909, titled *The Case of St. John's Chapel: Shall Christian Charity or Corporate Power Prevail?*[65] By April, the legal wrangling had been going on for some time, and this document wove together the legal arguments—based on chapel congregants' rights to suffrage and property with the parish—with the factual, good-faith appeals of the earlier petitions. In a markedly more polemical tone, the hand-sized pamphlet lays out clearly the history of the case, the vestry's rationales, and the congregation's counterarguments. There is no mention of the chapel's civic, secular history—that is, its founding, architecture, associations, and function as a visual and cultural landmark—even though this was a prominent part of the original petition. But this pamphlet stresses the congregation's attachment to worshipping *in that place.* It offers encomiums to Dix, stresses the need to continue the chapel's religious work for this particular quarter of the city, and expresses the congregation's overriding wish "to continue to worship within its walls."[66] The congregation, now fighting for existence with its last breaths, set aside any expression of its building's civic memory as it defended its collective memory *as a congregation.* The fear implicit in this emphasis, that the congregation's memory would soon be erased, would soon be realized.

On April 15, 1909, the *New York Times* reported that Justice O'Gorman had dissolved the injunction: Trinity Vestry retained full control over church and chapel affairs, just as the board of any private corporation would. The decision was appealed once in May, to no avail. The congregation's further appeals were heard and denied on May 28 and June 22. The congregation filed yet another suit, on grounds that its members' franchise as corporators had been denied, which was unsuccessful. All appeals were exhausted by August 1909, and the congregation and its committee were not heard from again.

To the congregation, though, the right to worship meant the right to do it *in that place*, within the four walls of the chapel, with the congregation's clergy. Having to relocate was tantamount to revoking the right to worship. (This is a constant theme in congregants' affidavits filed on appeal.) The congregation's worship was inseparable from its setting—exemplifying Maurice Halbwachs's principle that the collective memory of any social group is inescapably linked to the spaces in which its collective life is enacted.[67]

Throughout the court fight, the civic values of the building—historic associations and architectural quality—were trumpeted in support of the congregation's side. Historical associations were not the primary line of argument, but a backdrop. For example, the original complaint filed by the committee against the vestry read: "The edifice of St. John's [and its outbuildings] are all in a good state of preservation and repair and the said edifice itself, constructed after the Georgian style of architecture with a high steeple, and large porch is, for its beauty, grace, and grandeur, the best of its kind in the City of New York, and by reason thereof and its age and historical associations, has become a monument of peculiar value and worth from both a religious and civic viewpoint."[68]

Once Trinity's right to close the chapel was upheld, the building was briefly used for "evangelical work," but it then sat empty. (Rev. William Wilkinson based a ministry of street preaching there for a short time.) "The plans of the Vestry . . . call upon a small number of persons to suffer some inconvenience and to sacrifice associations which are dear to them but the number of those really so affected is very small."[69] The congregation took the high road, and lost.[70] "Rarely in our history have a body of Churchmen stood more reverently, patiently and courageously in defense of their church privileges and their spiritual home than have the people of St. John's chapel, New York." The congregants brought themselves nationwide respect by suing the vestry, "not for the preservation of their church building alone but of the congregation as a Christian family and community."[71]

As the building was closed, several pieces of the interior architecture of the chapel were removed and taken to St. Luke's, where remnants of the St. John's congregation began worshipping. The artifacts salvaged were those most important to the chapel's progressive, Anglo-Catholic liturgical practices—the rood and rood screen, marble pavements from the main altar, the altar table and candle holders[72]—suggesting that the congregation of St. John's in some way continued its religious life and memory. Without its place or beloved vicar Gomph, these pieces of St. John's were the congregation's only material links to its collective memory, which it struggled to maintain.

THE BROADER PUBLIC SPEAKS

As the St. John's case unfolded, it quickly spiraled beyond an interchurch dispute. A variety of people and organizations involved themselves in the debate over the chapel. Today they would be called stakeholders: the city's newspapers, other journalists, other leaders in the Episcopal Church, civic leaders and reformers (many of whom were Episcopalians), and preservationists. At first these groups participated on behalf of the congregation that was being displaced. As the congregation faded away and the chapel was closed, however, these groups—primarily the historic preservationists—became the main advocates for saving the chapel.

The chapel closing caused considerable public outcry, beginning when the news was leaked to the papers on the Saturday evening before its announcement. This precipitated public reactions focused on two issues: threats to the integrity and memory of the congregation (the building's historic value was corollary to this at first, only later becoming a primary concern); and the responsibility of Trinity as a civic institution. The public reaction was stirred by the recognition that the chapel was a historic and visual landmark, and it was sustained by the public's memory of Trinity's real estate dealings, by the accusations that it was a slumlord, and by the decades-old debate over the church's civic responsibility (a debate of abiding interest to the press).[73]

The newspapers' interest in the St. John's controversy—and their plain advocacy of the congregation's cause against Trinity Vestry—fueled public debate over the meaning, memory, and use of the chapel. In a positive sense, many different views were represented in the press. Though articles often took a pro-congregation stand, the views of the vestry were reported just as often. Both the congregation and reformers forged close ties to newspapers, ensuring outlets for their views. Trinity, too, explicitly recognized the need for better public relations and the necessity of using newspapers' power to shape public opinion—and public memory.[74]

It was in the newspapers' interests to foment the controversy over a single site and congregation into a larger issue. The influence of the newspapers at the time was considerable.[75] For the congregation (and to a lesser extent, reformers), lack of money and influence made the media the most logical place to gain leverage in the controversy. Given the historical legacy of newspapers as agents for social reform, it is not surprising that the papers largely took a stance critical of Trinity. Dozens of articles appeared as soon as the controversy began, especially in the *New York Times, Herald,* and *Evening Post.* Headlines played up differences and fed the media flap: "St. John's Not Historic, So Dr. Manning Tells Clergymen . . ."; "Old St. John's Church is Marked for Destruction."[76]

Trinity's action closing the chapel came at a time when the destruction of historical landmarks, the fate of immigrant communities, and ways of dealing with poverty and neighborhood change all were on the public mind. Also on the public mind—and more importantly, on the agenda of the newspapers and some Episcopal clergy—was the responsibility of Trinity as a private corporation with a public face. Trinity had a long-standing reputation problem. Its trouble stemmed from the parish's wealth in real estate, from enduring issues about how this wealth was increased and shared with other Episcopal institutions in the city, and particularly from the "tenement" holdings in Trinity's portfolio. The city's leading religious institution, while preaching charity, was accused of being a slumlord, at a time when housing reform was a prominent public issue. The tenement question had come to the surface in the late 1850s, when a New York State senate committee conducted a lengthy and uncomplimentary investigation of tenements, an investigation widely reported in newspapers. The issue surfaced again in the first decade of the twentieth century, as housing reform picked up momentum as a citywide issue. The newspaper-reading public was primed for stories of Trinity misdeeds.

Typical sentiment against Trinity was found in a *New York Times* editorial on Christmas Day, 1908, remarking on the critiques of Trinity Vestry coming from elsewhere in the Episcopal church and quoting a "working man" who neatly summed up the public feeling about Trinity's decision to close the chapel no matter who protested: "They don't care for the public." Early in the conflict, the *Times* argued that the issue in this for the public was denying the congregation a say in its own governance.

Socialite Annie Gould was among the citizens pressuring Trinity in print: "When, twenty years ago, St. John's Park was sold for a railway freight depot everybody deplored it. . . . At the present time Trinity Vestry regrets having sold the park. Now, why not prevent the Vestry of twenty years ahead from feeling a more poignant regret at the destruction of that beautiful landmark of Old New York, a shining centre of Christianizing and civilising influences—venerable and noble old St. John's?"[77]

Richard Watson Gilder—well-known poet, editor, former member of the Tenement House Commission, and park preservationist—published this poem in the December 14, 1908, *Evening Post*, expressing the linkage reformers made between Trinity's history of tenement reform controversy, the St. John's imbroglio, and the church's larger public role:

> Guardian of a holy trust
> Who, in your rotting tenements,
> Housed the people, till the offence
> Rose to the Heaven of the Just—
> Guardians of an ancient trust
> Who, lately, from these little ones
> Dashed the cup of water; now
> Bind new laurels to your brow,
> Fling to earth these sacred stones,

Give the altar to the dust!
Here the poor and friendless come—
Desolate and templed home
Of the friendless and the poor,
That your laurels may be sure!
Here beside the frowning walls
Where no more the wood bird calls,
Where once the little children played,
Whose paradise ye have betrayed,
Here let the temple low be laid,
Here bring the altar to the dust—
Guardians of a holy trust![78]

Gilder's stinging verse stirred the pot. It neatly made Trinity's tenements and
its treatment of the poor part of the same issue as the destruction of the St. John's
landscape, which encompassed the park and its birds and playing children, as well
as the chapel altar. The poem notably joined issues of memory and landscape with
the more typical menu of urban-reform issues (such as housing, poverty, immigration, and congestion). Judging from Trinity's reactions and the poem's appearance
in other newspaper articles, it struck a popular chord of discontent over both the
larger and the more specific issues of the controversy. The poem provoked letters
to the editor from, among others, Trinity lawyer George Zabriskie, who weakly replied, "I am far from wishing to disparage Mr. Gilder's poetry; but I wish he would
be more careful about his facts."[79] Internal communications to and from Manning
referred obliquely and disparagingly to the trouble stirred up by Gilder's poem.[80]

Trinity had its defenders. *Harper's Weekly* published an article in February 1909
in which Manning and vestrymen William Jay and Frances Bangs were quoted at
length refuting the congregation's arguments, denying the historical value of the
chapel, and defending Trinity's real estate practices as part of the "improvement"
of the area. The article minimized all the criticisms by casting them in a light far
more friendly to the vestry's position.[81]

In a lengthy 1914 article reporting on one of the few public meetings on St.
John's (before the Manhattan Board of Estimate and Apportionment),[82] the *Herald*
offered a balanced view of the controversy, in the end posing a question:

This brings the attention of thinking men to the often asked question
about the duty of a church with trust funds. Is a religious corporation
justified in preserving steeples and stained glass simply to hold services

for empty pews, or is it better that it should employ the talents committed to its stewardship in providing churches in growing centres of population and leaving to secular subscription the preservation of landmarks?[83]

Critique from within the Church

As already mentioned, the strident New York Episcopalian reformer William Rainsford quickly weighed in on the debate on the side of preserving the congregation. Perhaps the more bothersome thorn in Manning's side was the position taken by the *Churchman,* a national periodical on church matters, beginning in December 1908. Editor Silas McBee took Manning and the vestry to task on the St. John's matter, mostly in support of worshippers' rights and church responsibilities in poorer areas, but also for neglecting the memorial value of the building. Lauding the congregation, McBee wrote, "Rarely in our history have a body of churchmen stood more reverently, patiently, and courageously in defense of their Church privileges and their spiritual home than have the people of St. John's chapel."[84]

The *Churchman* was the forum for other critics of Trinity: for example, the January 4, 1909, letter from Rev. Walter Laidlaw, of the Federation of Churches, arguing for the retention of St. John's on grounds of religious efficiency. He showed statistically that a large number of the unconverted—especially "churchless Italians"—lived around St. John's, representing an enormous opportunity to serve the disadvantaged. Manning and Bishop Greer exchanged a number of handwritten notes about intrachurch criticism, agreeing that the *Churchman* should be less critical, give the vestry more credit, and help "keep the public mind right toward Trinity Parish . . . instead of doing its best to stir up and strengthen prejudice against the parish."[85] These were devastating critiques because they came from *within* the Episcopal community. (McBee's editorial also was galling to Manning personally because he and McBee were contemporaries from their days at the University of the South in Sewanee.)[86] McBee, telling Manning, "I have been more or less pelted with petitions and complaints about St. John's," felt justified in staging the stinging critique because it represented true dissent among churchmen.[87]

Rev. John P. Peters also used the *Churchman* as an outlet for severe criticism of Trinity Vestry. Peters had charge of the independent (non–Trinity Parish) Episcopal church of St. Michael's (at Ninety-ninth Street and Amsterdam Avenue), from which he pounded on the class bias of Trinity's policies. While such criticism had been endured from newspapers and reformers, it had greater power coming from within the church community. Peters noted the continuing policy of leading New York churches, Trinity among them, to close churches and reinvest farther uptown:

"Churches had been sold and the proceeds used to build churches elsewhere, not because there were not people to be ministered to where the church was, but because the rich and the well-to-do had moved away." Legally, Peters conceded, it was Trinity land and a Trinity matter, but morally, he argued, Trinity had an obligation to "the City." Trinity's religious policies, in other words, also had a dimension of civic responsibility, which it was abrogating in this most recent example of closing a church in a poor or working-class area of the city. Peters also gave his position some historical context by observing that in the 1830s and '40s, Trinity had closed St. Matthew's and the City Mission Society, to much public outcry.[88]

In the same issue of the *Churchman,* Rev. Walter Laidlaw argued for the preservation of St. John's, saying that population figures showed a great need for the church and many opportunities for new congregants among the ethnic groups. Laidlaw was a Presbyterian minister and executive director of the Federation of Churches and Christian Organizations in New York. As a minister and social scientist, he asserted St. John's importance as the only Christian church remaining in the Fifth Ward. The ward's population had decreased between 1900 and 1905, when 7,727 people lived there and an estimated 50,000 worked there. By 1905, about 5 percent of the resident population were German-born and about 10 percent were Italian-born. The "churchless Italians" (that is, nonobservant Catholics) were thought to be prime targets for conversion to Episcopal worship.

Privately, as in public, Manning simply dismissed all these criticisms from his fellow Protestant clergy. "Dr. Peters' articles are best met by silence," Manning wrote, and in the same letter he dismissed Laidlaw's claim that Trinity Vestry had misused his population figures, saying that Laidlaw's gripes would only be taken seriously "by the 'yellow' journals."[89]

ENTER THE PRESERVATIONISTS

Preservationists were engaged in the St. John's case from the very beginning, asserting the chapel's historical value. But when did St. John's become "old"? The controversy heightened preservationists' interest in St. John's, but in other ways the chapel was emblematic of the type of historic place around which the preservation movement was beginning to gel.

An 1869 article describing Richard Upjohn's addition to the chancel refers not at all to age or history, but an 1872 account of the interior redecoration called St. John's "among the oldest and best known of our downtown churches" and noted that former parishioners, though moved on, retain their pews.[90] The chapel was listed (but not featured) in some guidebooks and histories of the city and was described as a notable place in the 1850s and '60s and, by the 1890s, as a historic place.[91] The chapel's multiple historic qualities were first articulated in 1893–94 in parish documents relating to the planned consolidation and destruction of the chapel. These referred to details of the building's architecture, its history in the development of the neighborhood, and its congregation. By 1905 or so—and certainly by the time of the closing in 1908—the chapel was considered by preservationists as among the most important landmarks in the city, owing to its age, its association with the city's elite, and its fine design. The ASHPS wrote in 1909 that "the only concern of the Society was that this venerable landmark, which is intrinsically interesting as a fine specimen of church architecture and around which cluster so many traditions of the growth of the city, should be preserved."[92]

By 1912 St. John's was among the city's acknowledged secular monuments and totally emptied of the congregation's memory. Trinity's official view of the chapel had shifted. Now recognizing (as it had only begun to in 1908–9) the effectiveness of making public arguments on the basis of historic value, Trinity interpreted St. John's as old, but not "historic." It was contrasted to St. Paul's Chapel, Trinity Church, and the whole parish, all of which *were* truly historic—George Washington had even worshipped at St. Paul's—whereas St. John's was merely beyond its useful life. Vestry counsel William Jay assured his colleagues that he "could find there was no history or historical value connected with the church."[93]

In the 1908–9 controversy, the chapel's past was wrested from the memory of a congregation and the community it served and redefined as a historical memory. This sense included, though, both associational values (the chapel was tied to the ongoing life of the congregation, and it evoked "Old New York") and aesthetic or architectural values (it was beautiful, representing colonial architecture and the work of John McComb). Early on, the two kinds of meaning were conflated. Gradually, this distinction between associational and architectural was clarified as professional architects became more concerned with historic preservation. This was another aspect of the transformation of the *congregation's* memory into the *city's* history—and a shift in the building's function from container of meaning to symbol. ASHPS used this issue to take one of its occasional forays into theory. In a December 1912 essay, "Elements of Historic Value in a Building," Edward Hagaman Hall and George Kunz took note of the public discussions and teased out some distinctions: "There are two elements, either or both of which may make a building historic, namely time and notable use. . . . 'time-historic' and 'use-historic'. . . express different qualities of historic character of a building." And, they continued, "The architectural appearance is an interesting but different phase of the subject. It may or may not be related to the history of the building."[94]

William Jay's opposing statement to the Board of Estimate's City Plan Committee about St. John's lack of historical value was quoted at length in the *Herald*. Jay denied St. John's had any history or memory associated with it, blamed the "civic societies" for raising expectations of the building's preservation without raising the money to buy it (as had successfully been done with Boston's Old South Church in the 1870s), pleaded the economic illogic of maintaining services for St. John's, and argued that Trinity's preservation duties were satisfied by maintaining St. Paul's and Trinity.[95] (In the same article he admitted that the vestry had always assumed that the chapel would be destroyed after services there were discontinued.)

The shift in Trinity's rhetorical valuing is clear when the 1913 statements are contrasted with remarks made in 1902 that held memory of St. John's dear. In a 1902 memorial to Rector Dix, Jay and other vestrymen had complimented Dix for keeping the old chapels open, and they declared their support for the idea that downtown churchyards were valued for more than economic reasons: "We rejoice that these churchyards, pleasant and peaceful breathing places as they are in our crowded city, remain to remind the passer-by that there is a life beyond the grave. And though they might be sold for much money, we believe that they silently tell the story that there are some things which money cannot buy."[96] Having referred implicitly to the sale of St. John's Park, one would imagine that the vestry would be eager to reuse the chapel instead of selling it. But the vestrymen's change of heart was clear: They now valued St. John's not for the memories it embodied but for the economic value it represented.[97]

As with the first episode in the chapel case, most newspapers were notably reform-minded and were clearly critical of Trinity. A 1914 *New York Times* editorial reported: "There is a growing feeling in this community for the preservation of old buildings worth preserving. Nothing much would be gained by the destruction of St. John's except a few thousand dollars more in the coffers of the Trinity Corp. By its preservation much would be gained. It is an example of good architecture of its kind, it has historic associations worth recalling, it is worth saving."[98] The power of fine, historical buildings was advanced by the landscape architect H. A. Caparn in a letter to the editor of *Times*: "Would not the man or woman in the street, seeing obvious and expensive efforts made to save a building like St. John's, pause and think, and wonder why? Could he have a more striking object lesson in things worth saving?"[99]

The idea that St. John's was a historic landscape in the fullest sense was expressed in a long article, in the May 25, 1913, *New York Times*, relating an excellent history of St. John's. The message of the article is clearly antidestruction, invoking the memory of the destruction of St. John's Park, the building's historical associations, and the chapel's community connections (one of which was sustained after the congregation was moved—the Leake Dole of Bread, an endowment providing for the distribution of loaves to the poor every Saturday, had been held at St. John's since 1855 in the Sunday school building next to the chapel). The article is unmistakably close to the ASHPS's account of the controversy, which included a characteristically extensive site history; Edward Hagaman Hall, ASHPS secretary and ex-newspaperman, may well have placed this article with the *Times*. The article concludes that city planning (street widening), preservation, and architectural goals could all be met—all the reform ideas could be reconciled; there was faith that a rational solution could be reached. The end of the article is actually quite complimentary, noting that the new Varick Street would "clear a path for modern things to enter the Village," and it mentioned the common understanding that Trinity Vestry was waiting for the city to act to condemn the land: "It is understood that Trinity is waiting for the city to speak first. . . . in the gossip of the BP's office it is irreverently whispered that Trinity is quite resigned" to having the city tear it down.[100]

Preservationists offered their several reasons for preserving the building and began to propose its reuse, but no firm offers were put forward. Trinity seemed content to wait either for a sufficient offer to purchase the chapel for reuse or for city condemnation in advance of the street widening and subway construction scheduled for the next few years; the congregation, of course, was gone.

Alongside the congregation's efforts to appeal to and litigate Trinity Vestry were the efforts of preservationists and reformers. St. John's champions included some of the city's most prominent citizens, such as former mayor and Columbia University president Seth Low. From the start, they lighted on the multiple issues at stake over St. John's, both civic and religious. Even though these critiques and interventions began with the religious and corporate issue of the congregation's rights, they also revolved around the idea of the public good and the responsibilities of civic institutions like Trinity to support it—including public interpretations of civic memory. With the involvement of reformers and preservationists, the fate of St. John's shifted to become more a civic issue and less a religious and intrachurch issue. Correspondingly, St. John's became more a matter of historical memory and less one of traditional memory, and this resonated with preservationists.

In late 1908, as the congregation appealed to the vestry for the right to stay open, preservationists immediately weighed in by elaborating the chapel's historical associations *as well as* asserting the rights of the congregation. The charge was led by Isaac Newton Phelps Stokes and the American Scenic and Historic Preservation Society. They were joined in succeeding months by reformers of great public stature—most notably Seth Low, Robert Fulton Cutting, and Robert De Forest (prominent Episcopalians all)—who expressed shock at the lack of civic responsibility shown by the vestry and joined the chorus of those insisting that Trinity save the congregation and chapel.

Ideas about the chapel's value as a secular, historical landmark were just one aspect of the congregation's position, but it was the main motivation for historic preservationists' extensive involvement in the St. John's case. Preservationists supported the congregation's efforts to preserve its worship in place but continued their advocacy (by themselves) after the congregation dispersed.

Why did reformers and preservationists latch on to St. John's? The chapel embodied several types of meaning resonant with the preservationist ethos. The building layered several kinds of reform and "historic" values: It fit the criterion for a "historic" site according to the prevailing theory of history (it dated from very early in the nineteenth century and was therefore old enough to be "old"); it was a visual and aesthetic landmark, high-style, "colonial," and designed by the well-known architect McComb; it was in some sense a public building; it was associated with civic memory through the destruction of St. John's Park; and it related to pressing reform issues about immigrant culture, poverty, tenements, and parks. St. John's provided a venue for working out a social reform ethos by shaping a "historic" urban environment while taking on a curatorial project focused on the building itself—both of which were ideas at the core of emergent preservation work.

Preservationists' advocacy of St. John's clearly defined civic memory as a matter of social reform. The efforts of Isaac Stokes are the best illustration of this connection. In a letter to Bishop Greer of December 12, 1908, Stokes reiterated the civic history of St. John's, as well as the reasons for continuing the religious work there. Writing "as a Churchman and as a strong believer in the great uplifting and ennobling power of the beautiful monument which still remains to us from the past [sic]," the chapel should be sustained, he argued, "from both the standpoints of sentiment and the promise of continued usefulness." He felt that these uses justified the expense. He went on to quote Dix at length, from an 1899 speech, about the need for memory infrastructure to stem the chaos of destruction. The letter was accompanied by nine pages of history and statistics, documenting the chapel's historic value and the demographic character of the ward.[101]

Stokes's second effort to establish the historical value of the building and force the vestry to cooperate in its preservation was more remarkable. Apparently without consulting the congregation, he organized the creation of an "all-star" petition insisting that Trinity recognize the historical, aesthetic, and civic values of the chapel building and thus Trinity's public responsibility to preserve it. The petition called the St. John's case "a surprise and shock to the community," especially for those (undersigned) who revered "the ancient monuments" of the city and believed "in the uplifting power of venerable traditions and accumulated effort, and the refining and ennobling influence of dignified and beautiful architecture." St. John's, the petition went on, "ranks second only to St. Paul's Chapel, among the very few remaining monuments of our past." The vestry therefore had a "double responsibility" for its preservation, as a force in both religious and civic life. The petition was signed by national and city officials, politicians, and urbanists, including President Theodore Roosevelt, George McClellan, Levi Morton, Robert Fulton Cutting, W. Bayard Cutting, J. P. Morgan Sr., Joseph Choate, Anson P. Stokes, John B. Pine, Thomas Hastings, William Dean Howells, C. Grant LaFarge, George B. Post, Charles F. McKim, Robert W. De Forest, Seth Low, Elihu Root, and J. Mayhew Wainwright (son of a former Episcopal bishop).[102]

The petition fell flat. The impressive list of names was just that—a fairly hollow publicity effort. Like all appeals and offers of help, the petition was rebuffed by Manning and the vestry. (The congregation noted that if it had thought outsiders would carry any weight, it could have produced "many thousands of signatures of people of all denominations, and particularly those in the neighborhood of St. John's.")[103] The petition not only failed to move the vestry but also raised the question of why these wealthy, influential men did not just donate the money to buy the chapel for the congregation. Rev. Dr. William Reed Huntington of Grace Church came to Manning's defense, asking this very question.[104] Stokes's lack of strategic sense in bulling ahead with this petition showed a lack of political savvy and influence that seemed a general failing of preservationists. The petition's failure to have any effect revealed the ad hoc preservation movement at its most spectacularly flawed and politically ineffectual.

To Seth Low, the fact that the wealthiest church would elevate cost-saving measures over religious and historical values was "a shock to the idealism of the City of New York."[105] Reform mayor of Brooklyn and later of greater New York, president of Columbia, and heir of an old New York merchant family, Low was the leading critic of Trinity's narrow conception of its own public role, as expressed in its actions regarding St. John's. Citizens have the right, he believed, "to expect churches to have regard to the architectural monuments of the city, no less than individuals." Low argued that Trinity's quest for religious efficiency ignored memory and public responsibility and ran "counter to the highest aspirations and best ideals of the community to be affected by it." Low and kindred reformers believed civic memory to be essential for a healthy civic culture. The good-government/social-reformer community invoked what could be called a stewardship ethic toward the built environment, understanding it to embody historic, natural, visual, and other symbolic values in addition to the economic values routinely traded and fought over. Reformers like Low advocated some balance of these values, allowing the didactic landscapes of memory, nature, and social reform to perform their functions.

In his letters to the *Churchman* in 1909, Low linked the St. John's case to other mistakes in handling memory infrastructure issues, such as allowing the building of the Post Office in City Hall Park and selling St. John's Park (both in the 1860s). He wished to refresh Trinity's memory of these bygone affronts to the public memory and open space. The abandonment of St. John's, he wrote,

> seems to indicate that [Trinity] is entirely unaware of the change in sentiment as to open spaces in the city which the last few decades have wrought. . . . If I interpret the public sentiment of New York City correctly, and no one will deny that I have had many opportunities for forming a correct judgment upon it, Trinity parish cannot remove its work from St. John's and destroy the old building, without incurring the condemnation of the overwhelming majority of those who cherish any municipal idealism for the city.[106]

In a sarcastic take on environmental determinism and the tendency for real estate markets to erode memory, Low wondered whether "the office buildings that surround Trinity Church have not affected the Church more than the Church has affected the offices"![107]

Low did far more than write a few letters. He joined Robert Fulton Cutting, John Pine, and other prominent men in behind-the-scenes efforts to resolve the situation.[108] Low tried to organize a private meeting between Manning and prominent Episcopalians such as himself. Pine and others sent at least two specific proposals to the vestry, outlining "A Proposed Plan for the Maintenance of St. John's as a Mission Church . . . a possible means of preserving St. John's." Stating that a large body of churchmen wished St. John's not to be abandoned as a center of religious work, these gentlemen proposed to organize a corporation to carry on the work of St. John's, lease the whole site (chapel, rectory, and hospital) to this corporation, and split the $20,000 cost of operating the chapel between the vestry and the new corporation for five years.

The petition was signed by W. Bayard Cutting, John B. Pine, R. Fulton Cutting, Stephen Baker, and I. N. Phelps Stokes, among others.[109] Their interim plan would have eased the announced financial burden on the vestry and demonstrated whether St. John's had really outlived its usefulness or not. If anyone could raise the money to purchase the building, it was these powerful men.[110] But it was not to be. Manning, Jay, and Cammann quickly informed Cutting that such suggestions "cannot be entertained."[111]

Robert De Forest was a bellwether for serious, elite-minded reform in New York. A wealthy lawyer and philanthropist, with strong political connections in the reform community, he was involved at a high level in a wide range of social- and environmental-reform efforts—including the Tenement House Commission, Charity Organization Society, Art Commission, Russell Sage Foundation, and Metropolitan Museum of Art. De Forest wrote to Manning in December 1908, including a resolution of the Art Commission, which De Forest headed at the time. The resolution noted St. John's "exceptional architectural beauty and historic interest and associations" and cited the building's civic memory and the public interest Trinity should serve by preserving it. Manning and the vestry were urged to consider "whether in the public interest St. John's, as a landmark of the early religious and social life of the city [that is, not its present congregation or function] and as a work of art, may not be permanently preserved and maintained as a place of worship."[112] The Art Commission was a city agency with jurisdiction over publicly funded buildings and landscapes only, but on De Forest's private initiative it extended its mandate along preservationist lines by pressuring Trinity to save St. John's.

Why were Trinity officials so resistant to the efforts of even the most prominent Episcopalians to modify their plans for St. John's? Bishop Greer, for one, feared that the church's charter—the basis of its wealth and influence—would be endangered by the St. John's controversy. In a "Private and Confidential" letter to Manning in January 1909, Greer admitted, "From conversations which I have recently had with several prominent persons who are friends of Trinity Church, I am afraid that advantage will be taken of the present public feeling [re the St. John's case] to make an effort in the Courts to abolish or set aside the Charter of the Church. . . . I am sure you will agree with me that it is desirable to prevent this [long court battle] if possible."[113] Manning was unconvinced of any real threat and held fast to his plan to be rid of St. John's. (Greer's alternative idea for diffusing the situation was to use St. John's as a center for converting churchless Italians, an idea employed briefly in 1909 but quickly abandoned by Manning.)

Seth Low was motivated in part by this threat as well. He wanted to see Trinity and its public role strengthened by this controversy. In a series of letters to Manning in March 1909, Low suggested resolving the St. John's case privately: He would put the issues before an informal board of impartial leading citizens like himself—including none of the congregants or preservationists—instead of letting the matter spill further into the courts and the press. Manning's quick rejection of any such effort fueled Low's severe public criticism of Trinity published in the *Churchman*. Nevertheless, Low's interest in the St. John's case (as well as that of Stokes and De Forest) clearly situated St. John's as a civic issue, a matter of citywide significance beyond the world of the congregation and the vestry.

Preservation-minded reformers were well placed, wealthy, and in some cases Episcopalian, which makes it all the more surprising that they exerted no influence on Manning and the vestry, who stuck behind their property rights as owners of St. John's. Even their bishop, who advocated a softer stance, could not budge them from their hard line. Low, Stokes, De Forest, and others who signed petitions and passed resolutions through groups such as the ASHPS and the Fine Arts Federation spoke for a large, influential class of urban reformers and economic elite. Yet the vestry, led by the steadfast and stubborn Manning, ignored their collective voice. As a group, preservationists were not well enough organized or strategically savvy enough to break through Manning's stubbornness.

Ironically, the issues of historical and architectural values were also invoked by Manning: In a *New York Times* article headlined "St. John's Not Historic," he was reported to have told a meeting of the Churchmen's Association (a group of Episcopal clergy) that "unlike St. Paul's or Trinity itself, [St. John's] had really no historical associations, but that its claims to survival lay chiefly in its architectural beauty."[114]

In April 1909, the court challenges and vestry elections having been concluded, Manning immediately delivered and published his sermon "The Policy of Trinity Parish," which was part announcement of his new policy of public disclosure (and public relations) and part justification of the vestry's actions regarding St. John's and Trinity's tenements. The conclusion of his opening section is a masterful attempt at spin-doctoring, turning the wide criticism of Trinity's handling of St. John's into a celebration not just of Trinity's good works on behalf of the civic community but also of the civic memory of Trinity: "The outcry which has been raised in regard to St. John's chapel is a real, though faint and far-off, indication of the feeling that there is deep down in the heart of every true New Yorker for 'Old Trinity.'" Old St. John's had been erased by "Old Trinity."[115]

Despite their ultimate failure to save the building, what did preservationists' involvement in this first phase of the St. John's case say about the nascent preservation field? First, preservation had arrived on the urban scene in the sense that memory sites and civic historical consciousness had clearly arrived on the stage of public debate. Everyone on the side of the congregation adopted preservationist arguments. Even their main opponent, Manning, debated them about which buildings had greater value but *not* about whether historical and architectural values were relevant. Debate over preservation stopped at the threshold of property values. Second, the variety and public nature of the responses to a threatened St. John's highlighted preservationists' reformist, not antiquarian, posture. Joint appeals to the congregation's integrity and the building's historicity were used to advance ideological positions on social change, environmental design, and the linkage between the two: Americanization, class differences, the constitution of a proper public realm, and the need for an environment that represented stability in a world of change. These formed the core of Progressive cultural-reform strategies. Third, preservationists (probably unwittingly) helped expand the possibilities for memory by secularizing the value of the building even before the congregation was dispersed. Using St. John's, preservationists asserted a secular conception of the value of a religious building; they had pulled this very privately held place into public, civic discourse. Over the course of this first "episode," the remembrance of St. John's chapel had been transformed from memory to history, or more to the point, the congregation's collective memory was transferred to a secular identity of public, civic memory. With the building emptied of worshippers, St. John's was acknowledged to be a *civic* landmark, embodying the collective memory of "Old New York" and no longer that of the congregation.

Shortly after the legal proceedings regarding St. John's were exhausted, Manning embarked on a public relations campaign to improve the reputation of Trinity.[116] Central to this campaign was retelling the history of Trinity to shape the way the public should remember Trinity.[117] Manning went public with his "policy of candor"[118] to rehabilitate the historical reputation of the church by elevating the history of Trinity's record of philanthropic works over the history of controversies like the St. John's case. Observers in the *Churchman* felt this whole policy was indeed forced by the St. John's controversy, but Manning again minimized the chapel and insisted his motivation was broader. By taking the time to deliberately reinterpret the past and fix the historical memory of Trinity's actions, Manning acknowledged memorial issues as one of the currencies of public opinion.

IMPROVING VARICK STREET AND PRESERVING A CIVIC LANDMARK

By the end of 1909, the chapel was closed, emptied of both its congregation and some of its more meaningful artifacts. The building itself remained in stable, but deteriorating, condition. Badly needed repairs were noticeable on the outside; the interior remained unused.[119] But the story of St. John's Chapel wasn't nearly finished.

Little was done about the chapel for the next two years, apart from the brief interlude of Rev. William Wilkinson's street services. Why did Trinity not sell the property? This would have been logical, given the church's desire to use its physical and financial resources "efficiently."[120] And why did the St. John's controversy disappear from preservationist discourse? The movement was still in an ad hoc, "butterfly" stage—jumping from site to site, issue to issue. Preservationists responded, often individually, to immediate threats to specific buildings. But as an organization—and certainly as a "field"—they placed little effort on lobbying for sustained institutional action on broad preservation issues.

The reason for the two-year vestry inaction regarding the chapel was revealed in 1911 with the official announcement that the city's Board of Estimate and Apportionment was embarking on plans to improve the transportation infrastructure throughout the city. The second episode of the St. John's story started with this new threat from the municipal government's new city-planning ambitions. Specifically, $3 million was allocated for work on the Lower West Side, widening Varick Street, connecting it with the extension of Seventh Avenue cutting a new swath through Greenwich Village, and extending the subway line beneath the street.[121] The new hundred-foot width of Varick Street placed the chapel literally in the path of improvement.

The city's eminent domain action took the heat off Trinity, which had remained under some pressure to reuse or at least to not destroy the chapel. Trinity officials' knowledge of these impending municipal plans (along with the public criticism) explains why the chapel was not immediately destroyed and redeveloped in 1909: They knew the city would eventually act to tear down the chapel and erase its memory and were willing to postpone redevelopment of the lot if they could avoid taking the blame.

The new Varick Street destroyed more than two hundred old Greenwich Village and Lower West Side buildings on the east side of Seventh Avenue and Varick Street, including St. John's Chapel. Varick was being widened to one hundred feet and the chapel's portico extended twelve feet into this new street. The city had to condemn a strip of land, and Trinity was probably a much more willing seller than the railroad company that had the freight shed across the street. The ASHPS and several others made the simple suggestion that street-widening space should be taken from the depot, leaving the landmark intact, but this possibility seems never to have been taken seriously.

Trinity Vestry must have known that St. John's stood in the way of this street widening and "improvement," which was shown graphically in the 1907 Improvement Commission plan.[122] This strategy worked well. Even the ASHPS began to let Trinity off the hook, noting in 1912 that St. John's was "now threatened from a new source"—street widening.[123] This was not the only reason for Trinity to with-

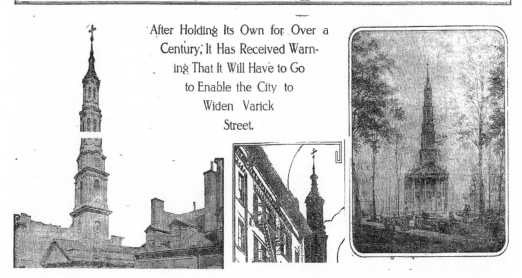

OLD ST. JOHN'S CHURCH IS MARKED FOR DESTRUCTION

After Holding Its Own for Over a
Century; It Has Received Warn-
ing That It Will Have to Go
to Enable the City to
Widen Varick
Street.

Figure 2.8. Newspapers, especially the New York Times *and the* Tribune, *were sympathetic to the plight of the St. John's congregation and to preservation of the chapel. These photos are from an article published in the* New York Times *on May 25, 1913. Courtesy of ProQuest, LLC/New York Times.*

hold action until the city's improvements were under way: The new, wider streets were planned to ease commercial traffic congestion and enable the further development of this district for industrial and warehousing uses, and these improvements would very probably bring a higher price for the chapel property. As the next several years unfolded, reformers' will to preserve the building complicated Trinity's plans and extended the St. John's case for years.

Led by reformer and borough president George McAneny, city planners and municipal engineers worked from public and private sectors to develop the armature for a burgeoning metropolis: building subways, designing a civic center, enacting zoning, and widening streets, including Varick Street, the extension of Seventh Avenue. These measures for stimulating and rationalizing the city's massive growth and geographic expansion were a major achievement of the early twentieth century. All these measures were designed and coordinated by government agencies and reformers working in concert to make the city more efficient and orderly as both an economic engine and a social organism. But they also raised conflicts within the broad reform movement: Though planners and preservationists both sought the improvement of society and the creation of a more orderly landscape, they clashed over the fate of some specific sites—such as St. John's.

Figure 2.9. This view looking north up Varick Street illustrates the cut-and-cover subway construction and the way the street was widened by demolishing buildings on the east side. The portico and spire of St. John's Chapel clearly stand in the way of the widened street. Courtesy of the New York Transit Museum.

The new conflict prompted public debates and proposed solutions, all documented in the newspapers, which continued to heap scorn on Trinity and to bring up the issue of Trinity's vast real estate portfolio, including its controversial tenements. The overall impact of the newspapers was heralded by writer Frank Marshall White: "Trinity Corporation can hardly claim the credit for [St. John's] survival. . . . Rather the vigilance of the newspapers has saved it. It is the newspapers again which have widely advertised those recent plans for street improvements to meet new conditions in the region of West Side warehouses which contemplated once more the sacrifice of St. John's rather than, for instance, any part of the ugly pile of brick across the way—the freight station which was the usurper of the park which once faced the chapel."[124]

Trinity Vestry could "afford to await" for the city to take the blame for tearing down the chapel—or as it turned out, take the credit for preserving it (temporarily). Apparently, the vestry's officers purposely deceived the public and the city about their plans for St. John's. In a June 14, 1912, letter to McAneny, vestry counsel William Jay expressed interest in McAneny's detailed proposal for the building and again repeated the vestry's party line that "Trinity Church has never taken any action looking to the demolition of St. John's." As indicated earlier, this clearly ignores the vestry's 1894 actions in which it secured the bishop's permission to tear down the chapel. In a letter dated the same day, Jay recounted his meeting with McAneny for vestry colleague Hermann Cammann. He reported that the vestry's stalling and stonewalling about its plans for the chapel would bear fruit, as McAneny would initiate the building's destruction: "Mr. McAneny admitted that he was strongly in favor of the retention of the Chapel and moreover he said that great pressure had been brought to bear upon him by the Members of the Architects Guild and certain other Societies, and that there would be a very great commotion if the building should be taken down. . . . I think we can afford to await further action on the part of the Borough President. It is the City of New York and not the Corporation of Trinity Church that is now threatening to destroy the building."[125]

George McAneny

George McAneny (1869–1953) forged a long career as a city builder and civic reformer, typifying the generation of professional reformers that built on Andrew Green's legacy. A successful politician as well as a dedicated preservationist, McAneny placed himself in the middle of such conflicts as St. John's (and in the 1940s, taking on Robert Moses, the preservation of Castle Clinton). A *New York Times* editorial memorialized McAneny shortly after his death as

> one of our finest and most useful citizens, whether in the role of civic
> reformer, public official or business man. He loved New York City, knew
> and well remembered its history and its landmarks, worked for its im-
> provement. He probably did more than anyone else in his generation to
> create and improve New York's public spaces and infrastructures. The list
> of public offices he held was extraordinarily long and only one index of
> his versatility and the esteem in which he was held.[126]

Epitomizing the Progressive reformer, McAneny devoted his career to the principled application of efficiency, rationality, and fairness in public affairs. He began his career as a newspaperman and became a protégé of Carl Schurz, the politician,

Figure 2.10. George McAneny (right) during his term as president of the Board of Aldermen, meets with a delegation from Japan. Courtesy of University of Pennsylvania Libraries.

reformer, Civil War general, and colleague of Abraham Lincoln. "Carl Schurz was a sort of Godfather of mine," McAneny remembered late in life.[127] Connections with Schurz put him in a circle of highly influential citizens and politicians, and he counted Seth Low, Robert De Forest, Theodore Roosevelt, and Woodrow Wilson among his acquaintances and colleagues. His social and professional connections came through his work, not his family. The young McAneny worked as a lawyer in the office of E. F. Shepard, counsel to the Pennsylvania Railroad, and he made his first public mark in civil service reform, working with good-government groups such as the watchdog Municipal Research Bureau.[128] Entering politics in 1910 as a reform and fusion candidate for mayor, he won office instead as Manhattan borough president, serving from 1910 to 1913. From 1914 to 1916, McAneny served as president of the Board of Aldermen—one of the powerful city officers making up the Board of Estimate and Apportionment, essentially the city government's board of directors.

Transit and city planning were his most noted contributions. The office of borough president, created as part of the 1898 Charter, wielded a great deal of power and influence over public works (public buildings, streets, and other services and infrastructure). With these large responsibilities, McAneny turned to the emergent field of city planning to tackle the problems of growth and congestion, and he built a substantial legacy. With lawyer Edward Bassett, he created New York's 1916 comprehensive zoning ordinance, the first in the United States and truly a landmark effort, addressing the trenchant problems of skyscrapers' blocking light and air without dampening the growth and densification of Manhattan's commercial districts.[129] At the same time, New York faced difficult expansion issues, with chaotic transit systems in need of reconciliation. Multiple companies and lines competed for public resources, and McAneny negotiated the immense Dual Contracts expansion of the IRT subway, which structured competition without stopping expansion. McAneny's administration oversaw such notable public building projects as the Municipal Building and the Manhattan and Williamsburg bridges over the East River, as well as more-pedestrian regulatory issues such as improving public food markets.

McAneny championed historic preservation, too, initiating and supervising the renovation and restoration of City Hall between 1913 and 1915. He helped lead an effort to build a memorial to Schurz at 116th Street and Morningside Drive. In his reminiscences, captured by Columbia University historian Allan Nevins in 1949, McAneny remembered his first encounter with the idea of historic preservation; writing stories for the *Herald* in 1887 about a 1740 house on Long Island was his "first job in preservation."[130] These early preservation activities foreshadowed a lifelong interest and involvement in historic preservation.

His influence on urban infrastructure extended to Manhattan's Fifth Avenue—the city's primary high-end retail district—where he widened the street and successfully battled against the sidewalk intrusions that had become the street-level expression of New York's chaotic growth and commerce. The success of his Fifth Avenue Commission in cleaning the vendors, stalls, and immigrant workers off Fifth Avenue sidewalks went hand in hand with the new zoning ordinance McAneny championed to control buildings' heights. Redesigning and rationalizing urban spaces—whether McAneny's Fifth Avenue, Green's Central Park of the 1860s, Grant's Bronx River valley in the second decade of the twentieth century, or myriad rearrangements of City Hall Park—required a certain amount of bullying and discrimination between proper and improper uses. So the altruism and objectivity for which Progressive reform is often remembered should be alloyed with the memory of the exclusion from the city's new "public realms" of immigrants and workers who did not fit the reformers' vision.

McAneny left his career as a public official in 1916 to work as business manager of the *New York Times* and later as president of the Title Guarantee and Trust Company. Straddling the worlds of business and governmental reform, he lamented in a 1914 speech that "among business men I am an advocate of the arts, and among artists I am an advocate of business." Though he regarded preservation and other matters of art as essential to civic culture, he also recognized them as secondary to concerns of growth and expansion. "When art or decoration or ornamentation is in conflict with commerce in the city, then commerce should and must prevail"—an idea rooted in the city's history: "New York is a commercial city. It had its origins in commerce."[131]

His retreat from civic life was only partial—in the true Progressive mold, his public service was constant and lifelong. McAneny took on important civic leadership roles as a volunteer, co-organizing the Regional Plan Association in the late 1920s[132] and the 1939 World's Fair. In the late 1930s, McAneny served as president of the ASHPS. His involvement in preservation deepened throughout the 1940s, both in New York (where he spearheaded the fight against Moses to save Castle Clinton) and nationally: McAneny was part of the small group who founded the National Trust for Historic Preservation in 1949. A memorial plaque devoted to his career and placed in Federal Hall anointed McAneny a "Pioneer in City Planning, Protector of Historic Places, Leader of a City, Friend beyond Compare."[133] His work as preservationist, city planner, and city builder exemplified the interweaving of these practices as part of the project of "improvement."

An Architectural Solution

In 1913, George McAneny, under pressure from "historical and artistic societies" and motivated by his own interests in historic preservation, offered a solution to the impasse over St. John's Chapel that had dragged on since 1909. McAneny and his activist administration proved to be the catalyst. McAneny supported a plan designed and advocated by architect Rawson Haddon that satisfied preservationists, accommodated the city planners' wider street, and convinced Trinity to postpone demolition.[134] Haddon had studied Greenwich Village and colonial architecture, and he presented his proposal to the ASHPS, which used its connections with McAneny to win its approval.[135] The street was still widened, but the new sidewalk was placed under the chapel portico. This also required reinforcing the columns to carry the building atop the new subway passing underneath. Such a design had been used in the United States—with St. Michael's Church in Charleston, South Carolina—as well as in London. The more remarkable part of the plan was McAneny's effort to secure the use of $15,000 of city funds to pay for the rebuilding of a private structure in the public right-of-way.

By reconstructing the portico as part of the subway and street-widening project under way by 1915, McAneny epitomized the preservationist as municipal reformer: He implemented a technical solution satisfying divergent demands on the place in question, avoided the zero-sum game of total preservation versus total destruction, and financed it using government resources in keeping with the Progressive ideological principle that an improved built environment is a public good. He managed to preserve, in effect, the memory *and* the efficiency of this environment. The Fine Arts Federation, an umbrella group of municipal reformers and artists, commended McAneny on his role "in regard to all matters which affect the art life of the City of New York," and in particular commended his "personal efforts that have played so large a part in saving Old St. John's Chapel in Varick Street."[136] A March 1914 letter to the *Times* celebrated McAneny as the chapel's white knight, lauding McAneny's commitment "to save old St. John's Chapel," "as New York City is almost ruthless in its destruction of sacred and historical places merely to make way for some sordid exaggeration of driveways."[137] McAneny would have disagreed that his new streets and sidewalks were "sordid exaggerations"—he was described as the "directing genius" of New York's scheme to alleviate traffic congestion by widening streets and clearing sidewalks[138]—but he would have agreed that new infrastructure did not have to exact a price of landmarks and historical memory.

McAneny's endorsement of Haddon's solution exemplifies the desire for accommodation among different streams of reform. Haddon worked out in three dimensions McAneny's kind of urban reform. Not only did it accommodate reform goals to the ultimate hegemony of property rights and redevelopment, but it also reconciled different reform goals where they clashed, in this case the wider streets of city planners and engineers that bumped up against the memory site preservationists wished to create. Ironically, the St. John's solution had McAneny effectively placing an obstruction in the public right-of-way—quite the opposite of his successfully eliminating obstructions along Fifth Avenue, which had won him great praise.[139]

St. John's as an Architectural and Historical Landmark

In this second episode of the St. John's case, the architectural profession showed a new interest in historic preservation. Architects' views of the chapel's value firmly situated the building as a civic landmark, an artifact valued primarily for its visual and artistic qualities. By 1913, the city's leading architects had begun taking an interest in St. John's, describing it as a beautiful and noble work of architecture, a source of authentic colonial design.[140] Leading colonial-revival architect (and one of Robert Moses's favorite architects) Aymar Embury described it as

> architecturally not quite so interesting as St. Paul's, though rather better than St. Mark's, and the narrow and crowded lot on which it stands, sur-rounded by tall office buildings, does not improve its appearance. . . . The tower is exceedingly tall, and rather heavy toward the top, but the porch is excellently designed, and the interior is extremely lovely. There have been fortunately no changes made in it.[141]

In the view of architects, the chapel was an artifact, related to its urban contexts only as a painting is related to the wall on which it hangs—the congregation was now a distant memory.

Architects' involvement in the St. John's case was orchestrated through their professional organizations: the Architectural League of New York, the Fine Arts Federation, and the New York chapter of the American Institute of Architects. In 1913, Aymar Embury presented a resolution of the Architectural League of New York supporting the preservation of St. John's;[142] another was addressed to Manning by league president Alexander Trowbridge in April 1917, expressing "deep concern at the possible loss of so valuable a work of art by the architect of our City Hall, John McComb, who by his talents and patriotic efforts marked an epoch in the history of our City."[143] The Historic Buildings committee of the New York chapter of the American Institute of Architects sent a similar letter. The hero-architect and his works of art dominated the architects' conception of New York's proper civic memory.

The architects' organizations did little besides periodically resolving to send more protests to Trinity. An April 12, 1917, resolution by the Architectural League asked for preservation of this "historic landmark," "valuable work of art," and "priceless souvenir to succeeding generations of our children." The league's com-mittee on St. John's included the most prominent architects of the day: Cass Gilbert, Stokes, Henry Herts, Christopher Grant LaFarge, Arnold Brunner, Grosvenor Atterbury, Henry Hornbostel, John Russell Pope, and Alexander Trowbridge. Atterbury, who had worked with McAneny and Robert De Forest in renovating City Hall in 1911–15, followed this with a letter of his own, noting that in bet-ter times—that is, before World War I—the money could have been raised to preserve the chapel for some semipublic, secular use. Trying to give Trinity an incentive to cooperate, he expressed confidence that the city, as the financial climate improved, would continue the investments in and around St. John's that had begun with McAneny's support of the portico reconstruction. Atterbury's letter to the vestry frankly acknowledged the difficulties facing both Trinity and the preservationists, recognizing that Trinity had been "misunderstood" and insisting (in anticipation of Trinity's quick dismissal of any suggestion) that he wrote "with the sole object of preserving for the public benefit, for the increased beauty and interest of the City and respect for its historic monuments which we know to be worth preserving." The "conditions for raising money to save the Church," made difficult by the war, was understandably frustrating to Trinity, he concurred. But Atterbury also assured Trinity that the city would continue making such investments of "esthetic and historic interest" when the economy improved. He noted that, had more money been available, McAneny would have created a park around a preserved St. John's, as had been done elsewhere in the city.[144]

There were two exceptions among architects: I. N. P. Stokes and Rawson Haddon. Stokes, as noted earlier, was an architect among his several other callings. His greatest impact on the city was as a housing reformer, historian, and philanthropist. Haddon, an otherwise unknown architect, had written about St. John's and its surroundings in a May 1914 *Architectural Record* article, in which the building of the chapel was chronicled and presented along with photographs and measured drawings documenting the building for posterity.[145] His article exemplified the architectural approach to preservation: If only the building mattered, not the people or their community bonds and social memories, then preservation could be achieved by graphic documentation. But Haddon was also drawn into studying the larger environment in which the chapel stood, and in effect he spoke to the social history narratives that gave the building meaning for the congregation and historic preservationists. He published a study of the ordinary dwellings in Greenwich Village soon to be demolished by the extension of Seventh Avenue, showing a sensitivity to the value embodied in the vernacular architectural context of landmarks like St. John's.

In the end, the architects' resolutions and proposals to preserve the chapel were summarily brushed off by the vestry (as it had done when anyone from Seth Low to Edward Hagaman Hall to other Episcopal clergy had made any similar suggestions). But one such resolution brought a fairly venomous reply from William Jay, who criticized the Fine Arts Federation for merely proposing and not acting to save the building: "Your society may be to blame that 'no effort has been made to avert the danger or to call to the defence of the Chapel the public sentiment which made

A PROSPECT OF OLD VARICK STREET, NEW YORK CITY.

⌐VARICK STREET⌐
Which is in Greenwich Village, Manhattan

A Narrative and Some Pen Sketches
By Rawson W. Haddon

Figure 2.11. Rawson W. Haddon's Architectural Record *article in 1914 elaborated on the history and significance of vernacular buildings of Greenwich Village, including the blocks of early-nineteenth-century houses around St. John's Chapel. Courtesy of Anne and Jerome Fisher Fine Arts Library, University of Pennsylvania.*

itself heard so forcibly three years ago.'" Jay continued the deception that Trinity did not intend to destroy the chapel, placing the blame on city planners: "The existence of St. John's Chapel is now threatened, not by any act of Trinity church but by an act of the public authorities of the City of New York."[146]

As artists, architects expressed the same deep cultural tensions at work in transforming the traditional memories of St. John's into the historical memory purveyed by preservationists. Historic buildings came to be rendered as artifacts, no longer as places rich in community association. But architecturally minded preservation brought with it a visual aspect that added to the rhetorical strength of historic preservationists. Architect and renderer Hugh Ferriss sketched St. John's in 1915, when the portico was being rebuilt, capturing this moment and its changing attitude to the past.

The visual aspects of the debate and preservation efforts signaled another important aspect of the joining of space and memory. For some preservationists, visual

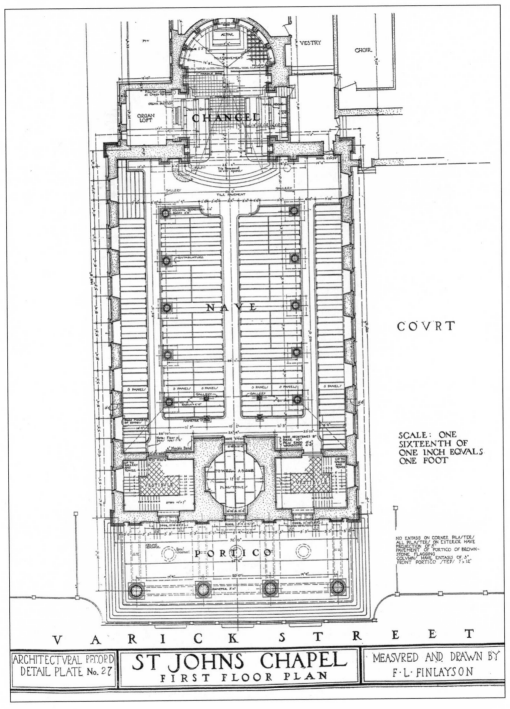

Figure 2.12. Haddon's Architectural Record *article on St. John's Chapel included several measured drawings of the building—elevations, section details, and the floor plan shown here. Courtesy of Anne and Jerome Fisher Fine Arts Library, University of Pennsylvania.*

Figure 2.13. Hugh Ferriss sketched this scene looking south down Varick Street in 1915. Famous for his renderings of futuristic skyscrapers, Ferriss here captured the tension between the disappearing architectural past (St. John's, carefully detailed at the center of the drawing) and the future (embodied by the Woolworth Building, the world's tallest when built; Ferriss worked in Cass Gilbert's office when the Woolworth Building was being designed). The drawing seems to reverse the interpretation one would expect from Ferriss: instead of celebrating the arrival of the future, he appears to be holding on to the past. Courtesy of the Museum of the City of New York.

appeals were the most important strategy. Several newspapers published lengthy, well-illustrated articles in their Sunday sections; the Art Commission hired a professional architectural photographer to "preserve" historic buildings they felt were going to disappear (see the portfolio of Frank Cousins's photographs for the Art Commission in this book); Haddon's articles used both measured drawings and impressionistic sketches to convey the architectural and artistic qualities of the chapel; Stokes's *Iconography of Manhattan Island,* William Loring Andrews's Society of Iconophiles, and Henry Collins Brown's *Valentine's Manual* relied on romantic engravings (aimed at an admittedly small audience); the Bronx River Parkway Commission, as detailed in chapter 4, relied heavily on visual strategies to explain, justify, and otherwise garner support for its work. The ASHPS, by contrast, used relatively few illustrations in its publications, and those tended to be simple, documentary images.

Between the first and second episodes of the controversy over the chapel, the public's interest in St. John's—as constructed by reformers and sampled through the press and Trinity Parish records—had turned from the congregation to the architecture. Architects' visions of St. John's as a work of art—as opposed to a setting for worship and community—were the epitome of this, describing an artifact and never the people inhabiting and using it. Even newspaper articles covering the greater destruction of the area by street widening and improvements show few people, only buildings, making the place seem already abandoned and suspended in time. Artifacts could be plucked from such an unpeopled landscape, but (traditional) memories could no longer be recovered. In other words, the chapel was transformed from a site of *memory* to a totem of *history.* As a historical memory, it was an artifact that managed only to be a weak link in the memory infrastructure.

A shift occurred in the memories being preserved: from congregation and civic responsibility to architecture; from local memory (in the traditional sense, as a process animated by people) to civic memory (in the modern sense, constructed, expressed as a relic, an artifact). Likewise, there was a shift in the grounds for the debate: It was no longer about sustaining a group's ability to remember, but about retaining spaces in which memories were expressed or the artifacts to which memory was attached. This was a change abetted by architects. Their narrow view of the building's value reflected the broad effects of modernity on Americans' use of the past.[147]

St. John's Fuels the Improvement of the Lower West Side

In March 1915, work progressed on St. John's portico, underpinning it and rebuilding street and sidewalk. Trinity agreed to McAneny's suggestion of a two-year stay of demolition. The stay was intended to give preservationists or civic organizations a chance to raise money to fund some kind of reuse. The vestry also agreed to sell the chapel for "public purpose" at a reasonable price (the valuation was set at $260,000, but estimates ran as high as $400,000).[148] As far as the vestry was concerned, the chapel's value was purely economic.

Preservationists had a concrete example on which to build: the heroic effort to preserve Boston's Old South Church, which historian Michael Holleran calls "Boston's greatest contribution to American preservation."[149] The Old South's congregation had moved to a new place, and the old building was purchased in 1876–77 and reused as a community center. Edward Hagaman Hall cited the Old South example, pointing out that the meeting house had been "purchased by private generosity" (a wealthy widow contributed $100,000) and with mortgages paid back by rents, land sales, fairs, and state funds (a financing package that today would be celebrated as a "public–private partnership"). Hall tried to shame New Yorkers into action: "New York has as much cause for civic and historic pride and as much generosity as Boston. Would that they might be stirred by the appeal for saving St. John's."[150] As suggested in the minutes of ASHPS meetings, the efforts of Hall and Kunz simply came up short. "The [Old South] suggestion met with hearty approval but no funds were forthcoming."[151] They found no one willing to donate the money for purchasing the chapel, even among the wealthier ASHPS board members (J. P. Morgan Jr., George Baker, Samuel Avery) and the Board of Education, which refused to consider acquiring the chapel for use as a school. Another option would have been for the city Parks Department to accept the donated building and surrounding parcels for the creation of a museum in a park, to be run by a civic organization, as had already been done in such cases as the Morris–Jumel Mansion, Poe Cottage, and Dyckman House. There is some evidence that McAneny proposed this, though money for the purchase was never allocated.[152]

Preservationists and other reformers still sought a "civic" use for the building. Its exterior could serve as a preserved artifact of an earlier time (the disembodied facade of the Assay Office comes to mind), and the buildings could serve as a sort of settlement house. A number of interesting ideas were offered for the chapel's reuse: as a war memorial, public school, or community center, or even, dismantled and removed to another site, as a church. The ASHPS led the way in proposing new uses: for example, calling for the Red Cross to use it during the war, and afterward making it the headquarters for the ASHPS and a center for other civic work, such as would go on in a community center.[153] Some of these uses would serve the population of the immediate neighborhood; others clearly would not. Moving the building proved technically impossible because of the rubble-filled construction of the walls.[154]

None of the proposals to adapt or reuse the chapel were realized, for lack of funds. Many preservationists thought the government should play a larger role and buy it. The failure could also be ascribed to the world war and war-related economic disruptions and to the fact that many leading historic preservationists had left the civic scene, either involved with the war or out of public life.[155] Stokes and Atterbury, for instance, were employed by the federal government on projects for the U.S. Shipping Corporation, designing communities for war workers. McAneny served the city as president of the Board of Alderman (and as interim mayor upon John Purroy Mitchel's death), but he was never in a position—such as borough president, directing all public building, infrastructure, and city-planning functions—to bring the St. John's controversy to a positive conclusion.

St. John's was demolished in 1918, under a contract jointly made with Trinity Vestry and the city. The two-year stay of sale or demolition was extended by Trinity, but the building meanwhile fell into disrepair. Newspapers and the ASHPS observed the demolition with resignation. The loss of a great historical landmark and beautiful example of colonial architecture was lamented. The papers noted the efforts of many prominent citizens to save it (Low, Gilder, Stokes) but ignored the congregation altogether.[156]

In September 1918, Morris Lamont, a demolition contractor, set to work tearing down St. John's. Under his contract with Trinity Parish and the city of New York, Lamont was permitted to sell materials he could salvage. "I had expected to make a profit on the material but said turned out to be quite a loss to me as the material was not usable and we had to sell it for fire wood." These "materials" were timbers from St. John's tall steeple. In contrast to the parts of St. John's that went up New York chimneys that winter, several furnishings and pieces of interior architecture—those most meaningful to the congregation's rituals and collective memory—were removed from the building and reused in worship at St. Luke's Chapel, where some of them remain in use today.[157] Memory and material, though linked, went their separate ways—some was kept and some was discarded, in keeping with the "natural" process of preservation and destruction.

With resignation, the ASHPS observed in 1919, "St. John's is gone, and remains now only a historical memory."[158] The memory of St. John's as a place of worship as well as a civic landmark did live on, though literally in pieces—some consumed for fuel, others reused in worship at St. Luke's, the hands and pendulum of the steeple clock taken to the borough president's office as a souvenir.[159] But as a souvenir to remember what? The substantial efforts of McAneny to preserve the chapel when he held that office? Or the ultimate failure of the government and civic sector together to halt the "juggernaut" of real estate redevelopment to preserve a landscape of some public meaning? Or just as a curious old artifact?

Figure 2.14. In the end St. John's Chapel was reduced to rubble, despite the efforts of preservationists. Only some archives, artifacts, and a street name (St. John's Lane, the small street behind the chapel) materially survived. Courtesy of University of Pennsylvania Libraries.

The site itself was cleared and readied for construction. Developer Adolf Prickin bought the land from Trinity and built an industrial loft building that stands on the site today.[160] A newspaper article noting that the site of the demolished building was up for sale also remembered the destruction of the park fifty years before and related the story of Trinity reneging on its promise to make it a public park.[161] To this day, Trinity's official histories note that the chapel was demolished by the city government, thus fulfilling the public relations strategy first implemented in 1909 to rewrite the historical memory of the chapel.

Conclusions

The controversy over St. John's was remarkable for its length and for the involvement of the city's leading citizens. But the social, cultural, economic, and environmental changes underlying this case were typical of what was happening in the whole Lower West Side, all of Lower Manhattan, and indeed across the metropolis. In the face of drastic changes in the social geography of downtown—spurred by economic growth and the need for a new commercial infrastructure of streets, warehouses, skyscrapers, and industrial lofts—a number of New Yorkers, not least of all the St. John's congregation, consciously spoke of the importance of preserving the historical memories attached to the building, and earlier to the park, as they tried to preserve the chapel. In one sense, the market had won out over memory: The pecuniary gain to Trinity Vestry from redevelopment outweighed the chapel's value as cultural heritage; the public value of preservation was in this case trumped by the private value of property rights. In another sense, though, creative destruction by the market was the memory of the St. John's landscape—harkening back to the sale and destruction of adjacent St. John's Park in 1867. Even though the market prevailed here, debate about memory infrastructure was seriously joined.

In the first few years of the debate over St. John's, the congregation's memory of worship and community was replaced with the reformers' notion of civic patriotism and secular, visual landmarks. The St. John's case illustrates the larger shift in the collective memory of the city in this era: from the congregation's traditional collective memory, characterized by continuities through time and space, a local and spatially bounded orientation, and strong religious values; to the modern historical memory constructed by preservationists and others, abstracted from the historical experience of the site, metropolitan, and secular in character. The chapel ceased to be valued as the center of a living community and was framed and valorized as an isolated landmark, an anomaly in space and time. Preservationists, in advocating for historical memory, drove this shift toward secular, modern forms of historical memory.

The point of St. John's story is not that Trinity Vestry was greedy and evil or that the congregation or historic preservation advocates were virtuous but powerless. Rather, the story of St. John's demonstrates how the memory of a particular landscape became a fulcrum for struggles to transform the meaning, use, and physical design of the urban environment. The construction of historical memory was interwoven as part of the urban development process.

Historical memory was a critical point of contention in directing the "improvement" of urban landscapes in early-twentieth-century New York. The negotiation of economic and cultural values through the construction of public memory was increasingly prominent in this era of intense redevelopment—it signaled the efforts of city builders to produce civic culture as well as economic wealth and social order. The struggle over the fate of St. John's was typical of this process of cultural production, but it was extraordinary in the variety of memories debated, the actors involved, and the length and complexity of the controversy.

The ultimate fate of the chapel—demolition—reflected the power of property and economic interests, though not necessarily the insignificance of public memory. At other sites across the city, elements of public memory were being built and preserved in a variety of landscapes. Though the St. John's landscape ultimately was not preserved as part of the memory infrastructure that was being built in modern New York, reformers succeeded elsewhere in the city: for instance, in City Hall Park, the Bronx River Parkway, and the many historic sites, restored buildings, and preserved parks studding the turn-of-the-century metropolitan landscape, and even Trinity's beloved St. Paul's Chapel. Provisionally, this was also the case at St. John's, when McAneny preserved the building from the threat of street widening. The construction of civic memory was not merely a matter of preserving old things; it was a process of building *and* destroying, remembering *and* forgetting. Also, it made evident that historical memory was a common currency of debate over cultural and urban change by 1908.

The fate of the building was, in a way, of less moment than what was signified by the debates over it: that collective historical memory of various kinds (of the congregation, of the chapel as a historic or architectural landmark of citywide importance) was one stage on which the meaning, use, and shape of the city was continually contested. The St. John's case could sensibly have been resolved in quite a different way—resulting, for instance, in the chapel's reuse as a civic center like Boston's Old South Church—but the lessons about the importance of memory and landscape would have remained substantially the same. The *process* of constructing memory, not just the outcome, is key to unlocking the cultural aspects of urban development.

Three

City Hall Park: Hearth of Official Civic Memory

> The Court-house board now proposes to erect on the site of the County
> Court-house an enormous structure. . . . If such a project be carried to
> execution, it will greatly reduce the open space of what has been the city
> common for over two centuries; It will encroach . . . upon land made
> sacred by venerated traditions of every period of our city's history; It
> will overshadow the city hall, which is one of the architectural treasures
> of the city; It will prevent symmetrical architectural development of a
> civic center around City Hall park commensurate with the dignity of the
> metropolis of the New World and similar to those of other large cities in
> America and Europe; It will increase the congestion of traffic . . . It will
> impair the city's financial credit . . . And it will establish a precedent for
> still further encroachments in this and other public parks.
>
> Edward Hagaman Hall, 1910

S PLENDIDLY SET APART FROM THE BUSTLING STREET, CITY HALL SAT PRO-
tected in its elegant park, surrounded by lawns and rows of elms. White marble
gleaming from the storied steps to the top of the cupola, City Hall and the old
Commons created a scene of civic grandeur and serenity—a mythic scene from
the 1830s, dreamed of by reformers in the 1900s as the centerpiece of the memory
infrastructure. "City Hall Park as it appeared before the Post-office was built, and
as it should be restored," read Edward Hall's caption to an 1830 engraving of an
idealized City Hall and its park. Hall's salvo was part of an intense debate over the
fate of City Hall Park—stretching back to the 1880s but peaking between 1910 and
1912—arguing over how the park could continue to function as the center of city
government and downtown political and social life while also reflecting the deeply
layered civic memories more evident here than any other place in the city.

Because it was geographically and politically so central and signified official
civic memory, City Hall Park provides a marvelous window on historic preservation's place in turn-of-the-century urbanism. Efforts to preserve City Hall Park and
City Hall itself were not just fights over the fate of an old building but a robust

City Hall Park as it appeared before the Post-office was built, and as it should be restored.

Figure 3.1. This 1830 engraving of City Hall and its park, showing what preservationists in the early twentieth century thought it should be, appeared in the 1910 Annual Report of the American Scenic and Historic Preservation Society. Courtesy of University of Pennsylvania Libraries.

and lengthy debate over symbolism, real estate, urban design, transportation, and politics—as well as over the role of collective memory in shaping the city's culture. As the official seat of government and a place of obvious historical value, there was no better place to put official memory on display. All New Yorkers had a stake in the memory and scenery of City Hall Park, and many spoke their mind about its fate. The multitude of proposals and changes envisioned for this landscape typified the complex, lurching, never-quite-choreographed character of "improvement" and the shifting roles that historic preservationists, planners, architects, elected officials, and real estate interests took in it.

The park's history stretched back to the days of the Dutch colony, and the layers of this history remained visible in its buildings, boundaries, and monuments. City Hall, the edifice at its center, was the city's most renowned and best-loved building—there was no greater single symbol of the city's ascendance and historical achievements.

Figure 3.2. By the end of the second decade of the twentieth century, the buildings in and around City Hall Park mixed the new and the old. City Hall, well preserved and restored, is at the center. The Tweed Courthouse is immediately behind it, to the left; behind the courthouse (across Chambers Street) rises the mansard roof of the new Hall of Records, or Surrogate's Court. The skyscraping Municipal Building, finished in 1914, dominates the civic center. The Brooklyn Bridge Terminal structure seems to be crashing into the right side of City Hall. Subway entrances are visible, for instance, at lower left. Courtesy of the New York Transit Museum.

By the 1890s, City Hall Park had long been a site of celebration as well as protest, the official center of politics and power, as well as a convivial public park. The rough triangle took shape on the edge of the seventeenth-century polyglot Nieuw Amsterdam colony, where two roads headed north diverged. For centuries, it had been a more or less open public space, alternately used, crowded, and revered by the city government and its citizens.[1] The symbolic and political functions of the park took on greater importance with the 1898 consolidation of the far-flung five boroughs into a metropolis with its seat of government in Manhattan.

The story of City Hall Park related here is of an old, long-evolving landscape becoming modernized, of how it survived this convulsive period in the city's history, and of how historical memory played a strong part in this process. As the center of Manhattan and of greater New York, City Hall Park functioned in several ways simultaneously. The park was the seat of city government (growing mark-

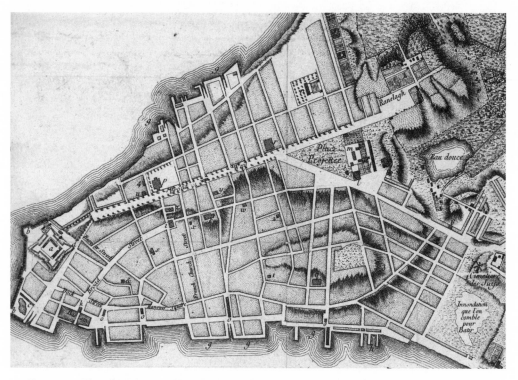

Figure 3.3. The colonial town of New York around the time of the Revolution (as rendered in this 1777 map by Rochambeau) reached to today's Chambers Street. City Hall Park—then the Commons, or Place Projettée—had already taken shape: follow Broadway from the Battery at the tip of the island to the right (northward), until it branches to the right, creating a triangle. This triangle, and the public buildings shown occupying it, formed the precursor of City Hall Park. Courtesy of the Lionel Pincus and Princess Firyal Map Division, the New York Public Library, Aster, Lenox, and Tilden Foundations.

edly in these decades), a transportation center (a nexus of Manhattan streets, the Brooklyn Bridge, streetcar and elevated train lines, and the new subway systems), the center of media industries (nearby Newspaper Row), part of the commercial downtown (the then world's tallest building, the Woolworth Building, opened across the street from the park in 1911), and a public park and town square. The newly imagined and expanded civic center (in the parlance of reformers and City Beautiful advocates) had to accommodate these uses and more (more government buildings, more traffic)—indeed, these new uses mirrored the whole city's growing complexity, disorder, and congestion. It also functioned as a commemorative center, a built environment constructed to shape ways of remembering the city's past and therefore to guide New Yorkers in the present toward better citizenship and morality. All this was in flux, up for grabs, by the time of greater New York's consolidation in 1898. How could the memorial functions of the place stand up to demands for expanded subway and mass-transit structures, for new municipal office buildings needed for the burgeoning bureaucracy that Progressives themselves envisioned? City-planning and historic preservation advocates promoted distinctly different ways of achieving this in City Hall Park.

Andrew Haswell Green and other reformers and civic leaders recognized that City Hall and City Hall Park anchored whatever civic memory would emerge from the tumultuous period of consolidation, expansion, and rebuilding that they were orchestrating: "[City Hall's] presence tends to keep alive associations that are near to very many of our citizens, a visible landmark, an object lesson to the people, that should not be destroyed."[2] Green and his followers saw preservation of important buildings and landscapes as a reform goal inspired by quasi-spiritual patriotism—and City Hall Park was the cathedral of the church of civic religion. Green's 1894 pamphlet detailing why City Hall must be preserved in situ spelled out the doctrine of preservation as cultural reform. Preserving City Hall Park was also a pragmatic goal—a means of creating good citizens, of turning public opinion against corruption, and of cultivating allegiance to the idea of the city and to the notion that the growing metropolis was a reality preordained by history—and in this sense memory sites were needed in order for the city to function properly. City Hall and City Hall Park were thus the subject of long and varied debate over how best to construct, sustain, and give form to civic memory. In the struggle to create a landscape of civic memory for the new metropolis, nowhere were the stakes higher.

City Hall Park was so symbolically important to the political debates of the time that it was given a new name—the "civic center"—to reinforce the fact that this landscape was the most conscious and conspicuous embodiment of civic culture. Leaders' ability to create a clear statement of civic culture—specifically, a statement or embodiment of civic, historical memory—reflected their ability to govern and grow the new metropolis. Just as the Croton water system connected the natural resources of pure water with a thirsty city and Central Park presented a congested, unhealthy city with salutary "nature," the efforts of preservationists gave concrete form to a social necessity as well as an ideal—a romantic, patriotic, normative notion of the city's past. City Hall Park played a central role in the way the city understood the past, the way citizens accepted the need for expanding urban government, and the way people moved around the city—in short, here citizens could be shown and could walk through the reconciliation of a city that was changing quickly and drastically while remaining rooted in a celebratory, unchanging past.

Creating a park that could facilitate these ends involved political control and urban design vision, but it drew equally from the power of place-specific narratives and memorial that preservationists sought to cultivate.[3] More environmental-reform and memory-building efforts were focused on City Hall Park than on any other place in the city, and the mixed results here accurately portended the city government's mixed results in building the metropolis of the twentieth century.

In this chapter, the book's central argument—that the construction of historical memory in the service of civic patriotism and the building of memory infrastructure were an essential part of urban development—is advanced by describing how efforts to spatialize historical memory shaped debates and plans for the City Hall and City Hall Park. The overarching goal for preservationists was cultivating order, grandeur, and historic memory in the park. Preserving buildings and open space was one side of the coin of historical memory; the other was destroying buildings with the "wrong" memory, as reformers wanted in the case of the Tweed Courthouse and the Post Office. As the oldest public building in the city and one of its oldest surviving buildings, a fine work of architecture, and the official headquarters of the city, City Hall was the most obvious kind of building to preserve—the charismatic megafauna of architectural preservation. The story of City Hall Park is full of paradoxes—preservation and destruction, competing proposals, political maneuvering, endless cycles of official action and popular protest—but this was typical of the larger process of preservationists' building historical memory into the urban landscape as part of the modern process of metropolitan expansion and redevelopment.

A STORIED PLACE

In 1910, the ASHPS published Edward Hagaman Hall's history of City Hall Park "with a view to showing the strong historical interest which attaches to this old public place."[4] Hall's chronicle of City Hall Park—also issued as a separate brochure titled *An Appeal for the Preservation of City Hall Park*—was imbued with a historian's scientific approach, using primary sources (Common Council minutes, old maps) and strictly adhering to chronology. The lengthy narrative was accompanied by detailed mapping of thirty-five structures that had existed on the site over the previous two and half centuries.[5] Hall's excellent history of the park was an indication of the maturation of the preservation field and an example of how preservationists combined advocacy, politicking, and historical research to shape places they considered important nodes in the memory infrastructure.

Preservationist interest in City Hall Park stretched back at least to the 1890s. By the first decades of the twentieth century, the park was understood as perhaps the most storied, deeply historic landscape in New York, and City Hall was the city's most treasured landmark.[6] If civic memory could be measured, it would be thickest here. The park was ground hallowed by patriotic events and civic achievement and had already become a showcase for the kind of historical memory preservationists worked to put on display.

Three kinds of powerful narratives were rooted in City Hall Park and cultivated as part of circa-1900 civic memory: First was the continuity and quality of City Hall itself, symbol of governmental power and evidence of the durability of city institutions. It was acclaimed as the country's finest work of civic architecture, an architectural expression of the ideal of disinterested and virtuous city governance. Second, important city-building achievements were celebrated or represented in the park, including the Croton water system, the buildings of city government (going beyond City Hall to include courts, offices, records-storage buildings, jails, and so on), transportation infrastructure (Brooklyn Bridge, subways), and park space (valued variously for its recreational, healthful, or aesthetic aspects—one of the tropes of a civilized place).[7] The third theme concerned national patriotism and the Revolutionary War. These were the most vivid narratives presented to the public, in the material and spectacular commemorations of protests against the Crown (liberty poles), of martyrdom and sacrifice (the Martyrs' Prison, Nathan Hale), and of the military and political genius of the founding fathers (the scene of the public reading of the Declaration of Independence before Washington and of Hamilton's first speech). Civic and national patriotism were seamlessly joined in these three themes.

The Commons

The Commons, or "the field," was located at the edge of the colonial town, "a wild, uncultivated tract, on the outskirts of civilization."[8] To the south lay the developing

EXPLANATION OF MAP.

The old Common was substantially identical with the triangle bounded by Broadway, Chambers street and Park Row. The north-east corner was gradually worn off until, with the opening of Centre street, the Park was bounded by Broadway, Chambers street, Centre street and Park Row. It thus remained until 1867, when the Post-office site was sold, since which time the Park has been bounded by Broadway, Chambers street, Centre street, Park Row and Mail street (the latter the shortest street in the city).

1. Site of ancient burying ground for negroes, paupers and criminals and for American patriots under British rule during the Revolution. 2. New Hall of Records. 3. Site of barrier gate and block-house in angle of second City Wall of palisades erected in 1746 (Marschalk's survey, 1755). 4. Large broken outline, 480 by 215 feet, plan of proposed new County Court-house. 5. Small broken outline, plan of second almshouse, 1797–1867; also site of Upper Barracks of larger extent 420 by 21 feet, 1757–1790. There were additional Barracks between sites 5 and 16 during the Revolution. 6. Solid outline, present County Court-house, begun 1861. 7. Present City Court-house, erected 1862. 8. Site of Rotunda, 1818–1870. 9. Site of dispensary and soup-house, 1817 and later; also of fire engine house, removed 1906. 10. New Municipal Building in course of erection. 11. Site of temporary fire engine house built 1859. 12. Subway kiosks. 13. Approximate site of old State Arsenal; later, Free School No. 1, circa 1809. 14. Fortifications built by Americans in 1776 (Hills' survey, 1782–5). 15. Postal Telegraph Building, 253 Broadway, site of Montagnie's Tavern, headquarters of Sons of Liberty, 1770 and earlier. 16. Plan of Bridewell, 1775–1838 (Mangin's survey, 1804); a Revolutionary prison. 17. City Hall, begun 1803; site of first Almshouse, 1736–1797. 18. Site of Gaol, the "Martyrs' Prison" of the Revolution. 19. Site of later Hall of Records, 1757–1903 (Mangin's survey). 19. Site of Powder Magazine (Marschalk's survey, 1755, and Montresor's survey, 1775). 20. New York World Building. 21. Nathan Hale Statue. 22. Approximate site of first building on the Common, early 18th century. 23. Fountain, built 1871. 24. Statue of Benjamin Franklin in Printing House Square. 25. New York Sun Building, built 1811, first permanent Tammany Hall. 26. Approximate site of grave of Jacob Leisler as located on Grim's recollection map, but may have been a little farther north. 27. New York Tribune Building; statue of Horace Greeley in vestibule. 28. American Tract Society Building; site of Martling's Tavern; rendezvous of Sons of Liberty and "Martling's Men"; Wigwam of Tammany Society, 1798. 29. Building formerly occupied by New York Times. 30. Site of Brick Presbyterian Church built 1768. 31. Site of Croton Water Fountain in what was once part of City Hall Park; triangle is now occupied by United States Post-office and Court-house. 32. Astor house, built 1834–38; site of Drovers' Inn and other early hostelries. 33. Nos. 21, 23, 25 Park Row, site of successive Park Theatres, 1798–1848, frontage of 78 feet on Park Row and 85 feet on Theatre Alley. Part of this site (No. 21 Park Row) is now occupied by the Park Row Building. 34. Saint Paul Building; southern half of this property is site of Spring Garden House. On this property stood Bicker's Tavern, bought by Sons of Liberty after they left Montagnie's and named Hampden Hall. Later site of Scudder's Museum and Barnum's Museum. 35. Saint Paul's Chapel, begun in 1764.

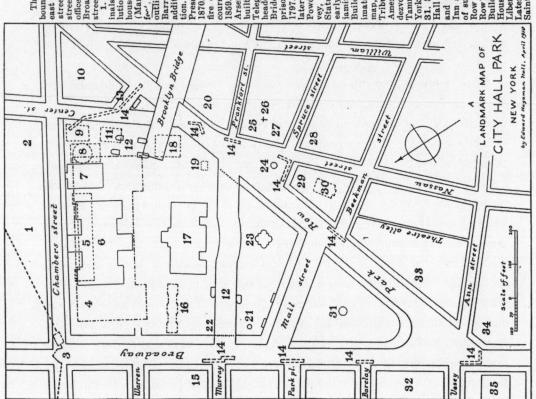

LANDMARK MAP OF CITY HALL PARK NEW YORK

by Edward Hagaman Hall, April 1910

scale of feet

Figure 3.4. Edward Hagaman Hall drew this map based on research for a history of City Hall Park, occasioned by threats to the park and published in the 1910 Annual Report of the American Scenic and Historic Preservation Society. He accurately documented the evolution of the park, squaring extant features with threatened and disappeared historical features. This rich base of information is identical to those created by preservation practitioners today. Courtesy of University of Pennsylvania Libraries.

town, to the north spread hills, wetlands, and the Collect Pond. One side of the Commons was marked by the road to Albany (Broadway) and the other side by the Boston road (Park Row). This marginal location hosted land uses of the economic and social margins: public space for pasturage, water supply, almshouses, prisons, gallows, "Negro burial ground" and Little Africa,[9] fortifications, a powder magazine (very dangerous in a town of wooden buildings), and more noisome industries such as tanneries. These land uses were marginal yet essential functions of the public sphere.

From the late seventeenth century onward, a separation between the built-up northern half of the Commons (north of the City Hall site) and the open southern half emerged. Echoes of this pattern remain today. Functionally, "the site visibly linked defense, charity, and control of crime, the major state functions in the eighteenth century."[10] By the end of the colonial period, the northern reaches of the Commons (north of Chambers Street) had been leveled, divided, and developed as private land, while the central and southern parts were evolving into a park, if not yet the "pleasure ground" to come in the 1820s through 1840s.[11]

The Commons was the setting for a number of Revolutionary War events, which lent this ground a great emotional appeal to turn-of-the-century preservationists. Liberty poles were erected in the 1770s to protest colonial rule (an "emblem of liberty" to preservationists, who re-created them in situ),[12] effigies of colonial officials were burned, and the first public reading of the Declaration of Independence to the assembled American troops took place here in July 1776, with Washington himself present. (To Hall, this was a "historic event which alone should have dedicated [the park] forever to the cause of liberty in the hearts of the citizens of New York.") The capture, imprisonment, and execution of Nathan Hale was supposed to have happened around the Commons, and the death of some of the four thousand other captured Americans in the Martyrs' Prison (Old Gaol) under post-1776 British occupation sanctified the ground.[13] Other events associated with the Commons included public protests against the Stamp Act in 1765–66 (including a protest of tradesmen and mechanics, and a drunken feast celebrating its repeal in 1766), Alexander Hamilton's first public speech (as a King's College student) at a mass protest of the Boston Port Bill,[14] and the camp of the American troops in 1776, including Hamilton and his artillery company, for their relatively short sojourn before British occupation.

By the time of the Revolution, the town had grown northward from the Battery to about Chambers Street, and as the town grew around and past the Commons— and became a significant port city of the newly independent country—the land uses and buildings of the area became more formal, more proper, and more developed. The town's growth and growing pretensions were reflected in the formalization of the Commons into City Hall Park. The Commons had already been the place of military parades, celebrations, and protests, stretching back to the colonial era, but in the postindependence era it became the new center of the growing town as well as "park," with all the convivial, positive social qualities implied by this new name.

The scene around the turn of the nineteenth century must have made for a strange congeries of people and uses—gentlemen and ladies promenading not far from the prisons and almshouses.[15] Stokes noted a "scheme proposed for beautifying" the Commons as early as 1785, and a plan to make inmates of Bridewell prison spread grass seed. Hall cites a 1784 letter—attributed to John de Crevecoeur—proposing that "the Fields" be made into a proper public park, called "Washington's Mall," and fitted out with public walks, fountains with wholesome water, and an obelisk bearing an "inscription the public might think proper."[16] The transformation from Commons to City Hall Park meant that "houses of ill fame"—all traces of undesirability—had to be cleared from the Commons.[17]

Large public assemblies and "stirring patriotic events" were again held in the park on the eve of the War of 1812, and later when the city was threatened with attack. Public figures renowned for Revolutionary War and Sons of Liberty exploits—Henry Rutgers and Marinus Willett, for example, war hero and mayors of New York—exhorted the crowds. Even early in the nineteenth century—decades before the preservation movement gelled—city leaders invoked the heady mix of memory and patriotism rooted in this place to stir civic feeling.

City Hall Park

The crowning moment of City Hall Park came in 1803, when the cornerstone of the grand new City Hall was laid, making this the official civic space of New York. (The city government had previously been housed at Federal Hall on Wall Street.) Through design and planning efforts both haphazard and intentional, the new park came into focus as a place of civic power, grandeur, and gentility. The park's new character did not, however, crowd out the utilitarian buildings and uses of the old Commons, which long remained cheek by jowl with the refinements of the new park.

Designed by John McComb, New York's foremost architect at the time, in partnership with Frenchman Joseph Mangin,[18] the neoclassical edifice of City Hall marked the northern edge of development in the decades following the Revolution. Its front entrance facing south, toward the historic center of the city,

City Hall was magnificently turned out in marble (on three sides, with brownstone on the north side, which faced the almshouse). The building featured a grand dome and rotunda, surmounted by a tall cupola with superb views of the city. It housed most, if not all, civic functions, from the mayor's office and those of other officials, the chambers of the city's legislative bodies, and the courts. It also held an office for the state governor. The fine architecture expressed civic pride and confidence in the commercial future of the city. Nearly a century after it was built, architecture critic Montgomery Schuyler called City Hall a triumph of civic classicism.[19]

Most older buildings around City Hall remained in use; only the first almshouse was demolished, as it occupied part of City Hall's site. The stature of City Hall as the town's foremost political and visual landmark grew in succeeding decades as commercial activity and wealth grew quickly, prompting intense shifts in the city's social geography. Amid these shifts, City Hall and its park functioned as a reference point—a landmark in the most basic sense—a public space whose public architecture and openness provided continuity. But the park was by no means unchanging over the next decades. In addition to the litany of buildings erected and demolished, changes in land and building use, and park improvements, there were also shifts in the social character of the park, which at various times served as a stage for the elite's gregarious social displays and promenading and for the workingman's Sunday retreat for somewhat rowdier amusements.[20]

The shifting social geography of downtown constituted the improving park as well: The residences of the wealthiest citizens, the best hotels (including Astor's, just across from the park), and the most fashionable shops (A. T. Stewart's marble palace, the first department store, just across Chambers Street) gathered around the boundaries of the park.[21] A city of such wealth and aspiration, its leading citizens felt, needed a correspondingly fine pleasure ground.

City Hall Park was formalized in the early nineteenth century by redesigning the park as a public space and segregating it from its surroundings: planting trees and lawns, paving paths, installing lamps and benches, and building fences (wooden, followed by fancier iron fences) to visually mark the boundaries of public space. In 1807, a British traveler described the park as "planted with elms, planes, willows and catalpas; and the surrounding foot-walk is encompassed by rows of poplars: the whole is enclosed by a wooden paling."[22] Spatially defining the park was important to defending its civic status among the commercial bustle of downtown. Without defining the sanctity and the boundaries of the park, protests over "encroachments" and "intrusions" would have had little force. City Hall was opened in 1811, and by the end of the 1820s, the place had became known, simply, as "the Park."[23] McComb designed an iron fence with neoclassical marble piers and topped with lamps for the southern end of the park in 1820–21, matching the civilized neoclassicism of City Hall.[24]

"During the period between the War of 1812–15 and the Civil War, City Hall Park was the focus of almost every festive demonstration of a public character that occurred in the city"—Independence Day celebrations, Lafayette's reception in 1824, celebrations for the opening of the Erie Canal in 1825 and for the laying of the transatlantic cable in 1857 (fireworks from this celebration started a fire in the City Hall cupola). These and other events—as well as its site and symbolic architecture—"marked City Hall Park as the civic center of the city."[25]

Also in the 1830s, the Revolutionary-era Bridewell prison, located adjacent to City Hall, was demolished (some of its stone was used to build its replacement further uptown, the Tombs), marking the further development of the park as a more specialized, "monoculture" space with fewer buildings and City Hall as its unchallenged center. This ideal—of the park as the setting of City Hall rather than a multifunctional place—became the flashpoint of preservation debates at the end of the nineteenth century.

The Croton Fountain, dedicated in 1842, commemorated the inauguration of the Croton water system, a civic achievement of vast symbolic weight. The infrastructure memorialized by the fountain transformed everyday life for many, protecting the city against disease as well as fire. The system, stretching far beyond the city into the northern hinterlands, was enormously important to the city's growth. The location of the fountain, at the southern end of the park, was a place of pride—the foreground of widely circulated views of the park ideal. A hundred-foot-wide basin featured the tall fountain sprays and was surrounded by the gravel paths and trees marking the park as a genteel and civilized domain. A grand celebration, parade, and nighttime illumination marked the arrival of Croton water in October 1842. Hall wrote of the fountain and this era as the apogee of the park's beauty and civic excellence.

Other buildings were added to the northern end of the park before 1850. The Rotunda, a circular building erected in 1818, was used as an art gallery and for the display of panoramas, a popular art form and spectacle. It later housed a post office and other public offices, including that of the Croton Aqueduct commissioners. The growing needs of the city government were reflected in the decision to build a new city courthouse in 1851. The structure was built next to the Rotunda, on the south side of Chambers Street, and opened in 1852. (It was demolished in 1928.)

From 1810 onward, the two ideals of the park—historically, as the site of a

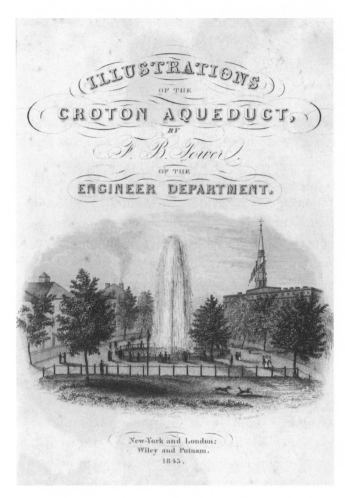

Figure 3.5. The introduction to the city of water from the new Croton aqueduct system in the early 1840s was a public work attended by great civic pride. A fountain celebrating and memorializing this feat was placed in the spot of greatest prominence and respect: the triangle at the southern end of City Hall Park. Courtesy of Library of Congress, Prints and Photographs Division, Historic American Buildings Survey.

number of public uses, and more recently, as the formal setting of municipal government—competed to define the place. In seesaw fashion, official efforts to make a more refined City Hall Park were counterpoised with New Yorkers' active use of the park for their own reasons. In the 1840s and '50s, the balance tipped toward the degradation of the park. The wealthy had moved uptown, to escape the bustle, noise, and congestion of the business district, leaving City Hall Park without its most refined social visitors. The whole area around the park became seriously congested with traffic. The lower end of the park, which had been kept clear of the varied buildings jammed into the area north of City Hall, was thick with maturing trees, park furniture, kiosks, the Croton Fountain, and people, while horse-drawn streetcars, delivery carts, and a crush of people jammed the surrounding streets. Newspapers complained of the "mutilation" of the park; a corrupt city administration even sold off the marble piers of the park fence. During the Civil War, the park was given over to utilitarian purposes, housing barracks, recruiting tents, and a hospital.[26]

Post Civil War

The 1860s and 1870s were seen as the time of the park's degradation. To turn-of-the-century reformers, the post–Civil War era was a dark age of civic life: The city struggled against the Tammany political machine, the tensions surrounding the war itself, chaotic urban growth, and immigration until the rise of more-effective civic improvement movements by the end of the century.[27] The crowding of the park continued through the war and its aftermath. Downtown congestion and traffic made increasing claims on the park and its surrounding streets. Some of the first skyscrapers were built along Park Row for newspaper companies (later to be eclipsed by early-twentieth-century architectural landmarks such as the Woolworth Building and the Municipal Building). In the 1860s and '70s, the Tweed Courthouse and Post Office changed the character and use of the park dramatically. These two large buildings became the hotly contested "encumbrances" debated by future generations—because they crowded historic City Hall and because they embodied political meanings opposite to those advanced by Progressive reformers.

Constructed between 1858 and 1878, the Tweed Courthouse (officially the New York County Courthouse) was placed between the north side of City Hall and Chambers Street.[28] The city's "second almshouse" was taken down in 1857 to make way for it.[29] This "monumental piece of extravagance"[30] is an imposing neo-classical building ostensibly meant to provide sorely needed government space. What made it famous was the scandal and political corruption associated with its construction. Commissioned by the Tammany Hall administration of Boss Tweed, the courthouse represented the worst excesses of Democratic machine politics in the eyes of good-government reformers. Left incomplete (though usable) after an estimated $16 million had been spent on its construction, the Tweed Courthouse was an expensive, controversial monument to the dominant political faction of late-nineteenth-century New York and therefore a negative symbol to Progressive reformers. A *New York Times* editorial called it "a monument to the malice, ignorance, and greed of its era."[31] The Tweed Courthouse embodied corruption:

> The new Courthouse, in City Hall Park . . . illustrates in all its parts, from
> the foundation-stone upward, the various stages in the rise, progress, and
> prosperous career of the paternal ruler whom the World calls a fraudulent

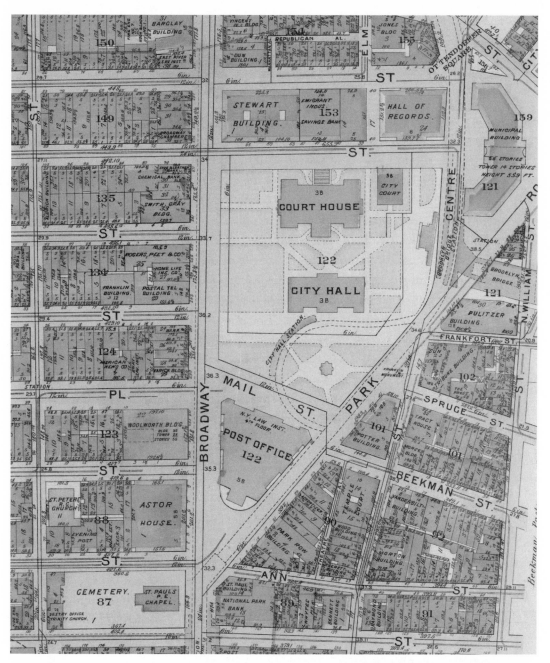

Figure 3.6. This 1911 Bromley map (a common type of real estate map) of Lower Manhattan conveys the dense commercial and residential development that had surrounded City Hall Park by the early twentieth century. Apart from Broadway, Park Row, St. Paul's Chapel, and City Hall Park, little remained of colonial or early federal New York. Courtesy of the Lionel Pincus and Princess Firyal Map Division, the New York Public Library, Aster, Lenox, and Tilden Foundations.

bankrupt. It was there that the "Boss" laid the foundation of his fortunes, both pecuniary and political. . . . Let the new Court-house, then, be adopted by popular acclamation as the fit and appropriate monument to the Boss.[32]

Though William Marcy Tweed himself died in 1875, he formed such an archetype of corrupt politician that his name was invoked for decades.

The Tweed Courthouse further crowded the already built-up north end of the park. Its architectural qualities and age value were beside the point.[33] The courthouse was a perfect expression of the Tammany hegemony in political culture, against which the Progressive reformers were specifically organized. The result, to reformers, was that City Hall Park no longer performed its proper symbolic function as long as this monument to Tweed overshadowed City Hall. Proposals for the destruction of the Tweed Courthouse appeared as early as the 1890s.

The Post Office, added to the southern tip of the park in the 1860s, provoked even more controversy than the Tweed Courthouse. Alfred B. Mullett's second-empire Post Office was "the crowning disaster" of City Hall Park's degradation as a civic space in the post–Civil War era.[34] Consuming more than half the open, lower part of the park, its mass completely blocked views of the front of City Hall, and the beloved Croton Fountain had to be removed to make way for it. These affronts to the civic symbolism of City Hall and its park were compounded by the fact that the Post Office's new Mail Street loading dock—the back of the building—faced the front of City Hall!

The saga of the Post Office began in 1857, when the Board of Aldermen—dominated by Tammany pols—approved the sale of this portion of park land to the federal government. Filling municipal coffers with $500,000, the transaction touched off protest. But the land sale was a fait accompli; the intervening Civil War delayed ground breaking until 1869. The edifice completely blocked views of City Hall from the south and added greatly to the feeling of congestion at this already crowded intersection of Broadway and Park Row. A new fountain, designed by Jacob Wrey Mould, was placed south of City Hall, replacing the Croton Fountain. Comfort stations and commercial kiosks and new paths and benches were also added to the newly constricted spaces of the park.[35]

The Post Office was another monument to corrupt machine politics—along with the Tweed Courthouse, perfectly bracketing City Hall! The politics and symbolism of the land sale and the placement of the building itself could not have been more contrary to Progressive politics or to the three-dimensional civic ideal preservationists, planners, and civic reformers were trying to cultivate in the first two decades of the twentieth century: a relatively open park in which City Hall would be couched as the city's greatest adornment. Reformers all agreed on calls to demolish the Post Office—though for a variety of reasons, including urban design, the creation of recreational space, architectural style, and the degradation of the civic and patriotic narratives of City Hall Park.[36] Until it was actually pulled down on Robert Moses's watch in 1939, the Post Office was the subject of a constant refrain of reform-backed iconoclasm: It was mentioned regularly in ASHPS reports and newspaper articles; typically, a 1927 *New York Times* editorial was headlined, "Is City Hall Park Ever to Be Freed of the Encumbrance of the Old Post Office?"[37]

For good-government reformers, looking backward from 1900, the Tweed Courthouse and the Post Office signaled the downfall of the park. Other projects, generally praised by reformers, also threatened the park. The construction of the Brooklyn Bridge had an immense impact on City Hall Park. The Manhattan side of the iconic bridge, which opened in 1883, emptied directly into the northeastern corner of City Hall Park, and the streetcar and pedestrian traffic obviously required some new facilities. Terminal structures occupied park space, spanning Park Row just north of City Hall. Later improvements to the bridge terminal led to demolition of the Martyrs' Prison and shared the eastern corner of the park with subway kiosks representing the *next* generation of transportation infrastructure to inhabit the park.

By the 1880s and '90s, as urban growth, congestion, and political battles intensified, the winds of reform began to blow across this symbolic center of Manhattan. The city's lurch uptown, the downtown redevelopment into a skyscraper district, transportation congestion, and burgeoning municipal government sparked many proposals to rebuild or move this center of city government. The building of the first subway line, opened in 1904, helped cement the centrality of City Hall Park. The IRT line terminated in a station underneath the park, where the tracks, platforms, and Guastavino vaulted ceilings turned in graceful curves and headed back uptown. While it temporarily tore up the park landscape during construction and installed a number of entry kiosks, the subway's greatest impact was in fueling the traffic congestion centered on the park—tens of thousands of New Yorkers daily commuted, worked, strolled, or otherwise moved through the park because it was such an important node in mass transit.

In the last decades of the nineteenth century, City Hall Park had become a very complex, crowded place. Space demands for transportation infrastructure, government offices, and park space—added to the tense political symbolism of every action and proposal—made the park a punching bag of urban politics. Issues of urban design, historic preservation, traffic congestion, the size of municipal government, fiscal responsibility in public works, and the sanctity and preservation of parks and open space all came to bear on this most visible civic space.

Shaping City Hall Park

Making It "Historic"

Michele Bogart has described 1875 to 1935 as a period of "memory, conflict and reclamation" for City Hall Park, a time when matters of historical memory took center stage.[38] By the turn of the century, City Hall had become not only crowded but "old," and even "historic," signaling a new dimension of public space and civic consciousness needing to be factored into the equations for managing the park into the next century. The historic and architectural values of City Hall, lauded on all political sides, made preservation and restoration of City Hall the centerpiece of most proposals (and certainly of the most successful ones). City Hall was indeed preserved—it remains part of the city's extensive architectural and historic legacy today—and the significance of City Hall and City Hall Park as places of historic (and scenic) value shaped the complicated debates about redesigning a new "civic center." The contentious story of the park in this era featured many building and rebuilding proposals—often revolving as much around moving, replacing, or expanding City Hall itself as around the urban design of the whole civic center precinct.

Andrew Haswell Green was among the first to proclaim the historic values of City Hall Park publicly. In 1894, responding to the proposed removal of City Hall to Bryant Park, Green threw his considerable public and political influence behind the preservation of City Hall and its historical memory: Green argued that the construction of City Hall, as a historical achievement for the city, state, and nation, was on par with that of the Erie Canal, the 1811 grid plan of Manhattan, and even Thomas Jefferson's national coast survey (all of them visionary works of planning and infrastructure). The building and its park were inseparable: "It [City Hall], and the ground upon which it stands, are memorable" as witnesses to the bravery and vision of the founding fathers, the events leading to the Revolution (from Hamilton's speech consecrating the liberty pole to the first reading of the Declaration of Independence to the American troops "in the presence of Washington"), the receptions of Lafayette and Andrew Jackson, and, more vaguely, "imposing displays" for four generations of New Yorkers. Green's argument went beyond antiquarian and associational interest in City Hall and the narratives attached to it; his unique contribution was insisting on the in situ preservation of the building in its park: "The Building [City Hall] is indissolubly connected with its site and surroundings. Remove it and interest in it vanishes."[39]

City Hall was celebrated not simply as a historic place but as *the* most historic place in the city. "No spot in New York contains such a wealth of historic material as City Hall Park and its vicinity," wrote John D. Crimmins in 1910.[40] And ASHPS president George Kunz, writing a Sunday feature for the *New York Times* in 1911, used City Hall as the lens through which to appreciate the city's history. In his role as chair of the City Hall Celebration Committee, marking the one-hundredth anniversary of the building's completion, Kunz penned "New York 100 Years Ago, When City Hall Was Built."[41]

In the next several pages, Kunz surveyed many of the changes (and proposals for further change) to the park, ranging from ideas about the shape of the whole civic center district, to preservation efforts focused on particular buildings within the park, to consideration of specific memorials and monuments erected therein. When overlaid to make up a history of this place over the few decades surrounding 1900, these changes demonstrated how issues of historical memory took center stage in the urbanism of this period.

As Edward Hall's detailed 1910 mapping and narrative show, dozens of structures had existed in the park over the centuries.[42] Each had its own particular history, and several had historic value and were the subject of preservation activity. But the whole collection of buildings was greater than the sum of its parts. It was the whole ensemble—park spaces, buildings, and monuments, the whole concept of "the Commons" and then "the park"—that placed City Hall Park at the center of the memory infrastructure. This, at least, was the view presented by historic preservationists.[43]

Proposals for Improvement

By the end of the nineteenth century, there was broad consensus that City Hall Park needed to be modernized, improved, cleaned up, and embellished. Reinforcing its role in the historical geography of Manhattan would ensure that it remained the center of greater New York. The park was crowded; skyscrapers, street vendors, and transit structures crowded the park; the ballooning city and state governments needed more space for offices and courts. The government of the new metropolis—the emergent capital of capitalism—warranted a correspondingly grand and arrogant civic center.

City Beautiful ideas for creating a civic center were a dominant theme, but they were challenged by preservationists. This would not be a tabula rasa project. Too many existing conditions and political realities of the site intervened: The historic and scenic qualities of City Hall Park were too dear to be erased; the vested interests of real estate and political stakeholders were too avariciously held to give urban designers wide latitude; New York politics were sufficiently fragmented and volatile that no grand proposal ever garnered enough support. The real question became how some coherent civic center functions could be conjured out of the confusion and richness of the park. Tracing the different ideas for how to achieve these political and urbanistic goals will help reveal the centrality of the commemorative function alongside the other demands made on City Hall Park space and preservationists' varied strategies for conjuring historical memory out of bricks and mortar, granite and bronze, trees and fences, stories and images.

Turning the park into such a place presented both political and architectural problems—and opportunities. Most advocates recognized the need to retain the public-space, "commons" function of the park, and even to build some commemorative, symbolic functions into the reimagined civic center. Urban politics and efforts to reform city government form a key backdrop to the changes in the park. Struggles to install a new, Progressive politics translated into an expansive government, one in need of new, powerful symbols to sustain its messages of self-sacrifice, disinterest, and public interest. Public opinion was divided, and political control of City Hall seesawed back and forth between Tammany-supported and reform-driven alliances.[44] Not only did political considerations shape the possibilities for approving projects and getting them funding, but patronage and political ideology also shaped the content of historical memory that preservationists wished to represent in the City Hall Park landscape.

The clearest political fault line—Progressive reform challenges to the Democratic machines—were expressed in the struggles over the Tweed Courthouse, the Post Office, and the new Hall of Records. In 1903, Herbert Croly lamented New Yorkers' poor stewardship of public space and urged preservationists on in their work. Referring to the building of the Tweed Courthouse and the Post Office in formerly "spacious and delightful" City Hall Park, Croly raged:

> What must we say of a city whose oldest and most beautiful public build-
> ing possessed every advantage of location and environment, and which
> then wantonly threw these advantages away? This incident is unfortu-
> nately typical of the time-honored attitude of New York toward all the

proprieties of its public appearance. The city has no public squares which, either because of the sacredness of their associations or the excellence of their encircling buildings, have aroused in the minds of its inhabitants any feelings of pride and affection.

Croly went on to blast Tammany for its greed and selfishness—and reformers for their lack of cohesion and their failure to sustain success in beating back Tammany.[45] This was the challenge preservationists and reformers took on.

The various functions of City Hall Park need to be understood in terms of the city's changing geography. Broadly, two geographic processes were operating: (1) stratification of spaces according to function and in increasingly fine granularity (producing smaller, more bounded, unifunctional, socially stratified spaces and forms); (2) integration of these specialized spaces as components of whole districts—that is, the newly conceived "civic center."[46] The new urban geography was marked by a growing number of increasingly distinct functional spaces and systems (infrastructures) as well as by new institutions, practices, and discourses (such as those associated with historic preservation, city planning, transit systems, and good-government reform). The first of these forces was an ineluctable process of capitalist urbanization; the second was a contest between different urbanistic practices just beginning to distinguish themselves from one another.

The controversial proposals for the park in the four decades around the turn of the twentieth century included both gross and subtle reconfigurations of City Hall Park's character and function. The most notable of these controversial proposals included the location of new courthouse and municipal office buildings, the demolition of older buildings adjacent to old City Hall, the new Brooklyn Bridge terminal (but, surprisingly, not the subway station), and Frederick MacMonnies's status *Civic Virtue,* in a fountain directly in front of City Hall.[47] Reform groups (including preservation organizations) took a leading role in nearly every debate over the park, pressuring, cajoling, protesting, or encouraging agencies of the local and state governments to act in the public interest, as called for in Progressivism.[48] Different visions and strategies developed *within* the reform community. Though they focused on different aspects of the City Hall Park environment—its material forms, social uses, meanings—taken together, the different approaches formed a common basis for reforming City Hall Park. In every case, the park's built environment was shaped by what Michele Bogart calls "the intensified role that memory played in the process" of urban change.[49]

There were three distinct strategies of environmental reform:

- The *design-driven* strategy, that of the American City Beautiful movement, focused on decorative, aesthetic means and control over the urban plan to represent governmental power and authority in architectural
  forms. Derived from European, neoclassical architectural language, it
  was exemplified in plans for Chicago and Washington, D.C.
- The *memory-based and site-specific* strategy, the primary one of preservationists, was achieved through material conservation and interpretation of old buildings, the creation of memorials, and the preservation
  of open space. Decisions about which parts of the environment would
  change and which would be conserved were based on the historical narratives associated with particular sites.
- The *functionalist* strategy, providing for utilitarian needs such as mass
  transit, government office space, park space, and an overall framework
  of economic growth and efficiency, constituted the basic strategy of city
  planning.

These approaches to reforming City Hall Park were not mutually exclusive.
Indeed, there was a great deal of complementarity among them. There was little
or no disagreement on the need for a multifunctional civic center that would accommodate some ceremonial and social functions. Likewise, all reformers and officials agreed on the need for growth, improvement, and rational planning of the
whole metropolis.[50] The gist of the debate was not over which conception would
win out over the others, but over how the three would be merged, combined, accommodated, and negotiated.

Because of its symbolic importance, efforts to reshape City Hall Park were
particularly intense. The tugs-of-war over City Hall Park were of great interest to
the public. Reform organizations devoted a significant share of their publications
and meetings to civic center and other City Hall Park issues. Not surprisingly, this
generated voluminous newspaper coverage—not only because partisan politics
were being played out or significant public policy issues were at stake (use of public
money, representational issues of what the city was "about"), but also because the
newspapers, keenly interested in exploiting political wranglings of any kind, were
especially interested in their own front yard—many newspapers were headquartered on Park Row across the street from the park, where City Hall was ground
zero for the metropolitan news beat.

The proposals and changes discussed below include efforts to create an ideal
civic center, to prevent encroachments on the historic open spaces making up the
park, to preserve or destroy specific buildings within the park, to restore City Hall

itself, and to place monuments and memorials in the park. The common denominator of all these proposals was the feeling that the purest, most powerful, most effective message of civic patriotism would stem from a landscape in which City Hall stood isolated in its historic park, restored to its original (mythic) dimensions and cleared of other buildings.

CIVIC CENTER VISIONS

Creation of a civic center was the framing question for many of the debates and discussions regarding the redevelopment, redesign, and memorialization of City Hall Park. Civic-center ideals occupied the center of the American city-planning and urban-reform movements. The civic center required wholesale invention or reinvention of downtowns to create ideal government centers, rather than incrementally shifting and evolving existing cities to a state of design more in keeping with urban politics. Without a proper civic center, it was felt, New York would fail to fulfill its promise as a leading American and world city.[51] Municipal Art Society leader John DeWitt Warner wrote in 1902 about "the urgent need, from a practical as well as aesthetic standpoint, of dignified, effective, and convenient Civic Centres for our great cities . . . and the overwhelming educational advantage that would thus be secured."[52] Like historic preservationists, City Beautiful advocates sought to create places that would embody and transmit their urbanistic ideals.

Civic centers were the stock-in-trade of the City Beautiful movement, which pulled the design idea of a highly ordered, neoclassical grouping of public buildings from the imperial capitals of Europe. There were many ideas behind City Beautiful schemes — functional, aesthetic, and political — but none more overriding than the desire to express in architectural and urban form an ideal vision of the city as beautiful, orderly, useful, meaningful, and well managed.[53] The City Beautiful movement also stemmed from the village-improvement movement in the United States and its concerns with small-scale aesthetic interventions driven by a more subtle reform ideology.[54] Both these sources of City Beautiful plans drew strength and purpose from environmental determinism. A seamless connection was imagined between the design of clean new environments and the reinvention and reform of the political and social life of American cities.

Apart from a shared root in environmental determinism, historic preservation and City Beautiful strategies sometimes diverged. City Beautiful ideology included representation of historical narratives in the public space of the civic centers — using figural sculpture, often allegorical and having little to do with the site-specific narratives preservationists drew upon. In their architectural decoration and urban design, civic centers invoked the history of European cities. Civic centers were seen to compensate for the lack of a history in American cities and also invoked the idea that the public square of any village or town was bound up with the history and notable achievements of that place.[55] Preservationists and planners alike agreed that New York City sorely needed a multifunctional civic center, and they passionately worked to fuse City Beautiful and historic preservation visions for City Hall Park.

A number of civic center proposals were ventured for New York. None of them were wholly realized. Henry Hornbostel, with George B. Post as consulting architect, drew a plan for a new civic center around City Hall in 1903, at the behest of the bridge commissioner, Gustav Lindenthal (who controlled land east of City Hall Park around the Brooklyn Bridge approaches).[56] This plan shared many characteristics with the numbers of other City Beautiful schemes published in architectural journals, newspapers, and pamphlets. The park was to be emptied out, clearing accumulated patterns and establishing visual order around the park, the center of which would be old City Hall set in an open green space. Surrounding the park, a series of matched, neoclassical, symmetrically placed midrise buildings would accompany some tower element. The tower, unmistakably, was the symbol of modern government, while City Hall and the neoclassical setting legitimated the whole place as a symbol of authority and refinement by linking it to the past (of the city itself, and of European capitals).

Explanations of this plan drew favorable comparisons to European cities; the design references to Italy, in this case, are unmistakable — the office tower is a 650-foot "campanile," and the whole scene resembles a sketch of some iconic Italian piazza. The city "square," cleared of buildings except for old City Hall (to be used as the mayor's office and "for museum purposes"), was embellished by, not dwarfed by, skyscrapers — a meaningful statement in the context of the haphazard skyscraper development then characterizing downtown. Like the skyscrapers, subway and bridge transit stations are sublimated to the whole scene; one can barely discern where they would be, and the absence of people or traffic from the scene "hides" the sources of congestion.

Hornbostel and Post wrapped a series of buildings around the east side of the park as well, including court and municipal office buildings plus a multimodal passenger terminal at the base of the Brooklyn Bridge to solve the "bridge crush." This ambitious, expensive ($50 million) plan gained much support but was dashed by the 1904 mayoral election, in which Tammany candidate George McClellan replaced reformer Seth Low.

In Hornbostel and Post's plan, City Hall is treated as a jewel in a jewel box — a solution amenable to preservationists, who routinely sought a green verge sur-

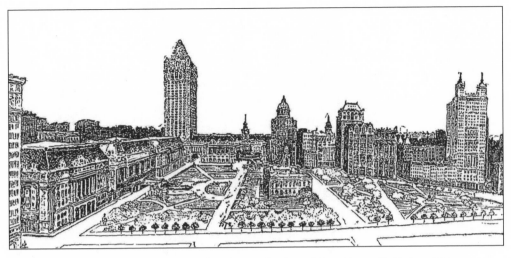

Figure 3.7. This proposal drawing, taken from a plan by architects George B. Post and Henry Hornbostel published in the New York Times *in 1903, looks east at City Hall in a cleared-out park. Courtesy of ProQuest, LLC/New York Times.*

rounding buildings of great significance. In other civic center schemes, though, City Hall is transformed, added to, or rebuilt as a skyscraper. Architect, reformer, and preservationist Charles Rollinson Lamb's bold proposal (undated, but probably from 1900–1910) renders an enormous skyscraper complex spanning Chambers Street while dwarfing old City Hall. The scheme imposes a clumsy symmetry to the new buildings and decorates the asymmetrical park with a profusion of symmetrically placed monuments, arches, and obelisks. As a dedicated preservationist, Lamb's plan would eliminate the Tweed Courthouse (replacing it with a complex of neoclassical buildings, including a hulking municipal office skyscraper, flanking pavilions modeled on the new Hall of Records, and matching sets of triumphal arches and obelisks) and remove the Post Office (replacing it with a reconstruction of the old 1842 Croton Fountain).

As sweeping as these schemes were, elements of such civic center plans were partly realized in the early twentieth century. Fragments of the City Beautiful vision were achieved: The new Hall of Records was the archetypal liner building that should have been repeated around the park, the Municipal Building was the skyscraper form (a true tall office building, not a campanile), and City Hall was restored in its park setting—though without the hoped-for openness.

Preservationists were less interested in what kind of buildings would surround the park, focusing instead on protecting City Hall and clearing the Tweed and Post Office buildings out of the park itself to create an "open" context. City Hall

Figure 3.8. Charles Rollinson Lamb proposed this treatment of City Hall Park (probably 1900–1910). Balancing beauty and utility, new architecture and preserved landscape, the centerpiece of his scheme (and most others) was a restored City Hall. Courtesy of Avery Architectural and Fine Arts Library, Columbia University in the City of New York.

preserved in a park setting was always the centerpiece of civic center plans, but its preservation was treated as an assumption rather than a real focus of energy, investment, and rhetoric. Preservationists paid a great deal more attention to City Hall itself, and their work on the building is detailed below.

City Beautiful advocates had specific ideas for new buildings to elevate the meaning and appearance of the place and to provide contrast and counterpoint to the chaotic commercial landscape. Their neoclassical midrise buildings arrayed symmetrically around the park—often set off by a single tall building—were responses to the commercial culture embodied in the changeful, visually chaotic downtown landscape. While skyscraper office buildings represented the ascendance of commerce, low-rise Beaux-Arts structures signified the dignity and power of government. Architecturally, skyscrapers crept into civic center plans to meet space needs as well as to make a statement in the architectural culture of downtown; the early newspaper buildings along Park Row were followed by a litany of skyscrapers, including, by 1911, the Woolworth Building. The Municipal Building, commissioned from McKim, Mead, and White in 1908 after four competitions stretching back to 1888, was under construction by 1909 and completed in 1914. The Beaux-Arts, skyscraping public office building was a fusion of architectural cultures.

Architects' proposals—whether offered by preservation-minded designers or not—tended to include tall buildings as an element of New York civic center plans. The Municipal Building—a civic skyscraper—was the realization of this idea. Looming over the park, it provided a great deal of office space, extended the civic center northeastward to continue the slum clearances there, and also served as a sort of memory site (through its neoclassical style as well as through the statue of *Civic Fame,* topping the building and representing the consolidation of the five boroughs in 1898). The skyscrapers around the park did not threaten the historic landscape so much as change the context for any redesign of the park.

Much has been written about the emergence of the skyscraper city.[57] Germane to City Hall Park was the relation of new, corporate infrastructure (skyscrapers and other office buildings) to the other parts of the burgeoning, functionally and spatially segregated metropolis. Many proposals called for a skyscraper in or next to the park to solve the government office space problem. Vertical and horizontal visions of the civic center were synthesized in McKim, Mead, and White's Municipal Building, completed in 1914. Many non-professional-reformer observers in this era saw the building of skyscrapers as the signal moment in the city's ascendance. Preservationists' general lack of attention to (or embrace of) skyscrapers also conforms to Daniel Bluestone's argument that the creation of a horizontal, civic landscape was intended to counterbalance the vertical landscape of the market.[58] Bluestone, for instance, argued that City Beautiful civic centers countered the skyscraping assertions of commercial culture—creating a horizontal, historically anchored landscape testifying to the elevation of civic culture.[59] Indeed, the modernity of the skyscrapers—notwithstanding the historicist details applied to them—highlighted the need for continuity of old buildings and other park elements (statues, plantings). They produced a useful contrast to City Hall's low-rise, historical qualities. They also produced a crowding effect, apparent in historical photographs, that doubtlessly made the removal of the Post Office a more urgent task. Thus, the ten or so tall buildings fronting the park by 1910—soon to be joined by the Woolworth Building—did as much to advance the cause of historic preservation, perhaps, as the avid preservationist arguments detailing the patriotic associations of the park.

It was difficult to form a civic center out of the old park in the midst of so much privately owned and developed land. The ceaseless change driven by the real estate market—at this point untempered by zoning ordinances and fueled by transit development and business expansion—made any kind of intervention a challenge and made it hard to achieve an overarching order. That would take massive, sustained government will and investment, two very rare commodities in the changeful politics of the day. Speculation in the real estate market continued to raise prices very high in the vicinity of City Hall Park, making it increasingly expensive and difficult for the government to purchase sufficient land to make the kind of grand civic center City Beautiful advocates envisioned. As Charles Mulford Robinson observed:

> In New York, where chaste City Hall occupies the centre of a green that has not been . . . protected, dozens of millions of dollars have been expended on structures that edge the square and that shut it in with lofty walls which utterly dwarf the municipal building [City Hall]. The same huge sum of money might have secured a series of structures that would have been civic ornaments.[60]

The Municipal Art Society and other good-government groups offered cost-benefit analyses proving that condemning surrounding land was more cost-effective for the municipal government than continuing to rent offices on the market. But every passing day of government inaction made condemnation more expensive, and no administration could muster the will to act comprehensively.[61] The reality, of course, was the production of greater density, and the emergence of the skyscraper downtown—a process of creative destruction that no administration could resist—demonstrated the ultimate reign of market forces over the shape of downtown.[62]

The new Hall of Records was debated for more than ten years, before finally being completed in 1907. This building was a City Beautiful success and testified to the fact that such schemes depended on far more than individual works of architecture. As far back as the 1880s, the need for more records storage was recognized, the city having outgrown the old Hall of Records located in the northeast corner of the park. Proposals to build a new structure in the park having been defeated, the site on the north side of Chambers Street was chosen. The building had its own civic memory infrastructure—the ambitious program of historical sculpture and murals described in chapter 2. The success of the new Hall of Records resided in advancing the (sometimes conflicting) purposes of both City Beautiful and historic preservation advocates, making a strong aesthetic contribution to the emergent civic center while presenting a rich tableau of memory sites through the sculptural and decorative program.

If City Hall Park was the official center of the city, could not the city government exercise sufficient control to express one ideal vision or another? No. Power to control even the municipally owned landscape was too fragmented and fleeting to realize such an extensive, long-term project. Controversies abounded: How would the civic center be designed, how would it be financed, and how would the

Figure 3.9. In this image of City Hall Park from 1922, one can barely find City Hall. The second-empire Post Office, occupying the southern tip of the park since the 1870s, seems to be lodged between the Woolworth Building (left) and the newspaper headquarters buildings of Park Row. The white cupola of City Hall is barely visible to the left of the Post Office's rear dome. Author's collection.

different meanings of this landscape be balanced? How could the unambiguous City Beautiful and Progressive ideals be created out of a deeply layered, haphazardly developed, ambiguous landscape at the center of the city's swirl of buildings, streets, and political battles? It was no surprise that the civic center ideal—a "dignified, effective, and convenient" landscape—was ultimately too ambitious for

Figure 3.10. The newspaper buildings of Park Row overlook City Hall Park, City Hall, and the Mail Street rear of the Post Office in this commercial postcard from the early twentieth century. From left, the Park Row buildings are the domed World Building, the spired Tribune Building, and the New York Times Building. Author's collection.

New York. No singular vision for City Hall Park was ever realized, let alone one as pure and controlled as the one the McMillan Commission and its consultants had created for the monumental core of Washington, D.C.

PREVENTING ENCROACHMENTS

While competing proposals for creating a new civic center out of City Hall Park were ventured, another constant refrain dominated the debate about the preservation and development of the area: preventing encroachments. Historic preservation often consists of preventing something from happening rather than making something happen. Regarding the park, "the question was not so much where to put [a new municipal building] as where not to put it, and the park should be held sacred."[63] One of the most persistent themes in the struggles over City Hall Park was preservationists' defense of open space, an issue joining scenic and historic preservation.

The motives for preservation were several: the sanctity of the park's historical associations, defense of open space and parks, and fiscal efficiency.[64] Reformers of all stripes rallied against the merged evils of park encroachment, and the nature of their appeals was telling: They tended not to cite any one reason over another—fiscal responsibility, historical value, sanctity of park space—but, rather, each one cited the full range of reasons, whether it was the Bar Association, the City Club, or the ASHPS talking.

Preservationist theory held that City Hall's historical associations would be compromised, even destroyed, by moving the building or crowding it with new structures. Further, commemoration of events that had happened in the Commons would be crippled if the open park setting ceased to exist. A courthouse proposal was resisted because it would "encroach further than heretofore upon land made sacred by venerated traditions of every period of our city's history."[65] Retaining the shape and open, parklike qualities of the land—its integrity, and therefore its sense of duration and continuity—was a condition for preserving its historical memory. And its memorial capacity was threatened by existing encumbrances and proposals to build in the park. Preserving open space around City Hall was thus part of preserving the historical value of the whole place as well as the building itself.

This strong conviction was supported by the second rationale for preserving the park as recreational space. Belief in the salutary influence of green space in the city, a reform axiom traced back to Olmsted and Vaux, at least (the so-called lungs-of-the-city argument), led to the diligent fight to preserve whatever open and natural spaces existed in the dense parts of the city and also to lobbying for the creation of additional parks on the city periphery. Related to this was the belief that parks were a part of the city's material heritage, that these green landscapes (no matter the design: Central Park, the Battery, or City Hall Park) represented the city's distant past (in contrast to the built-up areas representing, to reformers, the chaotic present) and were part of the legacy of civic works that should be passed on to future generations. Parks were seen as essential elements of civic memory because, like some old buildings, they had dear associations with events or simply with the city's antiquity, and also because the preservationist ideology modeled "scenic" and "historic" environments as equally valuable to the task of social reform.

It was often argued that not an inch of the city's park space should be taken for building because of the public health function it served. Andrew Green pointed to the absurdity and wastefulness of spending great sums to put new buildings in existing parks, having already agreed (rightfully) to spend a million dollars on park creation ("Breathing places"), especially in crowded downtown districts (as provided for by the 1887 Small Parks Act).[66]

Ironically, one could have argued that the park's historical significance drew on all the buildings that had been built there over the generations. Because the history of the place was utilitarian — it had housed plenty of uses before and after it became "the park" — there was a long history of proposals to put more uses and buildings in the park. The Bridewell prison, the almshouse, the gallows, and other buildings of the Commons set the stage. Isaac Newton Phelps Stokes's famous compendium of New York history noted a "wild scheme to fill [the park], with buildings, 1833."[67] Other buildings inhabiting the park at one time or another included Civil War barracks, Brooklyn Bridge structures, kiosks, and milk shacks.[68]

The main encroachments were the new buildings proposed for City Hall Park. They included courthouses, office buildings, a new city hall, commercial venues, and transportation structures. The park's central location in the city made it nearly inevitable that transportation construction would cause some disruption. Located at the center of downtown, the center of business, City Hall Park was a logical nexus of the modern transportation systems that ended up reinforcing its centrality — streetcars, elevated trains, the Brooklyn Bridge, and then the subway.

Transportation infrastructure was a potentially enormous disruption in the park; preservationists kept a vigil about such proposals because other parks — especially the Battery — had been greatly harmed by the construction of elevated railway tracks from the 1870s into the twentieth century. As early as 1880, alderman William Sauer protested plans to take park land for the Brooklyn Bridge approaches and structures, which would have involved tearing down the old Hall of Records.[69] "The latest proposal of the Department of Bridges for squatting on City Hall Park with an ugly headhouse omits to take account of the public opposition to the spoliation and disfigurement of the public parks."[70] But Brooklyn Bridge traffic had an urgency that preservation interests could not match. The streetcar traffic on the Brooklyn Bridge created a crush at the base of the bridge next to City Hall Park; an angry mob of fifty thousand people was endangered by stalled streetcars and the ensuing crush on April 24, 1907.[71] Several buildings in the northeast corner of the park were demolished — the Old Gaol/Martyrs' Prison (in 1903), the brownstone courthouse (in 1928), the fire station (in 1906) — to make way for both subway and bridge construction. The iron structure built over Park Row in 1907 to funnel passengers more quickly from the platform into the park was intended as a temporary solution, but it remained until 1945. Many City Beautiful proposals included a new bridge terminal; the need for it eventually dissipated with the opening of the second and third subway lines serving the park. Subways had a much less disruptive impact on the park, even though the first subway line looped under the park. Excavation and construction of the City

Hall Park station of the original IRT line—a magnificent underground curving station—generated protest only because the excavations undermined the old Hall of Records and helped spell its demise.

The more powerful and destructive impulse behind park encroachments was the economics of building on land that was "unbuilt" and already in public owner-ship. It would be cheaper, in present dollar terms, to build in a park (where land-acquisition costs are zero for the government) instead of buying a site on the market. This came up time and again: Debate on a new hall of records, and whether it should be located inside or outside the park, began in 1888. In 1889 a new municipal office building was proposed for the park; public protests led to new siting commissions that alternatively were tasked with locating the new struc-ture anywhere or anywhere outside the park. In 1896, a decision was reached on the eventual site on the north side of Chambers Street. The history of City Hall Park mirrors that of other major parks (for example, Central Park and the Battery, both of which have extensive chronicles of buildings proposed to occupy park space).[72]

The most intense and broad fight over the preservation of City Hall Park cen-tered on efforts to build a new city courthouse. Proposals for a new, modern court-house were first put forward in the late 1880s. Existing courthouses in City Hall Park (the Tweed Courthouse and the old brownstone building at the northeast corner) were crowded wrecks, and the courts needed to expand. The litany of con-troversies, commissions, and plans proposing a new courthouse stretched almost continually from 1890 through 1910. State laws authorizing a new courthouse in Manhattan flip-flopped many times: In 1888, don't build in the park; in 1889, do build in the park; in 1890, after much protest, back to no building in the park; in 1892, another commission was appointed to find a site in the park.[73] And so on. "The action of the Legislature and of the local authorities with reference to the matter [of building new municipal buildings in City Hall Park] has been strangely vacillating and dilatory."[74] The 1893–94 round of proposals to remove City Hall and build a grand new complex of buildings in the park (this was the proposal that inspired Andrew Green to pen his 1894 pamphlet on preserving City Hall)[75] resulted in yet another impasse. In late March 1910, the issue again came to a head when the Court House Board, appointed by Mayor William Gaynor to reach a decision on a building site, decided for financial reasons to build in the park.[76]

All stripes of reformers and politicians agreed that a new courthouse was needed and that it should be much larger than the Tweed Courthouse—probably a skyscraper complex. The practical point of contention was whether it would be built on land the city already owned (City Hall Park), thus reducing the gross present cost, or whether the city should purchase land on which to construct the new building (in most proposals, the site would be north of Chambers Street, either directly north of the Tweed Courthouse or near the eventual site of the courthouse, between Centre Street and Park Row, in what became Foley Square).

As with earlier instances when a decision was taken to build in the park, the 1910 announcement met with immediate and vigorous protests. Architectural, planning, preservation, and political interest groups—those vanguards of Progressive environmental reform—militated to change the decision, working through personal and political channels and through public exposure of the debate in the city's newspapers. They sought to convince the state and city to build around but not in City Hall Park.

The ASHPS weighed in with a lobbying effort resting on seven points of opposition. Its statement of these points (quoted as the epigraph to this chapter) synthesized the array of arguments that had come to define the preservationist position as strongly antiencroachment.[77] The same ASHPS annual report contained Hall's 1910 history, documenting in a careful, deliberate, fifty-page chronology the litany of historical values and narratives that were the core reason offered for preventing encroachments.

The protests against building a new courthouse in the park were sustained by the artistic and historical organizations. The Architectural League, American Institute of Architects, Municipal Art Society, National Arts Club, and other groups spoke out.[78] The ASHPS remained a cheerleader for the effort. The society—and Hall's history of the park in particular[79]—were greatly praised on the editorial page of the *New York Times*:

> The ASHPS is doing effective work in support of the movement to prevent the erection of a new Court House in City Hall Park and to restore that park and preserve it permanently as a park. . . . The history of the various buildings that have occupied or now occupy sites in the park is interesting reading. All the buildings now there, except the fine old City Hall, should be removed. The present General Post Office has always been an architectural eyesore, its site was transferred to the Federal Government in the careless old Tweed days.[80]

Other newspapers—the *Evening Post, Tribune, Brooklyn Daily Eagle, Evening Journal, Globe,* and *World*—editorialized in the same vein, in many cases also echoing the idea that building a courthouse and civic center worthy of New York's greatness should not include destroying the old one.[81] The ASHPS's preservation-based solutions to the multiple problems of City Hall Park were thus taken up as the leading critique of the Tammany-backed proposals to use public parks as building sites.

The preservation and allied reform organizations were not alone. The City Club, Merchants Association, Chamber of Commerce, and Bar Association—led by civic crusader Albert Bard—actively protested against building on park land.[82] These business-oriented associations implored politicians not to give in to "a misplaced sense of economy" by agreeing to the "injury of the City Hall and the unnecessary sacrifice of City Hall Park."[83] The goal of all was to "restore the Park to original uses"—recognizing not only the contemporary uses of the park but also the memorial qualities and the symbolic function that City Hall Park played in downtown.[84]

Public protests sustained the preservation effort, effectively challenging and changing the balance of power in managing the City Hall Park site, which ultimately rested with the state legislature. The *New York Times* editorialized in April 1910 that "the plan of forming a civic centre around the park by erecting the law courts on land just north of it, where other public buildings will also be situated in time, has already received a large measure of public approval."[85] Politicians were not left to decide the fate of the park themselves. Reform groups made a significant impact

Figure 3.11. This pamphlet published by the reformist City Club in 1910 outlined a proposal that balanced preservation concerns with fiscal issues when considering the placement of new buildings within City Hall Park. Like many other proposals addressing preservation, urban design, and fiscal matters, it calls for preserving City Hall in situ, clearing other older buildings from the park, and establishing sites for new, tall municipal office buildings. Its underlying argument was that the preservation of City Hall and its (overrestored) park was worth the cost of purchasing new building sites outside the park. Courtesy of Art Commission of the City of New York.

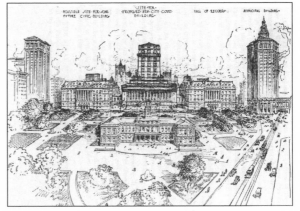

on the decision, and they in turn counted on other citizens who wrote letters, sent postcards, and attended public hearings. John Winfield Scott, chair of the City Hall Preservation Committee that had helped preservationists prevail in 1894, exhorted fellow citizens to repeat that success. He appealed to patriotism and the rarity of the city's "ancient monuments," and he trumpeted the power of "postal card" and individual and association appeals to effect the place's preservation *again*.[86]

In March 1910, the Court House Board held a hearing at which two dozen proposals to place the courthouse in places other than City Hall Park were presented, including an influential plan presented by Grosvenor Atterbury, chair of the Court House Site Committee of the American Institute of Architects. Proposals were made for the area of the Public Library, Battery Park, Greenwich Village, and the area just north of Chambers Street.[87] The powerful Board of Estimate and Apportionment formed a committee on the matter in May. It was led by Manhattan borough president George McAneny, who, along with the comptroller, William Prendergast, and the president of the Board of Aldermen, John Purroy Mitchel, investigated twenty-two sites around the city that had been proposed as courthouse sites.[88] McAneny advocated preservation of the park and, as demonstrated elsewhere in this book, championed preservation within the context of improvement and growth.

Editorials urged the Board of Estimate to reject any City Hall Park site, often citing the "intelligent work" of the ASHPS, Municipal Art Society, American Institute of Architects, and other reform groups.[89] The Society of Columbia University Architects weighed in, defending the value of City Hall as "the sole architectural ornament of the city's oldest park, a park to be restored to its old uses, and preserved for all time."[90] Atterbury was a member of most of these groups (it was typical of these groups to have overlapping and sympathetic memberships). So, not surprisingly, his plan spoke for the whole reform movement.

Despite the public support and preservationist logic of Atterbury's proposal, the Court House Board decided, in 1911, to build in City Hall Park for reasons of fiscal prudence, and it had the support of the majority of New York State justices (the powerful "client" group). But civic activists and reform-minded city officials did not give up. Though fiscal prudence was an important Progressive ethic, it did not trump the broader, longer-term value of preserving the park. Arguing that the long-term benefits of preservation would outweigh any short-term fiscal savings, preservationists developed what would become some of the most important signal contributions of preservation to American urbanism: the logic of long-term public benefits as a critique of short-term financial returns; the idea that the benefits of preservation cannot be measured in dollars.

In New York State, many powers are reserved to the state government and have to be explicitly ceded to lower levels of government. This dynamic has long had a dramatic effect on New York City politics. The Stillwell Bill of 1911 forced the issue, giving the city (its Board of Estimate) four months to decide on a final plan for the courthouse; if it did not, the state supreme court justices would be authorized to take as much park space as they required, and the courthouse would go in City Hall Park. Some argued that the bill violated home rule for the city, taking from the Board of Estimate the power to decide the site of the courthouse and forcing its location in City Hall Park. The bill passed the state senate, with its proponents using questionable tactics reported as "scandalous" in the *Times*; it was then passed unanimously in the assembly on May 2 by an "unconstitutional" voting procedure following a public hearing filled with reformers, including Bard; the bill was signed by the governor on October 12, 1911.

By July 5, 1911, the Board of Aldermen, though they had no direct power over the matter, had passed a resolution "favoring the preservation of the City Hall as a historic monument, and protesting against further encroachment of the park surrounding it."[91] To no avail: The Stillwell Bill was approved by the state senate and assembly, "passed in defiance of public opinion" by means of a "shabby trick."[92] The final Stillwell Bill gave the Board of Estimate a six-month window to choose a courthouse site, after which the decision would go to the Court House Commission (controlled by the state justices). A City Hall Park site was now off the table—public protests by the associations, leading citizens, and others had worked.[93]

In January 1912, the Board of Estimate and Apportionment adopted a resolution choosing the site that became Foley Square, the area north of Chambers Street and east of Centre and Lafayette streets, contributing to the eastward growth of a civic center that had begun to emerge with the new Hall of Records and Municipal Building.[94] The matter of a courthouse site outside the park was settled. McAneny was credited with preserving the park and with being "a potent factor in crystallizing the idea for a Civic Center and making the Court House a part of it."[95] Indeed, this understates the reason and balance McAneny brought to this chaotic fight to spare the park from a massive new building campaign.

The Jewel in the Jewel Box

Edward Hagaman Hall's statement about the proper urbanistic treatment of City Hall—destroying the courthouses and Post Office[96]—was the perfect expression of the preservationist idea that historical memory is best communicated by a monument restored to the grandeur of its distant past and couched in a green park setting—setting the jewel in its jewel box (see chapter 1).

City Hall was indeed the jewel in the jewel box of New York's official civic memory. As preserved, the building's authentic attachment to the city's past and government authority and its beauty and design made it the most important building to preservationists—and the fact that it remained the literal, official seat of power certainly reinforced this. "Our own age builds more quickly than McComb's—but not more sincerely; our age builds higher—but not more beautifully. Surely in this we can honor our fathers, that we reverence the work of their hands, and preserve intact our inheritance," wrote architectural historian Charles May.[97]

As noted above, the suggestion was made multiple times over the nineteenth century to abandon old City Hall and build a new one elsewhere—an idea completely in keeping with the overarching narrative of Manhattan, that progress rolls northward and the built environment needs constant revision to reflect and abet this process.[98] The old City Hall stubbornly resisted the uptown trajectory of Manhattan. In 1860, for instance, the city council opposed a state legislature bill to build a new City Hall in Madison Square.[99] In 1888, 1893–94, 1903, and 1910–13, politicians, business groups, or other interest groups proposed destroying City Hall and building a new one elsewhere, moving the historic edifice to a new site so it could be replaced with a more modern and spacious facility. Adding onto the historic structure was another strategy proposed. These new buildings or complexes often included skyscraper towers (including schemes designed by Lamb, Hornbostel and Post, and even the Regional Plan Association in the late 1920s). In some cases, these efforts failed because they were simply too costly or too architecturally ambitious, lacked the requisite political support, or were otherwise infeasible. That all these efforts to alter City Hall failed is alone testament to the value of some civic memories or the power of historical associations to shape certain aspects and sites of the changing metropolitan landscape.

When the threats to City Hall seemed genuine, preservationists mobilized the public relations and political forces at their disposal. The best example of this was Andrew Haswell Green's 1894 defense of City Hall when a proposal was made to move the old building to the newly created park on the former site of the reservoir (today's Bryant Park). In a pamphlet, Green laid out his theory on the power of historical associations; he outlined the bonds between City Hall, its specific site and context, and the memories attached thereto; and he made an eloquent case for the civic importance of this complex. Green made a spirited argument for the spatiality and groundedness of historical memory: "The Building is indissolubly connected with its site and surroundings. Remove it and interest in it vanishes."[100] Another principle of preservation was the heightened power of historical buildings set in parks, which was thought to make a purer narrative.[101] In the case of City

Hall, a solitary setting was not in fact authentic, as the park had always had a number of buildings in it. No matter. It was memorial effect, not historical accuracy, that preservationists most desired. Hornbostel and Post's plan, for instance, is a rather severe (over)interpretation of this principle. Though Green foregrounded the importance of City Hall as spatialized civic memory, he did not fail to mention the economic and logistical rationales behind preservation. Fiscal prudence, after all, was the basis for Green's considerable public reputation: It would be "wanton wastefulness" to tear down City Hall and move it to Reservoir Square, and its stone could not easily be reused, so City Hall should be left alone "solely as a measure of prudent economy."[102]

Ultimately, preservationists won multiple victories on City Hall as an *urbanistic* issue: where it was located, how it was affected by other developments in downtown, and whether the old structure was to be preserved, destroyed, or altered. Not only did the building remain on its original site, but additional buildings were not allowed to "encroach" on the historic edifice, and a major restoration of the building was carried out in the first two decades of the twentieth century. The restoration of City Hall—its story as the object of architectural preservation—fixed and increased the building's value as the centerpiece of the city's memory infrastructure.

Over the course of the nineteenth century, City Hall had been heavily used and abused, damaged by fire, and many times adapted according to the changing demands of city bureaucracy and politicians' tastes. As with the park as a whole, turn-of-the-century preservation efforts were meant to bring a sense of order and grandeur to this important civic symbol. In 1897–98, architect John Duncan combined and rearranged rooms to accommodate the Board of Aldermen, other city agencies, and newspaper reporters. Following the 1898 reorganization of city government, architect William Martin Aiken carried out further interior changes, including moving the mayor's office from one corner of the building to another and creating an office for the Manhattan borough president. Work on building systems and conservation was also undertaken—lighting was changed from gas to electric between 1899 and 1903; the exteriors were sandblasted in 1905—and a "heavily criticized" interior redecoration was carried out in 1907.

Robert Buckell Insley, superintendent of public buildings and offices, presented this appraisal of City Hall's condition and potential in his 1912 annual report to Borough President McAneny:

Speaking generally, the building is in a condition of disrepair, which is out of harmony with its importance. The application for an appropriation for this purpose, which was made by the Borough President last year, was not approved by the Board of Aldermen, but it is hoped that necessary funds may be provided in the near future for the checking of further deterioration and the thorough restoration of the building. Such a restoration is due the old City Hall, not only as a recognized architectural masterpiece, but by reason of its historic value to the city and state and its dignity as the center of the government of the second largest city in the world.[103]

Addressing both the challenges of an old, deteriorating building and the opportunities to make better memory infrastructure, the modern restoration of City Hall was carried out by leading architect Grosvenor Atterbury and sponsored by the borough president, good-government reformer, and preservationist George McAneny. Funding came via the industrialist fortune of Mrs. Russell Sage (Olivia Slocum Sage), whose philanthropy was secured through the efforts of Robert De Forest, who was a leading real estate lawyer, head of the Art Commission, chairman of the Tenement House Commission, benefactor of the Metropolitan Museum of Art, and McAneny's friend.

Atterbury was a well-known figure in architectural circles, active in the Fine Arts Federation among other artistic and reform groups.[104] Atterbury's full-blown, scientific restoration of the whole building—interior and exterior—was completed between 1912 and 1915, and he replaced a fire-damaged cupola in 1917.[105] His preservation work on City Hall, combining scientific research, design skills, and respect for historical authenticity and aesthetic canons, is an excellent illustration of architects' emergence on the preservation scene in the first decade of the twentieth century. The assignment was to restore the brilliance, beauty, and authenticity of the original design—to restore to City Hall its luster as the centerpiece of civic pride and, a century having passed, civic memory. Rooms also had to be refitted and rearranged to accommodate the new organization of municipal government (new aldermanic chamber, offices for the Manhattan borough president). Atterbury began his work by researching original McComb drawings "discovered" in the archives of the New-York Historical Society. A lot of damage, neglect, and "unsympathetic" renovations had to be repaired to make City Hall functional enough to sustain its use as the seat of government. Charles May described "a series of alterations, repairs and renovations which have ranged at various times from intelligent restoration to barbaric vandalism" following an 1858 fire and the subsequent neglect by Tammany politicians.[106] But just as important, the restoration of City Hall was a significant opportunity to showcase the power and persuasion of historic preservation and ensure City Hall Park's status as the seat of civic memory.

Figure 3.12. Architectural journals began publishing detailed articles — such as this one — about the historical documentation used to support increasingly professional efforts at architectural restoration, including the major restoration of City Hall by Grosvenor Atterbury in 1913–15. Courtesy of Anne and Jerome Fisher Fine Arts Library, University of Pennsylvania.

The work consisted of reestablishing the several public and official rooms to a suitably historical style, reinstalling the collection of great-man portraits cherished as the city's art collection (literally civic art), and installing modern infrastructure such as heating and plumbing systems and fireproofing.[107] Special focus was placed on the Governor's Room, which was the ceremonial greeting place — Lafayette was welcomed there — and was furnished with the city's portrait collection and two pieces of furniture from George Washington's New York residence. The room was immediately opened to visitors and schoolchildren as a museum of civic patriotism. "Let no one question the value of a municipal museum such as the Governor's Room."[108]

This detailed summary of Atterbury's approach to restoration of the Governor's Room — which opened as a public museum in 1909 — lends an appreciation for the professionalism and scientific approach he applied to all his work on City Hall:

When the work was undertaken, it was not known that any of the original drawings were in existence, but after painstaking search some of these drawings were discovered in the library of the New York Historical Society [*sic*] and others in the possession of the McComb family. In addition to these a copy of Sir William Chambers' "Treatise on the Decorative Part

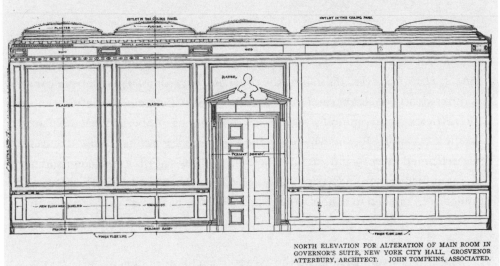

NORTH ELEVATION FOR ALTERATION OF MAIN ROOM IN
GOVERNOR'S SUITE, NEW YORK CITY HALL. GROSVENOR
ATTERBURY, ARCHITECT.   JOHN TOMPKINS, ASSOCIATED.

Figure 3.13. Architectural Record *carried a lengthy two-part article detailing the architectural history of City Hall written and illustrated by Charles May, an architect who worked in Atterbury's office. This cross section and wall detail are typical of the historical and contemporary drawings reproduced as part of the documentation. Courtesy of Anne and Jerome Fisher Fine Arts Library, University of Pennsylvania.*

Figure 3.14. The Governor's Room was the centerpiece of City Hall's public spaces. Operated as a museum in the early twentieth century, the room displayed the city's portrait collection and other valuable historical artifacts, such as President Washington's desk. Author's collection.

of Civil Architecture," published in London in 1791, which had been owned by McComb, and contained his annotations, was also found. After careful study of these drawings and of the condition of the room when the work of renovation was commenced, it was ascertained that the only details dating back to 1814 were the window trim, the inside shutters and sashes, and the trim of the three doors opening from the three rooms to the main corridor. These details have been preserved, but the remaining work, which was of a later date, has been removed. . . . The mantels, which had neither association nor merit to commend them, have been replaced by others of a design and character contemporary with the erection of the building. . . . it has been the aim of the committee and of the architect to carry out the ideas of the original designer, and to make the room accurately expressive of his personal taste and representative of the style of his period.[109]

In his appendix and bibliography, the exact sources used for each design element in Atterbury's restoration are listed. They included William Pain's "Practical House Carpenter," McComb's own portfolios, William Davenport Goforth and William J. McAuley's "Old Colonial Architectural Details in and around Philadelphia," elements sketched and copied from other parts of City Hall, E. A. Crane and E. Soderholz's "Examples of Colonial Architecture in South Carolina and Georgia," and "a pitcher belonging to George Washington."

Figure 3.15. The creation of new transportation infrastructure in and around City Hall Park at the turn of the century had an impact on the preservation of park buildings. The Martyrs' Prison, pictured at upper right in this subway-construction photograph, was destroyed, over the protests of preservationists, to make way for subway construction under Park Row and at the foot of the Brooklyn Bridge (the terminal is seen at upper left). This view looks south along Park Row, where a trolley passes excavations in the corner of City Hall Park. Courtesy of the New York Transit Museum.

The restoration was a fine example of methods of "scientific" architectural restoration emerging as a dominant way of spatializing memory. Atterbury's work was praised as an accurate, transparent, and authentic restoration of rooms, each of which had "gathered round itself a wealth of association"[110] The project was acclaimed by political leaders as well as architectural critics. (The mode of architectural preservation and design Atterbury practiced evolved as the architectural–aesthetic preservation of the 1920s and '30s and became the dominant mode, overshadowing preservation organized around the meaning of a building's historical associations.)[111]

Destroying Buildings

It is a caricature to say that historic preservation is an ideological position—"save all old buildings." This criticism has an element of truth to it—the religious tenor of preservation advocacy is an abiding part of preservationist discourse, from John Ruskin and William Morris through to today's activists. But the reality of preservation practice has always been rooted in discernment between buildings of greater and lesser value, and the simple but powerful principle that some buildings should be preserved while (tacitly) others should not. The discernment between buildings is not only based on their age (though this is a precondition), but on the particular kinds of memories with which buildings are associated and whether those memories are politically and culturally resonant or not. The practical result, made evident by early preservationists in New York, was that discernment between different buildings and their memorial meanings led to preservation of some and destruction of others. To create politically resonant, useful kinds of historical memory, buildings with valuable associations were jealously preserved and restored, while buildings with undesirable associations were slated for destruction. The destruction advocated by preservationists was not the neglectful sort—because there were too many buildings and not enough resources to address them all—but was the result of unabashed iconoclasm: destroying buildings because they were associated with unwanted values and negative meanings. By looking more closely at a buildings within City Hall Park, the destructive impulse of historic preservation becomes clear.

In City Hall Park, preservationists regarded some buildings as beyond their useful life, safety hazards, and not particularly meaningful, so their destruction was a nonevent—for instance, the brownstone firehouse (its demolition was noted, without regret, in 1906). Other buildings, with strong associations, were objects of great interest, and debates or decisions about them are extremely revealing. Some were defended by preservationists on the grounds of their memorial or architectural value; some of these were successfully saved (City Hall), others regretfully destroyed in the real estate market or by government "improvement" (the Martyrs' Prison). Yet other buildings were targets of iconoclasm fully supported by preservationists because the buildings embodied the wrong meaning and represented undesirable values—in particular, the Post Office and the Tweed Courthouse.

Memory is famously selective, and the memory infrastructure was selective, too. Edward Hagaman Hall, spokesman for the preservation field, embraced this idea: "Let us keep our City Hall where it stands and set it forth as the gem that it is by removing the Court Houses and in due time the old Post Office."[112] The

Municipal Art Society agreed, recommending in 1902 "that all buildings, except the old City Hall and County Court-house, be promptly removed from City Hall square. The City Hall is the one structure within the park which is so creditable in its architecture and of such historic interest that its preservation should be indefinitely provided for. The removal of these buildings will afford great relief where it is most needed."[113] Clearing the park of other buildings would not just make for a beautiful civic center design but would also make the space more effective for commemoration. "A City Hall Park between the Post-office and Chambers street cleared of obstructions, [would be] attractive and spacious to an extent that can now be scarcely imagined, and a fitting site for generations to come for every class of adornment that may make beautiful the place, or commemorate historical events or characters."[114]

Martyrs' Prison

The Martyrs' Prison (also known as the old Hall of Records and the Old Gaol) was located in the park to the northeast of City Hall. It presented early-twentieth-century preservationists with a more subtle case of trade-offs rather than a clear-cut instance of preservation or iconoclasm. It was built in 1757 in the north precinct of the Commons and demolished in 1903, by which time it was "the oldest municipal building in town." Replacing the Old Gaol (which predated City Hall), it was used as a debtors' prison. During the Revolution (and the long British occupation of New York), captured Continental soldiers were confined there as prisoners of war. Many of them died in the dreadful conditions of this jail's dungeon cells, leading turn-of-the-century preservationists to coin the name "Martyrs' Prison" and advocate for its preservation as a sacred patriotic site associated with heroic loss of life. As Edward Hagaman Hall wrote, "This old building [was] hallowed by the sufferings of American patriots during the Revolution and many other [civic] traditions."[115]

The building was converted in 1830 for offices and storage, and a Greek-revival facade was added to one front. It was so used until 1897, when the city government made plans for the new Hall of Records across Chambers Street.[116] As subway construction gathered pace in 1903, the Subway Commission applied for the building's demolition. The Old Gaol stood in the way of new stairs accessing the subway station under City Hall Park (terminus of the first IRT line) and of expanded elevated-train platforms stretching from the foot of Brooklyn Bridge across Park Row. Though subway baron August Belmont offered to reerect the building on another site, this option could not be realized and demolition plans proceeded.[117]

The ASHPS opposed the demolition because the site was hallowed by patriotic sacrifice and was also the oldest civic building in the city—easy qualifications for the pantheon of civic patriotism. Hall's political and legal efforts yielded to the Subway Commission's power to condemn the site. "After earnest arguments in opposition," wrote Hall, "Justice Leventritt announced . . . an order for its demolition, and by April, 1903, the sunlight was shining into the uncovered dungeons of the cellar in which Continental soldiers had suffered for their country's sake."[118]

The *New York Times*, realizing that the martyrs would be well remembered in Brooklyn at the Prison Ship Martyrs Monument, launched a vehement bit of constructive criticism of the preservation field. The *Times* had been quite supportive of preservation in this period. Feeling that the cause of preservation was ill served by advocating for the preservation of such a nondescript, decrepit building as the old Hall of Records had become, the paper insisted that arguing for its preservation was absurd—and even worse, would discredit the whole preservation field in the public mind. The two *Times* editorials on the issue were among the most passionate arguments for (and against!) preservation in the period:

> It is only the site [of the Martyrs' Prison] that has any historical interest. That could be preserved by the erection of a tablet on or near the spot. . . . The existing building is entitled to no respect whatever, either on architectural or historical grounds. It is an ugly and ridiculous sham, and it is a modern sham.

Concurring with the Municipal Art Society's report that all buildings except City Hall should be removed from the park, the paper continued:

> The removal of the absurd Hall of Records building should be made at the earliest moment. . . . Perhaps the most discouraging thing about the agitation for the retention of this absurd building is that it discredits, in the minds of sensible people not especially interested either in art or local history, any future agitation that may arise for the preservation of buildings really worthy of preservation, on artistic or historical ground, or both. There are such buildings in New York. But when the question of demolishing them comes up those who oppose the demolition will be seriously handicapped by the zeal, not according to knowledge, with which the removal of the old Hall of Records is resisted.[119]

The next year, in February 1903, the *Times* again weighed in to both praise and damn preservation, making an example of Hall's advocacy for the old Hall of

Records: "The demolition of the old Hall of Records is proceeding as rapidly as could be wished. . . . We do not know any example of what may be called local piety more misdirected than the agitation to save this ugly old sham. . . . But we have, within the limits of Manhattan, two old buildings that are very well worth preserving"—the Morris–Jumel Mansion and Fraunces Tavern.[120]

The preservationists clearly lost the argument over this building—this piece of the memory infrastructure was destroyed. Hall and the ASHPS dropped their defense of the old Hall of Records for two pragmatic reasons: First, subway excavations in 1903 began undermining the structure (already in poor condition), making it materially more difficult to preserve the building, let alone find a viable use for it; second, and more to the point of the memory infrastructure thesis, the same martyrs who suffered here in the Old Gaol were already being commemorated across the East River, in Brooklyn's Fort Greene Park. A Prison Ship Martyrs Monument had existed near Wallabout Bay since the early nineteenth century, later to be moved up the hill to Fort Greene Park. As the Old Gaol was threatened with demolition, plans and fund-raising were already underway for the new ossuary and grand new obelisk and monumental plaza adorning the hill at the center of Fort Greene Park. Completed in 1908, the new monument effectively made the preservation of City Hall Park's Martyrs' Prison redundant.

Hall and other preservationists seemed to realize the pragmatism in the *Times*'s assessment of the situation. The sense was that the brownstone courthouse, fire house, and old Hall of Records must give way to progress—an effective civic center, another of the preservationists' goals, relied on good transit infrastructure—and in the end, the city's memory infrastructure was not really damaged.

Tweed Courthouse and the Post Office

Preservationists' iconoclasm was motivated by politics. Preservation was not animated by objective study of history and technical practices of restoration; their choices were shaped strongly by reform politics, and the historical memories valued by preservationists were those useful in the present—the "usable past."

The main political cleavage of the day was marked by reformers' Progressive fusion politics wresting control from Tammany Hall and Democratic machine politics. As part of the Progressive reform fold, it makes perfect sense that preservationists would denigrate narratives and sites associated with Tammany—the Tweed Courthouse and the Post Office. What is remarkable is that this politicization of historical memory could lead preservationists not just to ignore but to recommend the destruction of some relatively old, architecturally fine, but Tammany-associated buildings.

The Tweed Courthouse is a critical example because its political symbolism could not have been more fixed in the public mind, nor could there be a greater contrast to the political ethic of the preservationists. From the 1890s onward, the Tweed Courthouse (its very name dripping negative association) emerged as one of the primary obstacles to realizing a proper civic center. Not only did it symbolize Tammany greed and corruption, but it also crowded and detracted from the character of City Hall. Preservationists therefore insisted that this building—already a couple generations old, its neoclassical style echoing that of City Hall—be demolished. Having been constructed by Boss Tweed to the great benefit of him and his cronies, this edifice stood for just the political values that reformers opposed, a legacy that reformers were eager to eliminate by erasing the building and its memory from the landscape. A City Hall Park free of the memory of Tweed and machine politics would improve the civic mind, preservationists felt, just as preservation and creation of filiopietistic monuments and sites of civic patriotism did.[121]

The Post Office, constructed in 1867 at the southern end of City Hall Park, had long been an affront to civic pride. There were several motivations for the militant feeling about the Post Office's demolition: It was tainted by association with Democratic machine politicians who controlled the city legislature when the land was sold to the federal government (a sale that reportedly lined Tammany pockets); the Post Office took the place of the popular Croton Fountain; the design of the building was seen by preservationists and taste-makers as garish and Victorian and thus unbecoming of the messages of civic and republican virtue intrinsic (it was thought) to neoclassical architecture; and it occupied a great deal of park space and blocked preservationists' favored nostalgic view of City Hall shining like a gem in its park. (Adding insult to injury, the building's loading dock faced the front of City Hall.) By the 1890s, when the need for an expanded, coherent civic center was gaining voice among reformers, calls for the removal of the Post Office were renewed. As with the Tweed Courthouse, the preservationists' voice was not alone in advocating demolition. Newspaper editorials joined in advocating its removal and the building of a new post office elsewhere.[122] The facility had already become overcrowded, and despite a condition of the original sale that would deed the land back to the city if the building were to cease to be used as a postal facility, the building had long been used for other federal, nonpostal functions.

Preservationists, planners, and other reformers projected their desire onto the public: "New Yorkers look forward hopefully to the time when the City shall

Vol. LVI.   NEW YORK, AUGUST 31, 1912   No. 2906

Figure 3.16. *As downtown New York grew skyward, it afforded a new perspective on the district's past. This workman adorned a spectacular photograph in a 1912 issue of* Harper's Weekly, *emphasizing that progress and redevelopment were not completely effacing the city's heritage: City Hall and its park remained the center of downtown. Courtesy of HarpWeek, LLC.*

reclaim the southern portion of City Hall Park, which was inadvisedly sold to the Federal Government in 1867."[123] But wide agreement on the removal of the Post Office went unrealized for decades. Hopes were raised in 1914 when, on the heels of preservationists' victories in preventing the removal of City Hall and a new courthouse in the park, the executive functions of the Post Office were moved to the new Post Office on Eighth Avenue and Thirty-third Street. Ineffectual efforts to demolish the Post Office and restore the park continued—a 1924 *New York Times* article enticingly showed what the park would look like after removal of the Post Office—but the building remained until 1938–39, when Robert Moses's authority managed to sweep it away in favor of a quasi-historic reconstructed park.[124]

Iconoclasm directed at prominent buildings demonstrated that historic preservation was foremost concerned with shaping memory, meaning, and values—by whatever means necessary—and not simply with protecting historic fabric in and of itself. Preserving and restoring old buildings was a means to the end of creating useful historical memory; destruction was another useful means, in certain circumstances, for editing civic memory.

City Hall Park: Official Commemorative Landscape

In her brief history of City Hall Park, Michele Bogart writes of "the possibilities of memory accreted over time, certain aspects of memory [becoming] crucial to the representation and politics of the park as public space."[125] When this period of the park's evolution ended, the mythical, historic vision of City Hall commanding an open park, conjured by Hall and others, remained a myth. Nor was the unified, orderly civic center landscape envisioned by City Beautiful enthusiasts ever achieved. The politics were too fractious, and the fiscal obstacles too great, to achieve such spatial order and control. The city lacked a permanent, powerful planning body to control this or other public spaces. The Municipal Building provided much-needed offices, while the courthouse need was only solved in the mid-1920s with the development of Foley Square. The plurality of forces pushing and pulling civic life were accurately reflected in the chaotic, partly realized civic center.

As the twentieth century turned, City Hall and its park were not becoming old and useless. Quite the opposite: They were becoming modernized and highly efficient in performing more and more functions. City Hall Park was at once a landscape of civic memory, transport, and active governance. While there certainly are ways in which these uses conflicted, what must be stressed is the *interweaving* of these different infrastructural projects. In combination, they made an appropriately modern center of this quintessentially modern city, with all the attendant

contradictions—old and new, rich and poor, visible majority and hidden minori-
ties, destruction and preservation, solid and thin-air.[126] This civic center was an
accurate reflection of the whole contradictory city.

But preservationists were successful enough in implementing their vision to
qualify City Hall Park as the "official" commemorative landscape—where the historical memory of civic patriotism was best represented. In City Hall Park, civic
memory and the need for a memory infrastructure framed designs, plans, and
actual changes in the park landscape. It is evident in the debates and proposals
for individual buildings and sites that City Hall Park was a deeply meaningful landscape, richly layered with historical associations that competed and won against
other meanings and uses. The park accommodated a broad range of functional
needs and the infrastructures to support them. Conflicts arose less over the overall
vision of City Hall Park as the center of the city and more over how the existing
landscape—with all its contingencies—would be incrementally rebuilt and preserved in order to communicate civic ideals.

Historian Gregory Gilmartin has observed that "City Hall Park is a vivid demonstration of the city's incompetence at planning facilities for its own use."[127] While
this captures the overall difficulties, it loses important nuances: First, it wasn't just
"the city" that was trying to shape the park but, rather, a plethora of public agencies, shifting political alliances, private property owners, and third-sector reform
groups (planners and preservationists foremost among them, but not alone); and
second, at least in the cases of the IRT subway, the East River bridges, and finally
the Municipal Building, "the city" and its many partners were quite successful in
realizing large-scale projects to support the modern metropolis. While the memory infrastructure was not as comprehensively planned or masterfully realized as
these projects, the park nevertheless became an enduring part of the fabric, public
space, and civic culture of modern New York. And the place *functioned*—then as
now—as the political and memorial center of the city.

City Hall Park had all the right narratives to put on civic display: great men,
patriotic acts, martyrdom, civic achievement, symbols of the power and authority
of municipal government. Andrew Green's 1894 pamphlet exhorting the preservation of City Hall in situ effectively put to rest proposals to remove City Hall, and
the narrative values he and his colleagues fixed in the public's mind linked the
city's political achievements with its material progress.

The visual qualities of City Hall Park were critical to its function as memory
infrastructure. The iconic edifice of City Hall in its park surroundings were just
the kind of landscape to clearly express notions of civic patriotism to the public.
The scenic and historic effects of the park foregrounded the narratives embed-

Figure 3.17. Frederick Mac-Monnies's statue of Revolutionary patriot Nathan Hale, dedicated in 1893, was one of several monuments and memorials placed in City Hall Park. Legend had it that Hale had been executed nearby. Author's collection.

ded in City Hall and the park's other buildings and monuments, and in turn the value of the park landscape was heightened as the surrounding buildings grew to great heights.

The ability of the city builders to create a sense of control and order in City Hall Park was tied in their minds to the ability to govern and grow the new metropolis. The result in both cases was partial success — the city grew, but not without its chaotic aspects; the park has been retained, though not without significant threats and changes.

City Hall Park is indispensable for understanding the ideology of historic and scenic preservation as it emerged as a means of urban reform in the early twentieth century. Debates about specific buildings and sites in the park — City Hall, the Tweed Courthouse, the Post Office, the Martyrs' Prison, the liberty pole, the

Nathan Hale and Horace Greeley statues, the park space itself—revealed preservationists' theories about the power of place-specific association, the visualization of civic patriotism, and the use of preserved and destroyed memory sites. The process of debating and managing City Hall Park in these decades demonstrated how the construction of memory could be the driving force of urbanism, and how the memory-rich environment resulting from preservationists' work kept City Hall Park at the center of civic culture.

Historic preservationists were the imagineers of the civic memory infrastructure, and they considered City Hall Park to be among their most important works. Their achievements included what did *not* happen (a new courthouse in the park, the removal or disfigurement of City Hall) as well as what did happen (the preservation of the park's shape and general character despite the breakneck growth of skyscrapers downtown, the restoration of City Hall, ensuring its enshrinement as a civic landmark). Of course, there were disappointments in not achieving the complete preservationist vision of the place—the Post Office, the Tweed Courthouse, and some other "encroachments" remained in the park—but some of these goals eventually would come to fruition, too.

The City Hall Park story illustrates clearly that preservationists were most concerned with shaping *memory,* not with saving fabric. This was evident in the irony of preservationists' insisting that some old buildings be torn down because the buildings' narratives (more than their form or placement) did not fit the civic ideal. City Hall Park's history also illuminates the connections between the historic preservation and city-planning fields: The fields agreed on redevelopment, the need for movement, the elimination of congestion, and the cost-effectiveness of planning and investing comprehensively and with foresight; they agreed on the need for memory infrastructure; but they had different ideas about how to build civic memory into the landscape. While planners and civic artists looked to abstract narratives, architectural styles, and decorative schemes to satisfy the need for memory sites, preservationists cultivated place- and site-specific narratives represented by authentic buildings.

Though most discussions about the future of City Hall Park took place among professionals, reformers, and government officials, the place evidently mattered to the general public. The plan to erect a new courthouse in the park "aroused the most earnest protest from the public. Popular sentiment on this subject was unmistakably manifested at the hearing before the Board of Estimate and Apportionment in the City Hall on March 18, 1910, when the chamber was crowded almost to suffocation and when the limits of the hearing did not suffice to allow all the protestants to speak."[128]

The legacy of this preservation work from a century ago is quite evident today: City Hall Park and its environs remain the place where the history of the city and the struggles to cultivate memory as well as improvement are best appreciated. A colleague visiting from another country recently remarked, upon seeing the City Hall Park landscape for the first time, "This makes New York feel like a European city, all this oldness and contrast." Still, preservationists' editing of historical memory created silences that are disturbing today. The 1863 draft riots, for instance, revolved around City Hall Park, among other Manhattan locations, but were never spoken of nor commemorated in public memory discourse of the early twentieth century, belying the idea that "the memory of the riots lingered, especially for blacks and the governing elite."[129]

The park's chaotic mix of old and new, treasured and intrusive, historic and modern, is something the preservationists helped nurture. It characterized the whole of New York and would remain the backdrop for any victories preservationists later achieved. Today, as in the early twentieth century, City Hall Park is a magnificently imperfect and richly textured landscape shaped through struggles over defining and representing civic life at the heart of the city.

Four

Bronx River Parkway: Modern Highway, Environmental Improvement, Memory Infrastructure

The Bronx River, from its original condition of natural beauty so charmingly described, had degenerated into a sewage laden stream, its channel obstructed by fallen trees, old iron and other debris, with stable yards, manure piles, and cesspools of human and other animal filth encumbering and defiling its banks. The river valley restored for all time, improved and utilized as the route of one of the finest motor parkways in the world, is the final picture closing our chapter on the Bronx River Parkway. This great improvement stands forth as a triumph of civic achievement of incalculable value to present and future generations.

> Jay Downer and James Owen, Bronx Parkway
> Commission engineers, 1925

T HE BRONX RIVER PARKWAY WAS MUCH MORE THAN A ROAD THROUGH THE country.[1] This remarkable project was really many projects in one: a major regional landscape improvement effort, involving environmental restoration, billboard removal, and slum clearance; a new model of modern automobile highway design; a triumph of corporate organization and real estate investment; and a work of memory infrastructure.

Planned and built between 1906 and 1925 on an expanding edge of the New York City metropolis, the parkway was an ambitious regional-planning project integrating several kinds of infrastructure—transportation, public health, recreational, social, economic, administrative. It was planned and executed by a tightly controlled, quintessentially modern planning process and organization. The parkway embodied all the facets of "improvement" that were the proudest achievements of Progressive reformers. While the road-building or environmental-reform aspects have dominated nearly every account of the parkway[2] (it is most widely known as the world's first automobile highway), this chapter shows that the goal of building a *memory* infrastructure was an essential part of designing and planning this modern urban landscape. Likewise, the parkway embodied a more sinister kind of environmental reform: Eugenics-driven environmental determinism and real estate speculation fed an aggressive program of slum clearance, not just the usual patriotic, tacitly anti-immigrant reach for cultural hegemony otherwise common in historic preservation.

The Bronx River Parkway was the first automobile parkway, the precursor to the Westchester County parkway system and later the American interstate highways.[3] But to its builders the road was never the most important part of the project. The parkway clearly followed the line of development of nineteenth-century "park ideology,"[4] synthesizing country and city, normative cultural reform and economic development, totally designed and comprehensively planned as a differentiated, specialized urban space. The more pressing goals voiced by parkway commissioners were cleaning the environment, creating a park, spending public funds conservatively, and, tacitly, encouraging suburban real estate development.

The notion of "improvement" was often invoked by the parkway's makers, civic boosters, and kindred reformers. This was a multivalent idea—it referred to physical as well as social change and included aesthetic, sanitary, economic, and political dimensions.[5] "Improvement" is interesting analytically because it invites consideration of the landscape *before* and *after* transformation—that is, historically, comparing the unimproved to the improved. The visualization of improvement—a central strategy for the Bronx Parkway Commission—raises the question of obscure costs as well as obvious benefits. What is lost, what costs are incurred, in making the dramatic improvements so proudly illustrated? The purposeful construction of civic memory of the Bronx River valley landscape was a necessary part of its "improvement" into the first modern parkway—it was the story to accompany the pictures. Just as improvement required the destruction of some landscape features and the wholesale creation of others, the success of the parkway required that historical and scenic memory be taken apart and reassembled.

Engineering feats often obscure the cultural processes and narratives that necessarily accompany them.[6] The cultural aspects of the parkway's design and implementation (the memory work) should not be dismissed as incidental, merely decorative, or unintentional. While the narrative qualities of parkway improvements were not the point of the project, they were key enabling strategies, deliberately represented both in the landscape built and the rhetoric officially describing it. The stories, images, and designs created as part of the parkway project were the result of great, deliberate effort on the part of the builders and served important functions: justifying social reform, providing political support, fulfilling the environmental- and

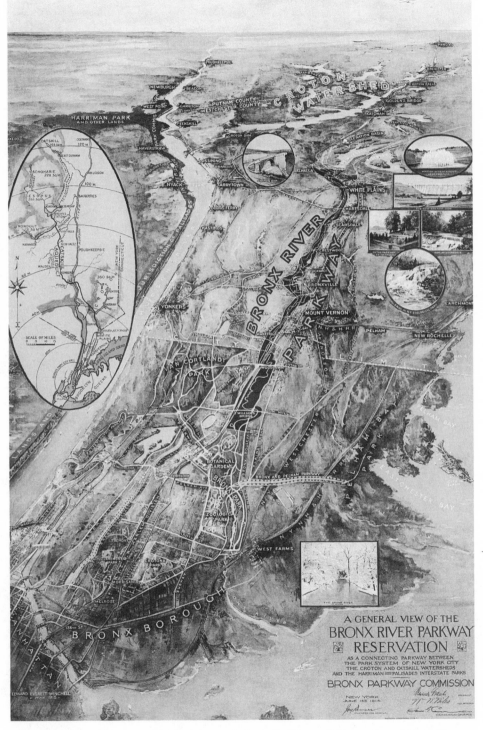

Figure 4.1. This color painting, which hung on the wall of Bronx Parkway Commission offices, shows the ambitious scope of the Bronx River Parkway project and its location on the periphery of the city. The fifteen-mile-long Parkway Reservation is shaded in slightly darker color at the center of the image. Courtesy of the Westchester County Archives.

Figure 4.2. This oblique aerial photograph taken near Scarsdale in the 1920s shows the close relationships among the parkway, rail- road, and suburban development. Courtesy of Westchester County Park Commission.

Figure 4.3. These before-and-after photographs in the area of Williamsbridge in the Bronx, from the extensive photographic archives of the Bronx Parkway Commission, were part of a small portfolio used for presentations about the progress of the parkway during its planning and construction. Courtesy of the Architectural Archives, University of Pennsylvania.

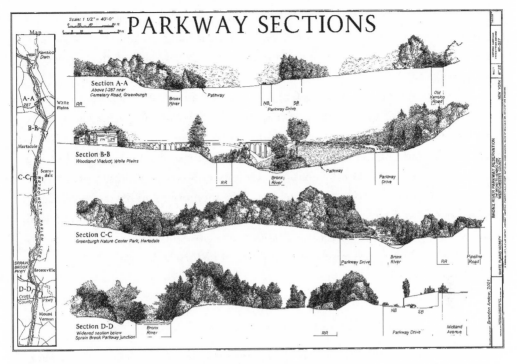

Figure 4.4. This drawing, from the National Park Service's Historic American Engineering Record, depicts the Bronx River Parkway's design and evolution and interprets its significance as a work of design and engineering. Courtesy of Library of Congress, Prints and Photographs Division, Historic American Engineering Record.

social-reform legacies of its landscape-architecture and city-planning precursors, and emphasizing the parkway's character as a model public space.

Reconstructing the public memory of the valley landscape was essential to the parkway's success as a comprehensive project of landscape transformation and modernization. The way the valley should be seen, thought of, and remembered was defined through the design of the landscape and the Bronx Parkway Commission's canonical, autobiographical *story*: the once-beautiful valley and its virtuous colonial life, the despoliation of both, and the place's subsequent redemption by the commission and its experts. The naturalistic designs of a "regained" valley landscape, the rusticated bridges, the redrawn boundaries of property ownership, property condemnation and slum clearance, the institutional setup of the commission, and the extensive use of before-and-after photography all contributed to the "spatialization" of historical memory and the creation of an ideal modern landscape. These strategies fell in line with the preservation ideology of the time, as projected in the ASHPS's work: selectively preserving, destroying, and building urban spaces to project stories celebrating the civic past; joining scenic and historic values to create a sense of civic heritage; relying on the work of reformers and professionals; and contributing to the overall political project of Progressive reform.

This chapter interprets the rich chronicle of the Bronx River Parkway as a plan to create different kinds of infrastructure.[7] The parts of the parkway's memory infrastructure are described first: restored natural landscape and landscape architectural and engineering designs, reports, photographs, and stories (like the one quoted at the head of the chapter). Other sections of the chapter present the commission and its leader, Madison Grant; the memorial and narrative strategies integrated into the parkway project; and the slum-clearance program that paved the way for implementation. Like the other two case-study chapters, the parkway case sheds light on the construction and use of historical memory and the role it played in urban development.

CHRONICLE OF THE BRONX RIVER PARKWAY

The Bronx River Parkway is best known as the world's first modern automobile parkway.[8] It was the successor to the intra-urban parkways of pioneering nineteenth-century landscape architects Olmsted and Vaux, Horace Cleveland, Charles Eliot, and others and was the precursor of today's highways. Before the parkway, though, there was the valley. As completely as the Bronx Parkway Commission transformed the valley, Joseph Rodman Drake's romantic poetry offered them useful images and narratives suggesting an older, unspoiled Bronx River as an opening chapter to their story of improvement.

Designed and built between 1906 and 1925, the parkway followed fifteen and a half miles of the course of the Bronx River, connecting New York City's Bronx Park with Kensico Dam in Westchester County, and points between. The parkway "reservation" covered 1,155 acres, averaging about six hundred feet wide, and included twenty miles of cinder footpaths as well as thirty-seven innovative steel-and-stone bridges. The reservation land was acquired from 1,400 separate owners, and the project cost over $16.5 million. Two million cubic yards of earth were moved.[9]

State legislation establishing the Parkway Commission was passed in 1905 and 1906, followed by years of surveying, planning, and efforts to secure the funds to begin property acquisition. In effect, the commission was created as a separate, autonomous local jurisdiction. The vast work of negotiating deals and condemning property and of cleaning, clearing, destruction, and construction began in earnest

Figure 4.5. Though the Bronx River Parkway was intended to look natural, as if the historic valley had been "regained," a great deal of earth, river, and vegetation had to be moved. Courtesy of Library of Congress, Prints and Photographs Division, Historic American Engineering Record.

Figure 4.6. The Bronx Parkway Commission used this sort of environmental degradation to rally support for its work. Courtesy of the Architectural Archives, University of Pennsylvania.

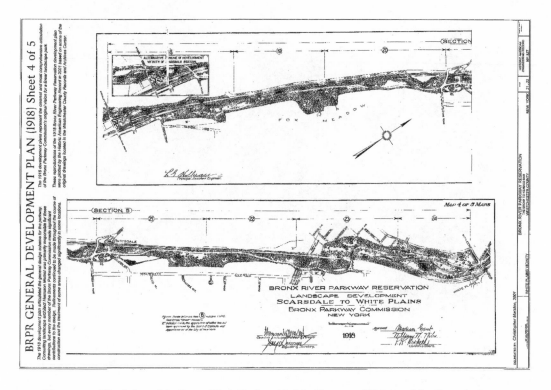

Figure 4.7. The design of the Bronx River Parkway, led by Hermann Merkel and Jay Downer, integrated the roadway and park features (lawns, paths, grouped plantings, forest environments) with the reengineered river. The ample land acquired by the Bronx Parkway Commission allowed the designers enough room to create a consistent park resource for the entire length of the parkway, even though the width of the reservation varied widely. Courtesy of Library of Congress, Prints and Photographs Division, Historic American Engineering Record.

in 1913. The work was halted in 1918 because of the war and was restarted with double shifts in 1919, once equipment and men became readily available. The first sections of park and roadway opened to the public in September 1922, and the 1923 season brought a crush of users. Difficulties in getting the New York City government to release its share of construction funds brought more delays in 1923, and even layoffs of senior staff, before work was completed in 1925. Once the full parkway was opened to the public, jurisdiction was transferred to the respective parks departments of Westchester County and New York City's Bronx borough.

The idea of the parkway stemmed directly from the degraded condition of the valley's natural environment. Because of residential sewage, and to a lesser extent industrial pollution, the stench of "the open sewer" was "indescribable," and, since the Bronx River flows into the zoo, birds began to die in the Bronx Zoo's lake.[10] The valley lands were also susceptible to flooding, which left the riverside land in need of reclamation but also made it relatively cheap and therefore a sensible, cost-effective place to build a park.[11] Solutions to this environmental problem—what kind of park or parkway to build?—drew on the extensive New York tradition of park building and park-driven residential development, as well as on some examples of ecological reclamation from other American cities (Boston's Muddy River and Philadelphia's Wissahickon Creek). The leaders of the Bronx Parkway Commission went beyond these precursors to imagine a more ambitious project, designed to address not only environmental difficulties but issues of transportation, economic development, slum clearance, social reform, and civic culture.

Throughout the nineteenth century, waves of development washed through the Bronx and Westchester. The large estates and industrial villages were transformed beginning in the 1840s with the arrival of the Harlem Railroad. Built along the course of the Bronx River, the railroad spurred the growth of satellite cities such as Mount Vernon and White Plains and laid a necklace of smaller towns and pockets of industry. All the while, private developers and town boosters eagerly sowed the seeds of housing development along the axis everyone knew was destined to absorb the expansion of New York City. In the last third of the nineteenth century, New York itself was looking to this metropolitan future, having annexed the Twenty-third and Twenty-fourth wards in 1873. Andrew Haswell Green and other city leaders commissioned Frederick Law Olmsted to draw up comprehensive development plans for these "annexed districts."[12] As development proceeded northward, so too did advocacy for parks. Civic groups such as the Metropolitan Parks Association, landowner groups, and municipal officials lobbied for public investment to acquire land and build parks in advance of land speculation. In 1884, four thousand acres were acquired for parkland in the Bronx, including Bronx Park, which would later become the home of the Bronx Zoo and the New York Botanical Gardens and the southern terminus of the Bronx River Parkway.[13]

The march of development and rapidly increasing population brought drastic changes to the physical and social landscape of the valley, including major environmental stress and ugly features such as small industries, refuse dumps, and billboards. Land was consumed, more water was needed, and pollution (from industries and residential sewage) combined with increased runoff to seriously degrade the quality of the immediate Bronx River environment and tributaries such as Davis Brook and Troublesome Brook. The use of storm sewers in urbanizing areas of the watershed and continued development in the floodplain further destroyed wetlands and their ability to act as natural sponges and filters, so flooding as well as pollution became a serious problem.

The Bronx Sewer Commission was organized in 1895 to study the public health issues that had emerged in the valley and explore options for addressing them through a public works project. The commission included future parkway commissioner William White Niles, and its report was written by engineer J. J. R. Croes:

> Into this stream of varying flow, all kinds of sewage, refuse and factory wastes finds [*sic*] its way. Barnyards, privies, cesspools, gashouse refuse, the watery part of the White Plains sewage disposal works, and drains from houses in Tuckahoe, Bronxville, Mt. Vernon, Woodlawn and Williamsbridge deposit their unsanitary and foul-smelling contributions. The observation of the commission and the complaints of citizens at the several hearings all confirm the undisputed fact that the Bronx [River] has become "an open sewer."[14]

The transforming and degrading role of the New York and Harlem Railroad, constructed along the valley ridge in 1844, was consistently underplayed or ignored in the Bronx Parkway Commission's narrative of the valley's decline. Instead, blame for the valley's decline was placed on the inhabitants of the bottomlands. Without doubt, the land was made cheap enough for working-class homesteads and small industries not only because it was susceptible to flooding but also because values had been degraded by the coal-burning railroad. And it doubtlessly would have been awkward for the Parkway Commission to have criticized the railroad's role in degrading the land immediately next to the river — and then approach railroad executives for donations of land and their approval of grade-crossing structures.

What was the shape of the valley around 1900? And who lived there? By the 1880s, around thirty-five thousand people lived in the valley. Below Bronx Park, the river was tidal, flattened and widened. From Bronx Park northward, the river possessed the raw material for a picturesque landscape: dramatic gorges and a valley otherwise well defined by ridges, the course of the stream meandering through a succession of open, built, and forested areas.[15] The valley was quite heavily urbanized from its Bronx sections (the Williamsbridge and Wakefield neighborhoods) through Mount Vernon. The river then traced through a succession of workaday villages and small towns (Tuckahoe, Crestwood, Scarsdale) and burgeoning White Plains, before terminating at the newly completed Kensico Dam.[16]

By 1900, a few waves of urban development had rippled though the Bronx River valley, but traces of its bucolic past remained — just the kind of country-life trappings Olmsted sought to bring back into (sub)urbanism. Late in the century, a local historian wrote, "The rapid growth of the City of New York has already destroyed much of its natural beauty, and in a few years its appearance will be changed. A plain, old-fashioned country road is already the exception. . . . Still, there is much of natural beauty left."[17]

ENVISIONING A PARKWAY

On the face of it, the parkway was a winning idea. The Bronx River was in desperate condition. The parkway would solve a number of problems and create opportunity as well. Each of the proposed goals met a pressing need. The 1898 consolidation of New York fueled suburbanization and a raft of efforts to build and expand metropolitan transportation infrastructure.[18] The congested, polyglot citizens, meanwhile, were ever in need of reform. Reform principles, boosterism, and the emergent ideology of rational city planning, married to park ideology, presented a full kit of tools to address these crises. The parkway project drew fully on the accomplishments of previous Progressive reforms. The state law creating the Bronx Parkway Commission mandated the following goals for the parkway, in order:[19]

First, clean up pollution. This was a public health issue as well as a political issue concerning the responsibility to protect existing public investments in parks—especially the Bronx Park and Zoo.

Second, create a reservation of land (a park). Restoring the land, and not just the river itself, was a critical part of the parkway's success. Owning and controlling substantial strips of land was key to remaking the river aesthetically and environmentally, providing visual and ecological buffers. The reservation was also the commission's real power base. Land ownership gave the commission total control, allowing it to implement its plans—not only to rebuild the river, but also to clear existing development, shape new development around the reservation, and effect social reform. The commission wanted to control and reshape this land, not simply move cars through it (the idea of the roadway, fully formed, came later in the parkway's evolution).

Third, form a commission. This body was empowered by the state to implement a multijurisdictional project, encompassing several jurisdictions in Westchester County as well as New York City. It was afforded eminent domain powers and the right to regulate and police the property it owned. The commission had at its disposal a well-organized workforce of seasoned experts, dominated by engineers and lawyers, to carry out its plans. The three commissioners represented the moneyed, the elite, the city builders, and conservative Progressive social reformers, and they took great pride in the efficient, impartial, businesslike conduct of the commission's affairs.

Fourth, build a roadway. A road was always part of the scheme—going back to Croes's recommendations in 1895—but it was secondary. The road only came to the forefront when it was clear (after 1910) that the roadway would be heavily used by commuters and not just for pleasure driving, as had originally been envisioned.[20]

The Bronx Parkway Commission chose to be remembered according to the four points outlined above, and it often reinforced this litany of goals in publications and speeches in which it never failed to tell the story of the valley and the commission's heroic efforts to bring about the happy ending of the parkway. Historians have mostly remembered the parkway for the fourth point—the roadway. It remains remarkable, though, that the Parkway Commission was so successful on so many fronts.

In what became the definitive study of early parkways, landscape architects and planners John Nolen and Henry Hubbard wrote in 1937 that a parkway was simply "an attenuated park with a road through it." Without emphasizing the design of the parkway too much—because the design was a means to the end of reform, not an end in itself—some sense of the parkway's scope and physical plan suggests the extent of the transformation and "improvement" that was envisioned and carried out in the Bronx valley.[21]

Like previous urban parkways, the Bronx River Parkway was quintessentially modern. It was intended to wholly reorganize the social and physical landscape and create a new experience of space and time (moving through a thoroughly urbanized nature in an automobile). The design rationalized different functions and functional spaces by separating them, and it integrated the whole in a controlling physical plan and administrative structure. The parkway was envisioned as both bone and muscle—both the armature for urban development (on the model of Olmsted's Riverside Park) and the tissue connecting old and new elements of the landscape. In addition to separating kinds and speeds of traffic, parkways were also "the first demonstration of the clear separation of traffic and housing," as the architectural historian Sigfried Giedion saw it.[22] Though Giedion imagined this separation as an invention of the automobile age, it simply continued the modern urbanism that had already been established as a hallmark of nineteenth-century Olmstedian "park ideology."[23]

Landscape architect Hermann Merkel executed the design implementing these principles. Physical elements of the Bronx River Parkway included

- A "reservation" of more than one thousand acres of land, in the shape of a sixteen-mile-long strip, varying between 200 and 1,200 feet in width,

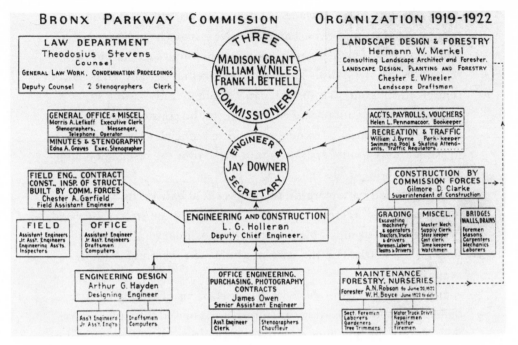

Figure 4.8. The Bronx Parkway Commission was a quasi-public institution, organized with a strict corporate hierarchy of separate departments and functions. Modern management structure, as this illustration from the commission's annual reports suggests, situated the parkway as part of the Progressive reform movement. Author's collection.

following the river course and between the ridge lines. This was the area over which the commission could exercise near-total control.

- A restored and renovated Bronx River. Eight miles of river were dredged and cleaned, 154 sources of pollution were found and stopped, and about six miles of the course of the Bronx River itself was relocated and straightened.

- A naturalistic design integrating the parts (plantings, road, river, structures) and fitting the road alignment and profile to the (revised) topography. More than two million cubic yards of earth were moved.

- A roadway, forty feet wide and paralleling the river and railroad. The design was notable for its limited access, with few crossing streets intersecting at grade (since the parkway had been primarily designed for pleasure driving, an uninterrupted driving experience was important, though providing access to growing suburban communities was essential), and for the use of grassy median strips as lane separators, which were both a safety measure and an aesthetic feature.[24]

- Thirty-seven bridges and viaducts to carry streets, rails, and paths over the roadway and river. The innovative designs by parkway staff and consultants married rustic, historicist aesthetics (in harmony with renovated naturalistic landscape) and technologically advanced, reinforced-concrete structural design.[25] A number of existing streets crossing the reservation were eliminated (to the consternation of some local residents, business owners, and elected officials),[26] and all remaining streets were grade-separated and carried over the reservation and roadway on bridges.
- Heavily planted park margins, serving as visual barriers and forming discrete areas for recreational "park" use. The design strategy stressed preservation of as much plant material as possible, yet the commission often remarked on the scale of wholesale replanting that was required.[27]
- A more open and naturalistic landscape. Dozens of billboards, 370 buildings, and other existing structures were removed from the reservation. Most of the buildings were houses; they were auctioned off by the commission and were then often moved and reused nearby. The commission established a rule that no building could be placed within three hundred feet of the roadway.[28]

THE BRONX PARKWAY COMMISSION AND MADISON GRANT

Who was behind the Bronx River Parkway? The three original members of the Bronx Parkway Commission—Madison Grant, William White Niles, and James Cannon—were the real movers and shakers. Given power and funding to acquire and control the reservation lands, they effectively had a free rein in building and managing all aspects of the parkway. Throughout the twenty years of parkway planning and building, the commissioners often asserted their nonpolitical, objective, and disinterested motives—beauty, health, and efficiency, they held, were above mere politics. W. Delavan Baldwin, president of Westchester County Park Commission, noted that the commission "endeavored to and have succeeded in keeping politics out of this work and have gone ahead on business principles."[29] This, of course, is impossible—when have politics and business ever been separated except in the pronouncements of public officials? What it effectively meant was that the commission's reformers won out over the occasional resistance of Tammany politicians. Indeed, interpreting the political goals of the commissioners is essential to understanding the real goals and achievements of the parkway project.

The Bronx Parkway Commission was chartered by New York State laws passed in 1905 and 1906 as a quasi-public body independent of local governments but dependent on them for funding. Its mission was to study the feasibility of an environmental cleanup and park-building project and then to design and implement it. The prospective commissioners lobbied heavily to get these laws passed, planting stories in the media and writing letters to and holding dinners for politicians, landowners, railroad executives, local business and booster groups, and officials of cultural organizations (including the ASHPS, the Municipal Art Society, and the Metropolitan Parks Association). They worked hand in hand with executives of the New York Central and New York and New Haven railroads, as well as with members of the Bronx Sewer Commission, as the commission's work stood to benefit greatly from the successful completion of the sewer.[30]

Where did the parkway idea come from? By the 1880s, the Bronx River had become an "open sewer," a conduit for residential sewage and industrial waste, as a consequence of unfettered urban development not simply along its banks but throughout its watershed. In response to these obvious public health dangers and environmental evils, a number of prominent citizens and parks advocates lobbied state legislators to fund the Bronx Sewer Commission to study the feasibility of constructing a massive new sewer system in the valley. The engineer commissioned to conduct the study—Olmsted's collaborator, J. J. R. Croes—recommended not only a sewer along the river's course but also a roadway and park reservation built atop the completed underground sewer system: "This highway, and the reservation with the river flowing through it, can be made a beautiful and picturesque feature of the section at very small expense, as the population increases and the needs of the section demand it, since it is naturally very picturesque."[31] The echoes of Thomas Cole are unmistakable. Parkway Commissioner William White Niles was a member of this earlier Sewer Commission, so it is little surprising that the very same arguments were made on behalf of the parkway a few years later.[32] In the end, the Sewer Commission recommended constructing only a few sections of road, keeping the effort focused on the river and sewer itself, and dealing only with controlling floods and eliminating pollution. This recommendation languished until 1905, when state politicians did create a separate commission to acquire land and construct the sewer.[33]

William W. Niles was a prominent Westchester citizen and longtime state legislator. Though he clearly knew of the parkway–sewer idea proposed in the 1890s—and could even have proposed it himself—Niles had a better story about the beginning of the Bronx River Parkway. While on holiday in Scotland, he had an epiphany:

In 1901 I went abroad with Dr. Hornaday, the director of the New York Zoological Society. He had occasion to visit Mr. Carnegie at Skeibo Castle and I accompanied him as far as Inverness, where I remained for three days while he was visiting the Laird of Skeibo.

Having nothing better to do during his absence, I spent most of my time in walking in the vicinity, and on one occasion, coming upon a little park which bordered the River Ness beyond the limits of the city, I followed the river down through the city, and was greatly surprised to find the water as it issued from the limits of the city as clean, so far as appearance went. . . . My astonishment was due to the fact that I had rather assumed that a stream could not go through a built up community without being defiled. I was familiar with many streams running through cities in America, but recalled no instance in which the sewerage and much of the refuse of the city was not dumped into the stream and its banks devastated and shorn of all beauty and in most instances disfigured and rendered offensive by public dumps, dilapidated structures, coal yards and other unattractive activities. The experience set me thinking as to whether it was possible to arouse any interest in America in protecting its streams where they flowed through urban communities.

When I returned home I happened . . . to be walking through northerly parts of Bronx park along the Bronx river . . . and was distressed to see the conditions prevailing there. . . . I determined to make an effort to see if something could not be done to improve matters.[34]

Meanwhile, back in the Bronx, the foul smell and obviously unhealthy quality of the water only worsened. Birds were dying in Bronx Park (the zoo) because the river fouled their lakes (a great offense against a public park that reportedly attracted more than two million users a year). Threatened "wildlife" was a call to action for Madison Grant. As head of the New York Zoological Society, he joined William Hornaday and Niles in lobbying for a state-funded parkway spreading up the whole valley—from the zoo northward to what later became Kensico Dam in Valhalla—spreading the gospels of nature conservation, sanitary reform, and governmental efficiency.[35] Niles, who had been elected to the state legislature in 1895, drafted a bill for establishing a parkway commission and persevered in the capital to get it passed (over the opposition of senators who thought it would wastefully duplicate the efforts of the Sewer Commission). It took several sessions to build the requisite political support for starting the parkway.[36]

From start to finish, the commissioners drove the project and retained a very strong hand in the day-to-day operations. For nearly twenty years, the three com-missioners met weekly (702 meetings), almost without fail, to manage and direct the project in all its details![37] The biography of this remarkable group of men suggests a great deal about the multiple "improvement" goals of the parkway, the ambitious nature of this reform project, and the far-reaching connections between the parkway and other important social movements of the era (such as suburbani-zation, eugenics, and reform politics).

William White Niles was the original spark for the Bronx Parkway idea and a longtime commissioner. A son of privilege, lawyer, civic reformer, Democratic politician, and former state legislator, Niles owned a home along the Bronx River and shared a mutual friend with Madison Grant: Bronx Zoo director William Hornaday.[38] Niles had participated in earlier efforts to advocate for parks in the Bronx and Westchester (his father had been active in the earlier Bronx parks movement) and seems to fill the role of a classic local booster-politician.[39]

The second original commissioner was James G. Cannon, a banker and West-chester real estate developer, whose Scarsdale Estates company was both a con-tributor and vendor of land to the commission.[40] When the commission was first formed to study the feasibility of the project, Cannon housed the commission of-fices at Scarsdale Estates and appointed the engineer from his real estate develop-ment company (J. Warren Thayer) to perform the surveying work for the parkway reservation. Cannon's involvement testifies to the priority placed on the park-way's function in facilitating suburban development. Cannon formed Scarsdale Estates in 1898 to develop housing and a golf club. His interests also extended to moral reform (he was active in the YMCA) and patriotism ("The American home is the cradle and the centre of all our personal and national virtues. . . . When the American home loses its ancient dignity, scrutiny and sacredness, the country is doomed").[41] Cannon's sense for the historic extended to his work as a devel-oper: His golf club, commercial buildings, and residential architecture adhered to Tudoresque and colonial-revival styles. Upon Cannon's death in 1916, Frank H. Bethell, a partner of Cannon's in Scarsdale Estates and vice president of the telephone company, was appointed as commissioner.[42]

The third member, president, and leading light of the commission was Madison Grant, a lawyer, nature conservationist, and writer—a nationally known propo-nent of eugenics and scientific racism.[43] Building on patrician roots, Yale and Columbia education, and notoriety gained through his books (such as *The Passing of the Great Race* and *The Conquest of a Continent*),[44] Grant was connected to leading politicians and scholars of the day (for example, Theodore Roosevelt and geogra-pher Ellsworth Huntington).

Grant was a founder of the New York Zoological Society along with paleontologist and biologist Henry Fairfield Osborn (president of the American Museum of Natural History and Columbia professor, who wrote a preface to Grant's *Passing of the Great Race*), Teddy Roosevelt, and Andrew Haswell Green.[45] But his leadership of the Bronx Zoo and the Bronx River Parkway reveals some of the darker motivations behind preservation and other environmental-reform movements of the early twentieth century. Believing in the genetic superiority of the white, northern European race, Grant wrote popular books and articles detailing the inferiority of "nonwhite" peoples (including Jews and Italians) and the need to exclude them from the United States. Such views on race, racial purification, and reform were mainstream positions in Grant's day.

Beside his work in the Bronx, Grant's activities included organizing the Save the Redwoods League in 1918 with Osborn and working with the National Park Service to protect and interpret this quintessentially American natural ("native") landscape in California. On the national stage, Grant also lobbied for immigration restriction to prevent impurities from diluting "native" American racial stock. All Grant's causes were advanced by his connections (through class, education, and politics) to the highest political levels of the country; he regularly exchanged letters and met with presidents, cabinet secretaries, senators, and scholars.

The direct connections among Grant's many reform pursuits—wildlife conservation, zoo, parkway, eugenics, immigration restriction—are unmistakable.[46] His idea that purely American fauna and flora (such as the California redwoods) must be conserved paralleled the idea that purely American (Nordic) racial stock should be conserved. In both cases, Grant argued for the inherent advantages of the "native" and for using the logic of conservation/restoration to purify and protect what was native. Grant explained the connection he found between the heritage embodied in racial purity and historic heritage—one might call it his "native" narrative:

> Conservation of that race which has given us the true spirit of Americanism is not a matter either of racial pride or of racial prejudice; it is a matter of love of country, of a true sentiment which is based upon knowledge and the lessons of history rather than upon the sentimentalism which is fostered by ignorance.[47]

With his brother De Forest and others, Grant founded the patriotic Society of Colonial Wars in 1892, the kind of heredity-based group Richard Hofstadter and other historians have pegged as evidence of the old elite class's unease with the changing face of the country.[48]

Why Grant became so committed to eugenics and to conservation remains an enigma; the archival evidence that would permit one to draw solid conclusions is gone. Jonathan Spiro ascribes these commitments to childhood encounters with nature, a naturalistically inclined mind, and his rigorous education. Perhaps more straightforwardly, as a patrician he was brought up to look down on others.

For Grant, American history was full of justifications for his racist views and eugenic motives.[49] The kind of environmental designs, historical references, and justifying narratives that he placed at the center of the Bronx River Parkway restoration project were emblematic of this very selective version of the past. When matched with Grant's deterministic and racist anthropological theories, these narratives about patriotism and restoration led to the parkway's program of "improvement"— including slum clearance and ethnic-community displacement along with restoration of "original" natural environments.

Though they are anathema today, Grant's eugenic theories fit neatly into the mainstream environmental determinism of the time: Genetic purity should be accompanied by salutary environments; lesser racial stocks were identifiable by their degraded living conditions. Under the umbrella of environmental determinism, historic preservation and nature conservation could be tools of social reform supportive of the overarching racial project or something less malign.

Grant led the commission from its inception until its disbandment. He chaired weekly meetings for these twenty years and frequently inspected work along the parkway, traveling by car or canoe, or sometimes walking.[50] He got involved with the Bronx Parkway Commission through his longtime leadership of the Bronx Zoo (he was secretary and later president of the New York Zoological Society). Around 1905, with zoo animals threatened by Bronx River pollution, Grant and fellow conservationists sprang into action.

The deep involvement of Madison Grant in the project casts a whole different light on the parkway. Grant was a famous and divisive figure in the history of early-twentieth-century America, renowned and reviled as a proponent of eugenics, racial exclusion, and anti-immigration laws. Grant's ideas about American society, the American environment, and how the past was interpreted to create a particular kind of racially pure future were popular and mainstream in his time. Today, these same ideas demand a reinterpretation of the varied movements in which Grant was deeply involved—not only the parkway, but nature conservation.

Grant must have seen in the parkway an opportunity to pursue several of his interests and ideas at once: reform through nature and wilderness protection,[51] ridding the city of undesirable racial stock,[52] civic reform, and even recreational motoring. Nowhere in the historical record is there evidence that Grant saw his varied activities as part of one grand plan for what would be a truly sinister sort of "improvement." However, it is easy to infer, from his apparent interests, some private correspondence, and his incredible dedication to the parkway as well as his other reform activities, that Grant saw close connections between nature conservation, eugenics, and park and road building. On background, such a holistic view of environmental qualities and social dynamics abides by the overarching reform ideology of the time, hinging on the principle of environmental determinism. More particularly, some of Grant's surviving private letters and published writings shed light on the interconnections of his various pursuits. For instance, Grant wrote to lobby Senator Elihu Root in 1912 on a federal bill to limit immigration, joining the realities of urban slums to immigration policy:

> It is needless to urge on anyone like yourself, familiar with the conditions in New York, the absolute necessity of doing something to stop the draining into this country of the great swamp of human misery and degradation which has centered around . . . Poland . . . [and] Russia.[53]

In part of his voluminous correspondence with Prescott Hall, his colleague at the head of the Immigration Restriction League, Grant relates nature conservation to immigration restriction:

> I regard [immigration restriction] as equivalent to the Game Law where everybody has the right to carry a gun and kill every living thing except certain enumerated animals and birds during specific seasons. How much easier it would be to enforce the law and protect our wild life if no one was allowed to shoot any living thing except certain animals at certain specific seasons and other animals like rats at all seasons. . . . it would be very easy to say that we wanted Scandinavians and did not want South Italians, that we wanted Hollanders and not Syrians, and that we wanted domestic servants and agricultural laborers and not Jewish tailors or Greek banana vendors.[54]

Add to these views Grant's belief—shared among his colleagues in the parkway project, in conservation organizations, and indeed across the whole spectrum of civic reformers—that their work was at heart patriotic:

> Conservation of that race which has given us the true spirit of Americanism is not a matter either of racial pride or of racial prejudice; it is a mat-

ter of love of country, of a true sentiment which is based upon knowledge and the lessons of history rather than upon the sentimentalism which is fostered by ignorance.[55]

Explicitly historical aspects of Grant's devotion to patriotism were evident in his work cofounding the Society of Colonial Wars, an organization of those who had fought in past wars or their descendants. (Grant and his brother were charter members, as their father had had a distinguished career as a Civil War officer and surgeon.)[56] Grant also brought out a book in 1928 collecting quotations from the founding fathers interpreted to support policies of immigration restriction and Americanization. The foreword reads, in part:

> That the process of introducing discordant elements into the body politic is fraught with danger has been the opinion of the thoughtful for many years (see Hamilton, pages 49, 50. Jefferson, page 68. Washington, pages 89–92). The Founders of this Republic were not unadvised on the subject. These pages contain, without comment, extracts taken from the writings and sayings of a number of our early leaders. They will repay study.[57]

The small volume is a remarkable piece of historical justification for scientific racism. To Grant, these voices from the past, all objects of patriotism, answered imperative threats to the Republic and the need to preserve it from the pernicious influences of foreigners. Like much of his work, it is absolutely in line with the views of other preservationists and with their goal of Americanizing immigrants, but it rhetorically and politically takes a giant step further in that direction.

Grant's consuming interest in race and the environment was symptomatic of scientific and reform fields in the early twentieth century. Race stood for "accumulated cultural differences" as well as the biological-cultural notion of "blood." Discourse on race was the thread weaving together "immigration policy, mental health assessments, military conscription, labor patterns, nature conservation, museum design, school and university curricula, penal practices, field studies of both wild and laboratory animals, literary evaluation, the music industry, religious doctrine and much more," in Donna Haraway's analysis. Haraway cites Grant as being typical of mainstream thinkers who saw everything through the lens of race, advancing quasi-scientific racism as metatheory and cultural norm.[58] Thus, in his efforts for the California redwoods and the Alaskan wilds, the Bronx Zoo and the Bronx Parkway, Grant pursued a vision of sanitized, managed landscape as the moral environment needed to combat the degradation of American culture.

The other important group involved in the parkway was the cadre of experts and professionals who realized the commission's agenda as a program, a design, and a new landscape. At its peak, the professional and support staff numbered around fifty. The most influential of these included engineers Jay Downer (known as the "chief executive" of the parkway, he had previously worked building railroads and laying out Scarsdale subdivisions for James Cannon) and Arthur Hayden and landscape architects Hermann Merkel and Gilmore Clarke.[59] Assistant engineer George Hilty took many of the photographs and went door-to-door to negotiate with landowners and tenants. These executive staff members and the small army of workers under them were organized carefully into a model of an efficient public works department. The discipline and hierarchy maintained among the commission staff was almost military. Many of these experts went on to distinguished careers in city planning and other civic endeavors. The Bronx River Parkway was the apotheosis of the Progressive ideology of city planning. As engineer Jay Downer summed up in the commission's final report: "Our public wants a first-class job and will support a big work, if broadly conceived, honestly conducted, and economically administered on a non-partisan basis with all records open."[60]

As for actually building the parkway, the commission managed a seasonal workforce of laborers, many of them drawn from Italian immigrant communities surrounding the parkway reservation.[61] The work—"the rough grading, the moving of the river, the building of lakes, the planting, the topsoiling, and the seeding"[62]—was done by civil service workers; bridges and pavements were built by contractors and their less-well-paid laborers (including Italian stonecutters for the bridge facings). The commission put great trust in the engineers and designers; in contrast, it thoroughly distrusted the laborers and treated them as quite expendable. In 1920–21, Gilmore Clarke's annual salary was raised from $3,600 to $4,200, for instance, whereas common laborers' pay was reduced from fifty to forty-five cents per hour, in keeping with going rates in the vicinity.

Among these people behind the parkway, the balance of power was clearly in the hands of the commissioners. The experts and laborers took their direction—broadly and in the details—from Grant, Niles, and Cannon. As Gilmore Clarke remembered, "The idea came from the vision of the early commissioners."[63]

There was another source for the parkway idea, which the commissioners barely acknowledged: As part of a planned infrastructure and a designed landscape, the idea of parkways, park systems, and parklike suburban developments had been around for a while and had been applied many times in and around New York City. These began with the urban boulevard and the urban park. Olmsted and Vaux's roads and parkways—Central Park, Eastern Parkway in Brooklyn, first among others—stood as examples for New York. In these projects and other examples of what David Schuyler terms the nineteenth-century "park ideology," naturalistic design, creative transportation design, and efficient administration of large-scale public works were integrated to achieve social reform as well as to fuel real estate development. Perhaps the commissioners did not directly acknowledge the influence of these projects because the ideas were so well known and proven that they were considered to be common sense.

River restoration and environmental cleanup were uncommon at the time, though the commissioners certainly studied efforts to clean up Philadelphia's Wissahickon Creek and Olmsted's work on the Muddy River Improvement in Boston. The Muddy River project was sanitary reform, designed to prevent flooding and to reclaim land on the edge of Back Bay. It was planted with indigenous plants to restore the (pre)existing marsh landscape. The Bronx Parkway Commission went to inspect the Fenway and other Boston landscape projects in 1906, when they were about to begin designing their own plans.[64]

One certainty of the parkway was that the project would cost a lot of money. The commission's funding arrangements shaped the parkway effort in critical ways: The Commission had no direct source of funds allocated by the state legislature, nor did it have the authority to issue its own bonds. Funding was contributed by local governments, who had to issue bonds for this purpose. Three-quarters of the funds came from newly metropolitan New York City and one-quarter from Westchester County—despite the fact that three-quarters of the parkway's length fell in Westchester and only a quarter fell in the Bronx. The rationale for this was that New York City would benefit much more from the environmental cleanup than would Westchester and should therefore shoulder more of the cost (somehow this funding formula remained in force, despite the wide recognition that parkway-induced increases in land values and tax revenues would benefit Westchester far more than New York City).

This funding arrangement stalled progress on the parkway several times, as the commission needed to convince Tammany-related New York politicians to release funds in order to continue work. The constantly shifting political sphere of New York City gave the commission an uncertain base of support and source of funds. Some in New York City—government officials and even civic improvement groups such as the Municipal Art Society—felt that such a parkway (even if needed, and they were unconvinced) should be funded by the state and thus went to great lengths to stop or delay funding of the commission's work. Several times, New York City officials withheld the financial contributions required of them by state law, hampering and even halting work on the parkway. In 1917, bills to abolish the commission were introduced in the senate and assembly, instigated by New York Democratic politicians. They charged that the whole project was a misuse of public (New York City) funds benefiting Westchester County. Bronx Parkway Commission political connections were sufficient to quash such efforts, reflecting the ongoing pitched battle between state legislators and city politicians. This necessary engagement with municipal politics was a source of consternation for the commissioners, who contrasted the morass of New York City politics and corruption with their own disinterested public service.[65]

SEVERAL KINDS OF INFRASTRUCTURE, ROLLED INTO ONE

In his classic text *Space, Time, and Architecture,* Sigfried Giedion wrote, "The meaning and beauty of the parkway cannot be grasped from a single point of observation."[66] In Giedion's perspective on the parkway, there is something valuable that forms the basis for its interpretation—the notion that the full significance of the Bronx River Parkway "cannot be grasped from a single point of observation." The parkway combined a varied set of activities and goals under the rubric of landscape "improvement," including environmental cleanup, road building, social reform, and the efficient administration of a large-scale public-planning project. Interpreting the parkway in terms of *one* of these aspects to the exclusion of others would miss the point of the project's original intentions and real significance as a legacy of American urbanism. Indeed, looking at the parkway in the context of the emergent historic preservation field and the whole Progressive environmental-reform movement, the project's construction of a purposeful, creative connection to the past—the preservation of a specific edition of historical memory—stands out. The memorial function of the parkway reinforced Giedion's encomium to parkways as quintessentially modern landscapes.

At the simplest level, the Bronx River Parkway was a typical, straightforward reform response to urban disorder—changing the environment to help change society, addressing space and people simultaneously, as if environmental determinism led reformers to see the world as some sort of holistic, continuous social-geographic fabric—a notion seemingly at odds with the increasingly segregated modern landscape. But what *kind* of response was the parkway, and on whose behalf? Was it a public health issue? Was it a recreation park? Was it transportation infrastructure? Was it social reform and slum clearance? Was it all of these and more? Taken at face value, the rhetoric of the commission proclaimed disinterested, objective goals for the parkway project: a healthier environment, better transportation, and new recreation opportunities. But a detailed look at the commissioners' biographies and their self-conscious archive of meeting minutes, official records, and before-and-after photography foregrounds a number of other goals as equally important: clearing ethnic slums, facilitating suburban development, eliminating threats to the Bronx Zoo, and radically reconfiguring historical memory of the valley.

Historians most often interpret the parkway as an artifact of a particular moment in urban history: The city rebuilds for the automobile.[67] Likewise, the commission itself interpreted the significance of its work as the logical conclusion of the valley's history: The modern highway recovered the legacies of natural beauty and pioneering spirit that had been spoiled by the industrial, immigrant mess that had accumulated by 1900. The parkway, in the commission's narrative, was the capstone of the valley's legacy, the final chapter in its history of the valley. This interpretation has held sway: Nearly every subsequent account of the parkway is silent on the nonroad, non–public health aspects of the project.[68]

In several senses, the Bronx River Parkway embodied the essential qualities of infrastructure: It consisted of physical, three-dimensional structures; it was designed to perform a particular function, addressing a particular problem or opportunity; it enabled further development; it was supported by the public sector in some manner; and it was perceived and used as essential equipment for urban development and social life, not a frivolous add-on.

The Bronx River Parkway was a roadway, hugging the gently undulating landscape and the course of the stream (a design formula later lauded by conservation guru and designer of regional landscapes Benton MacKaye). But this description is a bit misleading: The road conformed closely to the profile of the river, but the river profile was redesigned and changed by a massive amount of grading, excavating, and filling. The road was designed for traffic traveling at thirty to forty miles per hour, on a road without banked curves; the forty-foot-wide surface had room to expand to fifty feet; and the grassy, lane-separating medians used in a few sections were hailed as an aesthetic and safety improvement.[69]

The grade-crossing designs and structures were major features of the parkway's transportation infrastructure. Most at-grade crossings were eliminated; each crossing was individually studied, designed, and engineered, an excellent expression of the total aesthetic control the Bronx Parkway Commission sought over its newly restored landscape and over its points of contact with the surrounding, less-controllable landscape. The bridges were lauded as engineering works and beautiful rustic designs, incorporating modern structure and naturalistic or historicist facings (and presaging the attention famously paid to bridges in successor parkways, such as the Merritt).[70]

The Bronx River Parkway was a public park, incorporating facilities for active recreation (pleasure driving and, to a limited extent, sports such as baseball and swimming) and passive enjoyment (picnics and nature appreciation) among the many acres of lawn, meadow, and forest. Even while the parkway was under construction, the commission granted permission to use reservation land to local groups requesting space for baseball fields, and it constructed bathing houses, which signaled a remarkable improvement in the cleanliness of river water.[71] The commission also allowed victory gardens on bottomlands during World War I. Like other urban parks, the Bronx River Parkway was intended as an amenity, furthering development of the surrounding area as well as directly improving public health.

The Bronx River Parkway was a public health improvement and a flood-control project: It stopped sewage effluent flowing from tributaries and pipes and cleaned debris out of the river bottom, straightening and deepening the channel (the commission called this "river regulation")[72] and planting the stream verges to reduce outwash and erosion. As in the Muddy River Improvement in Boston, the Bronx Parkway Commission's redesign of the valley aimed to make the whole valley work in a more machinelike manner—cleaner, with better flow and less unpredictability.[73]

The Bronx River Parkway directed and channeled suburban development, not just by improving mobility to help decongest New York but also by reinforcing the desirability of Bronx valley land—including land developed by Commissioner James Cannon and his company, Scarsdale Estates. The close link between transportation, park building, and land value was well known to Olmsted and his contemporaries, was assumed by the supporters of parks and parkways throughout the metropolis, and was acted upon by Bronx Parkway commissioners.[74] The parkway epitomized modern New York City's drive toward "improvement." Complementing the skyscrapers, subways, wider streets, civic centers, and better citizens of Manhattan, Westchester County, and the Bronx River axis was a leading edge of metropolitan expansion, already established as a train corridor and primed for the "crabgrass frontier" of automobile-commuting suburbs.[75]

The Bronx River Parkway also worked as cultural infrastructure—multifunctional, totally reconfigured, professionally managed, a seemingly seamless integration of past and future. The cultural aspects of the project were just as central to its success as the engineering of the road. Without reconfiguring the valley's historical memory and scenery—erasing the conflict, disorder, degradation, development, marginal communities, and minority peoples—it would have been impossible to present the parkway as a model modern landscape.

PRESERVATION STRATEGY, MEMORY WORK

What held together the parkway's different goals, functions, and infrastructures as a coherent project? Three things stand out: the commission's rigid organization and administration; superb naturalistic landscape plans and designs that integrated many elements into a sensible and beautiful whole; and a comprehensive, compelling story about the valley, told over and over again and strongly reinforced by the design and execution of the project. It took all three of these factors, working together, to articulate a clear, normative memory of the valley and the parkway. This civic memory—conveyed in the form of the physical landscape, in photographs, in writing, and in rhetoric—wove together the varied goals, strategies, and infrastructures that made up the parkway project.

This section expands on memorial and narrative efforts that were so vital a part of the Bronx River Parkway enterprise. The official histories, before-and-after photographs, the extensive efforts the commission made to publicize its work—all were devoted to making the parkway effort appear to be a natural step in the valley's evolution, bringing back a history that had once existed and completely erasing the landscape and people of the valley as found circa 1900.

Storytelling: Narratives and Historical Memory of the Bronx Valley

The Bronx Parkway Commission told a story about this landscape in which its own efforts were the rightful, sensible final chapter—the story recounted by Jay Downer quoted at the start of this chapter. This story began with evocation of the valley's pristine original nature, moved to the pastoral (balanced) landscape of colonial settlement (later sanctified by Revolutionary War battles), to the despoliation of the place by nineteenth-century development, and to redemption and improvement by the Parkway Commission. In a nutshell: "The hand of man was laid heavily upon the valley of the Bronx until most of its beauty was destroyed, and its waters polluted to the point of foulness," and later, the valley was "restored to its natural condition of purity."[76]

The commission's story was echoed by others, including the *New York Times,* the *Bronx Home News,* and local historian John Wintjen, who wrote in 1933: "The industries which once obtained their motive power from the Bronx River, and the early military activities in its vicinity have now become history. Today we see only its beauties, enhanced by the splendid Parkway following its shores."[77] This narrative has been well sustained, as evident in an article from the 1970s: "In the nineteenth century as the railroad and settlers found their way into this fertile valley, the river slowly became an open cesspool and sewer. By the end of that century it was so badly polluted that it appeared doomed. Its reprieve came with the construction of the BRP."[78]

The Bronx River Parkway was new, modern, and efficient yet anchored in (and by) the past. This story was reinforced in word, image, and space: The overwhelming visual impression of the landscape was of lost nature regained, a timeless nature bereft of most reminders of contemporary activity. The plans self-consciously built on the positive civic memories of New York's naturalistic parks and saw parkway work as part of the preservationist effort to resist threats to park space ("The battle to preserve parks as parks is unending," the commission noted, with special reference to the encroachments threatening Central Park).[79]

The commission also adopted the preservationist strategy of recounting historical narratives associated with the valley landscape as a way of building the importance of the place in the public eye. "In addition to legend and tradition, literary associations and the recorded history of mankind cluster along the stream valleys of the world. The Bronx River Valley is no exception to the general rule."[80] Like other historic sites, the fact that these events and great men were authentically attached to the valley gave greater impetus to the "preservation" the commission was pursuing. Historical narratives routinely cited by the commission included the homesteads and agricultural landscape established by the first European settlers, including Jonas Bronck himself; the few rural mills located along the river in the eighteenth century (especially two of them associated with wealthy New York families, Delancey and Lorillard); Revolutionary War events (Washington's troops traveled up the Bronx valley between the battles of Harlem Heights and White Plains in 1776); and a few industries established in the valley in the nineteenth century (textile and saw mills and a tannery).[81]

Only the distant past was remarked upon, as this provided the kind of historical memory the commission could employ to justify its designs, and there was only a desire for justification (naturalizing the story), not for criticism or reflection. The narratives were based on the "facts" of history on the ground, but, being sufficiently distant from the present time, the narratives based on these facts were quite malleable. More recent versions of the past—memories alive in the minds of residents, for instance—would be more difficult to manipulate. For instance, memories of the destroyed valley communities never had a place in the official histories of the parkway, other than labeling them as hazards. Stories of the displaced and destroyed communities were not only neglected but erased altogether. The manipulation of historical memory by the parkway authorities echoed the fate of St. John's Chapel's congregation: The traditional memory (shared past) of the displaced community was erased and replaced with historical memories constructed and publicized by reformers and authorities. In the case of the Bronx River Parkway, historical memory was used in the service of destruction, whereas in the case of St. John's it was used in the cause of preservation (of the building, though, not the congregation).

The preservation sensibility and historical associations of the Bronx landscape were part of the appeal of the report of the commission led by John Mullaly in 1884 proposing a system of Bronx parks. In a section titled "Landmarks and Traditions of 1776," the report noted the Revolutionary War associations, including Van Cortland Manor's role as "Washington's Headquarters"—the gold standard of patriotism and historical memory—and the old mill that provided bread for both sides in the war:

> This tract possesses, in addition to its singular suitability for a grand public park . . . an historical interest which in these days of centennial celebrations gives it a special value—a value that will increase as time rolls on and those grand old days recede further and further into the past. . . . These are shrines where patriotism is taught, not by wordy harangues, but by stern example, and wherever possible they should be preserved; for no matter how glorious the succeeding years of the Republic have been, and the future may be, the roots of her power and her glory can be found only in the battlefields of the Revolution.[82]

In a May 1906 letter to New York governor Frank Higgins, Madison Grant lobbied for the law creating the commission, arguing the importance of the river and valley for beauty and public health *and* because of its historical associations (Revolutionary War battles and earthworks). Integrating different qualities of the landscape "improvement" was typical of reform rhetoric for this period, appealing to a place's historical memory as part of the fundamental preservationist argument. Grant's language could have been lifted from the pages of the ASHPS annual reports, and it places the parkway effort squarely in the historic preservation field:

> Besides its extreme beauty and its value to one of the most beautiful of the City Parks, the stream has historic associations which render its preservation very important. During the Revolutionary War it was the scene of a long contest between the Continentals and British troops. A few of the old earth-works still remain and many revolutionary relics are still picked up in the vicinity of the stream.[83]

So, along with its other works, the commission promoted standard turn-of-the-century commemoration: filiopietism toward the founding fathers and the first white men; associations with a landscape hallowed by battles; and idealized colonial life, including domestic architecture, mills, and place-names. The commissioners erected monuments to themselves, too. A memorial flagpole dedicated to the efforts of the commission was located at the southern terminus of Bronx Park. Commissioner James Cannon was memorialized upon his death. A bronze plaque on a boulder in the woods near Scarsdale celebrated the land gift of Miss Emily Butler, whose land donation was the largest given to the parkway effort. The commissioners lauded her as an example to follow—a conservationist and public-minded philanthropist.

As for spatializing these memories, the commission had mixed feelings about the presence of other memorials in the reservation—"other" in the sense of memorials commemorating narratives not associated with the building of the parkway and in the sense of not fitting with the parkway aesthetic. Allowing formal memorials of Revolutionary or other local narratives would in effect create a competing memory infrastructure. But communities surrounding the parkway saw the new park as space in which to place the memorials they wished to erect. These proposals had to be brought before Bronx Parkway Commission for approval, given that they were proposed for land within the reservation. The commissioners rejected most of them. Begrudgingly, a few were accepted. Bronx alderman Charles Halberstadt, representing a committee of Draft District Seven, requested permission to erect a soldiers' memorial in the reservation near East 226th Street. They had $5,000 and designs in hand and requested a location only. The commission replied that none of the designs "would harmonize with the informal development of the Parkway" and suggested that a flagpole or "a huge rough boulder or rugged mass of stone work" would be suitable, but nothing came of it.[84] A Mr. Southard from Valhalla proposed a memorial in the reservation to Valhalla residents who had served in the world war. After seeing sketches, the commission tentatively approved it but reserved final approval until seeing the final design of a bronze eagle atop a boulder.[85] The commission also removed "the Bronx River soldier," a life-size statue placed in the middle of the river near the Bronx–Westchester line, where it was accessible by footbridge. Upon removing it to dredge the river, the commission relocated the statue to the Bronx County Historical Society.[86]

The commission had a literary angle on historical memory as well. As early as 1820, some New Yorkers were beginning to divine a romantic and pastoral Bronx valley, to counterpoise the reality of the city's gathering urbanism, furor, and congestion. The early-nineteenth-century poet Joseph Rodman Drake (1795–1820), writing about the Bronx River valley in 1815, presented parkway planners with a neat—though florid—synthesis of history and nature. Drake also gave the commission the "literary associations" that any respectable historic landscape was expected to have. Drake was a Bronx resident, a physician who died young and tragically, and was popularly known as "the poet of the American flag"—for a popular verse he penned to the Stars and Stripes—making him further useful in tying the ideal natural history of the valley to patriotism.[87]

> The breeze fresh springing from the lips of morn,
> kissing the leaves, and sighing so to lose them,
> the winding of the merry locust's horn,
> the glad spring gushing from the rock's bare bosom:
> Sweet sights, sweet sounds, all sights, all sounds excelling,
> Oh! 'twas a ravishing spot formed for a poet's dwelling.
>
> And did I leave thy loveliness, to stand
> again in the dull world of earthly blindness?
> Pained with the pressure of unfriendly hands,
> Sick of smooth looks, agued with icy kindness?
> Left I for this thy shades, where none intrude,
> to prison wandering thought and mar sweet solitude?
>
> Yet I will look upon thy face again,
> My own romantic Bronx, and it will be
> A face more pleasant than the face of men.
> Thy waves are old companions, I shall see
> A well-remembered face in each old tree,
> And hear a voice long loved in thy sweet minstrelsy.

The histories, associations, and poetry stop around the 1830s—the period between the 1840s and 1890s is mute. There is no mention, for instance, of the single most important factor in the valley's nineteenth-century history: the construction of the New York and New Haven Railroad, completed in 1844. The past was kept at a distance, the better to construct historical memory from it. This break in the history of the valley's past, not incidentally, reinforces Leo Marx's insight about the 1840s being a watershed in American culture—when the railroad arrived in the garden.[88] This watershed moment in American culture, the onset of modernity one could call it, had many effects, including the valorization of "scenic" and "historic" places as representations of the simplicity, beauty, and virtues of the premodern world vanquished by the railroad.

Visual artists also found the Bronx River an appropriately romantic, pastoral subject—for instance, the American painter R. L. Pyne captured a wild, remote scene of the river in the 1880s. This painting helps locate attitudes toward the Bronx among the canonical approaches to representing nature as an American heritage, as mastered by Thomas Cole and the Hudson River school, and other romantic writers like Drake.

Memory is a selective process, and the intentionality behind representations of the public memory of the parkway highlights this clearly. Aspects of the distant past were celebrated and idealized, while the more recent past was ignored. Giving form, voice, and visualization to an idealized past (the "natural conditions" regained, and a few monuments) complemented the commission's efforts to erase parts of the landscape that spoke to the recent past and undesirable aspects of contemporary society: houses in the floodplain (many of which had been moved once already to make way for railroad or sewer construction); Italian and African American communities in White Plains, Mount Vernon, and the Bronx; billboards, river debris, and sewage.

Nature as Heritage and Historical Memory

Nature formed an important part of historical memory in turn-of-the-century New York. Nature and culture are strongly bound together in forming the canons of American memory. It follows that efforts to shape public memory would be most successful if they incorporated both scenic and historic places. American patriotic values and memories draw as strongly from natural elements—the shape, look, character, and meaning of the land—as they do from human achievement and "culture."[89] Think only of "America the Beautiful" alongside "The Star-Spangled Banner," or of the canonical shrines of American heritage, which include national wonders as well as historic sites. As with the use of cultural and individual narratives to construct historical memory, the "nature" contributing to public memory was itself thoroughly constructed, selectively framed, and managed to achieve a proper balance of wilderness, the sublime, and the pastoral.

Naturalistic design[90] was decidedly urban and was meant to catalyze social change. It was an aesthetic strategy proven as a civilizing force many times over in New York and other American cities. The values of naturalistic design were many: It created beauty, often "improving" landscapes seen as "degraded." It brought urban dwellers into contact with nature, which was believed to have a salutary and moralizing effect on them. It provided a commons in which democratic society could flourish. It provided open, green space for recreation. Urban parks and park systems were known to raise real estate values and therefore to be wise investments of public funds. Last but not least, park landscapes embodied public historical memory (implicitly and explicitly) in four ways.

First, nature was prized as an original, authentic cultural condition—as "native." The use of native plants was part of the landscape ideology espoused by the commission, a principle suggesting some connection between the intrinsic value ascribed to native plants, the intrinsic value of historic places, and eugenicists' belief in the intrinsic value of "native" peoples. The mutual reinforcement of racial purity and landscape design driven by "native" plants was not a novel idea; it was evident in the context of late-nineteenth-century Germany (both in landscape design and landscape painting) and in the work of Jens Jensen, a Danish landscape architect transplanted to the American Midwest.[91]

The second aspect of shaping public memory was the interpretation of "scenic" places—which included a range of natural landscapes—as an important part of the national legacy and the object of historic preservation. Naturalistic design was underpinned by a consensus belief that wilderness and sublime nature was part of the heritage of Americans and therefore part of the patriotic canon—in recompense, many have argued, for the young Republic's dearth of human history. Along with heroic deeds, nature lent American culture historical depth and distinction. The canon of American monuments are Washington's Headquarters *and* Yosemite, Gettysburg *and* Niagara Falls. To use a more contemporary notion: "Scenic and historic objects" together made up the "heritage" that was the raw material for public memory and the object of the work of preservationists and other memory shapers. By putting scenic *and* historic together, preservationists were also making a statement that scenic value was a version of historic value. This scenic-(as)-historic synthesis was a commonly held principle in New York's preservation and conservation circles, expressed, for instance, in the name and mission of the most dedicated preservation advocacy group of the period, the American Scenic and Historic Preservation Society:

> It would seem a fitting time that conservative methods be devised by means of which objects of historic value, localities where patriotic struggles have taken place, where peculiar natural scenery obtains, or made interesting by association with illustrious personages, should be rescued from the grasp of private speculation and preserved for public enjoyment, subject only to such restrictions as make for the public pleasure.[92]

Third, by the early 1900s, New York City's parks were newly valued as civic memory sites in themselves, as cultural achievements and for their utility as aesthetic, recreational, economic, and public health resources. Civic pride in the city's parks had taken on a new dimension; parks like Central Park, the Battery, and Bowling Green were part of the pantheon of civic patriotism that memory shapers were trying to build, preserve, and convey. Central Park, for example, was lionized as a monument to the reform tradition to which preservationists and other civic reformers saw themselves as successors. As part of its preservation advocacy, the ASHPS published a history of the park along with excerpts of Olmsted's biography.[93] The Battery and City Hall Park were somewhat different examples: Their heritage was embodied in their history as long-standing open spaces, in the centuries of ongoing use if not in intentional design as a public space. Public spaces, in this sense of a long-shared, communal resource, inherently have historic value. Thus, preservationists continually fended off proposals to alter or build in parks, as compromising the open spaces of parks would destroy an aspect of their historic value.

Fourth, the creation of a designed, naturalistic landscape brings with it a narrative element: the notion of nature being lost and then regained. This "redemption" storyline was particularly important to these efforts to clean up the Bronx.[94] The commission invoked a story of nature balanced, nature lost, and nature regained. Augmenting this, the commission touted the extent to which it "preserved" the existing landscape (while, ironically, also citing the statistics measuring how completely that preservation remade the valley landscape).

Naturalistic design was in part a strategy for constructing civic memory, and it follows that naturalistic landscapes (both created and preserved) are elements of a civic memory infrastructure. The genealogy of this idea is clear in the Olmstedian model, which was woven out of several traditions relating physical design and natural landscapes to normative ideas about social and moral reform, and relying on faith in the intrinsic value and moral power of historic and scenic places.

Before and After: Landscape Improvement and Photographic Storytelling

The trigger for the parkway project was the "degraded" condition of the valley landscape. "Degraded" had at least three dimensions to it: The natural landscape was physically degraded, which is to say flood-prone and polluted; the landscape was aesthetically degraded, being strewn with billboards and the workaday yards behind plain wooden houses; and the people who lived in the valley bottomlands (slated to become the Parkway Reservation) were of degraded racial stock. Such judgments are, of course, in the eye of the beholder, and the Bronx Parkway

Commission made great efforts to establish these degraded conditions as the unarguable view of the public eye. It achieved this with an extensive photographic campaign—spanning decades of survey, design, and construction—relying on the device of before-and-after photographs of particular locales and scenes to convey its official narrative of the valley's history.

The commission took great pains to construct a positive identity for itself, its actions, and the parkway landscape—such an identity was needed to ensure public accountability and continued funding. It stood on the legs of efficiency, fiscal thrift, and public health, as well as on narrative constructions of history and nature. These ensured public and political support. The commission's tools for this process included published reports, an archive of its weekly meetings over nearly twenty years, presentations to conferences and business groups, articles in professional journals, friendly articles placed in newspapers,[95] and a remarkable archive of photographs. The commission took thousands of photographs documenting its work and the preexisting conditions in the valley. In effect, these photographs were a tool for (re)constructing the landscape and a landscape narrative—and, like Frank Cousins's work, they "preserved" this place. Storytelling photographic preservations were key to the commission's effort to construct the historical memory and public image of the Bronx River valley.

These photographs recorded existing conditions and the progressing work of parkway construction. They were published in nearly every one of the commission's publications and were used in lantern slide presentations. They constituted a pictorial strategy to justify and promote the work of the commission in making the planned "improvements."[96] The photographic strategy had an inherently historical, narrative logic to it: These plain, inartistic images were almost always displayed in before-and-after pairs, which succinctly and convincingly conveyed the commission's declension-and-redemption story. The "before" photos presented the most unflattering aspects of the valley and were usually taken in winter. The images of "improved" landscapes showed the lush greenery of spring and summer, with nearly all traces of buildings and people removed.[97] The before-and-after strategy followed Humphry Repton's famous "Red Book" methods of the eighteenth century, in which he advocated for landscape "improvements" designed by him through arguments that were at once visual and narrative.

Photographs legitimated not only the restoration of degraded land but also the removal of working-class, often immigrant, housing. The photographs also documented the removal of all signs of production and commerce from the landscape—billboards, factories, small farms, and stables—in favor of the new parkway landscape of consumption.

Figure 4.9. These two pairs of before-and-after photographs taken by the Bronx Parkway Commission (of 210th Street in the Bronx and a site at Bronxville in Westchester County) capture the transformation that the parkway builders achieved. Courtesy of the Architectural Archives, University of Pennsylvania.

Historian Tim Davis calls the pictorial strategies of the Bronx Parkway Commission "deliberate" and "deceptive." "Disingenuous pictorial strategies" were used to promote the social and spatial agendas of the commission. The photos were used to legitimate the expert, reforming roles of landscape architects and planners. More important, they legitimated the commissioners' goals: reform along with suburbanization; keeping the whole project funded by getting legislative approvals and bond issues; constantly proselytizing the case for the parkway to landowners.[98]

The parkway story, with all its inclusions and elisions, was *part of* the improved landscape of the Bronx valley, constantly retold in words and photographs and built in earth, water, stone, and plants. The landscape forms themselves told the story, but only partly:

> The parkway by the beauty of its planting, its fine driveway, with the evidence which is manifest to all using it of the care and thought exercised in its locations, the architectural features in the way of bridges and viaducts, will teach a valuable lesson . . . which should go into any such improvement. . . . [But to avoid the same dangers in the future] it will be necessary to have reference to [this] written record and to the convincing photographic evidence which will be preserved among the records of the Commission.[99]

Despite the commission's exhaustive efforts to shape memory in word and images, it did not persist in the ways the commissioners intended. Memory, like physical landscapes, erodes and shifts, is added to and subtracted from. As the parkway was being completed, the city-planning field was taking a highly rational, technocratic turn, destining the parkway to being remembered for its technical achievement, not its social goals. And even in this vein, the parkway was quickly eclipsed. When Gilmore Clarke wrote about the parkway in subsequent years, he cast it mostly in terms of landscape and roadway design—the reform aspects of the project had already faded. When the National Trust for Historic Preservation placed the Bronx River Parkway on its 1995 list of "America's 11 Most Endangered Historic Places," it was remembered because the roadway—the "scenic drive"—had become historic.[100]

SLUM CLEARANCE AND SUBURBANIZATION

Like most efforts to create memory infrastructure, the Bronx River Parkway required some destruction. Buildings, communities, land uses, and other landscape features built up in the second half of the nineteenth century were defined as the problem—the "blighted conditions" at which the parkway efforts were aimed—so removing them was, for the commission, a logical precursor to building the new ideal landscape of the parkway. It is particularly important to recognize the destruction as well as the creation of landscape elements contributing to memory infrastructure, and in the case of the Bronx River Parkway it is also the easiest way of seeing the connection between "improvement" of the Bronx River valley and Madison Grant's belief in eugenics.

Destruction was a reality in the parkway project—eggs must be broken to make the omelet, as the saying goes—but there were vastly different interpretations of what destruction meant and how necessary it was. As the quotations above suggest, the commission and its professionals saw destruction, clearance, reclamation—call it what you will—as a logical and natural part of the process of improvement. Residents and others without official voice might have thought very differently about it. Like local resident Adele Priori, for instance, they could have seen some value in the existing landscape and envisioned a different way to transform it, a different ideal to construct. The destructive aspects of the Bronx River Parkway, and the detailed records of the condemnation and construction processes through which we can reconstruct them, provide a glimpse into the reception of the parkway by valley residents soon to be displaced.

Taking Ownership

The parkway provided the mobility to enable Westchester residents to commute by car to New York City, making a great deal of land ripe for suburban residential development and increasing its value.[101] Suburban landowners, developers, and real estate companies were a key constituency for the parkway. They provided political support through their influence on state legislators, through the financing this achieved for the parkway, and through land they directly contributed for the reservation.

The connection between park and parkway construction and increasing land values was well known. Olmsted often mentioned it as one of the rationales for park building, and civic boosters and owners of adjacent property were well aware of the benefits.[102] Increasing land values meant greater property tax receipts, and thus, parks and parkways were understood to pay for themselves. The clear memory of Central Park's success as a real estate venture was fresh in everyone's mind. John Mullaly's New York Parks Association led the charge in creating a system of parks through the Bronx for the dual purposes of ensuring "breathing space" and ensuring the quality of residential development that was clearly on its way. Nolen and Hubbard demonstrated this effect in their 1937 study of parkways, using the Bronx River Parkway as an example.[103]

The commission wanted to replace "the wrong sort of development" with "the best class of development."[104] Degraded or "blighted" environments were known to prevent new development of high quality, and their transformation was known to provide economic opportunity. Bronx Parkway Commission engineer Warren Thayer reported to Madison Grant in November 1910 a discussion Thayer had had with Bronx Borough engineer Amos L. Schaeffer: "River lands and old erosion bottoms periodically flooded. Unfit for healthful residence. Increasing plague zone. Permanent detracting influence on better property growth—retarding desirable community development and normal increase of taxable valuations."[105] With the existing landscape devalued, the way was paved for "improvement." Thus, to begin the process of removal, existing communities and homes near the river were routinely portrayed—in photographs and words—as unsanitary, chaotic, unaesthetic, and decidedly unpastoral to justify evictions, land acquisition, and expenditures on parkway improvements. Even properties that were clearly *not* in such poor condition were condemned and cleared if parkway designs required it.

Once the commission gained title to a parcel, it would immediately raze or move the buildings in order to compel adjacent landowners to sell their property soon, on the commission's terms.[106] Most of the 370 buildings removed were houses. Some were small businesses. These were places where immigrant and working-class folks could own or rent a house with a bit of land, form a community, perhaps run a business, and still be in close proximity to transit.

About a third of the properties acquired by the commission came through condemnation (454 of the total of 1,338 properties). The condemnation of so much property disrupted community life even in those places not stigmatized as slums. Correspondence in Parkway Commission property records indicate several examples of commission actions that put small merchants or manufacturers out of business—either by directly displacing them and not paying a high enough price for land or buildings to enable the merchant to open a business elsewhere, by closing streets that provided access to business locations, or by displacing the businesses' customers.

The details of the commission's land-acquisition policies and experiences shed light on how the owners and tenants of property within the reservation saw the construction of the parkway and on the kinds of places those policies were destroying. As a group, owners and tenants had mixed feelings. Some owners were happy to be bought out and were eager to move on; others were reluctant to leave their homes. Tenants had no power and were simply evicted. Most owners negotiated, and many quarreled with the commission over the price to be paid for properties. The commission went through a thorough appraisal procedure on each property, after which they tendered an offer. The owner would usually counteroffer. If a price could not be agreed on following this, the commission would condemn the property. But these proceedings were lengthy and were usually more expensive for the commission: It very often had to pay a higher price in condemnation than it otherwise offered. These proceedings also took a good deal longer and delayed the work—obviously earth moving and construction work could not proceed in

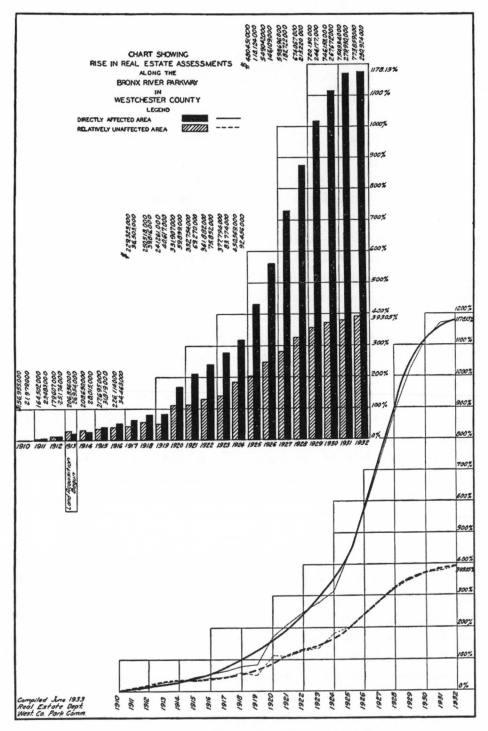

Figure 4.10. John Nolen and Henry Hubbard included this graph in their 1937 treatise on parkway planning and design, demonstrating the crucial economic development principle behind the plans of the Bronx Parkway Commission: The public cost of parkway construction and improvements raised adjacent land values enough that tax revenues paid back the cost to the state. Courtesy of University of Pennsylvania Libraries.

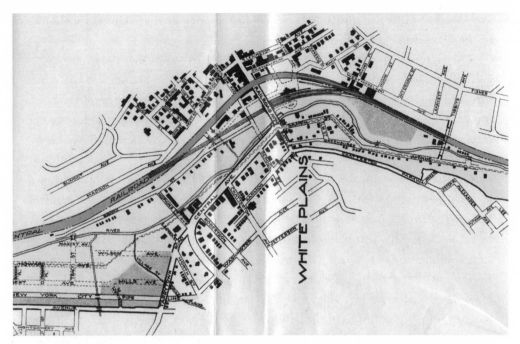

Figure 4.11. This detail of Bronx Parkway Commission development plans around downtown White Plains shows the extent of planned removal or demolition in the shaded area of commission reservation land surrounding the river. In this area, 101 buildings are marked for removal. Author's collection.

places where the commission did not yet hold title. Thus, it did everything it could to convince owners to sell and obviate the need for condemnation proceedings.

The commission went to great lengths describing its fair and objective approach to land negotiations, including its reluctance to use condemnation unless absolutely necessary. More than a few owners accused the commission of treating them poorly, "like dogs," in the words of one. There was a fundamental difference in the way the commission valued property and buildings and the way owners did. The commission selected an architect and an appraiser to independently price the property and based its offer on these numbers. That was, it said, the most "scientific" method, and it seemed truly disbelieving when owners rejected its offers. The commission appraised the present value of the property, but owners routinely protested that these prices were too low to allow them to actually relocate—to build a new house or relocate a business—because they did not account at all for moving costs, lost business revenue, or other costs. The commission rejected all such claims, and the judges sitting at condemnation proceedings generally gave them little weight. Of course, no aspect of cultural value—whether expressed as historical association, family history, personal attachment to home, or the like—was acknowledged.

The commission steadfastly appraised all property—whether house, business, garden plot, or church—only on the basis of the material qualities of the structure and the size of the lot. Never was an allowance made for the use of the land, the consequences (economic and otherwise) of halting those uses, or the costs of relocating. Generally, the commission offered somewhat less than half what owners asked.

On the surface this was simply a case of state-sponsored redevelopment and creative destruction with the intended effect of gentrification, but the motives behind it were not merely economic. The existing landscape was scarred not only by refuse, flooding, tumbledown houses, and billboards; it also harbored undesirable immigrants of "races" (Italians, blacks, and assorted other non–northern Europeans) detested by eugenicist and commissioner Madison Grant. The commission worked to sanitize the valley's social landscape as well as its ecology. This meant getting rid of "undesirable conditions" by the river's edge, including "Italian shacks" as well as billboards, and replacing them with an aestheticized, naturalistic park landscape. Both the disappearance of the extant landscape and the appearance of the new park landscape were a boost to the "best class" of suburban residential development. Tim Davis notes that while most reformers tried to improve inhabitants by bettering the environment, the Bronx Parkway Commission tried to improve the environment by getting rid of the inhabitants.[107]

Riverside Communities

The social impact of clearance and destruction on existing communities and homes was most apparent in the few larger clusters of homes in the Parkway Reservation at White Plains, Mount Vernon, and northernmost Bronx. These clusters were on the physical and socioeconomic margin of towns and villages that had grown up in the valley—some dating back to the preindustrial era, others having grown around railroad stations in the second half of the nineteenth century.

The bottomlands of the Bronx River formed a kind of transient landscape. Periodic flooding made the land of marginal value; more disruptive were major infrastructure projects such as the building and expansion of railroad facilities and the construction of the trunk sewer. These projects resulted in a lot of house moving; perhaps a fifth of the 370 buildings the commission removed had been moved once in the past.[108] The large majority of buildings in the reservation were sturdy and permanent, though quite utilitarian. The residents of the bottomlands were mostly working-class and were largely immigrants.[109] Cartographic and census data suggest that some of these communities were mostly Italian; others were quite mixed, with foreign- and native-born residents; and some, at least in the Williamsbridge section of the Bronx, included African Americans as well as European immigrants. The majority of the houses were owner-occupied, and many of them had substantial mortgages, suggesting that these properties were the first purchases for working-class families working their way into property ownership. Anecdotal evidence (from property-file data including interviews with owners) suggests that some of the resident property owners were eager to be bought out by the commission and then to move out and up in the housing market.[110]

Significant clusters of houses were located at Williamsbridge (in the Bronx, just north of Bronx Park), Mount Vernon, and White Plains (the largest, with over one hundred buildings cleared). Analysis of Sanborn Fire Insurance Company maps and other maps suggests that the riverside land was often the last to be developed in a particular area and was often given over to industrial land uses and lower-class dwellings.[111] These dwellings and communities were judged by the commission to be marginal and worth little, a conclusion drawn from outward appearances that also made the work of acquisition and clearing more expedient. Bottomland dwellers, especially immigrants, were disdained by the commission and seen as simply another environmental "condition," suitable for their engineering approach of clearing away and constructing anew.

To what extent did these clusters constitute "communities"? In the case of White Plains, there is compelling evidence that the parkway destroyed a close-knit community—a cluster of small houses owned and occupied mostly by Italian-Sicilian immigrant families. The 104 buildings in this cluster, located on Smith Street, across the river from downtown, surrounded a small Catholic parish church, Our Lady of Mt. Carmel. The residents of Smith Street worked as hod carriers, gardeners, stonemasons, laborers, and hotel bartenders. Most of them had arrived in the United States between 1890 and 1910.[112]

The commission property-acquisition records provide a few glimpses into the social status of residents, the character of their houses, and the relationship between the commission and the residents.[113] Salvatore Falsorano, at 97 Bronx Street, had earned his U.S. citizenship, and with his wife Eugene held a $700 mortgage on their two-story shingle house. The commission's architect (sent out to describe the condition of every acquired building for appraisal purposes) reported the house to be "run down" and continued, "This house is of a very inferior kind; has practically no improvements. No sewerage, cold water plumbing . . . light frame, mostly second hand lumber."

Figure 4.12. These two photographs show part of downtown White Plains before and after removal of residents, building demolition, and landscape reconstruction. Courtesy of the Architectural Archives, University of Pennsylvania.

Likewise, Joseph and Vicenza Palermo's property was described as a "poor type of building . . . very old," moved here not long ago. The appraisal also noted that the house had cement foundations and water but no sewer, and that the tenants were "Negroes." Mr. Palermo wrote asking the commission to speed up the acquisition because he had a new property in mind. A few doors down, at 85 Bronx Street, Domenico and Anna Disalvo ran a bakery in the rear half of their building, and a second building served as a stable for six horses. Another appraisal report described a Smith Street property as a "tumbled down vacant house and inhabited by goats," further noting that "it was in this house that the murder of Carida by Bova took place." Of another Smith Street house, assistant engineer George Hilty wrote to his bosses: "It is an old grade building, and the dismantling and removing of same, particularly in this section, would have a wholesome effect in inducing other vendors in that vicinity to negotiate the sale of their holdings to the Commission"; he was keeping an eye on the commission's goal of acquiring and clearing property cheaply and quickly. In the eyes of commission staff, there was nothing redeeming about most of the buildings standing in the reservation.

But this part of White Plains also had some very substantial buildings. A hotel with fifteen guest rooms, a bar, and a dining room, five minutes' walk from the train station, stood in the reservation. It had been moved there from the railroad right-of-way about fifteen years previously. At the center of this community was Our Lady of Mt. Carmel chapel and parish house. The commission dealt as severely in acquiring this church as in acquiring any "tumbled down" house.

Commission appraiser Edward West visited the chapel and reported attractive, well-built buildings (the chapel and rectory) in fair condition and grounds with good shade. He also took note of stained glass windows. His appraisal of $16,575 included neither the costs of relocating nor compensation for the interior furnishings of the church. This was a matter of commission policy; it was not required to compensate owners for such costs, nor for hardship, and it never offered. The appraising architect reported the 320-seat chapel and rectory to be in good condition, but set a price of just $9,000.

Rev. Joseph A. Marinaro was the founding pastor of Mt. Carmel (according to the commission's architect report, the church was "his life blood"). Leaving the chapel was a foregone conclusion—the commission freely used its eminent domain power—so the only recourse for a property owner was to negotiate a price. In this vein, Marinaro wrote to the commission on April 8, 1913:

> Honorable Dear Sirs, In reference to your letter, dated March 15th . . .
> concerning your buying this Church's property I should like to inform
> you that having consulted my Superiors at the Cardinal's Residence, in
> New York, the said property can be purchased by you for the price of thirty
> thousand dollars, with the understanding that we will take the church and
> parish house and transfer them in a suitable place nearby. We can prove
> that we cannot replace the same in this neighbourhood with less money.

Meanwhile, Hilty reported to the commissioners: "While in White Plains, I was informed by an Italian who did not wish to be known in the matter, that the Rev. Joseph A. Marinaro wants to get enough money for the above premises to go to Europe. He is trying to get $28,000 for this purpose. He has been sick for some time and wants to leave America."[114]

After a series of accusations, counteroffers, and refusals, the commission made its final offer of $16,540 in late 1915. On February 8, 1916, a lawyer for the dioceses, Edward McGuire, was sent to negotiate for the chapel. Having obtained an appraisal of $17,600, which did not include any allowance for moving, he said the church was willing to settle for $20,000. Commission executive Jay Downer did not budge. On February 19, 1916, McGuire wrote, exasperated, "After consulting with the officers of the church corporation, the Church of Our Lady of Mt. Carmel, White Plains, I have received authority from the corporation to accept the offer of $16,540 made by you for the purchase of its real property." Characteristically, the commission got its way—it played hardball, and won—and the way was cleared for the parkway to sail through White Plains.

In the town of Mount Vernon, just across the New York City line, the commission removed thirty-one buildings.[115] The residents there were mainly immigrant (about equal parts German-born and Italian-born) and worked as laborers, bakers, janitors, and stonemasons; one was a street railway conductor.

In negotiating for each property, there was typically a series of counteroffers, often leading to a compromise on the part of the owner, or otherwise leading to a condemnation proceeding, at which the commission usually paid substantially more than it had first offered. The negotiations were quite intense. A Mrs. Roper visited the commission office in December 1913 to discuss the offer on her property. As Hilty recounted in his report: "She considered the offer ridiculously low."

In Mount Vernon, a number of small businesses were displaced. Mr. and Mrs. Herbison spoke to commission engineer Jay Downer in January 1915, saying they could not take less than $10,000 for their multibuilding property. Even $7,500, they said, would not be enough to buy a parcel across the street, move the buildings to it, and reopen their ice business—which depended on the great accessibility of this area to trolleys and trains. To no avail.

Elise and Peter Nantz operated a delicatessen at 504 Bronx River Road. Mrs. Nantz explained in a December 1913 letter to the commission that she could not accept their offer, which did not take into account the income she counted on from the operation of the store. Hilty reported in a memo that "[Mr. Nantz] further stated that the Commission in acquiring his property is not only depriving him of his home but of his earning capacity, and that the amount offered by the Commission is insufficient inasmuch as he cannot reestablish himself elsewhere, and that the Commission would therefore subject him and his family to future privation and suffering."[116] Hilty swiftly replied that the commission "finds no tangible basis that would justify an increase in its offer." Wanting to avoid the "hardship" of condemnation, Nantz pleaded in more letters, in visits to the commission office, and in conversations with Hilty for a high enough price for him to at least break even and continue business in a nearby location; he wanted to remain "in place." In March 1916, Nantz wrote: "Since my original offer on May 21, 1915, a good many of my customers living in the Parkway have moved away, with the result that their trade is no longer available and to that extent my business has been destroyed by your Commission."

Adam Danner, who was president of East Yonkers Realty Company as well as Ad. Danner Co., a manufacturer of brewers' and bottlers' machinery ("the globe porcelain stopper a specialty"), was moved from his group of shops and dwellings, but he planned to reopen elsewhere.

In Mount Vernon as elsewhere, some of the buildings cleared by the commission were far from "blighted." For instance, Incoronata De Pasquale, who lived in White Plains, owned a three-year-old building, "in good condition throughout, well plumbed, sewage piped to river." It had a stone foundation; the metal-reinforced structure was covered in stucco. It housed two stores in front and had two flats behind and two flats on both the second and third floors. The commission increased its initial counteroffer and compromise price of $13,000. The successful bidder on this structure moved the building to a nearby corner (out of the reservation) and renovated it into "a high class steam apartment building with janitor's quarters in the basement."

In the Williamsbridge section of the Bronx, the story was largely the same. The commission acquired and removed thirty-seven buildings. This was a neighborhood of drivers, laborers, and laundresses living as renters. About half the residents were of Italian descent; they also included a number of southern-born African Americans and a few Irish.[117]

The commission saw the residents themselves as part of the problem to be fixed. They were blamed directly for the blighting influence, the degraded condition of the valley. Their lives, their stories, had no value in the eyes of the commission and no place in the narrative of the modern parkway. The reason for this was not simply that blight prevented the implementation of the parkway design or maximization of economic value through suburban development. It was driven by discrimination and racism as well. As is apparent from the eugenic theories elaborated in his books, Grant considered most of the residents to be of inferior race, and he worked avidly to exclude such people from immigration to the United States. The captions appended to photographs of riverside dwellings read: "Italian shacks" and "Slums." For Grant, Americanization wasn't enough: The Jews and other inferior races had to be kept out. Such racial impurities were worsened by their concentration in cities: "Cities are consumers of men and the country side producers of them. So we still have some chance for the future if we are able to keep the blood of the countrymen pure."[118] Though the commission never explicitly stated that the racial purity of the valley was one of its goals, the fact that racial purity and environmental reform were the fundamental beliefs of the commission's longtime president makes the connection clear.

Popular Resistance

John Bodnar suggests that public memory is an accommodation of official and vernacular memories, continually challenged and reformed.[119] It is difficult to get a handle on this historically. The vernacular motives for shaping memory too often are simply inferred, as little historical or landscape evidence is available. Therefore the memory constructed around the Bronx River Parkway, to the extent that it has been reconstructed and analyzed here, is mostly of the "official" kind. What means, if any, did ordinary citizens have to reshape or protest this official memory?

Commission archives and newspaper clippings provide a few shreds of evidence: Several communities, as noted below, proposed the creation of memorials on reservation land. These were mostly war memorials, and communities saw the parkway as a typical kind of park, in which green space would be punctuated with modest patriotic monuments. The commission allowed a few such monuments on the reservation, but they constituted less a challenge to the official parkway narrative than a harmless adding-on of another use of open space that did not detract from the parkway's functions.

One form of resistance to the parkway and its official vision was through real estate negotiations and transactions. Many property owners objected to the tactics of the commission and felt cheated. Some returned insults to the commission.[120] As the property files show, several times community groups (mostly homeowners' associations) petitioned the commission to change its designs—create a new grade crossing, make part of the reservation accessible to adjacent residents, eliminate plans for an artificial lake—but these comments were generally dismissed, as the commission stuck to its design vision.[121] While these protests were not aimed at the parkway's overall narrative, they show convincingly the disaffection among some of the public with the commission's efforts and tactics.

Finally, violence and vandalism, a more direct form of resistance, cropped up along the parkway now and then. In 1921, commission park-keeper John Siliano was attacked by two men while on patrol and "forcibly removed from his post."[122] Vandalism of signs and other parkway property worried the commission in the early 1920s. Vandals repeatedly defaced and stole signs marking the boundaries of the reservation and announcing the commission's control of recently acquired and improved land.[123] The commission offered rewards to find the vandals, to no avail. These nuisances, along with the need to control traffic, led in 1922 to a commission-requested change to its enabling legislation so it could create its own police force under park-keeper William J. Byrne.[124]

The commission established its own set of ordinances, which took effect January 1, 1924. They specifically prohibited not only disorderly conduct (such as throwing stones, setting off fireworks, gambling, littering, fighting, or climbing) but also activities such as advertising, soliciting alms and contributions, loitering at night, selling merchandise, littering, and dumping. They forbade animals (except dogs being walked), explosives, firearms, weapons, tools, and "fire-lighted cigars."

Vehicles were required to have proper licenses and safety equipment, and driving was regulated. The protection of the reservation itself prohibited injuring property, drives, bridges, and so on (including removing rock, gravel, and the like or defacing any structure or sign), harvesting or damaging plants, and hunting or fishing.[125]

Opening Day

The Bronx River Parkway opened officially in 1925 with a motor tour, leading out of the Bronx and north to Valhalla, and a day of speeches. Speakers included the commissioners, local politicians, Governor Al Smith (by telegram), and the director of the National Park Service, Stephen T. Mather, who spoke of memory—his own memory of the Bronx River of the 1840s, as related to him by his father:

> [The river's beauty] meant a great deal to them in those days and it is wonderful to think that the children that are coming will see it grow more and more aback to its original, natural beauty . . . back to that beautiful stream that meant so much to the people of old New York in the years gone by.[126]

The parkway was hailed as a success, a "triumph of civic achievement." The commission was showered with compliments, including the following private letter sent to Madison Grant by Robert De Forest, a dean of New York's upper-crust civic reformers:

> Dear Mr. Grant
>
> I was not able to attend the opening of the Bronx River Parkway, but I made up my mind that I would see it by myself, even without the advantage of special guidance. I went over its entire length last Sunday with great interest and . . . great appreciation.
>
> I unqualifiedly admire the great work you and your associates have done, both in its vision and in the way that vision has been carried out. To me there was no discordant element whatsoever in what you have done. All the landscape features—the planting, the use of native trees and shrubs—seem to me . . . quite perfect. And there was a remarkable separation of the parkway and its adjacent parks from discordant outside elements in the way of buildings and structures. . . .
>
> At a recent meeting of our Art Commission an exceedingly modest

Figure 4.13. Speeches at the official opening day of the Bronx River Parkway at its northern ter-minus in Valhalla in 1925 featured Madison Grant (in dark coat, without a hat) amid bunting, loudspeakers, and fellow dignitaries celebrating the transformation of the Bronx River valley. Author's collection.

tablet was brought up commemorating the opening of this parkway. Every member of the commission thought it was inadequate and wished that there could be some more important monumental record. I sympathized with this suggestion at the time. I am now, after seeing the parkway, quite urgent about it. Will not you and your associates think of this seriously?

Sincerely yours, RWD.[127]

Undeniably, the Bronx Parkway Commission did a fantastic job of cleaning up the Bronx River, improving the environmental and visual quality of the valley, and greasing the skids of suburban development in Westchester. But "improvement" was a goal of much broader ambition, and this chapter has illustrated its many dimensions. The broad ambitions of improvement included suburban expansion and racially motivated slum clearance as well as the bettering of public health and land reclamation for recreation, the enhancement of natural beauty, and easy automobile travel—and it centered on a particular reconstruction of civic memory to rationalize the resulting landscape. The parkway had a decidedly mixed legacy.

The parkway not only spatialized but monumentalized the idea of nature as heritage, as a rightful, patriotic inheritance and part of the civic memory canon. Madison Grant spoke of the project as one of landscape "restoration" of "a portion of our heritage."[128] With a chance to define the legacy and "meaning" of the project, he implored foresight so that preservation, instead of restoration, could save the American West (the East being too far gone already). The concluding thoughts of Grant's speech marking the opening of the parkway and the end of his twenty-year involvement lectured:

> We inherited a continent to develop or plunder, as we choose, and we
> have grown fabulously rich in its exploitation. These opportunities
> we have received from our ancestors. To those who come after us, we
> owe both the preservation and restoration of natural beauties [in effect,
> our "heritage"]. . . . Our descendents may never know what they have
> lost, but few of our generation would want to live in such a country in
> such an age.[129]

The commission placed itself at the dramatic, heroic conclusion of the story of the valley—having successfully regained, it felt, this heritage of the pastoral Bronx River valley. Constructing and telling this story was of direct political use to the commission in securing political support, cooperation from land owners, and funding. It held a quintessentially modern attitude toward the past and toward the possibilities for constructing a relationship with the past, a past rooted in place, with purpose. In rearranging time and space quite freely, a new narrative could be constructed, reflecting the "distance" between past and present that is a hallmark of modernity.[130] At the same time, the vision of the parkway accomplished other, equally modern goals: creating a space of pure mobility, enabling continuing creative destruction and metropolitan expansion.

The parkway was built with the intention that it be preserved and remembered, and the commission did what it could to ensure that legacy—thus the great efforts of documentation through photographs, records, published reports, articles, and speeches. All these materials were explicitly intended to shape the memory

of future generations.[131] In order to preserve, one first needs to remember, to select narratives and represent them (in words, images, and space), and these were
part of the commission's work. An older, pastoral, countrified Bronx River valley
was rebuilt, but the modern version of it included new sewers, a new automobile
roadway, and a new organization to effect the wholesale transformation of this
place. Nature was preserved, or rather, regained and "restored." The importance
of historical narrative in this remembering aspect of the parkway was twofold:
First, a story of the landscape's past was needed to explain the present and justify
future vision. The material for this narrative was readily available, in the work of
local historians, poets, and painters, as well as in the usual tropes of historical
memory—Revolutionary War and colonial narratives. Second, the commission
had to write the final chapter for itself, and of its own work. The commission's success in building the Bronx River Parkway and regaining the heritage of the Bronx
valley (in the service of its future) was the capstone narrative to the official, civic
memory embodied in this landscape.

The parkway was indeed an "attenuated park with a road through it,"[132] but it was
also a cultural project to reimagine and rebuild the periphery. Behind the veil of
"improvement" and modernization, histories were remembered and forgotten,
given form or destroyed; and nature was rearranged for proper aesthetic and
moral and marketing effect. All of this was carefully arranged by the powerful (and
mythically impartial) commission.

The Bronx River Parkway was a synthesis of planning, design, conservation, real
estate development, eugenics, and—tying it all together—public memory. While
the shaping of memory may not have been the *impetus* or the *cause* of the parkway's
building, it was an enabling strategy, a fundamental *means* of implementing this
transformation. The effort to control and shape memory was an essential part of
this development-preservation-improvement project. Constructing a relationship
with the past was part of constructing a modern urban landscape, and historic preservation was properly regarded—in the Bronx as elsewhere in the metropolis—as
an essential part of modern redevelopment and urbanism.

Grant, though a marginal figure to "historic preservation" per se, nonetheless
is a valuable lens on the intentions and achievements of the preservation movement in this era. The connections he made between ethnic-racial discrimination
and environmental reform revealed a spectrum of motivations behind preservation wider than simply taking the positive tenets of civic patriotism at face value.
Preservation and restoration projects cultivated public attachment to place, but
at the same time, the public sphere so-defined served the goal of purification and

protection of the native—whether it concerned redwoods and elk or the population of New York City.

Shedding more light on the cultural intentions of the project highlights the myriad contradictions and tensions of modernity: between destruction and conservation, between representing the past to enable a future vision, between history grounded in "place" and progress premised on mobility, between dominant and adversarial cultures, between the landscape that was replaced and forgotten and the one that was built to be remembered. These tensions were generated by creating the new "restored" landscape, totally designed and rigidly controlled, out of the chaotic, contingent, messy landscape of everyday New York.

The parkway landscape served cultural functions in a few different ways: First, the economic and engineering aspects of the parkway also performed social functions, at least implicitly. These functions were part of the emergence of scientific, rational modes of planning and urban regulation and were a continuance of the long-standing cultural belief in environmental determinism. The roadway improved mobility, facilitated recreation in the outdoors, and helped decenter congested city neighborhoods—all aspects of social reform. Flood control and cleanup measures improved public health and removed slum dwellers (at least the sight of them). It is important not to see these efforts as merely technical achievements.

Second, the Bronx River Parkway was a scene, an aesthetic creation. The reservation was designed partially for recreation on foot, but more for recreation by car, which was an essentially visual, scenic experience. Naturalistic park landscapes were conceived in part because of their scenic and iconographic functions, which, along with the healthful effects of being in nature, was the medium of moral and social reform. The encounter with nature—visually, experientially, and culturally (conveying meaning through symbols)—was one of the most compelling rationales for the Bronx River Parkway, and indeed was the raison d'être for the litany of urban natural landscapes going back to the cemeteries of the 1830s. The scenic quality of the landscape was one of the pillars of the Olmstedian synthesis and deployment of naturalistic landscapes as city-planning and social-reform instruments, a tradition to which the Bronx River Parkway very clearly was a successor. Scenic value was also one of the pillars of public memory that historic preservationists sought to cultivate.

Third, the Bronx River Parkway endeavored to construct historical memory: through masterfully orchestrated naturalistic design, with its powerful imagery and implicit narrative of nature lost and regained; through association of the valley landscape with place-bound narratives of heroic human achievement, namely, the Dutch colonial settlers and the patriots of the Revolutionary War; and through storytelling and memory making about the commission's own role in the narrative of this landscape. In creating the new valley landscape, materially and rhetorically and representationally, the commission created a "usable past" and put it to use. It built natural landscapes, erected monuments, wrote history, told stories, and used photography in a clearly narrative way to carry out this project of civic remembering.

The commission heaped praise on itself and its staff in the speeches marking the opening of the full parkway in 1925. And the commission was indeed very successful in meeting its goals. But the Bronx River Parkway was even more than the brilliantly executed infrastructure project that these goals defined. It was indeed a marvel of environmental restoration, design, engineering, administration—in short, a masterpiece of technical, rational, physical planning. Yet the parkway's meanings for its builders and turn-of-the-century New Yorkers were more complex. It was a work of imagination, vision, and cultural achievement. It was a public-planning project, a well-designed landscape, a modern transportation infrastructure, a feat of social engineering, and a monument to the heritage of the valley landscape, the rationally planned future, and a racially pure vision of what "American" means; it was a triumph of the civic will. For better or worse, a place to be remembered.

The Bronx River Parkway, lauded in its own time, continued to serve as a model for parkway building around New York, the United States, and the world. The twenty-year parkway project was a modern marvel of landscape transformation and infrastructure building, innovative in its design, planning, administration, financing, and "marketing." The parkway also exemplified the kind of historic preservation effort that came to define the preservation field as it matured and spread over the twentieth century. Landscape essayist J. B. Jackson, writing in the 1970s, could have been describing the Bronx River Parkway as he drew a portrait of the typical preservation project in his well-known essay "The Necessity for Ruins":

> It seems clear that the whole preservation and restoration movement is much more than a means of promoting tourism or a sentimentalizing over an obscure part of the past—though it is also both of those things. We are learning to see it as a new (or recently rediscovered) interpretation of history. It sees history not as continuity but as a dramatic discontinuity, a kind of cosmic drama. First there is that golden age, the time of harmonious beginnings. Then ensues a period when the old days are forgotten and the golden age falls into neglect. Finally comes a time when

we rediscover and seek to restore the world around us to something like its former beauty.

But there has to be that interval of neglect, there has to be discontinuity; it is religiously and artistically essential. That is what I mean when I refer to the necessity for ruins: ruins provide the incentive for restoration, and for a return to origins. There has to be (in our new concept of history) an interim of death or rejection before there can be renewal and reform. The old order has to die before there can be a born-again landscape. Many of us know the joy and excitement not so much of creating the new as of redeeming what has been neglected, and this excitement is particularly strong when the original condition is seen as holy or beautiful. The old farmhouse has to decay before we can restore it and lead an alternative life style in the country; the landscape has to be plundered and stripped before we can restore the natural ecosystem; the neighborhood has to be a slum before we can rediscover it and gentrify it. That is how we reproduce the cosmic scheme and correct history.[133]

The "dramatic discontinuity" of time and space and the redemption of a slum, as masterfully manipulated by the Bronx Parkway Commission, became the dominant trope of modern historic preservation—the "cosmic scheme and correct history."

Looking Critically at Preservation's Own Past

T HE ECONOMIST AND NEW DEAL TECHNOCRAT STUART CHASE WROTE A
series of articles for *Harper's Monthly* in 1929–30 appraising the prospects of
New York City. He reflected on the changes the city had undergone in the preceding generation—since becoming a true metropolis and the capital of capitalism.
Chase began by recounting the reception of modern New York as a place—how
the city *seemed* to the visitor and the citizen:

> Coming into Manhattan, I begin to feel a strange uneasiness like a slight at-
> tack of seasickness; leaving it, I suddenly grow more cheerful. Why? I am no
> confirmed bucolic; no city-hater in cheese-cloth and sandals. The thoughts
> which men generate in cities are as important to me as bread. For the past
> few weeks I have been noting specific impressions in an attempt to come to
> closer terms with this mysterious total feeling.[1]

The economist was smitten, even overwhelmed, by the city's "total feeling": the
combination of its environments, lives, rhythms, sensibilities. Among the "positive
reactions—pleasurable," he lists the Bronx River Parkway, the American Wing of the
Met, the Brooklyn Bridge, "Fifth Avenue below 14th Street—where fine old houses
and a ghost of dignity remain," and "the view of the city from a high roof garden,
particularly at night; towers indirectly illuminated." Chase's enduring impression
was the balance of old and new—the infrastructure of the modern city in balance
with that of the old. His account confirmed the success of preservationists and their
allied reformers in building a sense of the past into the modern metropolis.

Preservationists' efforts to fix historical memories as part of the built environment contributed a critical element to the "improvement" of modern New York.
Responding to tumultuous cultural changes and urban conflicts, as well as to society's innate need for collective remembering, historic preservationists made subtle
but critical urban interventions. Their memory works framed how the city was built
and attempted to shape how it was received. Beyond their more obvious results—old
buildings, historic markers, preserved landscapes—their works made the balance

between past and future an explicit question to be addressed by urbanists, designers, and decision makers. Memory infrastructure created in this period constituted a usable past specific to the tumultuous decades around the turn of the twentieth century; it also laid the groundwork—practically, philosophically, politically—for the preservation movement that continued to develop over the rest of the century.

"OUT OF THIS WELTER AND TURMOIL NEW YORK OF TODAY FISHES THE PAST"

The cultural moment of the early twentieth century was defined by looking backward and looking forward with equal intensity. In all spheres of culture, reconciling past and future was a dominant theme. In some cases, this meant iconoclastic rejection of the existing cultural tropes; in others, wholesale simulation of the ancient form. For historic preservation, the cultural crisis called for forging history and memory in the "real" architectural, urban, and artistic forms recalling the city's past.

The puzzle facing New York preservationists was captured in a *New York Times* cartoon from 1925: how to conjure a coherent past out of the seeming chaos of the contemporary city.[2] Their choices about which historical memories were important and how they should be made visible in the transforming urban environment are the core subject of this book. But these New Yorkers were not just fishing around. New York's early preservation advocates were deeply committed to the city's modernization, too, and regarded preservation—building historical memory into urban environments—as one aspect of the city's improvement. Their preservation efforts at once tried to connect and distance the past and present—a struggle shared by preservation advocates in all modern cities.

New York preservationists created a number of places meant to strategically remake the city's cultural landscape early in the twentieth century. (Their goal was never to preserve the whole city, or even the districts we preserve today. Rather, they sought control of some strategic anchors—often the oldest, most dearly associated, or most prominently located building remaining—as totems of stability against the overwhelming reality of change.) The sum of the era's preservation efforts was a scattered but substantial collection of "historic and scenic places" singled out, protected, and designed to maximize their ability to stimulate civic memory. Many of the buildings and sites making up this memory infrastructure remain today. One encounters them in any walk about the contemporary city. And they are not merely dead letters from a remote past; they still contribute to New York's cultural landscape. For example, the Historic House Trust and the city's Department of Parks and Recreation today steward many historic places first created as historic

Figure C.1. Joseph Webster Golinkin, "Out of This Welter and Turmoil New York of Today Fishes the Past," from the New York Times Sunday Magazine, *1925. Courtesy of ProQuest, LLC, and Webster Golinkin.*

sites around the turn of the century. And places like St. Paul's Chapel and Henry Kirke Brown's statue of George Washington in Union Square, fixtures of the memory infrastructure for nearly a century and a half, became substrates for vernacular memorials in the aftermath of the attacks of September 11, 2001.

CULTIVATING PRESERVATION'S HISTORY

The early history of historic preservation in American cities has mostly been uninterpreted or misinterpreted. *The Once and Future New York* endeavors to weave stories of historic preservation into the grander fabric of urban history, filling in some of these historiographical blind spots by drawing on the history of preservation's emergence in New York.

The main ambition of this book is connecting preservation to other urban dynamics—narrating its history in a hotbed of modern urbanization so that preservation will no longer be rendered in isolation. The ideas of historical memory, spatializing memory, and memory infrastructure advanced in this book describe the cultural and urbanistic challenges that preservationists faced in a key moment of New York's history. They create an analytical framework through which empirical histories of preservation practice and advocacy can be connected to

Figure C.2. New memorials layered on an old monument: in the aftermath of September 11, 2001, New Yorkers immediately began making their own memorials, often using the old memory infra-structure as a substrate. The base here is Henry Kirke Brown's statue of George Washington, dedicated in 1856. Photograph copyright Martha Cooper.

larger historical narratives of urbanism and cultural change. They offer an alternative to the more typical treatments of preservation: hero worship of individual preservationists or wholesale dismissal of preservation as an elitist hobby.

The roots of preservation are specific to cultural, historical, and geographic contexts. The emergence of urban preservation around 1900 in New York and other cities grew out of two larger dynamics: the evolution of modern metropolitan cities, with a new scale, complexity, and intensity of urban issues; and a newly reconfigured and reconfigurable relation to the past—a tipping point between memory and history. These dynamics together created the "need" for preservation.

The Once and Future New York offers historic preservation practices as a reading of cultural tensions. Reflecting the broader culture of modernity, preservationists transformed traditional, contingent cultural expressions and fixed them as concrete forms of "historical memory"—a term purposefully invoking the dialectical tension between memory and history as distinct, competing ways of apprehending the past. (As Pierre Nora put it, "Memory installs remembrance within the sacred: history, always prosaic, releases it again.")[3] The memory sites preservationists invested with meaning represented the persistence of collective memory as a distinct and essential social process and represented the emergence of history and architectural and landscape design as a way for experts to shape public historical consciousness.

Every act of historical interpretation and collective remembering invokes politics: The meaning of the past is controlled by someone and is often deployed against others in society to exert pressure, control, or even coercion. While these politics of historic preservation are undeniable, they are not foregrounded in this book. The political uses of memory infrastructure are, to contemporary sensibilities, fairly evident. They were overwhelmingly conservative, but not exclusively so. Revolutionary War narratives, colonial architecture, and great-man statues were, at one level, tools for social reform used on immigrants and the less educated—"for their own good," as the City History Club would have it, and also for the good of the conservative ruling classes who wished to control an unruly public. This book aims at a more preliminary argument toward a full understanding of the politics of public memory and historic preservation: namely, the assertion that issues of public memory had become part of the urban scene and had indeed begun to reshape urbanism so that experts, professionals, and decision makers responded to the cultural dimensions of city life (feelings of belonging and anomie, rootedness and dislocation) as well as to the aesthetic and economic dimensions for which the rationales are already well established. In other words, *The Once and Future New York* advocates taking account of culture (specifically, those core aspects of culture that construct social relations between the past and the present) when it comes to understanding urban dynamics, design, and planning.

Changing attitudes toward the past—as reflected in historic preservation, art, literature, and other cultural forms—are a central theme of modernity. And the long unfolding of modernity as an urban phenomenon can be read in efforts to preserve, design, and otherwise represent the past in urban environments. Several important scholars have dwelled on this topic. David Lowenthal described the history of this long moment in post-Enlightenment western Europe in terms of the estrangement of the past from the present and, metaphorically, as the distance and foreignness that came to be associated with the past and its material expressions. Pierre Nora lighted on the tension between memory and history as distinct ways of apprehending the past, the former traditional and the latter modern. J. B. Jackson, immersed in the ordinary landscapes of mid-twentieth-century mid-America, evoked the same long moment of modernity with the metaphor of ruins.[4] And New York preservationists such as Andrew Haswell Green, George Kunz, and George McAneny tackled it as a problem of cultural "stability" and worked to shape the city's culture by anchoring it in the past. The issue of squaring cultural conceptions of the past with stark environmental changes—whether termed "foreignness" or "ruins" or "memory versus history" or "stability"—is an old and abiding one, the ancestor of all preservation debates.

The other stimulus of the early preservation movement was the environmental reality of fin de siècle cities: intense growth, complexity, conflict, congestion, and innovation. Breakneck urbanization created engineering challenges and also brought cultural problems. Traditions and social relations were strained by the ascendance of corporate capitalism, by continuing innovations in popular culture and entertainments, and by a global influx of immigrants. The seemingly divergent culture of these new cities called forth ideas like "civic patriotism," the central didactic message New York preservationists designed their memory sites to convey. Drawing on themes of national patriotism and local history and boosterism, civic patriotism trumpeted to public audiences a sense of duty, obligation, and responsibility of citizens to their city. Politically, civic patriotism was clearly normative and sometimes repressive (ranging from the relatively benign war memorials erected in parks by the ASHPS, to the more aggressive Americanization of schoolchildren undertaken by the City History Club, to the virulent nativism advocated by Madison Grant). Shared, collective memories were thought to lead to greater social cohesion among the populace—countering the increasingly fractured social and cultural life of the city. Preservation narratives thus supported the dominant culture, offering narratives of social order and images of stability drawn from the past. Alternative narratives, or any real sense of empowerment of ethnic groups over "the public," were discouraged. (And when particularistic memories *were* asserted—as in the case of the Italian community insisting that Verrazano be acknowledged as part of the Hudson–Fulton Celebration—they still reinforced the idea of a civic patriotism pantheon.) Echoes of civic patriotism live on today—economic boosterism, rooting for sports teams, expressions of cultural ownership of "America" as a justification for anti-immigrant militancy, or expressions of regional identity[5]—and live on in the canons reinforced in preservation debates even though the hegemony of such normative commemoration practices is now thoroughly discredited.

As cultural reformers, preservationists wanted to fix important narratives in the public mind—not leave them to the vagaries of traditional, changeful collective memory—so they preemptively cast memories in stone, brick, and bronze. Threats to memory sites (from development) were forestalled by taking places out of the real estate market and putting them in public ownership. And these material and legal strategies were supported by aggressive communications and public relations campaigns. Preservationists' strategy was fairly successful: Today, restored houses, monuments, and historic parks are regarded as "natural"; they are as much a part of a modern city's environment as public buildings, clean streets, mass transit, tall buildings, and so on.

What many regard today as the core purpose of preservation activity—"the reverent protection from decay and destruction of historic sites and buildings"[6]—was only part of the story, however. Memory sites were not an end in themselves. They were envisioned as means to an end—a way to reform urban society and shape civic identity by exposing citizens to a memory-rich environment. Reformers and civic leaders sought stability to counter the gathering sense of cultural dislocation and the loss of memory in this period, and historical memory lent this appearance of stability to culture. The broad cultural imperative to reconstruct the past—Van Wyck Brooks called it creating "a usable past"[7]—gained greater momentum as the city developed more quickly, as expressed in the debate over St. John's Chapel in 1909: "There is little permanence upon which to fasten one's memories, affections and historical traditions. A city needs just such piles as old St. John's to give it some idea of firmness and stability in contrast with the fleeting changes around."[8] Likewise, Andrew Haswell Green argued that City Hall and City Hall Park anchored whatever civic memory would emerge from the tumultuous period of consolidation, expansion, and rebuilding that he and other New York leaders were orchestrating: "Its presence tends to keep alive associations that are near to very many of our citizens, a visible landmark, an object lesson to the people, that should not be destroyed."[9]

Core preservationist ideas about spatializing historical memory were also expressed in new construction, including public works such as the subway system (with its many plaques referencing local history themes), the bridges of the Bronx River Parkway, the Cathedral of St. John the Divine, public schools, banks, and other buildings built in colonial-revival and other historicist modes.

Taken together, these memory works are best thought of as a kind of infrastructure—a memory infrastructure—envisioned and designed to perform specific functions and meet reform needs. Materially and urbanistically, memory works required design, funding, construction, and maintenance just like any other kind of infrastructure. The old buildings and parks were maintained expressly so they would serve a reforming function, not just for the sake of safeguarding them as antiquarian artifacts. Memory works promoted a civic ideal, creating instruments of reform by touting social bonds drawing authority from historical precedent (patriotism, martyrdom, business achievement). These bonds were to instill respect and enforce obligations to advance the public and civic good. Aesthetically, memory works created experiences that were purposely a world apart from the everyday urban environment, where the past could be felt strongly and purely; they aspired to *look* different. Promotion of pastoral, colonial, Old New York visual culture was an essential aspect of cultural reform. Politically, the memory works folded into the core Progressive project to defeat machine politics and government corruption. The "impartial" experts advocating good government drew authority from the visible achievements of the distant past—City Hall and its park, for instance.

UNCONVENTIONAL WISDOM

The stories of early New York preservationists retold in these pages cast doubt on some of the conventional wisdom about historic preservation, its relation to urbanization in our market-centered cities, and its place in the New York narrative. The findings of *The Once and Future New York* advance a more subtle and accurate understanding of the history of preservation, based on a rereading of the archives and projects produced in this nascent period of preservationist thinking and practice. This section recasts some of the conventional wisdom commonly held by scholars, practitioners, and the interested public about preservation. Most simply, historic preservation is not a recent invention. The history of preservation as an urban practice stretches back more than a century. This history has been forgotten, however. The common understanding, especially in New York City, is that preservation was born in the 1960s, in opposition to postwar urban renewal. In fact, urban preservation emerged in the last decades of the nineteenth century, and there was a great deal of historic preservation activity in New York between 1890 and 1920. Dozens of successful historic preservation projects were completed in these pioneering decades, many of them resulting in the design of public historic sites preserved to this day. Vigorous debates, detailed scholarship, energetic advocacy, and an institutional life for preservation began in this period, evident, for instance, in the work of the American Scenic and Historic Preservation Society.

To the extent that the history of preservation is recalled, the field is usually regarded as having been, at root, a hobby of rich folks and dilettantes with nothing better to do. Preservation was not merely a concern of ineffectual, waning, blue-blooded elites. Though these upper classes often supported preservation and though their own histories were often among those preserved and celebrated, it is more accurate to regard urban preservation as part of the influential Progressive reform movement. As with most strains of Progressivism, preservation sought the "improvement" of cities and citizens and traded on environmental determinism as the mechanism of reform: creating better society and better citizens by creating better environments (in every sense of the word—natural, cultural, educational, moral, and political "environments"). Preservation's most important and forgotten pioneers were the leading city builders and public leaders of the era—as much professionals as well-to-do elites. Rather than being a pursuit of "old ladies in tennis shoes," preservation was closely connected to the cultural and urbanistic mainstreams that emerged in the Progressive Era. As evidence, consider the men leading early preservation efforts: Green, McAneny, Grant, De Forest, and others championed preservation while also directing the political consolidation of the five boroughs, zoning laws regulating skyscraper development, subway system expansion, street widening, and the building of suburban parkways, the Public Library, the Metropolitan Museum of Art, the Bronx Zoo, and an expanding system of public parks—modern infrastructure in all senses. Preservation was a little-known legacy of these leaders; their cultural entrepreneurship has long been sublimated by their other public works. They regarded cultural reform as a foundation for economic growth and political reform, and historic preservation, one important mode of cultural reform, was an essential aspect of modern city building.

Historic preservation was not simply and solely about saving individual buildings as works of architectural art. Though architectural preservation has long been a mainstay of the field—stretching well back into the nineteenth century— architectural connoisseurship began to dominate historic preservation only in the second decade of the twentieth century. (By midcentury, the increasing professionalization of the field, favoring architects and architectural historians, heightened the focus on works of architecture.) The first concern of New York preservationists was shaping collective memory, and all sorts of environments and fabrics were means to this end: architecture, landscapes (natural and designed), public art. Preserving buildings was the most frequent trope of this memory work, but preservation strategies ranged much more widely. A great deal of emphasis was placed on the visual qualities of historic sites—their "scenic" as well as "historic" values—expressed in preservation work on landscapes as much as on buildings. Redesigning historic places sometimes called for conserving architectural fabric, creating memorials, protecting or creating open space, and sometimes even destroying buildings. Making City Hall Park into an effective memory site, for instance, involved not just retention of some old architectural fabric but preservation of park space, destruction of certain old buildings, and creation of new historical art. What determined the mix was the desire to shape particular historical memories, not the sort of philosophical attitude toward physical fabric that is the bedrock of architectural conservation. By 1920, the ascendance of professional, scientific restoration was obscuring the cultural politics that had originally motivated preservation (such as was the case with many aspects of Progressive reform, as new professional cadres assumed control of what had previously been reform causes). This was not a completely positive turn of events. Though technical and design aspects of preservation improved with professionalization, the field had also embarked on a path to professional self-absorption and insularity. The marginalization of nonprofessional "historic preservationists" as "old ladies in tennis shoes" began in earnest in the 1920s and resulted in the defensive posture for which preservationists are well known today. The cultural politics of preservation activity—which never ceased to motivate preservation—were mostly obscured until the preservation boom of the 1960s and afterward.

The achievements of the historic preservation field add up to more than a collection of historic sites and heroic stories about saving dear old buildings from the jaws of the unthinking juggernaut. The "memory infrastructure" argument of this book (and the three cases of sites where cultural, economic, and political values intersected) attempts to get beyond a mere group biography or analysis of projects. The project- or hero-centered analysis of preservation tends to enforce a (mythic) view of preservation as a world unto itself, claiming the high moral ground by opposing destruction, in effect obscuring the intentions of early preservationists. The improvement-focused, modernity-embracing, mostly market-friendly preservation leaders had an influence that went beyond their collection of successful projects. Their way of thinking, their efforts to weave preservation into debates about the management and quality of urban spaces, and the institutions they built all had lasting effects on the city. Their broad and pragmatic outlook—epitomized in the career of George McAneny—was remarkable. And it is a legacy that the preservation field has recently, in indirect ways, begun to recover, with the broadening of the preservation field over the past few decades to tackle issues of community well-being, suburban sprawl, cultural landscapes, farmland, and more (witness the issues taken on by the National Trust for Historic Preservation in the last ten to fifteen years). These changes in very recent preservation history are not new inventions so much as a regaining of the roots of the field. Without a historical understanding of the field's sources, however, the contemporary preservation field is mostly innocent of these deeply rooted preservation ideas.

The attitude of early preservation leaders toward urban growth and change was remarkable. Corollary to the idea that preservation was led by people who were otherwise directing various aspects of New York's modernization and metropolitanization is the fact that historic preservationists were not, for the most part, opposed to the market-driven, mainstream ideology of growth. In fact, one of the main narratives celebrated by preservationists was the continuing commercial success of New York — the driver of growth. One of few historians to tackle the subject of preservation's relationship to urban development, Mike Wallace, drew conclusions that ring true to many:

> The historic preservation movement was born, over a century ago, in opposition to a free wheeling, free market era, when profit-seeking Americans — as disrespectful of the past as of the environment — routinely demolished what prior generations had constructed. Historicide, like ecocide, had become embedded in the culture.[10]

Wallace is right that preservation did emerge as a reform reaction. And "historicide" and "ecocide" are part of American culture (though they are not unchallenged). On one deeply important subject, his essay contradicts one of the main insights of this book: Historic preservation in New York City cannot be seen simply as a movement in opposition to markets. Early preservation was fundamentally pro-market and pro-growth. With many of their fellow reformers, preservationists in fact supported, participated in, and directed the creative destruction and redevelopment of other parts of New York City.[11] Progressive reformers (including preservationists) largely accepted the market and wished to complement it by tempering the culture of the market with a culture of historical memory. The "stability" preservationists sought to cultivate with historical memory was meant to save and strengthen market society, not replace it; to resist it only selectively, not as all-out "opposition." The market was not, in other words, the most important of preservation's "traditional enemies."[12] Preservationists had no illusion of being able to (nor did they want to) stop destruction and redevelopment altogether; their philosophy was that some places had such great cultural value that they should be spared destruction. Instead of broad sweeps, preservation consisted of a series of incremental, ad hoc, in themselves relatively minor adjustments to the course of "progress." This sort of urbanism is less visible, less well documented, and fairly discredited—developing as it did in the shadow of Daniel Burnham's "make no little plans, for they have no power to stir men's souls" bluster.

Historic preservation was, to its practitioners and leaders, an essential part of New York urbanism. The city needed to remember, just as it needed to grow, they believed. The definition of certain buildings and landscapes as "historic" or "scenic" implied license to destroy and redevelop the rest of the city. Without memory, growth would act as "the remorseless juggernaut," consuming all before it. This full picture of New York preservation would be impossible to understand if one only looked at individual sites; in exploring preservation as a field growing out of specific contexts, it is readily apparent.

Preservationists put themselves in the position (with more or less success) of determining which places had such great cultural value for the public and how those places should be preserved. The result of preservationists' accommodation with development was a shifting but particular geography in which destruction and redevelopment were mostly regarded as "natural," as long as certain "islands" of high historic or cultural value remained to lend the whole city some places where stability and permanence were made visible. The geographic logic was clear: In the historic core of Manhattan, the presumption was that preservation was primary and development would occur where cultural values were low. On the periphery, the presumption was that cultural value was unimportant and economic value could be maximized; here, only buildings of great antiquity or historical association or large-scale places of great scenic value would qualify for preservation. In both circumstances, guaranteeing the cultural value of preserved sites was assumed to raise the economic value of the rest of the landscape. Preservation cases such as Fraunces Tavern, Dyckman House, or Hamilton Grange constituted such islands of relative stability in the sea of change that, by consensus, had to result from the breakneck redevelopment of modern New York. It is more accurate, though, to understand these places (memory sites) as *part of* the process of improvement, urbanization, and destruction, not as sites of resistance. They were designed and implemented, after all, by the very leaders and institutions steering the juggernaut. Preservationists' mind-set saw more leverage between cultural and economic values than conflict.

A *New York Evening Post* editorial of 1915 acknowledged the subtleties of preservation's contributions to the city and its reform:

> Of the phase of city planning which consists in demolishing, rebuilding and extending, a new country naturally hears more than of the phase which consists in preserving and restoring. Even Manhattan, with its three centuries of history, we regard as a sort of palimpsest, where the erasure of old structures meets with little restraint.[13]

There is a subtlety in this passage—rare for its time—about the cumulative, evolutionary process of retention and erasure, preservation and development, that "naturally" characterizes the city. The writer acknowledged a place for preservation in the urbanization process (albeit a clearly secondary one)—a sentiment echoed in speeches by McAneny, Green, Kunz, and others in the early decades of the twentieth century. Historic preservation was regarded as a part of modern city building, not as opposition to it. That preservation and memory sites constituted a type of infrastructure—part of a holistic vision of Progressive reform of the modern city—was seldom voiced explicitly. Andrew Haswell Green, however, who truly looked for the big picture, opined in 1901: "What we should have is one plan for the unified city that will provide conditions of living, methods of transit and travel, and features of adornment [preservation], suited to advance the comfort, convenience and happiness of the whole."[14]

The final myth about the early preservation field highlighted here is that government agencies only got involved via New Deal and Great Society programs. Even in the early twentieth century, private, nonprofit, *and* public sectors played substantial parts in urban preservation. Quasi-governmental, reform, and professional organizations—mostly private, though public-minded—were the driving forces in preservation (as in many other aspects of Progressive reform). But local and state government institutions also participated in the preservation of historic sites. Local and state governments embraced preservation in a more ad hoc manner than through the deliberate public policy we are familiar with today. For example, the New York City government (the Parks Department, the Art Commission, and at various times the borough presidents and other elected officials), the New York State legislature, and state commissions such as those charged with the Bronx River Parkway project or the preservation of the New Jersey Palisades often played very strong roles in the creation and stewardship of historic sites. Acknowledging the interest of local governments in preservation is an important rejoinder to the overwhelming (if implicit) notion that federal government involvement is the best indicator of meaningful public-sector activity. To be sure, the federal government pioneered roles in historic preservation during the period of this study—the 1906 Antiquities Act, the creation of the first national monuments (mostly in the West), and the creation of the National Park Service in 1916 stand out—but for urban preservation the involvement of local government was (and is) the far more significant factor.

This book also debunks a myth about the history of New York: that New York City is all about tearing down and about making money, and never about remembering the past. The dominant New York City narrative is one of unalloyed commercial drive, destruction, building, and rebuilding. Corollary to this, as noted in the introduction, is the idea that "history is for losers" (turning the old canard that "history is written by the victors" on its head), that historic preservation has been the interest of New Yorkers on the losing side of the city's global economic ascendance. The stories in this book, reconstructed from archives, suggest that building a modern metropolis was *not* considered at odds with cultivating a relationship to the past as represented in old buildings and landscapes. Nascent efforts at urban preservation from 1890 through 1920 were *part of* city leaders' efforts to build bigger and better, more intelligently and more humanely. Preservation leaders—Green, McAneny, Grant, De Forest, and others—held powerful positions in the city's economic as well as cultural circles. They were, in real terms, in the group of New York's most powerful city builders. Seth Low (former mayor and president of Columbia University, leading reformer, scion of an old merchant family) celebrated this accommodation of permanence and change, elaborating on the uses of civic patriotism and historical memory in a speech on the City Hall steps celebrating the city's 250th anniversary in 1903:

> In a city where the old gives place so rapidly to the new; in a city where
> the population grows more rapidly from the outside than from within;
> in a city whose especial function it often seems to be, so large is the
> scale of immigration, to welcome the emigrant from abroad and to
> make him into an American citizen, it is not always easy to realize how
> very deep down into the soil of American history run the roots of the
> life that flourishes here. And yet there is great inspiration in the city's
> long and interesting past. Here great events have happened; here great
> deeds have been done; here great men have lived and labored, and here
> the fascinating story of the country's material growth and development
> can be read in epitome.[15]

Celebrating "material growth and development" along with "the city's long and interesting past," Low weaves together the projects of Americanization and the preservation of urban places. He speaks comfortably of the reconciliation — or perhaps the absence of conflict—felt by civic leaders when it came to celebrating the past as part of the future trajectory of the metropolis. The speeches went on that day, reciting history and calling for more monuments. One of the celebration's crowning moments was "the illumination of skyscrapers," acknowledging that the soaring skyline was of a piece with the city's celebrated past. Low and his peers created a visible and narrative sense of the continuity of history in order to patch over the *dis*continuities created by urban development.

Historic preservation emerged as a means for leading New Yorkers to create this engagement with the city's past. Memory works and the discourse of preservation provided a mediating, reforming influence on the bare-knuckled, unalloyed, economic force for which New York City has been made the poster child by generations of historians and other observers. Of course, the construction of the past represented in preservation activities was very selective, was self-serving to those writing it, and abetted discrimination, Americanization, and the like. Such was the story that bolstered the hegemony of ruling elites — a story in which troubling narratives about the Civil War, ethnic discrimination, machine politics, poverty, violence, and vice were purposely ignored in favor of celebrating colonial and commercial heritage.

Prospects

In the first decades of the twenty-first century, the preservation field finds itself at a crossroads, just as it was a hundred years ago. At the beginning of the twentieth century, preservation was pressed to demonstrate its relevance in a competitive urban milieu buffeted by national and international economic competition, the continual conflict of urban politics, a cultural scene rocked by immigration and new communications technology, and an urban environment at once enlivened and threatened both by new construction and by obsolescence. Does this sound familiar? The contemporary preservation field is challenged in many of these same fundamental ways—competing as an economic development strategy, ever morphing to resonate with the latest cultural stresses, seeking relevance in the most pressing issues of public consciousness and policy (such as sustainability and environmental conservation). The signal difference between preservation challenges in the early twentieth and early twenty-first centuries is that today's preservation leaders have a deep foundation to build upon. The historic sites, preservation institutions, and public debates of the last century have embedded the sense, idea, and reality of preservation in the urban scene. Every place—even creatively destructive New York—now pursues preservation as a matter of course.

(Corollary to this: Preservation fails today in many of the same ways it did a hundred years ago. Today's preservation field continues to be frustrated by the tendency of historic sites to hide deeper power relations and historical agency in favor of consensus or normative narratives; by the conflicts between preservation of architectural values and preservation of historical values; by the challenges of financing preservation work; by the shared and shifting responsibilities of the public, private, and philanthropic sectors; by the desire and difficulty of including both natural and cultural resources in memory sites; and by the fragile balance between urban development and preservation interests.)

In terms of New York's cultural landscape, this early period of historic preservation activity imprinted the past on the city in explicit, self-conscious ways. For today's preservationists, these historic sites make up a physical legacy. The many restorations completed and parks preserved between the 1890s and the 1920s are a remarkable collection, well stewarded by the Historic House Trust, the Parks Department, and other organizations.[16] Though these places are not all "correct" restorations by contemporary standards, they testify to the field's technical and philosophical evolution over more than a century of work. These early-twentieth-century accomplishments debunk the widely held idea that preservation is vastly more professional, sophisticated, and politically attuned today than it was a hundred years ago. It is hoped that, by using these sites to elaborate on the sophisticated work of early preservationists, the preservation field can sustain a more critical conversation about its past and its future—instead of simply celebrating its Progressive achievements.

Today, the historic preservation field enjoys considerable success as a popular movement and even as a voice in some urban debates. But preservationist *thinking* seems to be as influential as historic preservation activities per se. Historic preservationist thinking has a strong presence in contemporary urbanism, and this is anchored in the successes of the early twentieth century. It is apparent in openly historicist modes of design and planning, such as New Urbanism, and in the legions of preservation-centered urban success stories of the past generation (including the renewal of Central Park; the revitalization of cities like Providence, Rhode Island, or Charleston, South Carolina; the new generation of retro baseball stadiums; the ubiquitous district of warehouse or loft luxury apartments; and the strength of heritage tourism as a sector of economic activity). The presence of preservationist thinking—a concern for spatializing history on an urban scale—is strong in these market-driven projects and even in such avowedly avant-garde projects as those collected in the recent Museum of Modern Art exhibit Groundswell (many of the projects exhibited are explicitly historicist in form, but never in word). The recent resurgence of memorials as cultural vanguards is also a resurgence of preservationist thinking. In many recent design competitions for prominent memorials—including New York's World Trade Center site—the question of how to spatialize memory at the scale of building, street, and city remains an exceedingly important question in American urbanism and follows many of the lines set down by early preservationist thinking (the focus on footprints, for instance, in the World Trade Center redesign is a core tenet in preservationist thinking).

Prospects for the theoretical development of historic preservation continue to take inspiration from the field's history. Though preservation theory from this early period is regarded as unsophisticated and ad hoc, ruled by patriotism and unscientific restoration, early-twentieth-century preservationists formulated progressive and encompassing theories about why preservation matters for society and which kinds of places are valuable. Foremost among these ideas was the central role of landscape, or scenic value, in early preservation.

The historic preservation field was founded on a notion of landscape that encompassed both natural and cultural resources, dealing with whole environments as well as isolated sites and monuments. This was evident in the work of the ASHPS, the scope of the Bronx River Parkway project, and the development of the national park and national monument systems happening at the same time. Preservationists' interest in what would today be called the cultural landscape notion—then framed by the combination of "scenic and historic" places—was rooted in the work of nineteenth-century artists, philosophers, and scientists, such as Thomas Cole and George Perkins Marsh. And it was advanced by the influence of Transcendentalists, Hudson River school painters, and the early landscape architects, including (but not limited to) Olmsted. The "scenic and historic" connection was sustained as a preservation issue, through the ASHPS's preservation of battlefields and natural features, Green's efforts at Niagara Falls and the Palisades, Hall's work for the Adirondacks, the concept of urban parks as the objects of preservation (the Battery, Central Park, City Hall Park), and Grant's interests in nature conservation and the Bronx River Parkway.

Interest in "scenic" places was not a signal that preservationists were merely interested in aesthetics. Natural places evoked a deeply meaningful kind of heritage, these days associated more with the environmental movement. Over the twentieth century, the ecology, landscape design, and environmental conservation movements professionalized and marketed themselves to be distinguished and separated from traditional partners such as historic preservationists. This idea about landscape taken up by preservationists in the late nineteenth and early twentieth centuries, and shared with allied environmental fields, made important contributions to American urbanism: the synthetic, holistic framing of natural and historic environments; the logic of long-term public benefits as a critique of short-term financial returns; the idea that the benefits of preservation cannot be measured in dollars.[17]

But this encompassing, landscape-centered vision of preservation was undermined (after 1920) by professionalization and specialization, as well as by barriers in public policy and politics making it difficult to implement. We have mostly lost sight of these ideas today, even though they are remarkably resonant with calls for "sustainability" and "sense of place" that have reinvigorated the preservation field in the last several years. While many observers in recent decades have lamented the lack of connection between the historic preservation and environmental-conservation fields, few seem to realize that this is an old idea, a core philosophical tenet of early preservationists.

Preservation has never been the dominant discourse or mode of practice in American urbanism, but it was a constant contributor to it in the twentieth century. To demonstrate that fact, this book has crafted a sense of New York's emergent preservation field as a whole — covering ideas, institutions, debates, and projects — without confining the history of preservation to the details of a few sites. The process of preserving and remembering, not just the results, is the story.

New York's Landmarks Preservation Commission is one of the strongest local-government preservation agencies in the country, supported by a very strong local law enabling regulation of designated building. Many preservationists would conclude that because the commission only came into existence in the early 1960s, everything before was a priori unworthy.[18] Contemporary preservationists are more likely to devalue this whole era because there was no Landmarks Preservation Commission in early-twentieth-century New York. Instead, a narrative of preservation is imagined that begins with the destruction of Penn Station in 1963. This heroic story of preservation's birth in New York is hard to resist, but it should be opposed because it obscures many decades of meaningful preservation work that laid the literal and philosophical groundwork for the achievements of the 1960s and afterward. This ahistorical attitude toward the evolution of the field abets the preservationists' aversion to reflection and self-criticism. Early preservation activity brought results in the actual landscape and injected preservation in the debate about New York urbanism, creating the expectation that these concerns would continue to be addressed.

Acknowledgments

L ITERARY CRITIC EDMUND WILSON'S MEMORY OF ST. JOHN'S CHAPEL reveals one of the underlying truths of historic preservation and of this book: It takes words *and* images *and* buildings *and* landscapes to evoke memory. We cannot rely on one or another of these media to remember a city's past. Likewise, the work underpinning this book has relied on many sources of support, counsel, and help.

I am awed by the limitless generosity of the many people who have supported me in this project. The usual caveat applies: Notwithstanding the inspiration of colleagues, friends, and mentors, all errors herein are my own.

The beginnings of this project put me under the guidance of Daniel Bluestone and Elizabeth Blackmar at Columbia University. Both have been dedicated and generous mentors and are models of principled and brilliant scholarship. Daniel freely spent his inexhaustible critical energy on my work, inspiring me to dig more deeply, see more connections, and bring historical imagination to bear on preservation. Betsy has been a more constant supporter than I have deserved, urging me forward through thick and thin. Whether in her office or at one of our chance sidewalk meetings, I left every conversation filled with enough confidence to move ahead.

I am grateful to other teachers and colleagues, as well: at Columbia, Elliott Sclar, Peter Marcuse, Saskia Sassen, Matt Dalbey, and Luc Nadal; at Penn State, Deryck Holdsworth, Peirce Lewis, and Don Mitchell; at Bucknell, Ben Marsh; in other places, Michael Everett, Cathy Gudis, Paul Groth, Brooke Wortham, Mary Sies, Steve Hurtt, Tim Davis, Michael Holleran, and Max Page.

The Getty Conservation Institute afforded me great opportunities, and I owe most to the leadership and vision of Marta de la Torre. Her confidence in me was more important than can be imagined. Erica Avrami, my colleague at the institute and since, I thank for constantly challenging me to do better and be clearer.

For the last five years, I have had the pleasure of working at the University of Pennsylvania. Frank Matero, chair of the Graduate Program in Historic Preservation, has created a fertile and supportive place to teach and research preservation. My work has benefited in myriad ways from Frank's advice and support, as well as that of Genie Birch, Gary Hack, David DeLong, Lynne Sagalyn, John Dixon

Hunt, John Hinchman, John Landis, and Suzanne Hyndman. In all the places I've taught—University of Pennsylvania, University of Maryland, Rhode Island School of Design—I learned much from my students. Beyond their probing questions and curiosity, some of them contributed research assistance for this book: Alex Bevk, Robin Tannenbaum, Alison Merritt, Hillary Adam, and Lindsey Allen.

I feel very fortunate to have found Pieter Martin as an editor. He and his team at University of Minnesota Press have been a joy. Two reviewers commissioned by the Press provided thoughtful, constructive guidance for which I am grateful. Financial support from the University Research Foundation of the University of Pennsylvania is gratefully acknowledged.

Friends and colleagues Vicki Weiner, Laura Hansen, Chris Neville, Ned Kaufman, Jon Calame, Kirstin Sechler, Amy Freitag, Tony Wood, and Frances Foster have supported this project with ideas and other generous support. My family (Rick, Julie, Liv, Cooper, Kyle, Susan, and Jack) have been steadfast supporters, reminding me of life beyond work. Though my parents did not live to see this work between two covers, they took pride in it.

Ellen Ryan, my wife, is nothing less than a superhero, saving me repeatedly with her endless wisdom, care, forbearance, and love. Henry Mason, my son, is a great inspiration. Work on this book has been alloyed by many afternoons of baseball, storytelling, and homework, as well as by summers organized around the beach and trips abroad. Matching his curiosity and energy these fourteen years has been my constant challenge and delight. This book is dedicated to Henry and Ellie.

Notes

INTRODUCTION

1. "The destruction of Penn Station in 1963 and the subsequent creation of the New York City Landmarks Preservation Commission in 1965 marked the beginning of the American preservation movement" (Wolfe 1993, 57). Statements like this represent the common understanding of the role of Penn Station and are flatly wrong. The Penn Station controversy did, of course, help bring into being both the Landmarks Preservation Commission and the important 1965 city Landmarks Law, one of the strongest in the country (Allison 1996; Wood 2007).

2. American Scenic and Historic Preservation Society (ASHPS) 1912 (Seventeenth Annual Report).

3. The term "preservationist" is used very broadly, encompassing any person—activist, architect, artist, citizen, or public official—who worked on or advocated projects to preserve or create historical memory in some form, whether using buildings, monuments, or open spaces. "The preservationists," in other words, were not a discrete group; almost all those in the preservation field simultaneously worked in other professions, reform movements, or public offices. In this era, preservation was not yet a professional field unto itself.

4. Herbert Muschamp, "The Secret History of 2 Columbus Circle," *New York Times*, Arts and Leisure, January 8, 2006, 34.

5. There were, of course, more-radical critics of capitalist urbanization—Benjamin Marsh and Henry George were among the most prominent and influential—but anticapitalist critique remained marginal in the scope of the whole reform movement.

6. Hamlin 1902, 68.

7. Kenneth Jackson, personal communication, 1994.

8. Hofstadter 1955, 138n; Burrows and Wallace 1999, 1084.

9. Max Page narrates a few different dimensions of the interplay of market and memory in New York in his *Creative Destruction of Manhattan, 1900–1940* (Page 1999).

10. The term "city builders," as used here, is defined as public officials, reform group leaders, institution builders, leading citizens, and other social entrepreneurs. The closest synonym might be "civic boosters," though the city builders committed themselves to the building of infrastructure and organizations, not just to rhetorical boosterism. They were practitioners, not just supporters, of reform and building. City builders do not include property developers or corporate hacks whose concerns were confined to economic self-interest.

11. Croly 1903, 198.

12. McAneny 1914, 4.

13. F. S. Lamb 1897, 675. Lamb typified early preservation advocates in New York: an educated professional, accomplished, well-to-do, passionate about art and history, full of a curious mixture of tradition and progress. With his brother, Charles Rollinson Lamb, he ran a firm designing ecclesiastical art and was active in the municipal art movement, preservation, and other reform movements.

14. Many of the city's leading capitalists saw the value of historic preservation, though as philanthropic contribution or connoisseurship rather than urban reform.

15. This study stays focused on the environmental-reform impulse—just one among several important strains and expressions of the broad social and political movement of Progressivism. The interpretation of preservation's role in Progressivism presented here provides a counterpoint to Richard Hofstadter's pioneering *Age of Reform* (1955). Seminal works by Paul Boyer (1979), Samuel Hays (1959), and Robert Wiebe ([1967] 1990) trace the evolution of different moments in environmental reform; M. Christine Boyer (1983) added a powerful dimension in her Foucault-inspired interpretation of the rise of city planning. Casey Nelson Blake (1990), R. Jeffrey Lustig (1982), and Michael McGerr (2003) provide important contextualization of the political, economic, and cultural inspirations of Progressivism. Also see Dal Co 1979; Fairfield 1993.

16. ASHPS 1906 (Eleventh Annual Report), cover page, emphasis added. This mantra was frequently restated in ASHPS annual reports.

17. ASHPS 1916 (Twenty-first Annual Report), 19.

18. George McAneny, speech to Architectural League and Fine Arts Federation, February 9, 1915 (George McAneny Papers, box 1).

19. Hammack 1988; K. Jackson 1980, quotation at 347; Burrows and Wallace 1999.

20. K. Jackson 1980.

21. Van Dyke and Pennell 1909, 7.

22. The definition of "modernity" employed here: Modernity is a historical period and condition in which traditional, organic, slowly evolving social ties and ways of life (cultures) give way to social and cultural forms and processes in which relations are more abstract, distant, quickly and repeatedly reconfigured, and reliant on impersonal technologies and institutions. Under modernity, industrialization replaces crafts, markets replace barter, invention replaces inheritance, and so on. The concept of "creative destruction" coined by the economist Joseph Schumpeter captures the central dynamic of modernity: a continual process of destruction and invention bringing the benefits of greater prosperity and improving material conditions, as well as the dislocation of constant change and increasing disparity in how benefits and costs of progress are distributed. The period of modernity could be said to have begun in the United States in the mid-nineteenth century and to have lasted at least through World War II; its heyday was the 1890s–1920s.

23. Burrows and Wallace 1999.

24. Green, quoted in ASHPS 1901 (Sixth Annual Report), 57.

25. Croly 1903, 198, 204.

26. Marsh 1910, 39.

27. As David Harvey tells the story, these combined social, political, and technological forces led to a "crisis of overaccumulation" in capitalism that was attended by a "crisis of representation." This congeries of events—spanning all geographic scales and aspects of social life—resulted in a sea change, or what he terms a "time-space compression." Early-twentieth-century modernism was one of these convulsive movements, in which economic processes, social relations, political patterns, and cultural forms were up for massive revisions. Consider this raft of massive changes happening in a ten-year span, from roughly 1905 to 1915: "Fordist" industrial and corporate organization, Taylorist time management, the closing of the American frontier, the ascendance of the United States as a global military power, the mass use of new technologies such as automobiles, and revolutionary artworks by Georges Braque, Igor Stravinsky, T. S. Eliot, and others. Harvey's argument, fundamentally, is that this remarkable range and depth of social changes instituting "modernity" are not coincidental but rather are linked to reorganization of the capitalist economy (Harvey 1989).

28. Marx 1964; Lears 1981; Huyssen 2003.

29. "The more modern we become, in fact, the more desperately we cling to our Washingtons, to our old-fashioned heroes, to an imagined colonial past, to the good old days when patriots stood firm on their pedestals" (Marling 1988, viii).

30. The parallels between Brooks's work and the issues of this book are many: He was writing in the period considered here (his essay "On Creating a Usable Past" was published in 1915), he was writing about issues of cultural response to modernity, and his circle of peers and friends—including Lewis Mumford—suggests that the connections between different spheres of culture (literature, art, architecture, and so on) were an important dimension of his work (Blake 1990). Other memorable phrases inspired by this cultural watershed were "invented traditions" (Hobsbawm and Ranger 1983) and the past as a "foreign country" (Lowenthal 1985).

31. The ferment in modern culture begot countless forays into the past to construct meaning for contemporary society. Brooks's studies of American literature were one tip of the iceberg: a widespread cultural movement to cultivate historical consciousness. The upheaval was also expressed in art, music, architecture, and other cultural spheres—for example, historical pageants (Glassberg 1990), the revival architecture of Ralph Adams Cram and countless colonial revivalists (Axelrod 1985), the antique-centered business ventures of Wallace Nutting (Denenberg 2003), the opening of the American Wing at the Metropolitan Museum of Art in 1925, and of course historic preservationists. Antihistorical modernism, on the American horizon in the 1920s and '30s, was only beginning to enthrall the avant-garde in the first two decades of the twentieth century (Lears 1981).

32. Harvey 1989.

33. Bush-Brown 1899, 602.

34. "Gloss" in the sense of a surface applied to hide something, but also in the sense of a shorthand marker of some deeper meaning, as in "glossary."

35. P. Boyer 1979, 232, 190. Boyer did not specifically include preservationists among the reformers of this important generation, though he did link historical pageants and other expressions of civic ideals to the large body of environmental-reform work that was such an important legacy of this period.

36. Bush-Brown 1899, 602.

37. From a contemporary perspective, one can conclude that by representing the dominant class's version of history in the built environment, preservationists repressed critical, alternative views of the past but provided sites for later generations to contest and reinterpret, when, much later in the twentieth century, the politics of the day demanded a memory infrastructure more democratic than paternalistic.

38. The federal Antiquities Act was passed in 1906, and the federal Organic Act, creating the National Park Service, was passed in 1916. The first comprehensive zoning ordinance—championed by McAneny for New York City—was also instituted in 1916. The first historic-district ordinance in the country, however, was not created until 1931, in Charleston, South Carolina.

39. Hosmer 1965, the classic text on preservation history, represents this approach.

40. A number of critical analyses of the history of preservation are presented in Page and Mason 2004.

41. Notable works include those of James Lindgren on Virginia (1993) and New England (1991, 1995), Michael Holleran (1998) on Boston, Chris Wilson (1997) on Santa Fe, and Robert Weyeneth (2000) and Stephanie Yuhl (2005) on Charleston, South Carolina.

42. Exceptions include Charles Hosmer's perfunctory mention (1965, 93–101), tangential treatment in Gregory Gilmartin's chronicle of the Municipal Art Society (1995), and Max Page's account of creative destruction (1999).

43. Their colleague R. T. H. Halsey (later the curator of the Metropolitan Museum's American Wing) also contributed to the project, though he was not an Art Commission member at the time (see the Art Commission's 1913 annual report: Art Commission of the City of New York 1913, 28).

44. "The Camera to Preserve New York's Old Buildings," *New York Times Sunday Magazine,* May 10, 1914, 9. The Art Commission archives contain about fifty photographic prints mounted on small boards, images of which are reproduced here. Cousins's papers at the Phillips Library, Peabody Essex Museum, include additional images of New York landmarks taken at the same time but not included in the Art Commission project (Frank Cousins Collection, boxes B35/F5, F6, and F6a).

45. A dry-goods merchant from Salem, Massachusetts, Cousins gravitated to the business of photographing and popularizing colonial architecture, traveling up and down the East Coast selling pictures to architectural firms, collectors, and other connoisseurs of the colonial revival. His clients included the Metropolitan Museum, J. P. Morgan Sr., and Joseph Choate, each of whom bought hundreds of his photographs. He published books on colonial builder Samuel McIntire and collections of buildings and details in Philadelphia and Salem. Part of his business strategy was to contribute articles to architectural journals and popular magazines (he received as many rejections as acceptances; he was accepted at *Country Life,* rejected by *Ladies Home Journal*), and his photographs were used in the White Pine Series of historical architecture pamphlets (Frank Cousins Collection, folders 1–4).

1. MEMORY SITES

1. Calvino 1974, 11.

2. There are some notable exceptions to this, including the works of M. Christine Boyer, David Lowenthal, Françoise Choay, and Aldo Rossi.

3. "Memory site" borrows from Pierre Nora's term *lieux de mémoire,* indicating distinct sites (as opposed to whole environments or places—*milieux de mémoire*) around which collective memory is constructed and stored (see Nora 1989, 1996–98).

4. Green, quoted in ASHPS 1901 (Sixth Annual Report), 52.

5. Hamlin 1902, 68.

6. P. Boyer 1979.

7. Foord 1913; Hammack 1987, 1988; Johnson 1988; Mazaraki 1966; Rosenzweig and Blackmar 1992; and Spann 1981 are good sources on Green's life and work. Green 1894 and the ASHPS annual reports are the best sources for his work in historic preservation.

8. Rosenzweig and Blackmar 1992, 196.

9. Obituary in the *New York Sun,* November 14, 1903.

10. Foord 1913, 79.

11. Green, quoted in ASHPS 1901.

12. Quoted in Foord 1913, 228.

13. Preservation did not draw on contemporary advances in historical scholarship. The tight consensus represented in the public history presentations of this period contrasted with Progressive academic historians' efforts to foreground conflicts (between different classes or interest groups) as the drivers of American history, as in the work of Charles and Mary Beard

and other pioneering Progressive historians of this period. There was a disconnect between this vanguard in academic historiography and the sense of history being popularized and portrayed on the ground. See Breisach 1993; Higham 1989; Novick 1988.

14. Hall 1901, 356.

15. Bellah et al. 1985, 153.

16. Hood 2002.

17. Hall 1912, 14.

18. Glassberg 2001; Kammen 1991; Lowenthal 1985.

19. Hood 2002.

20. The preservation field, such as it was, consisted mostly of advocacy groups. Actual preservation work (building restoration, funding of memorials) was carried out on an ad hoc basis, with property owners or specially organized citizens actually serving as clients. Exceptions to this included the DAR, the City Parks Department, and the city's executive offices (mayor, borough president), each of which financed the restoration of a number of sites. Several other New York organizations, public and private, were involved periodically in preservation issues and projects. Their work is mentioned elsewhere in this study, and they included the Art Commission, the City Parks Department, the Fine Arts Federation, the Architectural League, the New York chapter of the American Institute of Architects, the City History Club, the Colonial Dames of America, and the Sons of the American Revolution. The Municipal Art Society, founded in 1893 and today the city's leading private advocacy organization on preservation issues, was silent on matters of historic preservation until around 1916. Its active involvement in preservation was in full swing only in the 1940s. The membership of the Municipal Art Society and the ASHPS overlapped a great deal, however, so Municipal Art Society reformers certainly were preservationists, but they channeled their interest through the ASHPS and work on individual projects.

21. ASHPS [1906].

22. The original name was Trustees of Scenic and Historic Places and Objects in the State of New York, following the Trustees of Reservations model. The name was changed in 1900. Its office was located in the Tribune Building, across from City Hall.

23. Green 1895, 4, 6.

24. The first Annual Report of the Trustees of Reservations expressed the organizational philosophy that every town's village green had undoubtedly been the site of acts worth commemoration and would be the worthy object of "care and adornment." Clearly, preservation in this respect fell under the wing of the village-improvement movement, as well as its urban analog, the City Beautiful movement.

25. The society also mounted public relations campaigns with the help of newspapers such as the *Times* and the *Evening Post*. Frances Whiting Halsey, an active, longtime trustee of the society, was editor of the *Times* Saturday Review section, and the ASHPS actively recruited editors from around the state as members. ASHPS Board Minutes, December 1 and 29, 1900 (American Scenic and Historic Preservation Society [hereafter ASHPS] Manuscript Papers, box 6).

26. The idea of land-use regulation as a preservation tool was not discussed in this era. Neither building listing nor historic districts had been invented (they appeared first in the 1920s in other cities), and the strong land-use regulatory tool in New York City was not instituted until the 1916 zoning law.

27. ASHPS Manuscript Papers; ASHPS 1895–1925 (annual reports).

28. Edward Hagaman Hall (1858–1936), long-serving secretary of the ASHPS, was known

as "a writer and lecturer on American history, scenery and archaeology." Born in upstate New York, Hall worked for twenty years in New York City and around the Northeast as a newspaper-man (for the *Tribune*), historian, administrator, and preservation advocate. Hall was perhaps the only individual in this period to make a living at preservation work. From 1898 until his retirement in the late 1920s, Hall carried the water for the ASHPS: handling correspondence and business affairs, drafting and producing the annual reports, attending numerous meetings, coordinating actions and sharing information with other organizations, and more. Without his efforts (as the primary employee and essentially the day-to-day director of the organization, and as the main spokesman and advocate for preservation citywide), the ASHPS would have been just a hollow shell. Extending beyond ASHPS duties, Hall wrote many histories and historical guides to such places as the Cathedral of St. John the Divine, McGown's Pass in Central Park, the Water Supply of New York City, Battery Park, City Hall Park, Philipse Manor Hall in Yonkers; some of these were published as ASHPS pamphlets or in the annual reports, others as commercially published books. Participating in other historical organizations, from the Municipal Art Society to the Sons of the American Revolution, gave Hall yet more venues to cultivate public memory. Hall also took on additional "secretarial" and writing duties for special events, including the New York Commerce Commission (1898–99), the Hudson–Fulton Celebration (1909), and the New York Commercial Tercentenary Celebration (1914) (which were essentially run by the ASHPS, with Hall producing and publishing extensive official reports of the events). He was also secretary of the Association for the Protection of the Adirondacks from 1902 to 1929. A devoted Episcopalian and head usher at the Cathedral of St. John the Divine, Hall's memorial service was presided over by Bishop William T. Manning (whom Hall and other preservationists had opposed in the fight over St. John's Chapel).

29. ASHPS 1923 (Twenty-eighth Annual Report), 8.

30. ASHPS 1902 (Seventh Annual Report).

31. Brunner 1912, 23.

32. For example, the Board Minutes of 1912 record activities such as Hall's supplying Manhattan's parks commissioner Charles Stover with maps and various information on Hamilton Grange, which the ASHPS wanted the city to purchase (January 22), or Manhattan's borough president George McAneny's asking the ASHPS's advice on preserving the facade of the Assay Office, demolition of which was proposed (December 23) (ASHPS Manuscript Papers, box 1).

33. McAneny 1949, 86.

34. ASHPS Board Minutes, November 25, 1901 (ASHPS Manuscript Papers, box 6).

35. The Virginians were suspicious of the northerners' intentions and refused help. Later, the Association for the Preservation of Virginia Antiquities contacted the ASHPS for fund-raising assistance (ASHPS Board Minutes, May 24, 1915 [ASHPS Manuscript Papers, box 1]; Lindgren 1993).

36. The Antiquities Act of 1906 enabled the first national monuments, places like Mesa Verde and Chaco Canyon, and the Organic Act of 1916 created the National Park Service.

37. Later, in keeping with policy shifts in conservation and parks more generally, the management of these sites was transferred to state or local government agencies.

38. See, for instance, ASHPS [1911].

39. Ibid., 13–14.

40. Many libraries around the country have at least a few of the reports.

41. ASHPS 1908 (Thirteenth Annual Report), 112–13.

42. Despite much newspaper reporting to the contrary, the African Burial Ground, just

north of City Hall Park, was not altogether forgotten between the eighteenth century and the 1990s. Hall clearly marked the "site of ancient burying ground for negroes, paupers, and criminals and for American patriots under British rule during the Revolution" on his 1910 map (ASHPS 1910 [Fifteenth Annual Report], map between pages 416 and 417); some of his contemporaries wrote about it as well.

43. The ASHPS was willing to stretch the canons of patriotic commemoration: It even advocated and published a memorial tablet to Harriet Tubman (ASHPS 1915 [Twentieth Annual Report]). In a 1909 dustup over the location of a memorial in Battery Park, Hall patiently explained why it was not a conflict to give both Henry Hudson and Giovanni da Verrazano credit for a role in the city's early history, bowing to Italian Americans' wish for a place in the civic patriotism pantheon. Hall also spoke proudly of the "Melting Pot" float included in the Commercial Tercentenary Celebration parades (ASHPS 1915 [Twentieth Annual Report], 560–63).

44. Ashbee 1901, 6.

45. Holleran 1998; Lindgren 1995.

46. ASHPS 1922 (Twenty-seventh Annual Report), 12.

47. ASHPS Manuscript Papers, box 10.

48. ASHPS Board Minutes, June 13, 1899 (ASHPS Manuscript Papers, box 6).

49. This was perpetuated by the constant retelling of Green's founding role, and by the creation of the A. H. Green Memorial Fund, endowed with $10,000 from Green's estate for the benefit of the society. Activist Mike Miscione's recent efforts at memorializing Green are trying to reverse the fact that he is little remembered today.

50. George Frederick Kunz Papers.

51. Kunz lectured on the subject (see Kunz 1923) and served on a 1912 mayor's advisory committee on park improvement and preservation with fellow American Museum of Natural History scientist William Hornaday and Bronx River Parkway commissioner William White Niles.

52. ASHPS Board Minutes, October 28, 1912 (ASHPS Manuscript Papers, box 1); "Dr. G. F. Kunz Weds Miss Opal Giberson," *New York Times,* May 16, 1923.

53. ASHPS 1905 (Tenth Annual Report) and 1906 (Eleventh Annual Report).

54. Dubrow and Goodman 2003; Morgan 1998; Hosmer 1965.

55. ASHPS 1901 (Sixth Annual Report).

56. Morgan 1998; Giffen and Murphy 1992.

57. The auxiliary was quite successful in preserving and opening the Morris–Jumel Mansion and Poe Cottage. Their efforts on Fraunces Tavern—supported by the society, which lobbied the Parks Department to acquire the property—were unsuccessful, though the building was later purchased and reconstructed by another patriotic group, the Sons of the American Revolution.

58. ASHPS 1900 (Fifth Annual Report).

59. Kammen 1991; Lears 1981; Lindgren 1993, 1995.

60. *Literary Digest,* January 1, 1910 (clipping in ASHPS Manuscript Papers, box 10, record book of 1909–10).

61. George McAneny was president of the ASHPS in the 1940s. He helped fulfill earlier goals, such as preserving and opening Hamilton Grange as a museum. But the reformist zeal of the second decade of the twentieth century was not sustained in the postwar boom years, and the society was progressively weakened. Larger, better-connected groups, such as the Municipal Art Society, took on a broader role, assuming the mantle of the now more professionalized

preservation field. McAneny's preservation work in the 1930s and '40s was impressive, though the society was seldom the venue for it. McAneny founded separate organizations and efforts to preserve particular buildings—Federal Hall Memorial Associates, the City Hall Park Association, and his successful defense of Castle Clinton against the effort of Robert Moses to build a Brooklyn–Battery bridge. This victory came back to haunt McAneny. Moses used his influence in Albany to end the stewardship agreements the society had for five state battlefield and park properties (McAneny 1949; George McAneny Papers). In the late 1940s he formed a national preservation organization—the National Council for Historic Sites and Buildings—a precursor to the National Trust. (The idea to form a national trust, on the model of England's trust, had been suggested in ASHPS board meetings at least as early as 1900 [ASHPS Manuscript Papers, box 6]).

62. Axelrod 1985; B. May 1991; West 1999.

63. Dozens of other buildings were preserved and restored between 1890 and 1920—some by hereditary and preservation groups (the forty-nine or so DAR projects in the five boroughs listed in Barrington 1941), others by private individuals (Smith's Folly) or institutions (New York University and Washington Square North), and others by the city's religious institutions.

64. ASHPS 1910 (Fifteenth Annual Report), 57.

65. Bolton 1903, 4.

66. John McComb was New York's leading colonial-era architect, thus adding value to the building in the eyes of the preservation field. Dates cited for Hamilton's occupation of the house differ, variously reported as 1802, 1803, and 1804.

67. Over one hundred years, actually: the siting and restoration of the house, now owned by the National Park Service, is still a matter of debate. In recent years, proposals to move the Grange into a nearby public park have been a contentious community issue.

68. The Grange was moved from a site that would become 143rd Street to Convent Avenue, near the corner of 141st Street, in what is now the Hamilton Heights section of Harlem.

69. The trees were said to have been transplanted from Mount Vernon (ASHPS 1909 [Fourteenth Annual Report], 81; "Hamilton's Thirteen Trees," *New York Times*, January 14, 1897).

70. ASHPS 1901 (Sixth Annual Report), 25; Stokes [1915–28] 1972, 3:775.

71. ASHPS 1912 (Seventeenth Annual Report).

72. David Dunlap, "Hamilton Grange Needs Furniture (and $2 Million)," *New York Times*, February 14, 1988.

73. The literature on house museums includes Hosmer 1965 and West 1999.

74. Bolton, an engineer and amateur archaeologist, was an active preservationist and ASHPS member. He published his historical research in several books, including Bolton 1903, 1926, 1934.

75. Bashford Dean had a doctorate in zoology from Columbia and held positions as both curator of herpetology and ichthyology at the American Museum of Natural History and curator of arms and armor at the Metropolitan Museum of Art. He was the author of many works on arms and armor, a trustee of the Metropolitan Museum of Art, and a member of the Century Club. His brother-in-law, Alexander McMillan Welch, was an architecture graduate from Columbia in 1890 and won the first McKim Fellowship to study at the École des Beaux-Arts. His architectural practice was extensive, including the restoration of Hamilton Grange. Welch, also an active reformer, served as trustee and vice president of the ASHPS and was a member of the New-York Historical Society, the Architectural League, the Society

for the Preservation of New England Antiquities, and the Society of Beaux Arts. *The National Cyclopedia of American Biography* 1898–1978, 21:29 and 34:303.

76. ASHPS 1914 (Nineteenth Annual Report), 1917 (Twenty-second Annual Report), appendix B.

77. Avery Architectural and Fine Arts Library; Haley 2002.

78. Dean and Welch 1916.

79. Haley 2002; West 1999.

80. K. Jackson 1995, 438.

81. R. Wilson 1896, 1099.

82. Peirce 1901, 8.

83. See Hayden 1981 for biographical background of Melusina Fay Peirce and an explanation of her housekeeping reform work and its significance in domestic reform. This appears to have been her sole historic preservation effort.

84. Peirce 1901, 8, 10.

85. ASHPS [1911]; Bolton 1903, 3; "Fraunces Tavern Park," *New York Times,* December 5, 1902.

86. ASHPS 1901 (Sixth Annual Report).

87. City History Club 1913, 48.

88. ASHPS 1911 (Sixteenth Annual Report), 79–83.

89. For sources of these ideas see Cole 1836; Novak 1980; Marx 1964.

90. D. Schuyler 1986, 2.

91. Intrusions meant new buildings, trains and widened streets, commerce (peddlers and signs), and ball fields.

92. ASHPS 1916 (Twenty-first Annual Report), appendix.

93. ASHPS 1909 (Fourteenth Annual Report), 62.

94. Croly 1903, 199.

95. Commissioners of the State Reservation at Niagara 1885–86; Bluestone, n.d.

96. Rosenzweig and Blackmar 1992.

97. "Noted Men to Lead Park Defense Fight," *New York Times,* June 25, 1912.

98. George Kunz and Edward Hall, letter to the editor, *New York Times,* January 26, 1924.

99. "Fight to Save Park Arouses Entire City . . . Appeal Also Sent to Estimate Board to Keep the 'People's Heritage' Intact," *New York Times,* March 15, 1924.

100. ASHPS 1911 (Sixteenth Annual Report), appendix G.

101. The limits to the historical vision of Hall and his contemporaries is made clear by works such as Rosenzweig and Blackmar 1992, which recovers and creates narratives unimagined in Hall's account.

102. ASHPS 1916 (Twenty-first Annual Report), 155.

103. Bogart 1989.

104. "Fight to Save Park Arouses Entire City," *New York Times,* March 15, 1924.

105. The park was renamed Fort Greene Park in 1897, after Revolutionary War general Nathaniel Greene; see "Fort Greene Park," New York City Department of Parks and Recreation, http://www.nycgovparks.org/sub_your_park/historical_signs/hs_historical_sign.php?id=179.

106. Others were imprisoned in the old Hall of Records, also known as the Martyrs' Prison and as the Old Gaol, in City Hall Park.

107. "Taft and Hughes at Martyrs' Shaft," *New York Times,* November 15, 1908.

108. "Prison Ship Martyrs Buried at Fort Greene," *New York Times*, June 17, 1900.

109. "Woodford, Stewart Lyndon," Biographical Directory of the United States Congress, http://bioguide.congress.gov/scripts/biodisplay.pl?index=W000713.

110. Before the new monument was installed, Memorial Day celebrations centered on Grand Army Plaza or other sites.

111. Bluestone 1987; Gilder 1936.

112. The location of the original fort, and thus of the original Battery emplacement, was researched by archaeologists and determined to be near Bowling Green and the site of today's Customs House.

113. Today, it has about thirty memorials.

114. By 1920, the Battery had several monuments—including the one to Verrazano; today, they number more than twenty. ASHPS 1903 (Eighth Annual Report), appendix D.

115. "City Tercentenary to Open Today," *New York Times*, October 25, 1914.

116. "Save the Park," *Harper's Weekly*, April 11, 1891, 259.

117. ASHPS 1915 (Twentieth Annual Report), 187. In 2007, subway renovations revealed eighteenth-century and perhaps earlier walls—so the Battery's historical value continues to unfold and compete with other infrastructural projects competing for public space.

118. "Rapid Transit and Parks," *New York Times*, June 20, 1895.

119. Caro 1974; Martin 2005; McAneny 1949.

120. D. Schuyler 1986.

121. Green 1866.

122. "Art in Memorial Form," *New York Times*, November 3, 1895.

123. Bogart 1989.

124. Ibid., 3.

125. Yates 1966; Young 1993.

126. See Bogart 1989 and Gayle and Cohen 1988 regarding New York City in this era; Savage 1997, writing specifically about Civil War memorials, is another excellent study.

127. See the excellent literature on the City Beautiful movement, including M. Boyer 1983 and W. Wilson 1980 and 1994. In 1893, Richard Morris Hunt founded New York's Municipal Art Society. Gregory Gilmartin's (1995) history is a vivid account of the vast array of subjects and issues taken up by the Municipal Art Society.

128. The architects who incorporated the faience plaques into the stations, George Lewis Heins and Christopher Grant LaFarge, were leading municipal artists whose other historicist architecture projects included the Cathedral of St. John the Divine.

129. Green 1895, 6.

130. Opinions differ on whether he was captured and hanged in the Commons or elsewhere in Manhattan, near what is today the East Sixties.

131. Bogart 1989, 135–54.

132. Robinson 1901, 217.

133. Ibid., 221. Robinson was a member of the ASHPS, but his main affiliation was with the municipal art and village-improvement movements.

134. Page 1999.

135. R. T. H. Halsey, in Metropolitan Museum of Art 1925, 9–10.

136. Glassberg 1990.

137. Others included the 250th anniversary of the municipal government of New York, celebrated in May 1903 ("Father Knickerbocker Celebrates Birthday," *New York Times*, May 17, 1903).

138. P. Boyer 1979, ch. 17, 258.

139. The most evocative and successful part of the Commercial Tercentenary was the parade of bands, school groups, and civic associations and a procession of historical floats rendering a narrative of New York history through a series of thirty rolling tableaux. There was no clearer or more comprehensive expression of the historical memory canon: "The Historical Division was . . . led by a body of real Indians secured from the New York State Reservations, followed by 30 floats representing scenes and incidents in the history of the City from 1614 to 1914. The floats were as follows: Primeval Manhattan in 1614; The Purchase of Manhattan Island in 1626; Bowling on Bowling Green, 1664; Fort Amsterdam before Surrender, 1664; The Summons of the English for the Surrender of Fort Amsterdam, 1664; Hamilton's First Speech, 1774; The Reformed Dutch Church of Harlem; The Bombardment of New York, 1776; The Great Fire of 1776; Betsey Ross Making the First American Flag, 1777; Washington Entering New York, 1783; The Impressment of American Seamen, 1812; A Sea Fight in the War of 1812; The Writing of the National Anthem, 1814; Apotheosis of the Star Spangled Banner, 1814; The Treaty of Ghent, 1814; The Erie Canal, 1825; The Hudson & Mohawk Railroad, 1830; The Clipper Ship, 1840–1855; The First Telegram, 1844; Liberty Progress; Industries of New York; Early Education; Education of To-day; Industrial Education; Commerce; Recreation; A Century of Peace and Progress; The Melting Pot" (ASHPS 1915 [Twentieth Annual Report], 560–63).

140. Metropolitan Museum of Art 1925; on Progressive politics and the use of historical memory in public pageants, see Glassberg 1990.

141. Glassberg 1990. The New York Commercial Tercentenary of 1914 built on the success of the Hudson–Fulton Celebration and replayed many of the tropes, events, and themes. The Commercial Tercentenary commemorated the Dutch charter granted in 1614 to create Nieuw Amsterdam—the "three hundredth anniversary of the beginning of the regularly chartered commerce of what is now the State of New York." It was similar in main respects to the Hudson–Fulton Celebration and was also organized by Kunz and Hall, among other reformers and financial elites, but the execution of the tercentenary suffered from bad timing. Money proved difficult to raise from private and public sources, and the Vera Cruz landing and European "state of war" sapped attention. The celebrations nevertheless went on, spread from March 27 to October 11, 1914. More than thirty thousand participants and 1.75 million spectators were reported, even though a decision was made in August to postpone all activities except children's gatherings, commercial exhibits, and the public parade and illuminations (ASHPS 1915 [Twentieth Annual Report], appendix B).

142. Good general sources on the celebration include Nye 1994, 153–65; the exhaustive two-volume report was published (Hudson–Fulton Celebration Commission 1910).

143. The Hudson–Fulton Celebration and other, more modest celebrations in this era—such as the 1914 Tercentenary of the City and the 1914 commercial celebration—were expressions of the national phenomenon of historical pageantry and public celebration. Pageantry is described in Glassberg 1990; on holidays and other celebrations, see Gillis 1994 and Bodnar 1991.

144. Historian David Nye (1994) points out that the illuminated cityscapes were closely related to City Beautiful efforts to create an ideal city in the chaotic here and now.

145. This metropolitan spread contrasts with the design of two of the Hudson–Fulton Celebration's precedents: Chicago's 1893 Columbian Exposition, an enormously successful and influential "event" staged in one newly constructed "city"; and the historical pageants documented by Glassberg (1990) across the country, which usually were confined to one place or even one parade.

146. Nye 1994, 155.

147. Several statues and monuments were dedicated during the celebration. A few permanent monuments were erected around the city as part of the commercial tercentenary as well,
but the grandest of them—a memorial Robert Fulton water gate to be located on the Hudson
River in Morningside Heights—failed to happen. See Bogart 1989.

148. "Verrazzano Remembered," *New York Evening Post,* July 24, 1909.

149. "Honor Verrazzano at Hudson Festival," *New York Times,* July 25, 1909.

150. "200,000 Italians Honor Verrazzano," *New York Times,* October 7, 1909; "Honor
Verrazzano at Hudson Festival." Another dispute attached to the celebration's music: Some
charged that Gustav Lindenthal, a Hudson–Fulton Celebration commissioner of German
descent, chose too many German orchestras to play.

151. Bush-Brown 1899, 605.

152. Examples include monuments to the Hungarian patriot Louis Kossuth in Riverside
Park and the Danish sculptor Albert Thorvaldsen in Central Park.

2. The Preservation and Destruction of St. John's Chapel

1. Several other Episcopal churches and chapels, both independent and part of Trinity
Parish, moved or were closed around the turn of the century. Trinity opened new chapels in
this period, including All Saints Chapel (East 60th Street) in November 1913 and the Chapel
of the Intercession (Broadway and 155th Street) in May 1915 (Hughes 1963). The story was
similar for many other Protestant and Catholic churches. Holleran 1998 notes several examples in Boston. Gough 1995 is a superb rendering of the story of Christ Church in Philadelphia,
which faced a predicament very similar to St. John's, though it was ultimately saved.

2. Trinity Parish was founded by in 1704 by the mother (Anglican) church in England
and was awarded a large bequest of land that has since been the basis for its wealth. As the
church of New York's political and social establishment, its governing lay body—its vestry—
has long been a list of the city's most prominent citizens.

Perhaps it goes without saying, but there was no law for designating official landmarks, nor
therefore for preventing their destruction if an owner wished to do so. In New York City, such
a law was not passed until 1965.

3. Today, the site of the park contains exit ramps for the Holland Tunnel.

4. Haddon 1914a. The chapel's footprint was 80 feet by 180 feet, and it had a 179-foot
spire boasting bells and a clock. See Haddon 1914a for drawings and photographs documenting the chapel.

5. St. John's Park, and the whole district, was sometimes known as Hudson Square.

6. Rosenzweig and Blackmar 1992.

7. Cardia 1987; Rosenzweig and Blackmar 1992.

8. Cardia 1987.

9. Stokes [1915–28] 1972, 5:1851.

10. Dix and Lewis 1950, 64.

11. See Annie Gould, letter to the editor, *New York Times,* April 22, 1909; *Evening Post Saturday Magazine,* July 26, 1913.

12. Dix and Lewis 1950, 68.

13. Congregation petition of December 29, 1908, 3 (Diocesan Archives, box 54, folder
"Legal Documents").

14. The chapel had been renovated and slightly expanded by Richard Upjohn in the 1860s (Dix and Lewis 1950, 69–70).

15. Bridgeman 1962, 81; Trinity Parish 1893. A note on using Bridgeman: I normally would hesitate to rely on this official church history as much I have. The pro-church bias is easy to read. However, this is the only window available on the vestry's minutes, a crucial source of information to which research access is currently denied by the Trinity Corporation.

16. The vestry was analogous to a board of directors with whom the rector, the chief religious officer, worked to run the parish. This analysis has to remain somewhat speculative, as Trinity's Vestry Minutes remain closed to researchers and the issue is not directly raised in available correspondence.

17. Hughes 1963, 108. In addition to his real estate business interests, Cammann was a trustee of Columbia University for thirty years, as well as of philanthropic institutions such as the Home for Old Men and Aged Couples (located at 487 Hudson Street, very near St. John's). He was further distinguished by his relation (through marriage) to Robert Fulton (*New York Times,* June 19, 1910).

18. The new, consolidated congregation was to be located on the site of St. John's Burying Ground. The bishop, as leader of the diocese of which Trinity Parish was part, was the highest ecclesiastical authority.

19. Excerpt of January 11, 1909, Vestry Minutes (Trinity Parish Archives, record group 7, subgroup 3, box 2, folder "St. John's Closing, 1909, Corr re The Rt. Rev WTM"); Dix to Rev. Charles Gomph, November 17, 1907, quoted in I. N. P. Stokes to Bishop Greer, December 12, 1908 (Diocesan Archives, box 54, file "Manhattan, St. John's Chapel, Correspondence 1889–1909").

20. Bishop Potter replying to Nash and Cruger, March 8, 1894 (Diocesan Archives, box 54, Correspondence; original in Trinity Parish Archives, record group 7, subgroup 3, box 2).

21. Clerk and comptroller of the vestry (S. P. Nash and S. V. R. Cruger) to Bishop Potter, February 24, 1894 (Diocesan Archives, box 54, Correspondence).

22. Dix to Gomph, November 15, 1907 (Trinity Parish Archives, record group 7, subgroup 3, box 2, folder "SJC Closing, 1909, Corr re The Rt. Rev WTM").

23. Reports and letters in William Thomas Manning Papers (folder 1, box 3).

24. St. Luke's status changed in 1891. It had been independent of Trinity Vestry, though financially supported by it. The congregation decided to move its church uptown (to Convent Avenue and 141st Street), while the Hudson Street building reverted to status as a chapel of Trinity.

25. Trinity Parish Archives, record group 7, subgroup 3, box 1, folder "Brief for Respondents 1909."

26. "Trinity Tenements," *New York Times,* March 14, 1897.

27. They exchanged accusatory letters over an incident in 1904 in which Dix (as rector, Manning's boss) had used Manning's St. Agnes's Chapel to conduct the wedding of Col. William Jay's daughter without consulting Manning (William Thomas Manning Papers, folder 3, box 64).

28. Dix was a New Yorker, born 1827; Manning was born in England in 1866 and had lived in Nebraska, California, and Tennessee (though his biographer insisted, "He had no trace of accent, British or southern" [Hughes 1963, 51]).

29. This is in keeping with Manning's generally more conservative theology and view of social issues, which, along with his building of the Cathedral of St. John the Divine, was

another hallmark of his tenure as rector of Trinity Parish and later as bishop of the Diocese of New York.

30. Vestry Minutes, excerpt of November 9, 1908 (Trinity Parish Archives, record group 7, subgroup 3, box 2, folder "SJC Closing, 1909, Corr re The Rt. Rev WTM").

31. Vestry Minutes, excerpt of January 11, 1909 (Trinity Parish Archives, record group 7, subgroup 3, box 2, folder "SJC Closing, 1909, Corr re The Rt. Rev WTM").

32. Manning to the congregation of St. John's, November 20, 1908 (Diocesan Archives, box 54).

33. Trinity Parish 1909.

34. Bridgeman 1962, 82–85.

35. Trinity Parish *Year Book* of 1874, "Policy of the Corporation," 24–26, quoted in *Burke, John, et al., v. The Rector, Church Wardens and Vestrymen of Trinity Church, et al.* 1896–1911, 113.

36. Quoted in *Burke v. Rector* 1896–1911, 63–64.

37. Dix and Lewis 1950; Gilmartin 1995; Page 1999; Stokes [1915–28] 1972.

38. As detailed below, several other parties beside the newspapers advocated the causes of congregation and building.

39. Biographical information about committee members is related below.

40. Letters dated February 10, 1909, and March 24, 1909 (Trinity Parish Archives, record group 7, subgroup 3, box 2, folder "SJC Closing, 1909, Corr re The Rt. Rev WTM").

41. St. John's Congregation to Rector, Church Wardens, and Vestrymen of the Parish of Trinity church in the City of New York, December 5, 1908 (Diocesan Archives, box 54; also Trinity Parish Archives, record group 7, subgroup 3, box 2, folder "St. John's Petitions re closing, 1908").

42. Ibid.

43. Trinity Vestry did not apply the same standards to all its chapels, nor did it consider closing all chapels because of declining congregations. St. Paul's, for instance, had steadily declined in the late nineteenth century, to about four hundred communicants around 1908, though closing this chapel was never envisioned. The age, landmark status, and especially the association of St. Paul's with George Washington undoubtedly contributed to the vestry's decision to preserve St. Paul's, no matter the "efficiency" of its religious work. Trinity Parish 1893, 1907, 1908, 1909, 1910; Bridgeman 1962, ch. 6.

44. Lewis Smith to Bishop Greer, December 10, 1908 (Diocesan Archives, box 54, correspondence folder).

45. Gomph to Manning, April 24, 1909 (William Thomas Manning Papers, box 4, folder 13).

46. St. John's Chapel increased from 563 to 656 communicants from 1907 to 1908; St. Paul's estimated that it had 500 communicants in those years. Financial contributions to the parish from St. John's also exceeded those from St. Paul's and three other chapels (Trinity Parish *Year Book* 1893, 1907, 1908, 1909, 1910).

47. *New York Herald.* That a significant number did live near the chapel is supported not only by statements from the congregation and its clergy but by the social geography discerned from communion lists. It is difficult to reconstruct a complete geography of St. John's congregants, as only partial records exist keying congregants to addresses (Communion lists [Diocesan Archives, box 54, St. John's Chapel]).

48. Congregation to Rector et al., December 5, 1908 (Diocesan Archives, box 54, Correspondence folder).

49. Charles Gomph to Manning, December 14, 1908 (Trinity Parish Archives, record group 7, subgroup 3, box 2, folder "SJC Closing, 1909, Corr re The Rt. Rev WTM").

50. Anonymous clipping, "St. John's v. Trinity Church" (Diocesan Archives, box 54, News Clippings folder).

51. Quoted in "Closing of St. John's Stopped by Court," *New York Times,* January 30, 1909; also in court briefs (Trinity Parish Archives, record group 7, subgroup 3, box 1, folder "Brief for Respondents, 1909").

52. *Burke v. Rector* 1896–1911; anonymous clipping, "St. John's v. Trinity Church" (Diocesan Archives, box 54, News Clippings folder).

53. Stokes's report to Bishop David Greer describes parishioners as American-born of German or Irish parents. The sampling of congregants' names from communion lists and from lawsuit affidavits supports this characterization. Stokes to the Bishop David Greer, Dec 12, 1908 (Diocesan Archives, box 54, Correspondence folder); communion lists (Diocesan Archives, box 54, St. John's Chapel).

54. First congregation petition, December 5, 1908, 3 (Diocesan Archives, box 54, Legal Documents folder).

55. Petition, December 29, 1908 (Trinity Parish Archives, record group 7, subgroup 3, box 2, folder "SJC Petitions re closing, 1908").

56. K. Jackson 1995.

57. Quoted in congregation petition to the vestry, December 29, 1908 (Trinity Parish Archives, record group 7, subgroup 3, box 2, folder "SJC Petitions re closing, 1908").

58. The few glimpses in the record come from "Fight for St. John's," *New York Tribune,* November 30, 1908, an article interviewing Gustow (see William Thomas Manning Papers, box 3, folder 8); affidavits in *Burke v. Rector* 1896–1911.

59. Anonymous letter, January 29, 1909 (William Thomas Manning Papers, folder "New York. Trinity Church. Statement. 1909. Responses. Folder no. 1 A–C").

60. J. M. Mackay to W. T. Manning, January 24, 1909 (William Thomas Manning Papers, box 3, folder "New York. Trinity Church. Statement. 1909. Responses. Folder no. 2 D–K").

61. Annie Gould was a wealthy civic advocate, "an old New Yorker and parishioner of St. Thomas," in her own words. *Who Was Who in America* (1998) notes her "many tours in Europe" and summer residence in Tarrytown.

62. See especially Annie Gould to W. T. Manning, letters dated January 28 and February 17, 1909 (William Thomas Manning Papers, box 3, folder "New York. Trinity Church. Statement. 1909. Responses. folder no. 1 D–K").

63. The icing on the vestry's argument was pointing out that the January injunction overstepped the jurisdiction of the court by assuming ecclesiastical authority and thus violating the separation of church and state!

64. *Burke and Others v. Rector, Warders, and Vestrymen of Trinity Church,* Brief for Respondents (Trinity Parish Archives, record group 7, subgroup 3, box 1).

65. *The Case of St. John's Chapel: Shall Christian Charity or Corporate Power Prevail?* April 5, 1909, pamphlet (Butler Library, Columbia University).

66. Ibid., 15.

67. Halbwachs 1980.

68. "Original Complaint," *Burke, et al. v. Rector, etc.,* January 28, 1909 (Trinity Parish Archives, record group 7, subgroup 3, box 1).

69. "The Policy of Trinity Parish," 22 (Trinity Parish Archives, record group 7, subgroup 3, box 2).

70. More accurately, the congregation *mostly* lost. Some members of the congregation did continue their worship at St. Luke's, surrounded by some of the fragments removed from

their former home (see *Year Book,* 1909, 1910), and thus continued practicing their religion even if it was tainted by blows to their memory and sense of justice.

71. Anonymous and untitled newspaper clipping (Diocesan Archive, box 54, News clippings folder).

72. Chris Jenks (St. Luke's parishioner and architectural historian) and Dr. Donald Gerardi (St. Luke's parish historian), personal communication, July 1996. The rood (a cross) in particular was a sign that St. John's practiced a more Anglo-Catholic liturgy, which meant incorporating more of the formal rituals, artifacts, and hierarchical practices normally associated with the Roman Catholic Church. Given the greater importance of such trappings of worship, the material artifacts of St. John's parishioners' worship—not only furniture, decorative art, and vestments, but also the interior architecture of their chapel—were particularly meaningful.

73. The lone defense of the vestry in the press was Inglis 1909, which appeared in *Harper's Weekly;* other defenders within the clergy wrote personally to Manning (William Thomas Manning Papers, box 3, folders marked "New York. Trinity Church. Statement. 1909. Responses").

74. In 1909 Manning hired a public relations consultant to spin the vestry's message (Bridgeman 1962, 92).

75. To reformer and borough president George McAneny, the papers were particularly influential in the chapel controversy (McAneny 1949).

76. "St. John's Not Historic, So Dr. Manning Tells Clergymen Who Table Resolutions Pleading for It," *New York Times,* December 24, 1908; "Old St. John's Church Is Marked for Destruction," *New York Times,* May 25, 1913.

77. Annie Gould, "St. John's Chapel," letter published in *New York Times,* April 22, 1909.

78. Richard Watson Gilder, untitled, *Evening Post,* December 14, 1908.

79. George Zabriskie, letter to the editor, *Evening Post,* December 15, 1908.

80. Various letters in William Thomas Manning Papers, folder 4; Manning's papers also contained a newspaper clipping of the poem.

81. Inglis 1909.

82. The Board of Estimate and Apportionment was a small, powerful executive body made up of the borough presidents, the New York City comptroller, and the president of the New York City Board of Aldermen.

83. *New York Herald,* June 6, 1914.

84. Editorial in the *Churchman,* undated, 1909.

85. Some of the letters were published in the *Churchman,* December 17, 1908.

86. Silas McBee was an Episcopal educator, writer, and amateur architect. He had several church designs credited to him, including Christ Church in Houston and interiors, windows, and furniture for St. James in Wilmington, North Carolina. In addition to serving as a trustee of prestigious Sewanee, McBee was mentioned as a friend in Teddy Roosevelt's *Autobiography.*

87. Silas McBee to Manning, December 1, 1908 (Trinity Parish Archives, record group 7, subgroup 3, box 2, folder "SJC Closing, 1909, Corr re The Rt. Rev WTM").

88. John P. Peters, in the *Churchman,* January 9, 1909. Indeed, as Trinity was closing down St. John's, plans were under way to acquire the Chapel of the Intercession at 155th Street and Broadway, completed in 1914 as the newest uptown chapel of ease. Peters also accused Trinity of usurping all church property in the city, which more properly should belong to all Episcopal congregations in New York (there were several independent churches, like St. Michael's), not solely to Trinity Parish.

89. Manning to Milo Gates (priest at St. Paul's Chapel), January 9, 1909 (Trinity Parish

Archives, record group 7, subgroup 3, box 2, folder "St. John's Closing, 1909, Corr re The Rt. Rev WTM").

90. Anonymous clippings, "St. John's" (1872) and "Re-opening of St. John's Chapel" (1869) (Diocesan Archives, box 54, folder "Manhattan, St. John's Chapel, News Clippings").

91. M. Lamb 1877.

92. ASHPS 1909 (Fourteenth Annual Report), 79.

93. Archivist's notes (apparently summarizing the closed Vestry Minutes) (Trinity Parish Archives, record group 7, subgroup 3, box 2, folder "SJC Closing").

94. ASHPS 1913 (Eighteenth Annual Report).

95. Internal vestry notes, anonymous summary (Trinity Parish Archives, folder "St. John's, 1912–20, Demolition & Widening of Varick St."); "Trinity Abandons St. John's; Would Aid Preservation," *New York Herald,* June 6, 1914.

96. *Burke v. Rector* 1896–1911, 110–11.

97. The St. John's case was now being handled by the vestry's secular officers, no longer by Manning or other clergy. Once the congregation had been moved, the St. John's case was seen as a secular matter, requiring only the real estate and public relations departments. Thus, the clerk (lawyer) Jay and the comptroller (accountant) Cammann led Trinity's side, not the rector (priest) Manning. Cammann tended to see all the church's work in terms of its effect on real estate values (Hughes 1963, 62; "St. John's Chapel vs. Trinity Church," anonymous newspaper clipping [Diocesan Archives, box 54, file "Manhattan, St. John's Chapel, News Clippings"]); for more of Jay's polemics, see his May 9, 1912, letter to the Fine Arts Federation (Trinity Parish Archives, record group 7, subgroup 3, box 2, folder "St John's Chapel 1912–20"), blasting it for inaction in preserving the chapel.

98. Editorial, *New York Times,* June 2, 1914.

99. H. A. Caparn, letter to the editor, *New York Times,* May 28, 1914.

100. "Old St. John's Church Is Marked for Destruction," *New York Times Sunday Magazine,* May 25, 1913, 5.

101. Stokes to Greer, December 12, 1908 (Diocesan Archives, box 54, folder "Manhattan, St. John's Chapel, Correspondence, 1889–1909").

102. A facsimile of the petition is reprinted in Stokes [1915–28] 1972, 5: plate 79.

103. Petition from congregation to rector, December 29, 1908 (Diocesan Archives, box 54, folder "Manhattan, St. John's Chapel, Legal Documents, 1908–09").

104. Quoted in "Dr. Huntington on Saving St. John's," *New York Times,* December 19, 1908.

105. Letter to the editor, *Churchman,* January 2, 1909.

106. "Abandonment by Trinity of St. John's," undated (but probably January 2, 1909) clipping from the *Churchman* (Diocesan Archives, box 54, file "Manhattan, St. John's Chapel, Correspondence 1889–1909").

107. Low to Silas McBee, January 2, 1909 (William Thomas Manning Papers, box 3, folder 5).

108. Cutting was a wealthy investor (his grandfather was Robert Fulton's partner in the steamboat and grew the fortune in railroads, among other businesses) and also treasurer of the Bureau of Municipal Research, and first president of the Citizens Union, a political party and organization of leading civic reformers that forwarded Seth Low for the mayor's office. Pine was a prominent lawyer and lay member of the Art Commission.

109. Petition, December 26, 1908, and January 7, 1909 (Trinity Parish Archives, record group 7, subgroup 3, box 2, folder "St. John's, Corr Re H. H. Cammann, Controller").

110. The assessed valuation of the property in 1908 was $333,000 (*Burke v. Rector* 1896–1911, unpaginated).

111. Manning, Jay, and Cammann to Cutting, January 12, 1909 (Trinity Parish Archives, record group 7, subgroup 3, box 2, folder "SJC, Corr Re H. H. Cammann, Controller").

112. De Forest to Manning, December 9, 1908 (William Thomas Manning Papers, box 3, folder 3).

113. Greer to Manning, January 18, 1909 (Diocesan Archives, box 54, folder "Manhattan, St. John's Chapel, Correspondence, 1889–1909").

114. "St. John's Not Historic," *New York Times,* December 24, 1908.

115. "The Policy of Trinity Parish," 4 (Trinity Parish Archives, record group 7, subgroup 3, box 2).

116. "The Policy of Trinity Parish" was his formal statement on the matter. The other mandates he pursued as rector and later bishop included implementing a more conservative social agenda and building a cathedral—St. John the Divine.

117. Manning's papers contained a June 29, 1908, letter from Henry C. Swords, a vestryman and president of the Fulton Trust Company of New York, suggesting that Trinity look into the public relations strategy lately employed by Standard Oil for taking the public "into their confidence": "Their methods are well worth studying" (William Thomas Manning Papers, box 3, folder 2).

118. Bridgeman 1962, 91.

119. "The Passing of St. John's," *New York Times,* January 29, 1909.

120. The answer to these questions is speculative. A more conclusive answer, if it exists at all in the historical record, is locked in the Trinity Parish Archives.

121. Hunt 1912; "Old St. John's Church Is Marked for Destruction," *New York Times,* May 25, 1913; "Landmarks Doomed for New Avenue," *New York Times,* October 5, 1913.

122. "Landmarks Doomed for New Avenue," *New York Times,* October 5, 1913; New York City Improvement Commission 1907. While the vestry would surely have known about the Improvement Commission plans, it was far less likely that such grand visions, produced by appointed officials to guide government decisions, would be public knowledge. The plans were not widely disseminated. It should be noted that the commission amounted to nothing, but several of the ideas represented in its vague plans were later realized. See Kantor 1973; Marcuse 1987.

123. ASHPS 1912 (Seventeenth Annual Report).

124. Frank Marshall White, in *Evening Post Saturday Magazine,* July 26, 1913.

125. Jay to Cammann, June 14, 1912 (Trinity Parish Archives, record group 7, subgroup 3, box 2, folder "St. John's, 1912–20, Demolition and Widening of Varick St.").

126. Editorial, *New York Times,* July 30, 1953.

127. McAneny 1949, 19.

128. Robert Moses also got his start at the Municipal Research Bureau (Caro 1974).

129. Edward Bassett actually credited McAneny with making the idea a reality: "I want to say—as I have said many times before—that zoning was in my opinion initiated by you. I was simply the pusher" (Bassett to McAneny, January 11, 1943 [George McAneny Papers, box 50]).

130. McAneny 1949, 67.

131. Speech to the Fine Arts Federation, 1914 (George McAneny Papers, box 1).

132. The Regional Plan Association, still thriving today, was originally funded by the Sage philanthropy, which had also paid for City Hall's restoration (see chapter 3); McAneny's connection with Robert De Forest enabled both these efforts.

133. George McAneny Papers, box 2; generally, see McAneny's oral history (McAneny 1949) and "Plaque Honors George McAneny," *New York Times,* May 17, 1956.

134. Haddon wrote articles on historical architecture for *Architectural Record* and other journals, including the White Pine Series. Later, he was director of the Mattatuck Museum in Waterbury, Connecticut. Among his mostly straightforward articles, his study of vernacular architecture in Greenwich Village and the Lower West Side stands out (Haddon 1914b).

135. ASHPS Board Minutes, May 27, 1912 (ASHPS Manuscript Papers, box 1).

136. Jos. Howland Hunt (secretary of Fine Arts Federation) to McAneny, December 2, 1914 (George McAneny Papers, box 54).

137. Louis Schliep, letter to the editor, *New York Times,* March 26, 1914.

138. Hunt 1912.

139. Ibid., 412.

140. Not all architects acted together, or even through the organizations I note below. Architects played active roles in ASHPS and other reform efforts. But the positions of the Architectural League of New York and the Fine Arts Federation speak to a uniquely architectural way of constructing the St. John's debate that was different from ASHPS's focus on association and the specificity of place.

141. Embury 1914, 166–67.

142. *New York Times,* May 7, 1913.

143. Alexander Trowbridge to WTM, April 12, 1917 (Trinity Parish Archives, record group 7, subgroup 3, box 2, folder "SJC, 1912–20, Demolition & Widening of Varick St").

144. Atterbury to Trinity Corporation, April 9, 1917 (Trinity Parish Archives, record group 7, subgroup 3, box 2, folder "SJC, 1912–20, Demolition & Widening of Varick St.").

145. Later, Haddon served for forty-five years as director of the Mattatuck Historical Society, a museum in Waterbury, Connecticut.

146. Jay to the Fine Arts Federation, May 9, 1912 (Trinity Parish Archives, record group 7, subgroup 3, box 2, folder "SJC, 1912–20, Demolition & Widening of Varick St.").

147. The ascendance of professional architects in the preservation field was a strong influence on this narrowing view of buildings' values; see Murphy 1992, and the other literature on professionalization such as Gutman 1988 and Larson 1979. Regarding the use of the past, see Lowenthal 1985; also see M. Boyer 1994, Nora 1996–98, and Terdiman 1993.

148. The city had condemned the piece of land needed for street widening.

149. Holleran 1998, 109.

150. Edward Hagaman Hall, "A Plea for Old St. John's," letter to the editor, *New York Times,* April 6, 1917.

151. "St. John's Chapel Razed," *New York Times,* October 6, 1918; ASHPS Board Minutes, March 22, 1915 (ASHPS Manuscript Papers, box 1).

152. Atterbury to Trinity Corporation, April 9, 1917 (Trinity Parish Archives, record group 7, subgroup 3, box 2, folder "SJC, 1912–20, Demolition & Widening of Varick St."); but there was no mention of a park plan in ASHPS or Parks Department records.

153. ASHPS Board Minutes, April 30, 1917 (ASHPS Manuscript Papers, box 1).

154. The walls were not solid—interior and exterior walls enclosed a rubble-filled cavity— so reconstruction on another site would have been prohibitively expensive and technically difficult (McAneny 1949).

155. Gilmartin 1995.

156. "St. John's Chapel Razed," *New York Times,* October 6, 1918.

157. Morris Lamont to Trinity Vestry, February 17, 1919 (Trinity Parish Archives, record

group 7, subgroup 3, box 2, folder "St. John's, 1912–20, Demolition & Widening of Varick St."); Donald Gerardi and Chris Jenks, personal communication, July 1996.

158. ASHPS 1919 (Twenty-fourth Annual Report).

159. *Trinity Parish Record,* November 1918 (Trinity Parish Archives, record group 7, subgroup 3, box 1, folder "St. John's, Articles"); "Historical Notes, 1820–1935, St. Luke's Chapel, Trinity Parish, at Hudson and Grove Streets, NY, NY, and a Guide Book for Its Interior, by a Curate" (George McAneny Papers, box 127); Chris Jenks, personal communication, July 1996; Donald Gerardi, personal communication, July 1996.

160. The price was $200,000 (Conveyance Liber 3157, 148, New York County, City Register Office, Department of Finance).

161. "Sell St. John's Site," *New York Times,* November 24, 1918, real estate section. The asking price for the property was reported to be more than $200,000.

3. CITY HALL PARK

1. Neville 1994.

2. Green 1894, 6.

3. An example of a place-specific narrative is that of the newly erected liberty pole, which would have been far less meaningful if it had not been erected on the same ground as the originals were in the 1770s; likewise, if City Hall were to have been moved to Union Square or Forty-second Street, as was suggested, it would have lost its meaning and its perceived power to shape public behavior through its historical associations (Green 1894).

4. Hall 1910, 385.

5. ASHPS 1910 (Fifteenth Annual Report), 385–424.

6. M. Schuyler 1908.

7. The park was also the place where celebrations and protests were most often staged— from riots to the mourning of Lincoln's death, from Lafayette's parade to ticker tape parades.

8. ASHPS 1910 (Fifteenth Annual Report), 385.

9. Kaufman 1998, 61.

10. Bogart 1999, 299. Bogart also argues that this divide had a racial dimension, as well, distinguishing the black, socially marginal landscape of the northern area around the Collect from the southern areas claimed as "civic" ground by the dominant white culture.

11. Kaufman 1998; Stokes [1915–28] 1972, 6:518; ASHPS 1910 (Fifteenth Annual Report), 385–424; Neville 1994.

12. ASHPS 1910 (Fifteenth Annual report), 411.

13. The Americans were crowded, starved, and tortured. "The memory of the sufferings which the Continental soldiers endured, adds still further to the sacred character of this historic place. . . . [These sacrifices] make the site of the building one ever to be held in remembrance" (ASHPS 1910 [Fifteenth Annual Report], 419).

14. "City Hall Park was the birthplace of Hamilton's public career" (ibid., 415).

15. Bluestone 1987.

16. ASHPS 1910 (Fifteenth Annual Report), 405.

17. Stokes [1915–28] 1972, 6:518.

18. There was some controversy over who actually designed City Hall. According to leading critic Montgomery Schuyler, it was Mangin alone. Grosvenor Atterbury interpreted it as McComb's work alone, a narrative more in keeping with the civic patriotism that inspired his restoration project (M. Schuyler 1908; Stillman 1964).

19. M. Schuyler 1908.

20. Blackmar 1989; Rosenzweig and Blackmar 1992; Spann 1988; Bluestone 1987.

21. Cardia 1987.

22. Quoted in Still 1956, 70.

23. Stokes [1915–28] 1972, 6:518.

24. Kestenbaum 1984.

25. ASHPS 1910 (Fifteenth Annual Report), 423.

26. Stokes [1915–28] 1972.

27. Spann 1988; P. Boyer 1979.

28. Willensky and White 1988, 62.

29. The second almshouse was built in 1797 as a replacement for the first. The poor were housed at Bellevue Hospital after 1812 and the almshouse was occupied by various private but public-serving institutions, such as the New-York Historical Society, the Academy of Arts, the Academy of Painting, the city library, the Lyceum of Natural History ("In 1824 the first Egyptian mummy ever brought to this country was exhibited here"), and the Deaf and Dumb Institute. Federal courts and a private bank also occupied rooms there for a time (ASHPS 1910 [Fifteenth Annual Report], 395). In 1870 the Rotunda was also taken down, clearing a bit of the crowded northern end of the park—a job that was finished by subway and transit construction demolishing the firehouse and the Martyrs' Prison in the 1900s.

30. ASHPS 1910 (Fifteenth Annual Report), 399.

31. Editorial, New York Times, July 5, 1911.

32. "Concerning That Monument," New York Times, May 11, 1871.

33. It is a fine building, though few dared praise it until the 1960s, when the courthouse was designated a city landmark by virtue of its architectural qualities and historical associations. Today, fully restored, it is the headquarters of the city's Education Department.

34. ASHPS 1910 (Fifteenth Annual Report), 387.

35. Art Commission of the City of New York 1984.

36. The demolition did not happen until a Robert Moses–led renovation of the park was initiated in the mid-1930s, even though the federal government had opened a new central post office in 1913 across from the new Penn Station and the federal government's deed stipulated that the land would revert to municipal ownership if the building ceased to be used as a post office.

37. "Is City Hall Park Ever to Be Freed of the Encumbrance of the Old Post Office?" editorial, New York Times, March 31, 1927.

38. In offering this interpretation, I am conscious of adding something distinct to the existing chronicles, descriptions, and interpretations of civic center controversies (Bogart 1999; Gilmartin 1995; Page 1999; Stern et al. 1983). Bogart's article comes closest to the conclusions I draw—that concerns about memory played a very important role in shaping City Hall Park (Bogart 1999, 227).

39. Green 1894, 6–7.

40. John D. Crimmins, "The Sentimental Side of City Hall Park," New York Times Sunday Magazine, March 27, 1910, 10.

41. George Frederick Kunz, "New York 100 Years Ago, When City Hall Was Built," New York Times Sunday Magazine, July 9, 1911, 11.

42. Other, more temporary structures were not mapped. See Stokes [1915–28] 1972.

43. ASHPS 1910 (Fifteenth Annual Report).

44. Cerillo 1973; Hammack 1987.

45. Croly 1903, 199.

46. The metanarrative of nineteenth-century human geography of the industrial city is the growing segregation and specialization of social space, sorted by use, function, class, and ethnicity. The classic example of this process, at a general level, is the changing nature of "the street" in the course of the nineteenth century, from a complex social space hosting many different kinds of activities to a space increasingly devoted to movement and transport, to the exclusion of other uses. See Bluestone 1991, introduction; M. Boyer 1985; Cardia 1987.

47. Bogart 1999.

48. It has to be noted, without going into detail, that the institutions of local and state government were numerous, frequently shifted, and were in great competition during this time. There has always been an adversarial relationship between the state government and the city government over how much and which powers the former cedes to the latter. And this was expressed through (and complicated by) a proliferation of governmental and quasi–governmental agencies for carrying out specific functions—such as constructing transit systems, governing the police, or managing historic sites and nature reserves. See Hammack 1987; Revell 2003.

49. Bogart 1999, 240.

50. See, for example, the ASHPS points of agreement on overall comprehensive planning goals and New York City Improvement Commission plan statements about the diverse elements of comprehensive "improvement" (ASHPS 1907 [Twelfth Annual Report], passim; ASHPS 1915 [Twentieth Annual Report], 165; New York City Improvement Commission 1907).

51. Warner 1902; Croly 1903.

52. Warner 1902, 2.

53. See Bluestone 1988, 1991; W. Wilson 1980, 1994.

54. Among other sources, see the exhibit catalog from the Art Commission's collection of European urban design photographs (Bershad 1986); on the roots of the City Beautiful movement in the village-improvement movement, see Peterson 1976; W. Wilson 1980.

55. This idea was voiced explicitly by Andrew Green (1894). See also Bluestone 1991.

56. "Plan City Buildings at Cost of $50,000,000," *New York Times,* July 2, 1903.

57. Domosh 1996; Willis 1995; Holdsworth and Fenske 1992.

58. The idea of the civic center as a horizontal landscape balancing the commercial skyscrapers is from Bluestone 1988, 1991; on the design competition for the Municipal Building, which yielded a number of "civic skyscrapers," see Stern et al. 1983.

59. Bluestone 1988, 1991.

60. Robinson 1903, 96.

61. Gilmartin 1995, 74–75; City Club, the People's Institute, and the Fine Arts Federation of New York [1910].

62. From the 1870s onward, corporations and entrepreneurs raced to build ever taller and more massive office buildings in downtown Manhattan. Though tall buildings sprouted all over downtown, many of the earliest (for example, the Tribune Building) flanked City Hall Park. In the first decade of the 1900s, City Hall Park was again placed at the center of the race as the Woolworth Building rose to be the tallest building in the world (from its opening in 1913 until 1930) (Domosh 1996; K. Jackson 1995; Willis 1995).

63. "Many Protests Entered. O. B. Potter and A. H. Green Value City Hall Park," *New York Times,* September 19, 1889.

64. Demands for open space were addressed by enormous park-building projects, such as

those creating Central and Riverside parks, by efforts to set aside park space ahead of residential space in the Bronx (see chapter 4), and by the Small Parks Act of 1887.

65. Edward Hagaman Hall, in ASHPS 1910 (Fifteenth Annual Report), 52.

66. Green 1894.

67. Stokes [1915–28] 1972, 6:518.

68. Bogart 1999.

69. "The Aldermen in Session: A Protest against Tearing Down the Hall of Records," *New York Times,* June 22, 1881. Sauer's protest was also informed by his belief that the bridge would benefit only Brooklyn, not New York (Manhattan) — all the more reason not to forfeit valuable and dear park land.

70. "The Bridge Crush," *New York Times,* February 25, 1905. A headhouse is a structure at the "head" (front) of a bridge, market, or the like.

71. "Record Bridge Jam in Evening Rush," *New York Times,* April 25, 1907.

72. Regarding Central Park, see Rosenzweig and Blackmar 1992 and ASHPS 1895–1925 (Annual Reports).

73. Details of the myriad laws proposed and passed to control the courthouse project can be found in "A Municipal Opportunity," *Harper's Weekly,* March 3, 1894, 198; ASHPS 1910 (Fifteenth Annual Report); and ASHPS 1912 (Seventeenth Annual Report), 103–12.

74. "Our Municipal Buildings," *New York Times,* July 11, 1889.

75. Green 1894.

76. "Court Site Decision Held Up by Gaynor," *New York Times,* March 19, 1910.

77. Edward Hagaman Hall, in ASHPS 1910 (Fifteenth Annual Report), 52–53.

78. For instance, a New York American Institute of Architects resolution against building in the park was reported in the *New York Times,* highlighting the architectural arguments in favor of preserving the park and redeveloping the surrounding buildings as a proper civic center. The *Times* included a plan and rendering of the institute's specific vision ("Architects Propose a Court House Site," *New York Times,* March 18, 1910).

79. ASHPS 1910 (Fifteenth Annual Report), 385–424.

80. Editorial, *New York Times,* April 15, 1910.

81. For a sampling of editorials, see City Club et al. [1910], 10–13; other newspaper coverage is collected in scrapbooks in the Art Commission of New York Archives.

82. "City Hall Park's Defenders Aroused," *New York Times,* June 17, 1911; Wood 2007.

83. "Lawyers Condemn Court House Site," *New York Times,* March 17, 1910.

84. "To Restore City Hall Park," *New York Times,* March 28, 1910.

85. Editorial, *New York Times,* April 15, 1910.

86. John Winfield Scott, "Urges Voters to Petition for Defeat of Stilwell Courthouse Bill," *New York Times,* June 22, 1911.

87. "Many Sites Urged for Court House," *New York Times,* March 29, 1910.

88. "Civic Bodies Try to Save City Hall," *New York Times,* May 6, 1911.

89. "Preserve City Hall Park," *New York Times,* March 20, 1910.

90. Quoted in "The Court House Site," *New York Times,* March 26, 1910.

91. "The Old Tweed Question Again," *New York Times,* July 5, 1911.

92. "City Hall Park Scheme," *New York Times,* July 6, 1911.

93. "Court House Sites to Be Shown Public," *New York Times,* September 26, 1911.

94. "Civic Center Plan May Be Restored," *New York Times,* May 6, 1912.

95. ASHPS 1912 (Seventeenth Annual Report), 103–12.

96. "Societies to Resist City Hall Park Grab," *New York Times,* May 7, 1911.

97. C. May 1916, 535.

98. M. Boyer 1985; Cardia 1987.

99. "Board of Councilmen. Pawnbrokers to Be Checked—Protest against the Removal of City Hall . . . ," *New York Times,* April 3, 1860.

100. Green 1894, 7.

101. This was a standard preservationist strategy in New York and elsewhere. Its apotheosis is Williamsburg, Virginia, where the better part of the town was cleared away to make way for selective restorations.

102. Green 1894, 8.

103. Manhattan Borough President 1912, 49.

104. Atterbury is an interesting and important figure in American architectural history, best known for his work creating innovative housing developments—Forest Hills Gardens in Queens is the most famous—often employing the experimental use of precast-concrete-panel construction and other innovations. Like many of the leading architects practicing in New York at this time and participating in the emergent preservation field, Atterbury had been educated at both Columbia's architectural school (under the tutelage of A. D. F. Hamlin, among others) and the École des Beaux-Arts. He also had worked in the office of McKim, Mead, and White and built houses for a number of wealthy, influential New Yorkers.

105. Art Commission of the City of New York 1984, 6–7.

106. C. May 1916, 317.

107. Various anonymous pamphlets in Art Commission of New York Archives; C. May 1916.

108. C. May 1916, 480.

109. Art Commission of the City of New York 1909, 13.

110. C. May 1916, 474.

111. Holleran 1998; Lindgren 1993, 1995; Hosmer 1965.

112. "Societies to Resist City Hall Park Grab," *New York Times,* May 7, 1911.

113. Warner 1902, 480–81.

114. Ibid.

115. Hall 1910.

116. An organization called the National Historical Museum used part of the old Hall of Records to display "historical relics" for a time.

117. Hall 1910; "The Old Hall of Records Again," *New York Times,* October 5, 1902.

118. Hall 1910, 9, 13–14.

119. Editorial, *New York Times,* October 5, 1902. It should be noted that the Daughters of the American Resolution and the ASHPS jointly placed a tablet (which remains today) commemorating the site and the martyrs who died there, thus preserving some of the memorial value of the site.

120. Editorial, *New York Times,* February 1, 1903.

121. Ironically—but predictably—the values ascribed to the Tweed Courthouse changed over the years, and preservationists successfully listed it as a city landmark in 1984; in the late 1990s, the city undertook a full restoration, and Tweed now serves as the gleaming headquarters of the city's Education Department.

122. Editorial, *New York Times,* April 28, 1912.

123. Stokes [1915–28] 1972.

124. "City Hall Park May Be Restored," *New York Times,* January 27, 1924. The federal government could not be budged until the late 1930s, when, after the new Main Post Office opposite Penn Station had been opened, Robert Moses managed to reclaim that end of City

Hall Park as open space. The Gilmore Clarke and Michael Rapuano plan from 1935 remains basically intact today.

125. Bogart 1999, 227–29.

126. Berman 1988; Bogart 1999, regarding the racialization of memory and City Hall Park.

127. Gilmartin 1995, 68.

128. ASHPS 1910 (Fifteenth Annual Report), 53.

129. K. Jackson 1995, 344, based on Iver Bernstein.

4. BRONX RIVER PARKWAY

1. The definition of "parkway" changed and developed between the 1850s and the 1930s: First it was a path through a park (Central Park) or an extension of a park or planted boulevard (Eastern Parkway); later it was a hybrid of park and roadway (the Bronx River Parkway was the tipping point); by the 1930s it had become a landscaped road (as used by Robert Moses). See Carr 1987; Davis 2007; Orlin 1992; Zapatka 1995.

2. See, for example, McShane 1994; Giedion 1974; Grava 1981; the exception is Davis 2007.

3. Giedion 1974; Zapatka 1995.

4. This is the main argument in D. Schuyler 1986, though his work primarily concerns the development of park landscapes in the middle of the nineteenth century.

5. "Improvement" also situates the Bronx River Parkway in the landscape-reform tradition of Humphry Repton and his successors, as well as in the tradition of Georges-Eugène Haussmann and, essentially, all of modern urbanism.

6. Consider the example of the Brooklyn Bridge, which, perhaps more than any other American engineering work, has warranted equal consideration of its cultural meaning and its technical achievement. See McCullough 1983; Trachtenberg 1965.

7. The enormous archive created by the Bronx Parkway Commission is held at the Westchester County Archives in Elmsford, New York. Eight public reports were published between 1906 and 1925, and commission staff published numerous articles in professional journals.

8. The official history of the Bronx River Parkway project is detailed in the final report of the Bronx Parkway Commission, published in 1925, and in the seven commission reports that preceded it, first published in 1907 (Bronx Parkway Commission 1907, 1909, 1912, 1914, 1915, 1916–18, 1922, 1925). This was recapitulated by Weigold (1980) as a prelude to a history of the Westchester County parkway system, for which the Bronx River Parkway was the model. A more extensive project of historical and graphic documentation of the parkway was recently completed by the Historic American Engineering Record of the National Park Service (published in Davis, Croteau, and Marston 2004 and at http://hdl.loc.gov/loc.pnp/hhh.ny2000). The "chronicle" contained in this section is not exhaustive, conveying only enough factual evidence to support the chapter's larger arguments.

9. Bronx Parkway Commission 1925; Carr 1987; Giedion 1974; Orlin 1992; Zapatka 1995.

10. Quotations from Clarke 1959; Wm. Niles to Jay Downer, March 6, 1929 (Madison Grant Correspondence, box 5, folder 1).

11. The parkway's builders thus followed the principle of building parks on land that was otherwise undevelopable for economic uses; compare Olmsted and Vaux's Morningside Park.

12. Such plans for the Bronx, drawn up by Olmsted and Croes in 1876–78 (Fein 1967), were ignored, and the arrival of mass transit in the 1880s and '90s filled in an expanded grid.

13. These four thousand acres also included Van Cortlandt and Pelham Bay parks. Generally, on Bronx development, see Fein 1967; Gonzalez 1993; Mullaly 1887.

14. Bronx Sewer Commission 1896, 4.

15. For overviews of the geological and ecological history of the Bronx River valley, see Frankel 1978; Loeb 1989.

16. Plans for Kensico Dam and Reservoir, part of the New York water system, were announced in 1902. By 1909, most of the properties had been sold or condemned, and their buildings razed by fire (including the village of Kensico). "Some sold out immediately, others held out to the bitter end through legal procedures and were almost forcibly ejected. . . . The majority simply followed the course of least resistance, awaited the decision of the commissioners, accepted their award and moved away." In 1916, the dam was complete and the area, including the small farm community, was flooded. "Thus Kensico village became a necessary casualty to the growing needs of New York City and southern Westchester" (Scarsdale Historical Society 1983, 25).

17. Scharf [1886] 1992, 802. He went on: "Historic associations, blended with natural beauties, tempt one who has known the territory all his life, in giving a description of its present appearance, to combine with it a short gossipy account of its present as well as former owners."

18. McShane 1994.

19. Chapter 594 of the Laws of 1907 (Bronx Parkway Commission 1907; Downer and Owen 1925). This was later amended in 1913, 1916, 1922, and 1925 (Bronx Parkway Commission 1925).

20. See, for instance, the letter from Grant to M. Jessup, Rapid Transit Commission, July 24, 1906 (Madison Grant Correspondence, box 5, folder 2).

21. Details regarding the design and construction of the parkway are contained in the Bronx Parkway Commission reports (Bronx Parkway Commission 1907, 1909, 1912, 1914, 1915, 1916–18, 1922, 1925); Nolen and Hubbard 1937; and the numerous articles written by Gilmore Clarke for professional design journals.

22. Giedion 1974, 832.

23. Fein 1967; D. Schuyler 1986.

24. Because automobile usage and speeds increased dramatically over the period when the roadway was designed and built, there were ongoing debates among the commissioners and engineers on how wide to make the paved surface. Making it too big would spoil the aesthetic effect of the parkway, while making it too small would hinder traffic. The width was initially planned as twenty-four feet, and the built road was forty feet wide, with room for expansion to fifty.

25. The bridges were a great source of pride and praise for the commission. Designers included prominent New York architects Delano and Aldrich, Thomas Hastings, Charles Stoughton (also a designer of the Soldiers' and Sailors' Memorial in Riverside Park), and Bronx Parkway Commission construction supervisor Gilmore Clarke (who designed several bridges in his spare time). The innovative engineering designs, often praised by critics and historians, were the brainchild of commission staffer Arthur Hayden.

26. "Taxpayers Win Fight to Keep Open Certain Streets in Williamsbridge," *Bronx Home News*, November 21, 1918; see also "Hylan Again Denounces Parkway Commission," *Bronx Home News*, November 24, 1918.

27. "Much of the present Bronx River Flora was planted during the construction of the BRP" (Frankel 1978, 19); the commission's final report (of 1925) states that 30,000 trees and

140,000 shrubs were planted and that an additional 68,000 trees were trimmed and treated (Bronx Parkway Commission 1925, 50).

28. All statistics and facts in Bronx Parkway Commission 1925; see Bronx Parkway Commission property-acquisition files for many examples (Bronx Parkway Commission Collection, series 109).

29. Bronx Parkway Commission 1925, 102.

30. See correspondence among commissioners organizing the lobbying effort (Madison Grant Correspondence, box 5, folders 1–5). This behind-the-scenes political maneuvering and lobbying included episodes such as Madison Grant's having American Museum of Natural History director Henry Osborn write to New York City mayor George McClellan for his crucial (financial) support for the Bronx Parkway Commission; if necessary, Osborn was to offer McClellan's brother-in-law a seat on the museum board! (Grant to Osborn, February 10, 1908 [Madison Grant Correspondence, folder 6]).

31. Bronx Sewer Commission 1896, 40–41.

32. Bronx Sewer Commission 1896.

33. Marilyn Weigold suggests that the 1896 report recommended sewer, roadway, and park but that "political consensus" only existed for the sewer, and even for that the financing could not be agreed upon (Weigold 1980, 3); Bronx River Road, which ran along the course of the river for several miles north of Bronx Park, was constructed as a local street on top of the sewer.

34. Niles to Jay Downer, Westchester County Park Commission, March 6, 1929 (copy) (Madison Grant Correspondence, box 5, folder 1). This story, one of the most wonderful tales associated with the parkway, is related in several places—anywhere, in fact, that anyone associated with the Bronx Parkway Commission gave any history of the project (see Downer 1917; Bronx Parkway Commission 1907, 1909, 1912, 1914, 1915, 1916–18, 1922, 1925). In fact, however, the idea for an environmental-restoration and roadway project along the Bronx River had been around since at least 1895 (Bronx Sewer Commission 1896). Pugsley Medal citation, 2006.

35. The "gospel" phrase is from Hays 1959.

36. Historians differ on whom to credit with the idea for the parkway. In Niles's account, it was his idea, and the official commission reports support this. Jonathan Spiro (2000) gives credit to Grant.

37. See Bronx Parkway Commission Minutes, Bronx Parkway Commission Collection, series 118; Clarke 1959; Bronx Parkway Commission 1925.

38. Niles was also, reportedly, friends with Samuel Tilden, and thus may well have been acquainted with Andrew Haswell Green (Scharf [1886] 1992, 804).

39. Mullaly 1887.

40. Bronx Parkway Commission Minutes, Bronx Parkway Commission Collection, 1921, series 118, 34. Scarsdale Estates was incorporated by Cannon in 1898. Lynne Ames, "The View from Hartsdale; Rolling Back 100 Years to Golf Club's Beginnings," *New York Times,* June 7, 1988.

41. Quoted in "James G. Cannon, Banker, Dies at 58," *New York Times,* July 6, 1916.

42. Hansen 1954, 142, 146–47, 221–22, 288–92.

43. Many of Grant's letters and papers were destroyed by his family after his death in 1937. The only comprehensive biographical treatment of Grant is Jonathan Spiro's doctoral dissertation (Spiro 2000). On Grant's influence on American society, see Higham 1955, 155–56, 265–72.

44. Grant 1916, 1933; one of his essays, "Failures of the Melting Pot," appeared in the *New York Times,* November 12, 1922.

45. New York Zoological Society 1916: Grant was first vice president, secretary, and chair of the Executive Committee; Osborn was president.

46. The connections remain mostly circumstantial, however, owing to the dearth of primary sources that could provide more direct evidence (Pierpont 2004; Spiro 2000).

47. Grant 1916, ix.

48. Spiro 2000, 16; Hofstadter 1955.

49. Grant even published a book about it—*The Founders of the Republic on Immigration, Naturalization and Aliens* (Grant and Davison 1928)—selectively quoting from the writings of the founding fathers to support anti-immigration policies.

50. Grant's interest in the roadway aspect of the parkway may also have been piqued by his apparent interest in automobile touring and fast driving. He "was a pompous fellow to those who didn't know him, and I can't say that I ever knew him very well." Clarke relayed a story of Grant's cruising along the under-construction parkway in his open Cadillac (with some young ladies) and showing off by demanding that Clarke explain the grading work he was doing (Clarke 1959, ch. 2). See Bronx Parkway Commission Minutes, Bronx Parkway Commission Collection, 1920, series 118, index number 80, for mention of Grant's auto tours of work in progress.

51. Grant was an advocate of preserving the American wilderness, and through the Bronx Zoo and other organizations he worked to preserve the American bison, the caribou, and California redwoods. He saw the American wilderness clearly as one part of the pure heritage that needed to be bolstered in the face of the racial "mixing" of American society.

52. On his desire to rid the city of nonwhite groups, see, for instance, Grant to Prescott Hall, March 3, 1913 (Immigration Restriction League [hereafter IRL] Records, series I); Grant 1916.

53. Grant to Elihu Root, May 10, 1912 (IRL Records, series I).

54. Grant to Prescott Hall, November 15, 1920 (IRL Records, series I).

55. Grant 1916, ix.

56. Spiro 2000.

57. Grant and Davison 1928, vii.

58. Haraway 1995, 338–40.

59. Merkel was the designer of the parkway and generated the layouts and planting plans. Previously he had been the construction and operations chief for the Bronx Zoo, through which he learned landscape design (Clarke 1959). He later consulted on Central Park (Rosenzweig and Blackmar 1992).

Clarke's biography is fascinating: He was construction superintendent and an occasional bridge designer for the parkway, though he is often credited, mistakenly, for the landscape design. From his Bronx Parkway Commission experience, Clarke went on to an illustrious career. He was hired as chief planner and landscape designer of the famed Westchester County parkway system and then was Robert Moses's landscape architect of choice, designing dozens of important public projects all over New York and the country (including parks, parkways, world's fairs, and corporate headquarters). Later, Clarke was a member of the national Fine Arts Commission and dean at Cornell University. See Clarke 1959; Campanella 1991.

60. Bronx Parkway Commission 1925.

61. Bronx Parkway Commission Minutes, Bronx Parkway Commission Collection, 1911–13, series 118, 282.

62. Clarke 1959, ch. 2.

63. Clarke 1959. It is interesting to note that in the next iteration of the modern parkway idea, the Westchester County parkways, the social-reform function was far less prominent—that parkway system was more strictly an attempt to improve mobility and facilitate suburban development—and the professional designers and engineers took the front seat.

64. Cannon to Grant, September 18, 1906 (Madison Grant Correspondence, box 5, folder 2); on Muddy River Improvement, see Howett 1998 and Zaitzevsky 1982; regarding Wissahickon Creek, see Fairmount Park Commission 1996.

65. Letter from MAS to Bd. of Estimate and Apportionment, April 12, 1910 (Bronx Parkway Commission Minutes, Bronx Parkway Commission Collection, 1909–June 1911, series 118); Bronx Parkway Commission Minutes, Bronx Parkway Commission Collection, 1917–18, series 118, passim.

66. Giedion 1974, 826.

67. Giedion seized on the parkway as the perfect expression of modern zeitgeist because parkways' land-hugging design and segregation as a space of pure movement enabled the driver to achieve the perfect "freedom" that comes with mobility (Giedion 1974, 83).

68. The only other reinterpretive work on the parkway, to my knowledge, is Tim Davis's (2007) essay on the commission's use of photography.

69. Clarke 1959; Bronx Parkway Commission 1925. By the 1940s, the parkway was obsolete by then-modern highway standards, and Robert Moses embarked on a major rebuilding (Historic American Engineering Record, "Bronx River Parkway Reservation. HAER No. NY-327." http://www.westchesterarchives.com/BRPR/Report_fr.html [2001]).

70. Radde 1996.

71. Bronx Parkway Commission Minutes, Bronx Parkway Commission Collection, 1915, series 118, index number 198, passim. See Gonzalez 1993 on the pressing need for park space in the Bronx. With regard to swimming in the river, the commission cautioned, however: "Care must be exercised to avoid swallowing the river water which is not sufficiently pure to be taken into the mouth" (Bronx Parkway Commission Minutes, Bronx Parkway Commission Collection, 1917, series 118, 199).

72. Bronx Parkway Commission Minutes, Bronx Parkway Commission Collection, 1917, series 118, 67.

73. For the river-as-machine metaphor, see White 1996.

74. The details of these connections between property value increases and parkway construction were later the subject of John Nolen and Henry Hubbard's study of parkways (Nolen and Hubbard 1937).

75. K. Jackson 1985.

76. Bronx Parkway Commission 1925, 13; note the precedents for narratives of natural reclamation as parables of social history—for instance, Thomas Cole's paintings and essays (Novak 1980; D. Schuyler 1995). Given Grant's desires for racial purity, the commission's phrasing seems to suggest that the "natural condition of purity" had social as well as environmental facets.

77. Diana Rice, "A Magical Parkway Leads Out of City," *New York Times Sunday Magazine*, August 16, 1925; "New Parkway Nearly Done," *New York Times*, March 7, 1920; "Bronx River Has an Interesting History," *Bronx Home News*, September 5, 1918; Wintjen 1933, 38.

78. Frankel 1978.

79. Bronx Parkway Commission 1925, 51–52.

80. Downer and Owen 1925, 976. This passage is a paraphrase of Edward Hagaman Hall's writing on the coincidence of scenic and historic places. See Hall 1912, 13–24.

81. This ties back to the other case studies and more obvious ways of collective remembering through form: historic preservation, public art, City Beautiful urban design, and civic architecture.

82. *Report to the New York Legislature* . . . 1884, 95–97.

83. Grant to Higgins, May 11, 1906 (Madison Grant Correspondence, box 5, folder 2). The ASHPS in fact supported the parkway commission's efforts; see Edward Hagaman Hall to Grant, January 15, 1907, and Grant to Hall, January 16, 1907 (Madison Grant Correspondence, box 5, folder 3, "BPC").

84. Bronx Parkway Commission Minutes, Bronx Parkway Commission Collection, 1922, series 118, 20, 25.

85. Ibid., 42, 117–18.

86. Bronx County Historical Society (hereafter BCHS), "Bronx River" clippings file.

87. The title of the poem is "Bronx" (see Pleadwell 1935, 224–26). Selections from the poem were used in several commission publications and journal articles. The last stanza of this poem is inscribed on a bronze plaque near the ancient hemlock stand in the Bronx Zoo (BCHS, "Bronx River" clippings file).

88. Marx 1964.

89. See Bodnar 1991; Olwig 1995; and D. Schuyler 1995. Kammen 1991 essentially ignores nature as a source of American public memory. Many of the ASHPS annual reports clearly express the intertwining of "scenic and historic" places as the raw material of American (and civic) memory.

90. Also known as the Olmstedian tradition, though this belies its many sources, contributors, and practitioners.

91. On Germany, see Koshar 1998. Research has been inconclusive regarding Jensen's nativist leanings; see Grese 1992 and personal communication, February 1999; Jensen 1990; Howett 1998.

92. Green 1895, 4.

93. ASHPS 1911 (Sixteenth Annual Report); the 1904 Annual Report included a lengthy history of the Battery; as noted in chapter 3, Hall published a detailed history of City Hall Park in the 1910 Annual Report.

94. The notion of ecological restoration as a redemptive or scientific goal is debunked in Elliott 1997.

95. For instance, the *North Side News* published an article titled "How the Bronx River Will Be Transformed into a Beautiful Parkway," May 7, 1914. Few critical pieces ever appeared; most of them were in one local paper, the *Bronx Home News*. Claiming over 100,000 circulation, the *News* was one of a series of local papers published by James O'Flaherty. The paper reported on local politics and business matters, as well as traffic accidents and local history. It criticized the commission and the whole parkway project in the years 1918–19, echoing the claims of Mayor John Hylan and other New York City politicians who complained of the rising costs of the project and argued that control of any city park should be vested with the city Parks Department (not with an independent commission seemingly working on behalf of Westchester real estate interests).

96. Progressive reformers and other experts used photography for many purposes in this period, both documentary and polemical, ranging from muckraker Jacob Riis's tenement photographs to Frederick Winslow Taylor's efficiency studies. See E. Brown 2005; Trachtenberg 1989.

97. Of the hundreds and hundreds of photographs, very few have people in them.

98. Davis 2007; Clarke 1959; Downer 1917, 1920. Davis argues that the photographs were an integral part of the Bronx Parkway Commission's process of appropriating the actual landscape. He concludes that it is important to challenge the objectivity of these photographs and other justifications and to use other sources to discern the causation behind such an ambitious, multifaceted project of "improvements."

99. Bronx Parkway Commission 1925, 11.

100. National Trust for Historic Preservation brochure, 1995, in author's collection.

101. McShane 1994. Before the parkway, the drive from Manhattan to Kensico took a whole day. The valley had long been a home to commuter communities because the first railroad, the Harlem line of the New York Central, followed the river just as the parkway later would.

102. Olmsted 1870.

103. Mullaly 1887; Gonzalez 1993; Nolen and Hubbard 1937.

104. Downer 1917.

105. Bronx Parkway Commission Minutes, Bronx Parkway Commission Collection, 1909–June 1911, series 118: Thayer conveying to Grant, November 3, 1910. Thayer was otherwise employed by Scarsdale Estates, the real estate company of Commissioner Cannon.

106. Bronx Parkway Commission Minutes, Bronx Parkway Commission Collection, 1914, series 118, 150.

107. Davis 2007, 125.

108. This estimate is based on a sample from the Bronx Parkway Commission property-acquisition records.

109. The detailed information comes from the 1910 U.S. manuscript census (Thirteenth Federal Census, 1910, microfilm in the collection of the New York Public Library). Many of the sheets for the areas cleared by the reservation were faded and unreadable in microfilm; other addresses were either incorrectly mapped or had not been visited by census-takers. The data therefore are partial. Other information on the occupation and ethnicity of residents was gleaned from Bronx Parkway Commission property-acquisition records (Bronx Parkway Commission Collection, series 109; Gonzalez 1986; and anecdotal sources such as McNamara 1989, 221).

110. The evidence for these generalizations is drawn from samples of manuscript census schedules (Thirteenth Federal Census, 1910, microfilm in the collection of the New York Public Library), from descriptions in local history sources and newspapers, and from names listed in the commission's property-acquisition files.

111. Sanborn Fire Insurance Co., 1911, Map Collection, New York Public Library; map of reservation, Bronx Parkway Commission 1912.

112. Additional information on the displaced Italian community in White Plains was provided in interviews by the author in December 1995 of Nick Bonaiuto, of Hartsdale, New York (who was born on Smith Street in 1909 and whose parents were married in Our Lady of Mt. Carmel in 1908); Sharalee Falzerano (WCAC archivist, whose grandfather Salvatore Falsorano—as his name is spelled in the records—sold his house to the commission in 1915), and Sister Marguerita Smith (archivist at St. Joseph's Seminary).

113. The detailed data that follow are found in Bronx Parkway Commission property files 25-2, 25-4, 25-6, 25-9, 25-16, 25-49, and 25-53 (Bronx Parkway Commission Collection, series 109). Each file contains appraisal reports, correspondence, internal memoranda, demolition contracts, and other records pertaining to the individual property.

114. The chapel is property file 25-5 (Bronx Parkway Commission Collection, series 109).

115. Detailed data on building acquisitions in Mount Vernon are drawn from Bronx Parkway Commission property files 7-17, 7-18, 7-28, 7-39, and 7-51 (Bronx Parkway Commission Collection, series 109).

116. December 8, 1914, internal memorandum in Bronx Parkway Commission property file (Bronx Parkway Commission Collection, series 109, file 7-28).

117. Commission property-acquisition records for the Bronx sections of the parkway were given to the city Parks Department in 1925 and were subsequently lost or destroyed.

118. Madison Grant to Prescott Hall, March 3, 1913 (IRL Records, series I).

119. Bodnar 1991.

120. Property owner Adam Danner "further complained of the manner in which he had been treated by the President and Secretary of the Commission; that they had treated him like a dog" (Bronx Parkway Commission property file 7-51, June 7, 1915, memo [Bronx Parkway Commission Collection, series 109]). "When Mr. Weinberger first called at this office he began a tirade upon the Commission and called them 'highway robbers'" (Bronx Parkway Commission property file 7-32 [Bronx Parkway Commission Collection, series 109]).

121. See also BCHS, *Bronx Home News* clippings, 1918–19.

122. Bronx Parkway Commission Minutes, Bronx Parkway Commission Collection, 1921, series 118, 120.

123. Bronx Parkway Commission Minutes, Bronx Parkway Commission Collection, 1915, series 118, 300.

124. Bronx Parkway Commission 1925.

125. Bronx Parkway Commission Minutes, Bronx Parkway Commission Collection, 1923, series 118, 135–40.

126. Bronx Parkway Commission 1925, 85.

127. De Forest to Madison Grant, November 18, 1925, Bronx Parkway Commission Minutes, Bronx Parkway Commission Collection, 1925, series 118, 77–78. Jonathan Spiro reports that De Forest and Grant were distant relatives (Spiro 2000, 639). Indeed, the commission did erect a monument to itself, a bronze plaque affixed to a boulder in Bronx Park, reading, in part, "THE RIVER CLEARED OF POLLUTION AND THE NATURAL BEAUTIES OF THE RIVER RESTORED" (photograph in Historic American Engineering Record, http://hdl.loc.gov/loc.pnp/hhh.ny2000).

128. Bronx Parkway Commission 1925, 90.

129. Ibid.

130. Regarding the notions of "distance" and "foreignness," see Lowenthal 1985; also Kern 1983; Matsuda 1996; Terdiman 1993.

131. Niles to Jay Downer, March 6, 1929 (copy) (Madison Grant Correspondence, box 5, folder 1).

132. This was Nolen and Hubbard's (1937) definition of a parkway.

133. J. Jackson 1980, 101–2.

Conclusion

1. Chase 1929, 82; 1930.

2. Joseph Webster Golinkin, "Out of This Welter and Turmoil New York of Today Fishes the Past," cartoon, *New York Times Sunday Magazine*, September 13, 1925, SM6.

3. Nora 1989, 9.

4. Lowenthal 1985; Nora 1996–98; J. Jackson 1980.

5. Gilchrist 2006. Confederate history in the South is perhaps the most pointed example of expressions of regional identity; see Horwitz 1998; Savage 1997.

6. Hamlin 1902, 68.

7. Brooks 1968.

8. ASHPS 1909 (Fourteenth Annual Report), 78.

9. Green 1894, 6.

10. Wallace 1996, 178.

11. Consider the pro-development core of the Bronx River Parkway; or George McAneny's expansion of the subways, regional planning exercise, or commercial boosterism through the World's Fair; or Andrew Haswell Green's legal work on behalf of railroad companies or in developing Riverside Drive or the southern wards of the Bronx.

12. Wallace 1996, 179.

13. Editorial, *New York Evening Post,* August 24, 1915.

14. Green, in ASHPS 1901 (Sixth Annual Report), 57.

15. Quoted in "Father Knickerbocker Celebrates Birthday," *New York Times,* May 27, 1903.

16. See History House Trust, http://www.historichousetrust.org/.

17. Dal Co 1979; Dalbey 2002.

18. See Wood 2007 on the midcentury development of preservation in New York leading up to the 1965 Landmarks Law.

Bibliography

ARCHIVAL COLLECTIONS

American Scenic and Historic Preservation Society Manuscript Papers. Manuscript and Archives Division, New York Public Library, New York.

Architectural Archives. School of Design, University of Pennsylvania, Philadelphia.

Art Commission of New York Archives. New York.

Avery Architectural and Fine Arts Library. Columbia University, New York.

Bronx County Historical Society. New York.

Bronx Parkway Commission Collection. Westchester County Archives, Elmsford, New York.

Butler Library Rare Books and Manuscripts. Columbia University, New York.

Columbia University Oral History Collection. New York.

Cousins, Frank, Collection. Phillips Library, Peabody Essex Museum, Salem, Mass.

Diocesan Archives. Episcopal Diocese of New York. Cathedral of St. John the Divine, New York.

Grant, Madison, Correspondence. Wildlife Conservation Society, New York.

Immigration Restriction League Records. Houghton Library, Harvard University, Cambridge, Mass.

Kunz, George Frederick, Papers. New-York Historical Society, New York.

Manning, William Thomas, Papers. General Theological Seminary, New York.

McAneny, George, Papers. Seeley Mudd Library, Princeton University, Princeton, N.J.

Metropolitan Transportation Authority Archives. Brooklyn, New York.

Museum of the City of New York, Photograph Collection. New York.

New York Public Library, Map Division. New York.

Trinity Parish Archives. New York.

Wildlife Conservation Society Archives. Bronx, New York.

REFERENCES

Allison, Eric. 1996. "Historic Preservation in a Development-Dominated City: The Passage of New York City's Landmark Preservation Legislation." *Journal of Urban History* 22, no. 3 (March): 350–76.

American Institute of Architects, New York Chapter. 1911–17. *Yearbook*. Avery Architectural and Fine Arts Library, Columbia University, New York.

American Scenic and Historic Preservation Society (ASHPS). 1895–1925. *Annual Reports.* Albany, N.Y.: J. B. Lyon.

———. [1911]. *American Scenic and Historic Preservation Society, a National Society for the Protection of Natural Scenery, the Preservation of Historic Landmarks, and the Improvement of Cities.* Pamphlet. Cornell University Library, New York State Historical Literature Collection, http://digital.library.cornell.edu/cgi/t/text/text-idx?c=nys;idno=nys598.

———. [1906]. *American Scenic and Historic Preservation Society.* Pamphlet. New York Public Library, New York.

———. 1901. *Historical Handbook No. 1: St. Paul's Chapel.* New York: Tribune.

———. 1895. *Trustees of Scenic and Historic Places and Objects in the State of New York.* Memorial to the Legislature. Geology Library, Columbia University, New York.

Architectural League of New York. 1889–1925. *Proceedings.* Avery Architectural and Fine Arts Library, Columbia University, New York.

Art Commission of the City of New York. 1984. *On City Hall, in City Hall: An Historical Survey of City Hall's Art, Architecture, and Landscape Architecture.* October. Art Commission of New York Archives, New York.

———. 1902–25. *Annual Reports.* Avery Architectural and Fine Arts Library, Columbia University, New York.

———. 1909. *The Governor's Room in the City Hall, New York City.* Avery Architectural and Fine Arts Library, Columbia University, New York.

Ashbee, C. R. 1901. *American Sheaves and English Seed Corn.* London: Essex House Press.

Axelrod, Alan, ed. 1985. *The Colonial Revival in America.* New York: W. W. Norton.

Ballon, Hilary. 2002. *New York's Pennsylvania Stations.* With a photo essay by Norman McGrath, and a contribution by Marilyn Jordan Taylor, of Skidmore, Owings and Merrill. New York: W. W. Norton.

Barkan, Elazar. 1992. *The Retreat of Scientific Racism: Changing Concepts of Race in Britain and the United States between the World Wars.* New York: Cambridge University Press.

Barrington, Lewis. 1941. *Historic Restorations of the Daughters of the American Revolution.* New York: Richard Smith.

Bellah, Robert N., Richard Madsen, William M. Sullivan, Ann Swidler, and Steven M. Tipton. 1985. *Habits of the Heart: Individualism and Commitment in American Life.* Berkeley and Los Angeles: University of California Press.

Berman, Marshall. 1988. *All That Is Solid Melts into Air: The Experience of Modernity.* New York: Viking / Penguin.

Bershad, Deborah. 1986. *Imaginary Cities: European Views from the Collection of the Art Commission.* New York: Hunter College, in conjunction with the Art Commission.

Blackmar, Elizabeth. 1989. *Manhattan for Rent, 1785–1850.* Ithaca, N.Y.: Cornell University Press.

Blake, Casey Nelson. 1990. *Beloved Community: The Cultural Criticism of Randolph Bourne, Van Wyck Brooks, Waldo Frank, and Lewis Mumford.* Chapel Hill: University of North Carolina Press.

Bluestone, Daniel. 1991. *Constructing Chicago.* New Haven, Conn.: Yale University Press.

———. 1988. "Detroit's City Beautiful and the Problem of Commerce." *Journal of the Society of Architectural Historians* 47, no. 3 (September): 245–62.

———. 1987. "From Promenade to Park: The Gregarious Origins of Brooklyn's Park Movement." *American Quarterly* 39 (Winter): 529–50.

———. n.d. "Rock, Scenery, and Preservation on the Hudson River Palisades." Unpublished manuscript.

Bodnar, John. 1991. *Remaking America: Public Memory, Commemoration, and Patriotism in the Twentieth Century.* Princeton, N.J.: Princeton University Press.

Bogart, Michele. 1999. "Public Space and Public Memory in New York's City Hall Park." *Journal of Urban History* 25, no. 2 (January 1999): 226–57.

———. 1989. *Public Sculpture and the Civic Ideal in New York, 1880–1930.* Chicago: University of Chicago Press.

Bolton, Reginald Pelham. 1934. *Indian Life of Long Ago in the City of New York.* New York: Joseph Graham.

———. 1926. *From Sheep Pasture to Skyscraper.* New York: Equitable Trust Company of New York.

———. 1903. *Washington's Headquarters, New York.* New York: American Scenic and Historic Preservation Society.

Boyer, M. Christine. 1994. *The City of Collective Memory: Its Historical Imagery and Architectural Entertainments.* Cambridge, Mass.: MIT Press.

———. 1985. *Manhattan Manners: Architecture and Style, 1850–1900.* New York: Rizzoli.

———. 1983. *Dreaming the Rational City: The Myth of American City Planning.* Cambridge, Mass.: MIT Press.

Boyer, Paul. 1979. *Urban Masses and Moral Order in American, 1820–1920.* Cambridge, Mass.: Harvard University Press.

Breisach, Ernst. 1993. *American Progressive History: An Experiment in Modernization.* Chicago: University of Chicago Press.

Bridgeman, Charles Thorley. 1962. *A History of the Parish of Trinity Church in the City of New York. Part VI, The Rectorship of Dr. William Thomas Manning, 1908–1921.* New York: Rectors, Churchwardens, and Vestrymen of Trinity Church in the City of New York.

Bronx Parkway Commission. 1907, 1909, 1912, 1914, 1915, 1916–18, 1922, 1925. *Reports.* Avery Architectural and Fine Arts Library, Columbia University, New York, and Westchester County Archives, Elmsford, New York.

Bronx Sewer Commission. 1896. *Final Report.* Westchester County Archives, Elmsford, New York.

Brooks, Van Wyck. 1968. "On Creating a Usable Past." In *Van Wyck Brooks: The Early Years; A Selection from His Works, 1908–1921,* ed. Claire Sprague, 219–26. New York: Harper and Row.

Brown, Elspeth. 2005. *The Corporate Eye: Photography and the Rationalization of American Commercial Culture, 1884–1929.* Baltimore, Md.: The Johns Hopkins University Press.

Brown, Henry Collins. 1922. *Old New York Yesterday and Today.* New York: Printed privately.

Brunner, Arnold. 1912. "The Meaning of City Planning." In *Proceedings of the Fourth National Conference on City Planning,* 22–29. Boston: National Conference on City Planning.

Burke, John, et al., v. The Rector, Church Wardens and Vestrymen of Trinity Church, et al. 1896–1911. *Papers on Appeal: New York Supreme Court; Cases and Briefs.* 522 Appellate Division. Albany: New York State Library.

Burrows, Edwin G., and Mike Wallace. 1999. *Gotham: A History of New York City to 1898.* New York: Oxford University Press.

Bush-Brown, H. K. 1899. "New York City Monuments." *Municipal Affairs* 3:602–12.

Calvino, Italo. 1974. *Invisible Cities.* Translated by William Weaver. New York: Harcourt Brace Jovanovich.

Campanella, Tom. 1991. "Motor Elysium: Gilmore D. Clarke and the Building of the Westchester Parkways." *Colloqui: The Cornell Journal of Planning and Urban Issues* 6 (Spring): 18–31.

Cardia, Clara. 1987. *Ils ont construit New York: Histoire de la métropole au XIX siècle.* Geneva: Georg Editeur.

Caro, Robert. 1974. *The Power Broker.* New York: Pantheon.

Carr, Ethan. 1987. "The Parkway in New York City." In *Parkways: Past, Present, and Future; Proceedings of the Second Biennial Linear Parks Conference,* 121–28. Boone, N.C.: Appalachian Consortium Press.

Cerillo, Augustus. 1973. "The Reform of Municipal Government in New York City: From

Seth Low to John Purroy Mitchel." *New-York Historical Society Quarterly* 57, no. 1 (January): 51–57.

Chase, Stuart. 1930. "The Mad Hatter's Dirty Teacup." *Harper's Monthly Magazine,* April.

———. 1929. "The Future of the Great City." *Harper's Monthly Magazine,* December, 82–90.

Choay, Françoise. 2001. *The Invention of the Historic Monument.* Translated by Lauren M. O'Connell. New York: Cambridge University Press.

City Club, the People's Institute, and the Fine Arts Federation of New York. [1910]. *Save the City Hall and the City Hall Park.* Pamphlet. Art Commission of New York Archives, New York.

City History Club. 1913. *Historical Guide to the City of New York.* Rev. ed. New York: Frederick A. Stokes.

———. 1909. *Historical Guide to the City of New York.* New York: Frederick A. Stokes.

———. 1905. *Annual Report of the City History Club of New York City for the Year Ending April, 1905.* New York: Frederick A. Stokes.

Clarke, Gilmore. 1959. "Reminiscences." Columbia University Oral History Collection, New York.

Cole, Thomas. 1836. "Essay on American Scenery." *American Monthly Magazine,* January, 1–12.

Commissioners of the State Reservation at Niagara. 1885–86. *Report of the Commissioners of the State Reservation at Niagara.* Albany: State of New York. In Butler Library, Columbia University, New York.

Croly, Herbert. 1903. "New York as the American Metropolis." *Architectural Record,* March, 193–206.

Dal Co, Francesco. 1979. "From Parks to Region: Progressive Ideology and the Reform of the American City." In *The American City: From the Civil War to the New Deal,* ed. Giorgio Ciucci, Francesco Dal Co, Mario Manien-Elia, and Manfredo Tafuri, trans. Barbara Luigia LaPenta, 143–297. Cambridge, Mass.: MIT Press.

Dalbey, Matthew. 2002. *Regional Visionaries and Metropolitan Boosters: Decentralization, Regional Planning, and Parkways during the Interwar Years.* New York: Springer.

Davis, Timothy. 2007. "The Bronx River Parkway and Photography as an Instrument of Progressive Landscape Reform." *Studies in the History of Gardens and Designed Landscapes* 27 (October–December): 113–41.

Davis, Timothy, Todd A. Croteau, and Christopher H. Marston, eds. 2004. *America's National Park Roads and Parkways: Drawings from the Historic American Engineering Record.* With an introductory essay by Timothy Davis and a foreword by Eric DeLony. Baltimore, Md.: The Johns Hopkins University Press.

Dean, Bashford, and Alexander McMillan Welch. 1916. *The Dyckman House: Park and Museum, New York City, 1783–1916.* New York: Gilliss Press.

Denenberg, Thomas Andrew. 2003. *Wallace Nutting and the Invention of Old America.* New Haven, Conn.: Yale University Press.

Dix, John A., comp., and Leicester C. Lewis, ed. 1950. *A History of the Parish of Trinity Church in the City of New York. Part V, The Rectorship of Dr. Morgan Dix.* New York: Columbia University Press for Trinity Church.

Domosh, Mona. 1996. *Invented Cities: the Creation of Landscape in Nineteenth-Century New York and Boston.* New Haven, Conn.: Yale University Press.

Downer, Jay. 1920. "Reclaiming a Polluted River." *American City* 22, no. 1 (January): 15.

———. 1917. "The Bronx River Parkway." In *Proceedings of the Ninth National Conference on City Planning,* 91–95. New York: D. C. McMurtie.

Downer, Jay, and James Owen. 1925. "Public Parks in Westchester County." In *History of Westchester County, New York*, ed. Alvah P. French, 2:962. New York and Chicago: Lewis Historical Publishing Company.

Dubrow, Gail Lee, and Jennifer B. Goodman, eds. 2003. *Restoring Women's History through Historic Preservation*. Baltimore, Md.: The Johns Hopkins University Press.

Duncan, James, and David Ley, eds. 1993. *Place/Culture/Representation*. London: Routledge.

Dupont, William A. 2003. "A Place for Authenticity at Lincoln Cottage." *Forum Journal* 18, no. 1 (Fall): 6–17.

Elliott, Robert. 1997. *Faking Nature: The Ethics of Environmental Restoration*. New York: Routledge.

Embury, Aymar II. 1914. *Early American Churches*. Garden City, N.Y.: Doubleday, Page.

Fairfield, John D. 1993. *The Mysteries of the Great City: The Politics of Urban Design, 1877–1937*. Columbus: Ohio State University Press.

Fairmount Park Commission. 1996. *Wissahickon Trails Master Plan*. City of Philadelphia. March. Collection of the author.

Fein, Albert, ed. 1967. *Landscape into Cityscape: Frederick Law Olmsted's Plans for a Greater New York City*. Ithaca, N.Y.: Cornell University Press.

Foord, John. 1913. *The Life and Public Services of Andrew Haswell Green*. Garden City, N.Y.: Doubleday, Page.

Frankel, Edward. 1978. "Natural History of the Bronx River Valley." Unpublished manuscript, fall. Bronx County Historical Society Library, Bronx, N.Y.

Gayle, Margot, and Michele Cohen. 1988. *The Art Commission and the Municipal Art Society Guide to Manhattan's Outdoor Sculpture*. New York: Prentice Hall Press.

Giedion, Sigfried. 1974. *Space, Time, and Architecture: The Growth of a New Tradition*. 5th ed., rev. and enlarged. Cambridge, Mass.: Harvard University Press.

Giffen, Sarah, and Kevin D. Murphy, eds. 1992. *"A Noble and Dignified Stream": The Piscataqua Region in the Colonial Revival, 1860–1930*. York, Maine: Old York Historical Society.

Gilchrist, Jim. 2006. "Urging Vigilance on the U.S.–Mexico Border." *All Things Considered*, National Public Radio, April 7.

Gilder, Rodman. 1936. *The Battery: The Story of the Adventurers, Artists, Statesmen, Grafters, Songsters, Mariners, Pirates, Guzzlers, Indians, Thieves, Stuffed-Shirts, Turn-Coats, Millionaires, Inventors, Poets, Heroes, Soldiers, Harlots, Bootlicks, Nobles, Nonentities, Burghers, Martyrs, and Murderers Who Played Their Parts during Full Four Centuries on Manhattan Island's Tip*. Boston: Houghton Mifflin.

Gillis, John, ed. 1994. *Commemorations: the Politics of National Identity*. Princeton, N.J.: Princeton University Press.

Gilmartin, Gregory F. 1995. *Shaping the City: New York and the Municipal Art Society*. New York: Clarkson Potter.

Glassberg, David. 2001. *Sense of History: The Place of the Past in American Life*. Amherst: University of Massachusetts Press.

———. 1990. *American Historical Pageantry: The Uses of Tradition in the Early Twentieth Century*. Chapel Hill: University of North Carolina Press.

———. 1987. "History and the Public: Legacies of the Progressive Era." *Journal of American History* 73, no. 4 (March): 957–80.

Gonzalez, Evelyn. 1993. "City Neighborhoods: Formation, Growth, and Change in the South Bronx, 1840–1940." Ph.D. diss., Columbia University.

Gough, Deborah Mathias. 1995. *Christ Church, Philadelphia: The Nation's Church in a Changing City.* Philadelphia: University of Pennsylvania Press.

Grant, Madison. 1933. *The Conquest of a Continent, or The Expansion of Races in America.* New York: Charles Scribner's Sons.

———. 1916. *The Passing of the Great Race, or The Racial Basis of European History.* New York: Charles Scribner's Sons.

Grant, Madison, and Charles Stewart Davison. 1928. *The Founders of the Republic on Immigration, Naturalization, and Aliens.* New York: Charles Scribner's Sons.

Grava, Sigurd. 1981. "The Bronx River Parkway: A Case Study in Innovation." *New York Affairs* 7, no. 1: 15–23.

Graves-Brown, Paul, Sian Jones, and Clive Gamble, eds. 1996. *Cultural Identity and Archaeology: The Construction of European Communities.* London: Routledge.

Green, Andrew H. 1895. "Memorial to the Legislature." Avery Architectural and Fine Arts Library, Columbia University, New York.

———. 1894. *The Preservation of the Historic City Hall of New York.* New York: New York State Society, Sons of the American Revolution.

———. 1866. "Communication to the Commissioners of Central Park." In *The People and the Park: A History of Central Park,* ed. Roy Rosenzweig and Elizabeth Blackmar, 199. Ithaca, N.Y.: Cornell University Press, 1992.

Grese, Robert. 1992. *Jens Jensen: Maker of Natural Parks and Gardens.* Baltimore, Md.: The Johns Hopkins University Press.

Groth, Paul, and Todd Bressi, eds. 1997. *Understanding Ordinary Landscapes.* New Haven, Conn.: Yale University Press.

Gutman, Robert. 1988. *Architectural Practice: A Critical View.* Princeton, N.J.: Princeton Architectural Press.

Haddon, Rawson W. 1920. *An Architectural Monographs on Old Deerfield, Massachusetts.* White Pine Series of Architectural Monographs, vol. 6, no. 5. St. Paul, Minn.: White Pine Bureau.

———. 1917. "The Roger Morris House (Jumel Mansion), New York City." Measured drawings by Joseph Palle. *Architectural Record* 42 (July): 126–39.

———. 1914a. "St. John's Chapel, Varick Street, New York City." Measured drawings by F. L. Finlayson. *Architectural Record* 35, no. 5 (May): 389–404.

———. 1914b. "Varick Street, Which Is in Greenwich Village, Manhattan. A Narrative and Some Pen Sketches." *Architectural Record* 35, no. 1 (January): 49–57.

———. 1912. "The Threatened Demolition of Saint John's Chapel in New York City." *American Architect* 102, no. 1 (July 31): 33–35.

Halbwachs, Maurice. 1992. *On Collective Memory.* Edited and with an introduction by Lewis Coser. Chicago: University of Chicago Press.

———. 1980. *The Collective Memory.* Translated by Francis J. Ditter Jr. and Vida Yazdi Ditter. New York: Harper and Row.

Haley, Jaquetta. 2002. "Dyckman House Furnishing Plan." New York: New York City Department of Parks.

Hall, Edward Hagaman. 1914. *The Commercial Tercentenary of New York, 1614–1914 . . . Containing a Brief History of the Beginning of the Regularly Chartered Commerce of New Netherland and the Permanent Settlement of What Is Now the State of New York.* For the New York State Commercial Tercentenary Commission. New York: New York Commercial Tercentenary Commission.

———. 1912. *Philipse Manor Hall at Yonkers, N.Y.: The Site, the Building, and Its Occupants.* New York: American Scenic and Historic Preservation Society.

———. 1910. *An Appeal for the Preservation of City Hall Park, New York, with a Brief History of the Park*. New York: American Scenic and Historic Preservation Society.

———. 1905. *McGown's Pass and Vicinity*. New York: American Scenic and Historic Preservation Society.

———. 1901. "Our Heritage of the Picturesque." *Municipal Affairs* 5: 349–59.

Hamlin, A. D. F. 1902. "The Preservation and Restoration of Historic Sites and Buildings in Europe." Appendix A in American Scenic and Historic Preservation Society, seventh annual report, 65–69. New York: Lyons.

Hammack, David C. 1988. "Comprehensive Planning before the Comprehensive Plan: A New Look at the Nineteenth-Century American City." In *Two Centuries of American Planning*, ed. Daniel Schaffer, 139–65. Baltimore, Md.: The Johns Hopkins University Press.

———. 1987. *Power and Society: Greater New York at the Turn of the Century*. New York: Columbia University Press.

Hansen, Harry. 1954. *Scarsdale: From Colonial Manor to Modern Community*. New York: Harper.

Haraway, Donna. 1995. "Universal Donors in a Vampire Culture." In *Uncommon Ground: Rethinking the Human Place in Nature*, ed. W. Cronon, 321–66. New York: W. W. Norton.

Harvey, David. 1989. *The Condition of Postmodernity*. Oxford: Basil Blackwell, 1989.

———. 1985. *The Urbanization of Capital*. Baltimore, Md.: The Johns Hopkins University Press, 1985.

Hayden, Dolores. 1995. *The Power of Place: Urban Landscapes as Public History*. Cambridge, Mass.: MIT Press.

———. 1981. *The Grand Domestic Revolution: A History of Feminist Designs for American Homes, Neighborhoods, and Cities*. Cambridge, Mass.: MIT Press.

Hays, Samuel P. 1959. *Conservation and the Gospel of Efficiency*. Cambridge, Mass.: Harvard University Press.

Hermalyn, Gary. 1982. "A History of the Bronx River." *Bronx County Historical Society Journal* 19, no. 3 (Spring): 1–22.

Higham, John. 1989. *History: Professional Scholarship in America*. Baltimore, Md.: The Johns Hopkins University Press.

———. 1955. *Strangers in the Land: Patterns of American Nativism, 1860–1925*. New Brunswick, N.J.: Rutgers University Press.

Hobsbawm, Eric, and Terence Ranger, eds. 1983. *The Invention of Tradition*. Cambridge: Cambridge University Press.

Hofstadter, Richard. 1955. *The Age of Reform*. New York: Vintage.

Holdsworth, Deryck, and Gail Fenske. 1992. "Corporate Identity and the New York Office Building: 1895–1915." In *The Landscape of Modernity: Essays on New York City, 1900–1940*, ed. David Ward and Olivier Zunz, 129–59. New York: Russell Sage Foundation.

Holleran, Michael. 1998. *Boston's "Changeful Times": Origins of Preservation and Planning in America*. Baltimore, Md.: The Johns Hopkins University Press.

Hood, Clifton. 2002. "Journeying to 'Old New York': Elite New Yorkers and Their Invention of an Idealized City History in the Late Nineteenth and Early Twentieth Centuries." *Journal of Urban History* 28, no. 6 (September): 699–719.

Horwitz, Tony. 1998. *Confederates in the Attic: Dispatches from the Unfinished Civil War*. New York: Pantheon.

Hosmer, Charles B. Jr. 1981. *Preservation Comes of Age: From Williamsburg to the National Trust, 1926–1949*. 2 vols. Charlottesville: University Press of Virginia.

———. 1965. *Presence of the Past: A History of the Preservation Movement before Williamsburg.* New York: G. P. Putnam's Sons.

Howett, Catherine. 1998. "Ecological Values in Twentieth-Century Landscape Design: A History and Hermeneutics." Special issue, *Landscape Journal* 17, no. 2 (Fall): 80–98.

Hudson–Fulton Celebration Commission. 1910. *Fourth Annual Report of the Hudson–Fulton Celebration.* Albany, N.Y.: J. B. Lyon.

Hughes, W. D. F. 1963. *Prudently with Power: William Thomas Manning, Tenth Bishop of New York.* West Park, N.Y.: Holy Cross Publications.

Hunt, Felix. 1912. "A Practical Detail of City Planning: Street Widening in Old New York an Object Lesson in Europe as Well as America." *American City* 7, no. 5 (November): 411–15.

Hunt, John Dixon. 2004. *The Afterlife of Gardens.* Philadelphia: University of Pennsylvania Press.

Huxtable, Ada Louise. 1997. *The Unreal America: Architecture and Illusion.* New York: New Press.

———. 1992. "Inventing American Reality." *New York Review of Books,* December 3, 24–29.

Huyssen, Andreas. 2003. *Present Pasts: Urban Palimpsests and the Politics of Memory.* Palo Alto, Calif.: Stanford University Press.

Inglis, William. 1909. "Trinity and Its Critics." *Harper's Weekly,* February 20, 15–16, 19.

Jackson, John Brinckerhoff. 1980. *Necessity for Ruins, and Other Topics.* Amherst: University of Massachusetts Press.

Jackson, Kenneth T., ed. 1995. *The Encyclopedia of New York City.* New Haven, Conn.: Yale University Press.

———. 1985. *Crabgrass Frontier: The Suburbanization of the United States.* New York: Oxford University Press.

———. 1980. "The Capital of Capitalism: The New York Metropolitan Region, 1890–1940." In *The Rise of Modern Urban Planning, 1800–1914,* ed. Anthony Sutcliffe. New York: St. Martin's Press.

Jensen, Jens. [1939] 1990. *Siftings.* Baltimore, Md.: The Johns Hopkins University Press.

Johnson, David A. 1988. "Regional Planning for the Great American Metropolis: New York between the World Wars." In *Two Centuries of American Planning,* ed. Daniel Schaffer, 167–96. Baltimore, Md.: The Johns Hopkins University Press.

Jokilehto, Jukka. 1999. *A History of Architectural Conservation.* Oxford: Butterworth-Heinemann.

Jones, Samuel M. 1899. "The New Patriotism: A Golden Rule Government for Cities." *Municipal Affairs* 3: 460–61.

Kammen, Michael. 1991. *Mystic Chords of Memory: The Transformation of Tradition in American Culture.* New York: Knopf.

———. 1979. "The Rediscovery of New York's History, Phase One." *New York History* 60, no. 4 (October): 379–94.

———. 1977. "The Quest for Tradition and the Role of Preservation in Upstate New York." *New York History* 58, no. 2 (April): 163–71.

Kantor, Harvey. 1973. "The City Beautiful in New York." *New-York Historical Society Quarterly* 57, no. 2 (April): 148–71.

———. 1971. "Modern Urban Planning in New York City: Origins and Evolution, 1890–1933." Ph.D. diss., New York University.

Kaufman, Ned. 1998. "Heritage and the Cultural Politics of Preservation." *Places* 11, no. 3: 58–65.

Kern, Stephen. 1983. *The Culture of Time and Space, 1880–1918.* Cambridge, Mass.: Harvard University Press.

Kestenbaum, Joy. 1984. "City Hall Park." Report prepared for Walmsley and Company. Exhibit 1947. Art Commission of New York Archives, New York.

Koshar, Rudy. 1998. *Germany's Transient Pasts: Preservation and National Memory in the Twentieth Century.* Chapel Hill: University of North Carolina Press.

Kunz, George F. 1923. "The Economic Value of Public Parks and Scenic Preservation." *Scientific Monthly* 16, no. 4 (April): 374–80.

Lamb, Frederick Stymetz. 1897. "Municipal Art." *Municipal Affairs* 1:674–88.

Lamb, Martha J. 1877. *History of the City of New York: Its Origin, Rise, and Progress.* New York and Chicago: A. S. Barnes.

Larson, Magali Sarfatti. 1979. *The Rise of Professionalism: A Sociological Analysis.* Berkeley and Los Angeles: University of California Press.

Lears, T. J. Jackson. 1985. "The Concept of Cultural Hegemony: Problems and Possibilities." *American Historical Review* 90, no. 3 (June): 567–93.

———. 1981. *No Place of Grace: Antimodernism and the Transformation of American Culture, 1880–1920.* New York: Pantheon.

Lindgren, James. 1995. *Preserving Historic New England: Preservation, Progressivism, and the Remaking of Memory.* New York: Oxford University Press.

———. 1993. *Preserving the Old Dominion: Historic Preservation and Virginia Traditionalism.* Charlottesville: University Press of Virginia.

———. 1991. "'A Constant Incentive to Patriotic Citizenship': Historic Preservation in Progressive-Era Massachusetts." *New England Quarterly* 64, no. 4: 594–608.

Loeb, Robert E. 1989. "The Ecological History of an Urban Park." *Journal of Forest History* 33 (July): 134–43.

Low, William. 2007. *Old Penn Station.* New York: Henry Holt.

Lowenthal, David. 1985. *The Past Is a Foreign Country.* Cambridge: Cambridge University Press.

Lustig, R. Jeffrey. 1982. *Corporate Liberalism: The Origins of Modern American Political Theory, 1890–1920.* Berkeley and Los Angeles: University of California Press.

Manhattan Borough President. 1912. *Report of the President of the Borough of Manhattan of the City of New York for the Year Ending December 31, 1911.* Municipal Reference Library, New York.

Marcuse, Peter. 1987. "The Grid as City Plan: New York City and Laissez-Faire Planning in the Nineteenth Century." *Planning Perspectives* 2:287–310.

Marling, Karal Ann. 1988. *George Washington Slept Here: Colonial Revivals and American Culture, 1876–1986.* Cambridge, Mass.: Harvard University Press.

Marsh, Benjamin C. 1910. "Causes of Congestion of Population." In *Proceedings of the Second National Conference on City Planning and the Problems of Congestion, Rochester, New York, May 2–4, 1910,* 35–39. Boston: National Conference on City Planning.

Martin, George W. 2005. *CCB: The Life and Century of Charles C. Burlingham, New York's First Citizen, 1858–1959.* New York: Hill and Wang.

Marx, Leo. 1964. *The Machine in the Garden: Technology and the Pastoral Ideal in America.* New York: Oxford University Press.

Matsuda, Mark K. 1996. *The Memory of the Modern.* New York: Oxford University Press.

May, Bridget A. 1991. "Progressivism and the Colonial Revival: The Modern Colonial House, 1900–1920." *Winterthur Portfolio: A Journal of American Material Culture* 26 (Summer–Autumn): 107–22.

May, Charles C. 1916. "[New York's City Hall] Part I—Historical Notes" and "[New York's City Hall] Part II—The Work of Restoration." *Architectural Record* 39, no. 4 (April): 299–319; 39, no. 5 (May): 474–535.

Mazaraki, George. 1966. "The Public Career of Andrew Haswell Green." Ph.D. diss., New York University.

McAneny, George. 1949. "Reminiscences." Columbia University Oral History Collection, New York.

———. 1914. Address to the Sixth National Conference on City Planning. In *Proceedings of the 6th National Conference on City Planning*. Boston: National Conference on City Planning.

McCullough, David. 1983. *The Great Bridge*. New York: Simon and Schuster.

McGerr, Michael. 2003. *A Fierce Discontent: The Rise and Fall of the Progressive Movement in America*. New York: Free Press.

McNamara, John. 1989. *McNamara's Old Bronx*. Bronx, N.Y.: Bronx County Historical Society.

McShane, Clay. 1994. *Down the Asphalt Path: The Automobile and the American City*. New York: Columbia University Press.

Metropolitan Museum of Art. 1925. *Addresses on the Occasion of the Opening of the American Wing*. New York: Metropolitan Museum of Art.

Moore, Peter. 2000. *The Destruction of Penn Station: Photographs by Peter Moore*. Edited and with an introduction by Barbara Moore, an essay by Eric Nash, and chronology and captions by Lorraine B. Diehl. New York: Distributed Art Publishers.

Morgan, Francesca Constance. 1998. "'Home and Country': Women, Nation, and the Daughters of the American Revolution." Ph.D. diss., Columbia University.

Mullaly, John. 1887. *The New Parks beyond the Harlem: With Thirty Illustrations and Map. Descriptions of Scenery. Nearly 4,000 Acres of Free Playground for the People . . .* New York: Record and Guide.

Municipal Art Society. 1903–35. *Bulletin,* various numbers. Municipal Art Society Archives, in the collection of Gregory Gilmartin.

Murphy, Kevin D. 1992. "The Politics of Preservation: Historic House Museums in the Piscataqua Region." In *"A Noble and Dignified Stream": The Piscataqua Region in the Colonial Revival, 1860–1930,* ed. Sarah Giffen and Kevin D. Murphy. York, Maine: Old York Historical Society.

The National Cyclopedia of American Biography. 1898–1978. New York: J. T. White.

Neville, Christopher. 1994. "Overlooking the Collect: Between Topography and Memory in the Landscape of Lower Manhattan." Master's thesis, Columbia University.

New York City Improvement Commission. 1907. *Report of the New York City Improvement Commission . . .* New York: New York City Improvement Commission.

New York Zoological Society. 1916. *Annual Report*. Wildlife Conservation Society Archives, Bronx, New York.

Nolen, John, and Henry V. Hubbard. 1937. *Parkways and Land Values*. Cambridge, Mass.: Harvard University Press.

Nora, Pierre. 1989. "Between Memory and History: Les Lieux de Mémoire." *Representations* 26 (Spring): 7–24.

———, director. 1996–98. *Realms of Memory: Rethinking the French Past.* 3 vols. Edited by Lawrence Kritzman, translated by Arthur Goldhammer. New York: Columbia University Press.

Novak, Barbara. 1980. *Nature and Culture: American Landscape and Painting, 1825–1875*. New York: Thames and Hudson.

Novick, Peter. 1988. *That Noble Dream: The "Objectivity Question" and the American Historical Profession*. New York: Cambridge University Press.

Nye, David. 1994. *American Technological Sublime*. Cambridge, Mass.: MIT Press.

Olmsted, Frederick Law. 1870. "Public Parks and the Enlargement of Towns." Paper read before the American Social Science Association at the Lowell Institute, Boston, February 25.

Olwig, Kenneth. 1995. "Reinventing Common Nature: Yosemite and Mount Rushmore—A Meandering Tale of Double Nature." In *Uncommon Ground: Toward Reinventing Nature,* ed. William Cronon, 379–408. New York: W. W. Norton.

Orlin, Glenn S. 1992. "The Evolution of the American Urban Parkway." Ph.D. diss., George Washington University.

Page, Max. 1999. *The Creative Destruction of Manhattan, 1900–1940.* Chicago: University of Chicago Press.

Page, Max, and Randall Mason, eds. 2004. *Giving Preservation a History: Histories of Historic Preservation in the United States.* New York: Routledge.

Peirce, Melusina Fay. 1901. *The Landmark of Fraunces Tavern: A Retrospect.* New York: American Scenic and Historic Preservation Society.

Peterson, Jon A. 1976. "The City Beautiful Movement: Forgotten Origins and Lost Meanings." *Journal of Urban History* 2 (1976): 415–34.

Pierpont, Claudia Roth. 2004. "The Measure of America." *New Yorker,* March 8, 48.

Pleadwell, F. L., ed. 1935. *The Life and Works of Joseph Rodman Drake.* Boston: Merrymount Press.

Radde, Bruce. 1996. *The Merritt Parkway.* New Haven, Conn.: Yale University Press.

Report to the New York Legislature of the Commission to Select and Locate Lands for Public Parks in the Twenty-third and Twenty-fourth Wards of the City of New York, and in the Vicinity Thereof. 1884. New York: Martin B. Brown.

Revell, Keith D. 2003. *Building Gotham: Civic Culture and Public Policy in New York City, 1898–1938.* Baltimore, Md.: The Johns Hopkins University Press.

Robinson, Charles Mulford. 1903. *Modern Civic Art, or The City Made Beautiful.* 3rd ed. New York: G. P. Putnam's Sons.

———. 1901. *The Improvement of Towns and Cities, or The Practical Basis of Civic Aesthetics.* 4th rev. ed. New York: G. P. Putnam's Sons.

Rosenzweig, Roy, and Elizabeth Blackmar. 1992. *The People and the Park: A History of Central Park.* Ithaca, N.Y.: Cornell University Press.

Rossi, Aldo. 1984. *The Architecture of the City.* Cambridge, Mass.: MIT Press.

Rub, Timothy. 1986. "The Institutional Presence in the Bronx." In *Building a Borough: Architecture and Planning in the Bronx, 1890–1940,* ed. Timothy Rub. New York: Bronx Museum of the Arts.

Savage, Kirk. 1997. *Standing Soldiers, Kneeling Slaves: Race, War, and Monument in Nineteenth-Century America.* Princeton, N.J.: Princeton University Press.

Scarsdale Historical Society. 1983. *Bronx River Retrospective.* Exhibit brochure. Greenburgh Nature Center. Collection of the author.

Scharf, J. Thomas. [1886] 1992. *History of Westchester County, New York.* Camden, Maine: Picton Press. Originally published Philadelphia: L. E. Preston. Page citations to the reprint edition.

Schnapp, Alain. 1993. *The Discovery of the Past.* New York: Harry N. Abrams.

Schuyler, David. 1995. "The Sanctified Landscape: The Hudson River Valley, 1820 to 1850." In *Landscape in America,* ed. George F. Thompson, 93–109. Austin: University of Texas Press.

———. 1986. *The New Urban Landscape.* Baltimore, Md.: The Johns Hopkins University Press.

Schuyler, Montgomery. 1908. "The New York City Hall: A Piece of Architectural History." *Architectural Record* 23, no. 5 (May): 387–90.

Spann, Edward K. 1988. "The Greatest Grid: The New York Plan of 1811." In *Two Centuries of American Planning*, ed. Daniel Schaffer, 11–39. Baltimore, Md.: The Johns Hopkins University Press.

———. 1981. *The New Metropolis: New York City, 1840–1857*. New York: Columbia University Press.

Spiro, Jonathan. 2000. "Patrician Racist: The Evolution of Madison Grant." Ph.D. diss., University of California, Berkeley.

Stern, Robert A. M., Gregory Gilmartin, and John Massengale. 1983. *New York 1900: Metropolitan Architecture and Urbanism, 1890–1915*. New York: Rizzoli.

Still, Bayrd. 1956. *Mirror for Gotham: New York as Seen by Contemporaries from Dutch Days to the Present*. New York: New York University Press.

Stillman, Damie. 1964. "New York City Hall: Competition and Execution." *Journal of the Society of Architectural Historians* 23, no. 3 (October): 129–42.

Stokes, I. N. Phelps. [1915–28] 1972. *Iconography of Manhattan Island*. 6 vols. New York: Arno Press.

Terdiman, Richard. 1993. *Present Past: Modernity and the Memory Crisis*. Ithaca, N.Y.: Cornell University Press.

Trachtenberg, Alan. 1989. *Reading American Photographs: Images as History, Matthew Brady to Walker Evans*. New York: Hill and Wang.

———. 1965. *Brooklyn Bridge: Fact and Symbol*. New York: Oxford University Press.

Trinity Parish. 1893, 1907, 1908, 1909, 1910. *Year Book and Register of the Parish of Trinity in the City of New York*. New York: A. Livingston.

Van Dyke, John, and Joseph Pennell. 1909. *The New New York: A Commentary on the Place and the People*. New York: Macmillan.

Wallace, Michael. 1996. *Mickey Mouse History and Other Essays on American Memory*. Philadelphia: Temple University Press.

———. 1986. "Reflections on the History of Historic Preservation." In *Presenting the Past: Essays on History and Public*, ed. Susan Benson, Stephen Brier, and Roy Rosenzweig, 165–99. Philadelphia: Temple University Press.

Warner, John DeWitt. 1902. "Civic Centers." *Municipal Affairs* 6, no. 1 (March): 1–23.

Weigold, Marilyn E. 1980. *Pioneering in Parks and Parkways: Westchester County, New York, 1895–1945*. Chicago: Public Works Historical Society.

West, Patricia. 1999. *Domesticating History: The Political Origins of America's House Museums*. Washington, D.C.: Smithsonian Institution Press.

Weyeneth, Robert. 2000. *Historic Preservation for a Living City: Historic Charleston Foundation, 1947–1997*. Columbia: University of South Carolina Press.

White, Richard. 1996. *The Organic Machine: The Remaking of the Columbia River*. New York: Hill and Wang.

Who Was Who in America. 1998. Chicago: Marquis Who's Who.

Wiebe, Robert. [1967] 1990. *The Search for Order: 1877–1920*. New York: Hill and Wang.

Willensky, Elliot, and Norval White. 1988. *AIA Guide to New York City*. 3rd ed. San Diego, Calif.: Harcourt Brace Jovanovich.

Willis, Carol. 1995. *Form Follows Finance: Skyscrapers and Skylines in New York and Chicago*. New York: Princeton Architectural Press.

Wilson, Chris. 1997. *The Myth of Santa Fe: Creating a Modern Regional Tradition*. Albuquerque: University of New Mexico Press.

Wilson, Edmund. 1958. *The American Earthquake: A Documentary of the Twenties and Thirties.* Garden City, N.Y.: Doubleday Anchor Books.

Wilson, Rufus Rockwell. 1896. "Historic New York Houses." *Harper's Weekly,* November 7, 1099–1102.

Wilson, William H. 1994. *The City Beautiful Movement.* Baltimore, Md.: The Johns Hopkins University Press.

———. 1980. "The Ideology, Aesthetics, and Politics of the City Beautiful Movement." In *The Rise of Modern Urban Planning, 1800–1914,* ed. Anthony Sutcliffe, 165–98. New York: St. Martin's Press.

Wintjen, John. 1933. "Bronx River." *Quarterly Bulletin of the Westchester County Historical Society* 9, no. 2 (April).

Wolf, Kevin. 1993. "Who Saves What and Who Benefits?" *Metropolis,* June, 54–67.

Wood, Anthony. 2007. *Preserving New York: Winning the Right to Protect a City's Landmarks.* New York: Routledge.

Yates, Frances A. 1966. *The Art of Memory.* Chicago: University of Chicago Press.

Young, James. 1993. *The Texture of Memory: Holocaust Memorials and Meaning.* New Haven, Conn.: Yale University Press.

Yuhl, Stephanie E. 2005. *A Golden Haze of Memory: The Making of Historic Charleston.* Chapel Hill: University of North Carolina Press.

Zaitzevsky, Cynthia. 1982. *Frederick Law Olmsted and the Boston Park System.* Cambridge, Mass.: Belknap Press / Harvard University Press.

Zapatka, Christian. 1995. *The American Landscape.* New York: Princeton Architectural Press.

Index

Randall Mason is associate professor of city and regional planning in the Graduate Program in Historic Preservation at the University of Pennsylvania's School of Design. He is coeditor of *Giving Preservation a History*.